serious
eats

serious eats®

A COMPREHENSIVE GUIDE TO making & eating DELICIOUS FOOD wherever you are

ed levine & the editors of seriouseats.com

clarkson potter/publishers

new york

All rights reserved.
Published in the United States by Clarkson
Potter/Publishers, an imprint of the Crown
Publishing Group, a division of Random House,
Inc., New York.
www.crownpublishing.com
www.clarksonpotter.com

CLARKSON POTTER is a trademark and
POTTER with colophon is a registered
trademark of Random House, Inc.

SERIOUS EATS is a registered trademark of
Serious Eats, LLC.

Library of Congress Cataloging-in-Publication
Data is available upon request.

ISBN 978-0-307-72087-0
eISBN 978-0-307-95331-5

Printed in the United States of America

Design by Amy Sly

All photographs are copyright © 2011 by Serious
Eats, LLC, except for on the following pages: 10
(top and second from bottom), 19, 21, 32 (top), 69,
70, 73, 83, 106 (bottom), 116, 124, 129, 157, 180,
181, 215, 217 (bottom), 229, 242 (bottom), 259,
262, 289, 292.

All photographs are by Robyn Lee except for on
the following pages. J. Kenji Lopez-Alt: 39, 47,
48, 75, 77 (top), 84, 87, 148 (top), 149, 160, 168,
179, 182, 184, 189, 190, 281, 282, 300. Nicholas
Chen: 61. Nick Solares: 72, 81 (below), 100, 123.
Bonjwing Lee: 79, 188. Adam Kuban: 98, 113.
Maggie Hoffman: 104. Carey Jones: 145.

10 9 8 7 6 5 4 3 2 1

First Edition

for the community OF SERIOUS EATERS WHO INSPIRE US every day with their ENTHUSIASM, DISCERNMENT, AND WELCOMING SPIRIT

CONTENTS

ARE YOU A SERIOUS EATER?
page 8

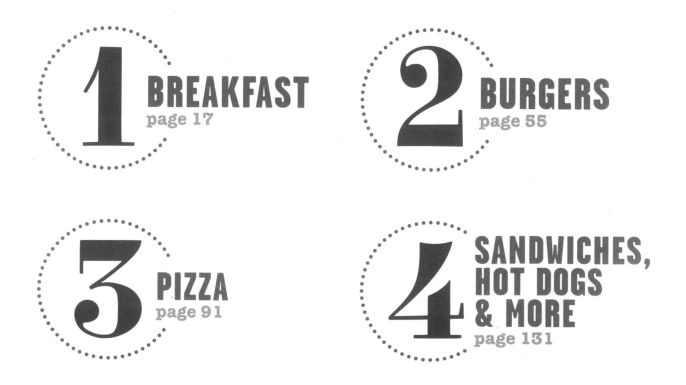

1 BREAKFAST
page 17

2 BURGERS
page 55

3 PIZZA
page 91

4 SANDWICHES, HOT DOGS & MORE
page 131

 **5 BARBECUE**
page 173

 **6 STREET FOOD**
page 205

 **7 FRIED FOODS**
page 239

 **8 SWEETS & BAKERIES**
page 269

 **9 HOME-GROWN & HOUSE-MADE**
page 305

MORE SERIOUS EATS
page 337

ACKNOWLEDGMENTS
page 355

DIRECTORY
page 356

INDEX
page 363

ARE YOU A SERIOUS EATER?

Answer these questions to find out:

1 » Do you plan your day around what you might eat?

2 » When you are heading somewhere, anywhere, will you go out of your way to eat something delicious?

3 » When you daydream, do you often find yourself thinking about food?

4 » Do you live to eat, rather than eat to live?

5 » Have you strained relationships with friends or family by dictating the food itinerary—changing everyone's plans to try a potentially special burger or piece of pie?

If you've answered yes to all five questions, you are indeed a serious eater. And you're not alone. There are millions of us out there in the world. We travel 80 miles to try a particular hot dog, and bring extra suitcases and coolers along on trips to transport our food souvenirs. We rhapsodize about sandwiches the way others do music, or literature, or art. We have loyalties to burger places or pizza styles the way others do to football teams. We read restaurant menus with wide-eyed wonderment and find ourselves in heated arguments about the merits of a particular taco truck.

Serious eaters are only distant cousins to "foodies." Whereas many foodies are trend focused and chef obsessed, and prefer ten-course tasting menus to the country's best burger, serious eaters are more democratic in their outlook. They're less interested in a celebrity chef's new restaurant or the latest Michelin rankings than they are in a genuinely delicious sandwich—and the story behind the person who makes it. They may not know the best food in any given place, but they'd like to and they love having a community that shares their enthusiasm and passion in equal measure.

meet the serious eaters

 **ED LEVINE** The Serious Eats founder, whom Ruth Reichl dubbed the "missionary of the delicious" in the *New York Times* (where he wrote for many years), had the good sense to gather up all the people mentioned below to help him spread the Serious Eats Gospel in this book.

 CAREY JONES The tireless, obsessively motivating and organizational force behind this book, and responsible for the sweets, sandwich, and fried-food chapters, Carey is an impassioned food explorer and the editor of Serious Eats: New York.

 ERIN ZIMMER Perhaps one of the world's leading oatmeal experts, Erin is the editor of the main Serious Eats site and a major contributor to this text, doing the spadework on the breakfast, street food, and farmers' market chapters.

 ADAM KUBAN A true new media pioneer who founded the blogs "A Hamburger Today" and "Slice," sites that now have a home at SeriousEats.com, Adam has written about pizza and burgers longer than just about anyone else on the Internet. No surprise that he worked on the pizza and burger chapters.

J. KENJI LOPEZ-ALT Chef-turned-writer Kenji is the recipe czar for this book—devising most of them himself and rigorously testing every one.

 ROBYN LEE Robyn is responsible for just about all of the spectacular images you find on our sites and in these pages.

 ALAINA BROWNE General manager of Serious Eats, she's another seminal food blogger and a certified member of the North Carolina Barbecue Society.

THAT'S WHERE WE COME IN

A food-loving community is just what I hoped to create when I started SeriousEats.com in 2006. Having written about food for years, I felt that the Internet was the perfect place to share my food finds while engaging readers and hearing about their own discoveries. Millions of visitors from all over the world have come to gather on Serious Eats. Whether looking to refine their knife skills or plan an eating tour of Chicago, share a gorgeous food photo, or just chew the fat with like-minded folks, they are all in pursuit of a tasty life.

And now, serious eaters have a book to call their own—a celebration of deliciousness across the country. These pages will make you smarter, make you hungry, and make you smile. You'll find the greatest breakfasts we've ever come across, 15 sandwiches that might change your life, photos that'll have you tasting fresh doughnuts and summer strawberries, and exhaustively refined recipes. We write about the greatest food in America 365 days of the year. But this book goes above and beyond the Serious Eats site, with new recipes, new photos, and a fresh look at the state of food across the nation. It's one long, impassioned search for the delicious—all in one place.

HOW DID THIS BOOK COME TOGETHER?

Did we eat at every sandwich shop, diner, and pizza parlor in the country? Of course not. But not for lack of trying. We've personally eaten from every place you'll read about in this book (and thousands of others along the way). We visited 41 states, took 92 plane flights, sat through dozens of bus rides, boarded many ferries, hopped more than a few trains, and drove our rental cars and ZipCars and borrowed cars thousands upon thousands of miles to bring you our favorite eats in the country. We had ice cream overnighted (packed in dry ice) from 15 states. We had friends and family ship us their favorite cookies or barbecue. We had days when we tried 25 slices of pie. We flew chicken wings and pancakes and sandwiches across the country for the rest of the Serious Eats team to dissect, reheat, and enjoy. We tapped local journalists, food bloggers, friends, family, and Serious Eats writers and community members for their expert opinions. We met up with Serious Eaters on the road and found that many of them are first-class tour guides and chauffeurs. In short, we ate our way across this country.

And in doing so, we got to know the remarkable people who make the food we came to love. Like Benjamin Wicks, of Mahony's Po-Boy Shop in New Orleans, who's breathing new life into the city's sandwich tradition—and whose grandmother happily delivered our po' boys to the table. And Bonnie Traxel, of Maria's Pizza in Milwaukee, with a bright red dress and a puffy bouffant; she's been slicing up enormous crispy pies just the way her mother Maria did, even using the same sausage supplier for 50 years. Or cheery Haitian-born Edwige Fils-Aimé, whose closet-size bakery tucked down an alley in Princeton, New Jersey, turns out some of the greatest pastries we've had this side of the Atlantic. And Rick Bishop, who studied agriculture at Cornell and now works 18-hour days to bring the sweetest strawberries we've ever tasted to New York City farmers' markets.

Behind every delicious morsel in this country, there's a baker or butcher, chef or farmer, burger mastermind or champion pitmaster whose skill and passion are to credit for the joy you take in every bite.

about our recipes

Every recipe you'll find in this book (unless otherwise noted) was developed by our managing editor, J. Kenji Lopez-Alt. The Serious Eats team would decide just what we were looking for in a given dish—say, light, buttery biscuits with exceptionally meaty sausage gravy—and Kenji would come up with a recipe that attempted to fit those criteria exactly. We'd try the results and discuss them to give Kenji feedback, and he'd refine the recipe until it produced just the biscuits and gravy we were looking for. It was hard work, all that taste-testing—but don't pity us too much.

SANDWICH AT OLYMPIC PROVISIONS, PORTLAND, OR

WHAT WE'VE LEARNED IN OUR SEARCH FOR THE DELICIOUS

Through our collective decades of searching out the perfect bite, we're now particularly attuned to the signs of deliciousness. We've found ourselves agreed on the following.

» Remarkable food is usually the product of one person's skill, craft, and imagination. True food artisans are passionate obsessives. They may become successful businesspeople over time, but first and foremost, they are food perfection-

ists. And the best purveyors and foodmakers know what *good* is. If you don't know what's tasty, you cannot replicate it consistently; without taste, you're flying blind.

» People who make something great usually have a story to tell. You'll be happy to meet many of these characters in the following pages. The passion that drives them inevitably means they're excited to talk about their craft and what it means to them.

>> Ingredients are important, but only in the hands of people who know what to do with them. The greatest tomatoes or cheeses or steaks are magical in the right kitchen, but not in every kitchen.

>> Chefs do many things well—but not everything. Experience in a high-end kitchen makes people more attuned to the nuances of taste and texture and flavor, and the best techniques for achieving what they want. But some cheffy dishes can be overthought or needlessly complicated, rather than improvements on an original.

>> *Authenticity* is a word that's difficult to define and ultimately not all that helpful. Some tortas look just like those sold in Mexico; others don't. Some pizza places look like they've been airlifted straight out of Naples; others serve a pie that couldn't be further from a Neapolitan-style pizza. But the fact that something is perfectly in line with a long tradition doesn't mean it's inherently good. Foods evolve, and we endorse those that evolve toward deliciousness.

>> All good food has some kind of history, but not all food with history is good. Many of our favorite hamburger joints have been in the same family for decades—they have legions of loyal customers and years of grease on the griddle. But that, in itself, doesn't indicate a great burger. We're all for the American classics, and there are reasons to support our local landmarks beyond the quality of the food. But in terms of finding the best bites out there? Older isn't always better.

>> The fact that a place is new and of a modern mind-set doesn't necessarily guarantee it's delicious. Particularly in urban centers, we've seen a huge resurgence of interest in food, especially among young people, with increasing attention to how foods are made and where they come from—a do-it-yourself movement that stretches from bakers to pickle-makers to pastrami-curers to chefs. We're all for those of every age and background jumping into the fray; the more people who devote time to making the best food possible, the more deliciousness results. But the best intentions don't always yield the best eats.

BURGER AT LE PIGEON, PORTLAND, OR

AND WHY NOW?

Serious eaters are having a moment. Forget about reality cooking shows, cupcake fanatics, and the cult of the celebrity chef. Today, people are paying more honest, careful attention to their food than ever before. Perhaps, in an age when so many

people eat from a drive-through rather than a home kitchen, there's an ever-greater yearning for carefully crafted food. Perhaps, as we become increasingly aware of the toll our food production methods take on the environment, the economy, and our own health, we pay more attention to the food we eat. And perhaps the last decades of American cookery have brought better, more thoughtful and delicious food to almost every corner of the country.

Some of the chefs and food crafters you'll meet in this book have been refining their art for decades. But others are the product of an exceptionally rich moment on our collective eating timeline. America has a wealth of culinary history, one that we hope to crack the doors of in this book; what we're seeing now is just the latest chapter in that history, but it's an exciting one. There's never been a better time to care about food.

HOW TO USE THIS BOOK

Read it for fun. Read it to discover how we approach the world of food, how we've learned to spot the true gems, and what we've learned about the stories behind them. Read it to see how others eat across the country. Read it to learn how to make 50 of our favorite foods. And read it to understand what drives some of the greatest chefs and sandwich-makers and farmers in the nation.

breakfast

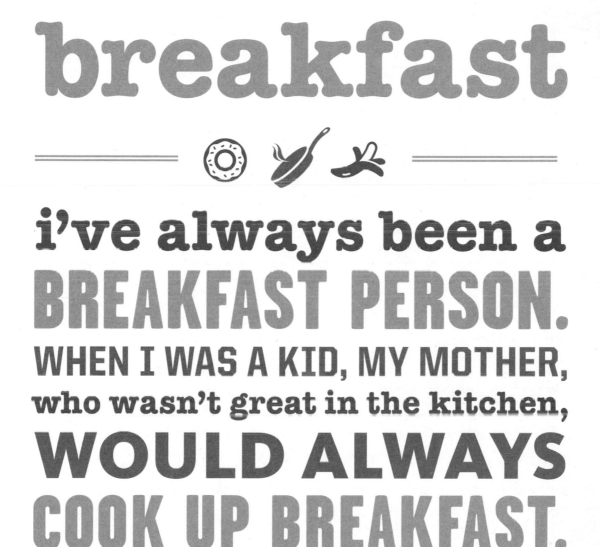

i've always been a **BREAKFAST PERSON.** WHEN I WAS A KID, MY MOTHER, who wasn't great in the kitchen, **WOULD ALWAYS COOK UP BREAKFAST.**

ON SPECIAL OCCASIONS, SHE WOULD MAKE US WHAT SHE CALLED EGYPTIAN EGGS, WHICH YOU MIGHT KNOW AS EGGS IN TOAST OR EGGS IN A HOLE (PAGE 40).

In fact, the family meal I remember most fondly was breakfast, when my dad and I would eat English muffins, farmer cheese, and lingonberry preserves. On the weekends my grandmother would visit and make us wondrously delicious breakfasts of blintzes, seemingly by the hundred. And Sunday breakfast was when my mother first entrusted me to do the food shopping. I would leave the house on my bike with strict orders to ask for a quarter-pound of nova sliced so thin you could see through it—plus cream cheese, bagels, and rugelach from Long Island's Cedarhurst Bake Shop.

Breakfast is the stuff of memory—and it's an empowering meal, eaten in or out of the house.

Why? It's the first meal you can make without help (what kid can't pour milk on cereal?) and one of the first you can make armed with a little bit of knowledge. I get a huge kick out of watching my college-graduate son make eggs and bacon at any time of the day or night.

It's the first meal for which you master your order when you're eating out. Everything on a breakfast menu tends to be recognizable—pancakes, French toast, omelets. It also may be the first meal for which you know your standards and preferences. Do you want your eggs over easy or scrambled soft? Almost everyone has an answer.

Breakfast means something different to everyone. It can be a perfect cappuccino or three plates at the hotel buffet. No other meal ranges so fully from sweet to savory, healthy to indulgent, nibble to feast. Breakfast can be a gooey, crumbly cake or a plate full of meat. Fruit, vegetables, eggs, cheese, fish—nothing is off-limits. In short, you can talk about the whole food universe by talking about breakfast. But breakfast is the meal at which we're most likely to fall into a pattern. Most people don't eat exactly the same thing for dinner every night. Breakfast, on the other hand, is habit-bound. Plenty of us microwave the same oatmeal every morning.

Venture outside your own pantry and there's much to see in the breakfast world. Diners and coffee shops and pancake houses can be found all over the country, all of which have their own traditions. And breakfast is the cheapest meal you can eat out—even at its most expensive, it's never all that costly.

In this chapter, you'll meet 25 of our favorite breakfast places (though we could easily have given you 250). You'll read about pancakes worth a detour. You'll find a killer corned-beef hash recipe and a guide to making the eggiest scrambled eggs the world has ever seen. And you'll find out why spending hours on waffles is worth it.

This chapter will help you enjoy a serious breakfast no matter where you are or what kind of kitchen you have. That's the other great thing about breakfast—all you need is a hot plate, a frying pan, and a spatula.

BREAKFAST PLATE AT SHOPSIN'S, NEW YORK, NY

25 BREAKFASTS WE LOVE

1 PENNY CLUSE CAFE
BURLINGTON, VT

Named after a pet pooch, "Penny," this always-jammed breakfast destination run by husband-and-wife team Charles Reeves and Holly Cluse serves gingerbread pancakes all year long—even when it's not snowman season (though this is Vermont, so it often is). With a batter packed with cinnamon and allspice, griddled into a fluffy flapjack body, they taste more like gingerbread than pancakes. Don't miss the namesake dish, either: two eggs any style with homefries and flaky biscuits, smothered in a basil and parsley–spiked cream gravy.

2 MIKE & PATTY'S
BOSTON, MA

Mike & Patty's only serves breakfast and sandwiches, and they do a mean lunch business, since they're so close to the offices of Boston's Financial District. But no matter what the hour, hang around their tiny Bay Village storefront and you'll hear multiple orders of the "Bacon and Egg, Fancy." It's easy to see why. Eggs and thick-cut smoky bacon with creamy avocado, sharp Cheddar, and red onion, all on a slightly sweet multigrain bread with a swipe of garlicky, barely spicy house-made mayo. What's in that swipe? "Garlic, cumin, cayenne . . . and secrets," says Mike. Want a sweeter sandwich?

Try the Grilled Banana, smeared with cinnamon-honey butter (don't even ask how much); butter creeps through both slices of bread, crust and all, dissolving it into a single griddled sugar-crusted creature, with sliced banana embedded inside.

3 BOULETTES LARDER
SAN FRANCISCO, CA

Amaryll Schwertner isn't just the best breakfast chef you've never heard of; she might be one of the best chefs you've never heard of, a locavore Alice Waters–type (page 313) who's stuck close to the kitchen. And her storefront is a must-visit in the Ferry Building Marketplace (page 335). The always-organic, always-mouthwatering menu changes with the season. One day, it's polenta with fresh crab and hollandaise; the next, perfectly poached eggs with sweet cherry-tomato bread salad and pesto. Even the toast is mind-blowing—an assortment of white and whole wheat from the legendary Acme Bread (right there in the market) and rye from Anna's Daughters' Rye; it's served with a ramekin of sweet butter and organic Italian fruit jams. Servings may be delicately portioned for the price (steel yourself for breakfast sticker shock), but they're satisfying on every level.

4 SHOPSINS
NEW YORK, NY

Half the reason to go to Shopsins is the wildly eccentric proprietor-king himself: Kenny Shopsin, alternately lovable and terrifying. You have to play by Kenny's rules: whipping out a cell phone will get you kicked out; so will showing up with a party of more than four. And if you don't like loud conversation, off-color remarks, or volleying obscenities, you're in the wrong place. But as he sees it, you're having breakfast in his house—with him and his equally colorful children. If none of that fazes you, you're in for one of the best and craziest breakfast menus we know, from mac-and-cheese pancakes and peanut butter–pumpkin Slutty Cakes to Postmodern Pancakes—pancakes chopped up, stirred into pancake batter, made into pancakes.

5 THE SANDS SOUL FOOD DINER
NASHVILLE, TN

When we walked into the bunkerlike building that is the Sands Soul Food Diner early one summer morning, we got in line to order breakfast. "What would you like, darlin'?" asked the kindly but sassy server-cook of the dignified gentleman standing in front of us. He didn't hesitate for a moment: "I'd like some wings, some country ham, two eggs scrambled soft, and a couple of pancakes." Two eggs scrambled soft? It seemed like a request that was unlikely to be heeded, but we admired that the cook seemed receptive to the notion. We ordered the same thing—the super-crunchy fried chicken was well salted and almost greaseless, our eggs were indeed scrambled soft, and the pancakes were a model for pancake-flippers everywhere: lovely crisp edges, a light and tender interior.

6 TASTY N SONS
PORTLAND, OR

When John Gorham, chef-owner of Portland tapas bar Toro Bravo, opened this brunch-minded joint, he brought along his small-plates philosophy. When we visited, every dish was under $11 and sharable at the long, wooden communal tables—and every dish is photogenic enough to be on magazine covers. The plates range from small (bacon-wrapped dates drizzled in warm maple syrup; golf-ball–size chocolate potato doughnuts)

MOROCCAN CHICKEN HASH AT TASTY N SONS, PORTLAND, OR

from the serious eats community

A TYPICALLY HAPHAZARD BREAKFAST PLATTER AT SHOPSIN'S, NEW YORK, NY

"Kenny [Shopsin] is just notoriously ornery. I would say, be amused, and let the anger go if you can. He's a real character, one of those New York treasures (though I'm sure it doesn't seem that way when he is calling you an [expletive] . . .). —CookiePie

to less small, like the shakshuka (a North African–Middle Eastern tomato stew with eggs). It shows up piping hot and glistening with about-to-burst yolky eggs in a lake of roasted tomatoes, house-made merguez sausage, and roasted red pepper strands that are so long you can twirl them up linguine style. You'll soak up the whole shakshuka swamp with their toasted country bread. Seasons are honored in the frittata, which, in the early summer, is a pile of delicious green—green beans, green olives, and snappy green peas—served in a burn-your-hand-off skillet, studded with feta and a single deep-fried feta ball.

talking to ina

I generally don't much care for cutesy retro breakfast-nook restaurants. You know the ones I'm talking about. They inevitably have cow creamers and all sorts of kitsch on the wall—or, in the case of Ina's, cheeseburger and hamburger salt shakers. But sometimes the cuteness at such a place is trumped by what comes out of its kitchen. After we made our way through a breakfast of delectable heavenly hots and fine fried chicken and waffles, Ina Pinkney herself wandered over to our table, a thermos of coffee in hand. I asked her how Ina's came to be. "Back in the early '90s, I was working in dessert catering, but I was always complaining about how there were no good breakfasts in Chicago. We just weren't a good breakfast town. And my friend said, 'You work with flour, butter, and eggs all day long. Why don't you open a breakfast spot yourself?' And the rest was history. If you want something truly delicious, sometimes you have to make it yourself." Truer words were never spoken.

7 INA'S
CHICAGO, IL

Ina Pinkney is breakfast royalty in Chicago's West Loop. But while her restaurant Ina's has the comfortable, worn-in feel of an old-time diner, the food is taken much more seriously; you'll notice with your first cup of coffee. From Chicago's own acclaimed roastery Intelligentsia, it's a good ten steps above your average diner brew. Ina's signature pancakes are the Heavenly Hots—coaster-size little cakes based on a recipe from Marion Cunningham of *The Fanny Farmer Cookbooks*, made famous at Bridge Creek Inn in Marin County, California. (Ina called Marion herself to ask permission to use the recipe.) Made with eggs, sour cream, and the smallest bit of flour, with potato starch to keep them from falling apart in the pan, they're creamy and custardy and cloudlike in their lightness; and though they need no adornment, they're served with an alluringly spiced fruit compote of peach, raspberry, and blueberry.

HEAVENLY HOTS AT INA'S, CHICAGO, IL

8 A'S BURGERS
DANA POINT, CA

What do burgers have to do with breakfast burritos? Nothing. But locals in this Orange County town know A's is just as famous for their flour tortilla bundles—full of fluffy scrambled eggs, buttery potato hunks, and melted cheese—as they are for

CRUMPETS AT CRUMPET SHOP, SEATTLE, WA

their burgers. You can also throw in steak, sausage, bacon, ham, or chorizo with the eggs. Given how mediocre most breakfast burritos are, we had to tip you off to A's. It's become a surfer breakfast staple, so don't be surprised if most of the clientele is sand-crusted.

9 BIG BAD BREAKFAST
OXFORD, MS

Venerable food writer John T. Edge once told us we couldn't leave Oxford without stopping by Big Bad Breakfast—and boy, are we glad we listened to him. Chef John Currence is a great cook with a lot of soul, and his modest, cheerful storefront lights up the generic shopping center where it stands. Picking just one dish from the menu is nearly impossible, but don't leave without a Cathead: that'd be a made-from-scratch buttermilk biscuit, helium-light with crispy nooks and crannies, piled with delicious sage-y sausage or sweet, salty ham, plus Cheddar cheese, all served with grits or hash browns.

10 CRUMPET SHOP
SEATTLE, WA

How often do you eat crumpets? Probably not enough. Slightly springier and puffier than English muffins, these edible sponges soak up honey, blackberry preserves, and thick pats of butter. The Crumpet Shop—its walls adorned with *Alice in Wonderland* tea party murals and signs announcing free tea refills—opened in 1976, the work of Gary Lasater and Nancy McFaul, a husband-and-wife team who aren't British, just pro-crumpet Americans. One of the staffers (we'll call him the "Crumpet Man") repeats the pour-batter-onto-griddle-shape-then-flip routine in the front window, over and over again, as Pike Place Market visitors stop to watch. He's kind of like the hand-pulled noodle men in Chinatown restaurant windows—you just can't stop staring.

11 THE HOMINY GRILL
CHARLESTON, SC

Chef Robert Stehling's artfully spartan but homey Charleston cafe has a way of making Southern

classics just the tiniest bit better—no surprise, from a James Beard Award–winning talent. In the mornings, when light streams in through the front windows, opt for the cheese grits and shrimp (sautéed with mushrooms and bacon) or the Big Nasty Biscuit, a huge, buttery biscuit with a tender crumble and a soft, moist crumb, smothered in smoky sausage gravy and sandwiching a superb fried chicken breast. These aren't just indulgent morning meals—with their clean, focused flavors, they're perfectly composed dishes.

12 TECOLOTE CAFÉ
SANTA FE, NM

Eating breakfast at the Tecolote Café in Santa Fe, you immediately understand the best of what New Mexico has to offer. The Huevos Yucatecos platter begins with pliable corn tortillas surrounded by tender black beans, green chile, and cheese, all topped off with two eggs and perfectly pan-fried bananas. Order any of their platters with a serving of creamy beans, posole (dried and rehydrated corn), or crispy hash browns. While all New Mexican joints serve carne adovada, a classic dish of baked lean pork in an earthy red chile sauce, Tecolote's version is exceptionally tender. And for those with a sweet tooth, the atolé piñon pancakes, light and fluffy, burst with real pine nut flavor.

13 THE FRIENDLY TOAST
PORTSMOUTH, NH

Every city has its local institutions—and small New England cities tend to be particularly devoted to their own. But hometown pride only partly explains the wild popularity of The Friendly Toast in Portsmouth, New Hampshire. The kitsch-strewn walls of this friendly spot, owned by husband-and-wife team Melissa and Robert Jasper, are as fun to look at as the whimsical menu: herb sauce–topped Green Eggs and Ham, Almond Joy Pancakes, and the toast, of course, baked right in their kitchen. The house special is the anadama, a hearty cornmeal-molasses bread—or, if you want to try the spiciest toast you've ever had, get the Ole Miss

breakfast plate. The dish comes with cayenne-Cheddar bread, which sits under chipotle-spiked sweet potato mash, scrambled eggs, and a mouth-cooling dollop of mango sour cream.

14 CAFÉ ESTELLE
PHILADELPHIA, PA

Philly is a pretty serious brunch town, but what about breakfast? At Café Estelle, they serve both. Casual and somewhat industrial-looking, it's set among parking lots in the ground floor of a big condo building. But don't let the stripped-down digs dissuade you—the food's worth a visit. The house-made bacon is deliciously smoky, porky, and crisp; they butcher from whole animals and make the bacon in a smoker out back (you can even call and make a date to watch that process). The buttermilk pancakes don't need syrup—they're thin and delicate, with brown-buttery flavor and crispy edges. And if French toast with home-made vanilla ice cream doesn't sound *too* much like dessert, dig in—the cream softens into the toast for a breakfast that's creamy and custardy and impossible to stop eating.

15 THE BREAKFAST KLUB
HOUSTON, TX

The Breakfast Klub is a clubby-feeling place, with a ridiculously friendly staff that makes sure everyone feels like they belong as they wait in the inevitable line to order. But unlike most clubs, this one has seriously tasty food. Order the poached eggs, super-crispy fried catfish, and creamy, tangy, cheese grits (for maximum enjoyment, break the yolks over those grits)—a true breakfast of champions. Their grilled biscuits, covered with house-made sausage cream gravy, are another fine option.

16 MATT'S BIG BREAKFAST
PHOENIX, AZ

Owners Erenia and Matt Pool met while working at nearby pizza mecca Pizzeria Bianco (page 104). In 2005, they opened this retro, mandarin orange–

countertopped diner where red-checkered apron-wearing waitresses serve basic breakfast fare made with the very best ingredients. "I pay more for King Arthur Flour, for Yukon Golds instead of russets; I pay $80 a gallon for real Vermont maple syrup," says Erenia. Their attention to quality shows everywhere. The pancakes and waffles are airy with golden-brown crusts, and served so hot that the clump of butter in the middle immediately slides off. The Five-Spot is the juiciest breakfast sandwich you'll ever eat: squeeze the fluffy roll and out spurt juices from the grilled onions, melted American cheese, and thick-cut peppery bacon, sourced from the Pork Shop in Queen Creek, Arizona. It sits alongside homefries; the potatoes are parboiled, roasted, pan-fried to get those beautiful charred edges, then tossed with soft onion strands and fresh rosemary sprigs.

17 TARTINE
SAN FRANCISCO, CA

Lines at this French-American bakery in San Francisco's Mission District often stretch down the block—even at mid-morning on a weekday, you're bound to spend half an hour inching your way toward the counter (perhaps making some new friends while you're there). Why the wait? It could be the double pain au chocolat, the flakiest, darkest, most buttery rendition of the pastry imaginable. Or the bowls of custardy bread pudding. Or the indecently oozy croque monsieur. There are no wrong choices on this menu. (There aren't many light ones, either.)

18 THE SILVER SKILLET
ATLANTA, GA

It's easy to love a place that opened in 1956 and still has the same swivel chairs—and that's served delicious breakfast the whole time, including exceptional biscuits. "I'd rather take my pants off than give away our recipe!" one employee told our curious food blogger friend Adam "The Amateur Gourmet" Roberts. Those tall, feather-light biscuits are best with the skillet-cooked ham: dark red and about twice as thick as typical country ham, served with red-eye gravy for spooning on top.

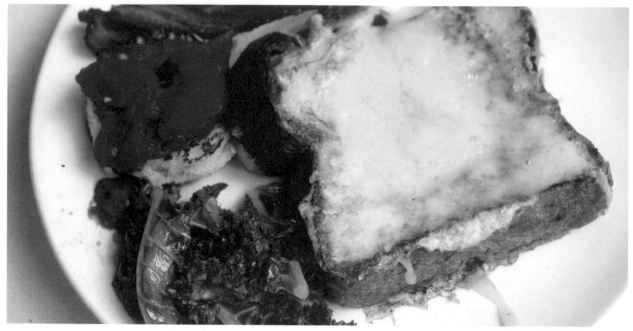

EGGS ROTHKO AT EGG, BROOKLYN, NY

19 SOFRA
CAMBRIDGE, MA

Sofra is a neighborhood bakery that takes its spices seriously. Owners Ana Sorton and Maura Kilpatrick have their hands full—they also run the highly acclaimed Middle Eastern–inflected restaurant Oleana—but we've spotted Kilpatrick at Sofra for the Sunday brunch rush, a sign of dedication that amazes us. Though the morning shakshuka (served with chewy house pita) is certainly worth an order, the real fun is at the pastry counter: Lebanese croissants with the Middle Eastern spice blend za'atar, morning buns with orange blossom glaze, and "dukka" doughnuts, covered in a salty, sweet Egyptian-inspired spice mix.

20 STANLEY
NEW ORLEANS, LA

Chef Scott Boswell has become a NOLA name for Stella!, his fine-dining destination, but sibling restaurant Stanley is also worth a visit—particularly for breakfast. We'd point you to the Eggs Stanley, essentially an eggs benedict with two enormous, delicately cornmeal-battered oysters. So plump that, when you slide a fork in, briny juices soak into the English muffin, just like the egg yolk. Delicious. A stack of fine banana pancakes, topped with a melty scoop of vanilla ice cream and Louisiana cane syrup, is perfect for those who like breakfast on the sweeter side.

21 HOT SUPPA
PORTLAND, ME

In 2006, two brothers from Portland turned this 1860 brick townhouse into a corned-beef-hash haven. The red meat shreds of their corned beef, which they cure in-house, aren't too fatty, are just beefy and tender, and are pan-browned to a crisp. It's a lot of meat for one person—with some potato, carrot, and onion slivers hiding in there, not to mention the two eggs and homefries served with it. If hash isn't your thing, go with their buttermilk pancakes. They have an "add Maine wild blueberries" option. You should take it.

22 EGG
BROOKLYN, NY

Egg's chef-partner George Weld really knows how to do up eggs—and these are from happy, free-roaming, local chickens—but anything on the menu is worth an order. If you're familiar with egg-in-toast, or one of its million nicknames (page 40), Eggs Rothko takes that dish to the next level: an easy-cooked egg hiding inside a slice of crusty

STURGEON AND EGGS AT BARNEY GREENGRASS, NEW YORK, NY

brioche, all topped with an oozy blanket of sharp Grafton Cheddar. Order a French press of excellent coffee to help wash down all the fatty deliciousness. Tip: to best enjoy the friendly-staffed Brooklyn restaurant, go during the week—unless hour-plus weekend waits are your thing.

bialys

"What's a bialy?" we overheard a new customer ask her waiter at Barney Greengrass. "A Jewish English muffin," he answered with a smile. Well, not really, but it's a great answer. A bialy is a bagel's lighter, smaller first cousin. Properly made, it's baked once instead of boiled and baked; it has a thumbprint of onion in the middle instead of a hole; and it has to be toasted unless you get it less than three minutes out of the oven. The good news about the toasting part? It means that good bialys can be shipped without losing anything in transit. Kossar's, the venerable bialy bakery located in what was once the heart of Manhattan's Lower East Side, ships their terrific bialys at a modest price.

23 BARNEY GREENGRASS
NEW YORK, NY

Breakfast at Barney Greengrass is a quintessentially New York eating experience, a rite of passage for any city visitor or newcomer. A plate of sturgeon, scrambled eggs, and onions is an incredibly ugly pile of food that nonetheless tastes like heaven. The salty, meaty, firm-fleshed sturgeon (still tasting of the sea), the creamy eggs, and the softened onions create an unbeatable combination that can only be had here. (They don't call themselves "The Sturgeon King" for nothing.) What completes the experience? Your gruff, constantly kibitzing waiter. Coming or going, say hello to third-generation owner Gary Greengrass, who sits behind the cash register just like his father and grandfather did.

24 DOTTIE'S TRUE BLUE CAFE
SAN FRANCISCO, CA

San Francisco may be a truly innovative food city, but Dottie's True Blue Cafe couldn't be further from the cutting edge; each of the diner's few tables are papered with photos of cinema stars, and the coffee is strictly diner-grade (not Blue Bottle French press). That said, the food is fantastic, from the house-baked bread that starts your meal to the ginger-cinnamon buttermilk pancakes and the sweet potato-butterscotch French toast.

25 HUCKLEBERRY BAKERY AND CAFÉ
LOS ANGELES, CA

Huckleberry chef and co-owner Zoe Nathan learned to bake at San Francisco's superb Tartine Bakery (page 25), which explains why the baked goods at Huckleberry are so insanely tasty, from croissants to coffee cake to doughnuts. But it doesn't explain why the breakfast menu is filled with so many irresistible-sounding items. Their Green Eggs and Ham, made with La Quercia prosciutto, pesto, and arugula (fresh from the Santa Monica farmers' market) on a house-baked English muffin, is one of the great breakfast sandwiches of our time. A Niman Ranch bacon-Gruyère sandwich with eggs, oozy and delicious, is just as good. And even though you will feel completely full and sated after eating breakfast at Huckleberry, it's hard to resist a container of chocolate pudding to go.

I grew up just outside the New York City limits, so I didn't discover the deliciousness of this classic Southern breakfast until I hit the road in college. At their best, biscuits and gravy are flaky, meaty, tender, savory, and creamy at the same time. Our recipe smothers feathery light biscuits with an intensely meaty gravy, giving you strong sausage flavor even in the meat-free bites. Folding the biscuit dough a few times helps our biscuits get super flaky.

biscuits
and gravy

MAKES 8

FOR THE BISCUITS

½ cup (1 stick) unsalted butter, frozen, plus 2 tablespoons melted and cooled slightly

2 cups (10 ounces) plus 2 tablespoons all-purpose flour

2 teaspoons baking powder

½ teaspoon baking soda

1½ teaspoons kosher salt

1 cup buttermilk

1 Adjust the oven rack to the middle position and preheat the oven to 425°F. Grate the stick of frozen butter on the large holes of a box grater into a medium bowl. Place it in the freezer until needed. Combine the 2 cups flour, baking powder, baking soda, and salt in a medium bowl and whisk to combine. Add the frozen butter to the mixture and toss with your fingers until it's thoroughly coated. Add the buttermilk and fold together the mixture with a rubber spatula until it is just combined.

2 Transfer the mixture to a well-floured work surface and knead it into a ragged ball (about six to eight kneads). Roll the mixture into a 12-inch square. Fold the dough into thirds by using a bench scraper or thin metal spatula to bring the sides of the square toward the center, one after the other, like a business letter (you should end up with a 12 × 4-inch rectangle). In the same manner, fold the short ends toward the center, folding into thirds again (resulting in a 4-inch square). Reroll the dough into a 12-inch square and repeat the full folding procedure.

3 Roll the dough into a square approximately 12 × 8 inches and ½ inch thick. Cut it into six 4-inch circles using a floured biscuit cutter. Transfer the dough rounds to an ungreased cookie sheet, leaving at least 1 inch of space between each biscuit. Gather the dough scraps into a ball, reroll them, and cut out two more 4-inch rounds and transfer to the baking sheet. Add the dough scraps to the baking sheet if desired, or discard them.

biscuit honor roll

We're always on the hunt for good biscuits at Serious Eats.
Some of the most impressive we've come across?
Big Bad Breakfast in Oxford, MS (page 23); the Silver Skillet in
Atlanta, GA (page 25); and Neal's Deli in Carrboro, NC
(page 43). Nowhere near the Biscuit Belt? Get some fine
mail-order biscuits from Callie's in Charleston, SC—the decisive
winner of an office mail-order biscuit tasting.

4 Brush the tops of the biscuits with the 2 tablespoons melted butter and bake until golden brown, rotating halfway through the baking time, about 16 minutes total. Let the biscuits cool for 5 minutes at room temperature.

5 Meanwhile, make the gravy: Cook the sausage in a 10-inch heavy-bottomed nonstick skillet over medium-high heat using a wooden spatula or spoon to break up the meat as it cooks. Once it is no longer pink (about 6 minutes), add the sage, fennel, and onion, and cook for about 2 minutes longer, until the onion is softened and the spices are fragrant. Add the remaining 2 tablespoons flour and cook, stirring constantly, until fully absorbed, about 1 minute. Add half of the milk and stir to combine. Add the remaining milk and allow the mixture to come to a simmer. Simmer until the gravy has thickened, about 3 minutes. Season to taste with salt and plenty of black pepper.

6 Split the biscuits, top with the gravy, and serve.

FOR THE GRAVY

1 pound bulk breakfast sausage

2 teaspoons minced fresh sage leaves, or ½ teaspoon ground sage

½ teaspoon ground fennel seed

1 small onion, finely chopped (about ⅔ cup)

2 cups whole milk

Kosher salt and freshly cracked black peppercorns

BREAKFAST PASTRY PARADISE

The great thing about breakfast is that it's an excuse to eat butter and sugar and call it a meal. Not that our favorite breakfast pastries are **all** butter and sugar, of course—restraint can be a virtue. Here are our top picks for flaky morning goodness across the country.

1 THE LITTLE CHEF
PRINCETON, NJ

Just across the street from the Princeton University campus, the Little Chef may be one of New Jersey's best-kept secrets. The cozy nook of a bakery is a one-man show: the charming Haitian-born Edwige Fils-Aimé rises before dawn each day and dons a flour-streaked baseball cap to bake the few hundred textbook-perfect croissants, scones, and brioches that inevitably sell out well before noon. It's the rare baker rigorously schooled in French orthodoxy who approaches his craft with a sense of humor, but Fils-Aimé (or "Pouchon," to friends) laughs and chats his way through the workday. Inside you'll hear French spoken as often as English—those who know their pastries know the Little Chef.

2 CAFE BESALU
SEATTLE, WA

Jamie and Kaire Miller's friendly neighborhood bakery, in the Ballard neighborhood of Seattle, is the kind of place you'll walk by and stop dead in your tracks, dizzy with delight from the doughy fumes wafting out. Their classic French pastries are unbeatable—croissants with shatter-crisp buttery shells, deliciously molten pain au chocolat—but their specials are perhaps even finer, such as a plum-mascarpone tart scented with cardamom. More of a savory person? Their pastry skill shows in their quiche crusts, too.

3 LES MADELEINES
SALT LAKE CITY, UT

Romina Rasmussen trained in French pastry at the French Culinary Institute in New York before she opened her Salt Lake bakery, and it's the French treats that are her best—particularly the Kouing Aman, so popular the bakery imposes a limit of six per person without advance order. Absurdly buttery, flaky dough is layered into a spiky, muffin-size package, a maze of caramelized edges cloaking a soft interior and wells of butter and sweet, gooey pockets within.

4 FLOUR BAKERY
BOSTON AND CAMBRIDGE, MA

These friendly, whimsical Boston bakeries, started by Harvard grad Joanne Chang, make homemade "Pop-Tarts" and tasty cookies—but it's the super-sticky sticky buns that everyone's really there for.

CAFE BESALU, SEATTLE, WA

BAKED GOODS AT BATCH BAKEHOUSE, MADISON, WI

Sticky buns should be sweet, and these are; the filling tastes like something between caramel and brown sugar, with cinnamon and honey rounding things out. Sticky buns should be *sticky,* and these are so thoroughly drenched with sticky goo that it drips all over the box, your hands, and everything within a three-foot vicinity. But even more important, the dough is tender and perfect, soft and just a little yeasty, airy in the middle and a teeny bit crisp around the edges. If your heart's set on one, call ahead to reserve—they often sell out.

5 LA FARINE
OAKLAND AND BERKELEY, CA

All the classics are tasty at this French bakery, which opened its first branch in Oakland in 1974, but it's the morning buns that really set the place apart; they're muffin-shaped but far from muffin density. Flaky, thin croissant layers swirl up around the top like a snail shell, and get a drizzle of cinnamon-sugar granules. You pull apart feathery

pieces like you're eating a cinnamon roll. Tan, crispy edges give way to tender pastry insides. And while any pastry is a little more magical when warm, these morning buns are even good in the afternoon, when they're not baked seconds-ago fresh.

6 BATCH BAKEHOUSE
MADISON, WI

It's open just five days a week, it's cash only, and it closes at 3 in the afternoon on the weekends, but it's worth making a date and getting there early to experience this charming closet-size Madison bakery. They have muffins and scones and crusty, hot rolls—all perfect expressions of their given forms. We're partial to the Vanilla Swirls, spirals of croissant dough with a sparingly sweet vanilla filling, as well as the uncommonly delicious blueberry muffins.

PASTRIES AT LOCANDA VERDE, NEW YORK, NY

7 LOCANDA VERDE
NEW YORK, NY

While Andrew Carmellini's Italian restaurant Locanda Verde is one of our favorite spots in New York City for any meal, pastry chef Karen DeMasco's baked treats, available both in the restaurant and for take-out from a counter up front, are the reason we find ourselves stopping by again and again. Even the most pedestrian breakfast bites are memorable here—including a supremely moist blueberry-polenta muffin and a zucchini bread with a crunchy sugar topping, delicate and sweet with notes of cinnamon. There's a pillowy hazelnut sticky bun and a syrup-soaked date cake and an apple-cinnamon roll with caramelized apple chunks tucked into the swirl of dough. Any of these, plus a cappuccino to stay, makes for an immensely pleasurable morning meal—especially if you add an order of their signature whipped sheep's-milk ricotta.

knaus berry farm's sticky buns

Miami chef Michael Schwartz (Michael's Genuine Food & Drink, page 312) and I once drove forty-five minutes to Homestead, Florida, to pick up produce from the extraordinary Teena's Pride farm. But right before we reached Teena Borek's farm, we needed some sustenance, so we pulled into the parking lot at Knaus Berry Farm, a farmstand famous in the area for baked goods. The only problem was the line snaking all the way around the parking lot and the farmstand. Michael had us on an aggressive eating itinerary and we didn't have two hours to spare, which was the time that the line-waiters estimated, so we calmly explained to one of the owners that I had come all the way from New York to try one of his sticky buns, hoping that he would take pity on us. We succeeded; he told us to meet him around the back of the small building that housed his retail operation ("Just make sure nobody sees you"), where he greeted us with two beyond fresh, insanely hot sticky buns. "Do not eat it now," he warned. "You will burn your mouth."

This sticky bun looked so good glistening like gold in the Florida sunlight, it was everything I could do to wait one minute before I tore off a piece. It was soft and tender with just enough chew to require teeth. The outer layers were as moist and buttery as the inner layers, which is how I judge cinnamon buns. I still don't know if I would wait two hours for a Knaus sticky bun—but if you show up anytime other than Saturday morning, you shouldn't have to endure those lines.

Our perfect waffles are crispy-skinned, fluffy-bodied, and tangy. An overnight rise in the fridge gives them a more complex flavor than any recipe using baking powder ever could. Trust us, it's worth the wait.

orange-scented
yeast waffles

MAKES FOUR 9-INCH SQUARE BELGIAN WAFFLES, OR SIX 7-INCH ROUND REGULAR WAFFLES

1 Whisk the flour, sugar, salt, and yeast together in a large bowl until thoroughly combined. In a medium bowl, whisk the milk, yogurt, eggs, orange zest, and vanilla until fully combined. Add the milk mixture to the flour mixture and stir with a rubber spatula until smooth, making sure to scrape and incorporate the dry flour from around the bottom and sides of the bowl. Add the butter and mix until it is incorporated. Cover the bowl tightly with plastic wrap and allow to rise in the refrigerator for at least 8 hours and up to 1 day.

2 Spray a waffle iron with nonstick cooking spray and place it over a medium-high heat, reversing sides until it just begins to smoke, about 4 minutes. (Alternatively, heat an electric waffle iron following the manufacturer's instructions.) Stir the waffle batter gently with a ladle, and add it to the iron (about 1 cup for a Belgian waffle or $2/3$ cup for a regular waffle). Cook the waffle, flipping the iron occasionally until it's golden brown and crisp on both sides, about 6 minutes total. Serve the waffles immediately or hold them in a warm oven (see below).

2 cups (10 ounces) all-purpose flour

2 tablespoons sugar (about $3/4$ ounce)

$1\frac{1}{2}$ teaspoons kosher salt

1 teaspoon fast-rise yeast

1 cup whole milk

1 cup plain low-fat yogurt

2 large eggs

1 tablespoon orange zest (from 1 orange)

1 teaspoon vanilla extract (or Grand Marnier)

$\frac{1}{2}$ cup (1 stick) unsalted butter, melted and cooled slightly

Nonstick cooking spray

NOTE Grand Marnier can be substituted in place of vanilla extract for a more pronounced orange flavor. If you are making a large batch or want to serve all the waffles at the same time, the waffles can be held for up to 20 minutes on a wire rack set in a rimmed baking sheet in a 200°F. oven.

We wanted sticky buns that were tender, light, and moist all the way through—not just any old dough dressed up with a sticky glaze. And we think these succeed beautifully.

caramel
sticky buns

MAKES 9 STICKY BUNS

FOR THE DOUGH

6 tablespoons (¾ stick) unsalted butter

½ cup full-fat yogurt, room temperature

2 large eggs, room temperature

1 packet (¼ ounce) fast-rise yeast

1½ teaspoons Kosher salt

3 tablespoons (1¼ ounces) granulated sugar

3 cups (15 ounces) all-purpose flour, plus more for working

FOR THE FILLING

½ cup (about 4 ounces) brown sugar, packed

2 teaspoons ground cinnamon

Kosher salt

2 tablespoons unsalted butter, melted

1 For the dough: In a large bowl, heat the butter in the microwave at medium power until it is just melted. Add the yogurt, eggs, yeast, kosher salt, and sugar and whisk until the ingredients are well combined. Add the flour and stir with a wooden spoon until the dough forms a ball. Transfer to the bowl of a standing mixer fitted with a dough hook attachment and knead on low speed for 10 minutes, adding flour as necessary until the dough just barely pulls away from the sides of the bowl. Transfer to a large greased bowl, cover with plastic wrap, and allow the dough to rise until doubled in volume, about 2 hours.

2 For the filling: Once the dough has risen, combine the brown sugar, cinnamon, and a pinch of salt in a medium bowl. Turn the dough out onto a floured surface. Roll the dough into an even 12 × 8-inch rectangle, with the long side facing you. Brush melted butter evenly over the surface, leaving a narrow border along the top long edge. Spread the cinnamon sugar evenly over the buttered area, using your hands to gently work it to the edges.

3 Starting at the bottom edge, roll the rectangle away from you into a tight cylinder 12 inches wide. Rest the cylinder seam side down and carefully even out the shape and square off the edges. Using a sharp knife, cut the cylinder into three even pieces. Cut each piece into three more pieces to create nine buns total. Arrange the cut buns in a well-buttered 8 × 8-inch baking dish. Cover the dish tightly with plastic. (The dough can be refrigerated overnight at this point.) Allow the buns to rise at warm room temperature until they are puffy and pressed tightly against each other, about 2 hours.

4 While the buns are rising, adjust the oven rack to the lower middle position and preheat the oven to 350°F. Remove the plastic wrap from the dish and bake the buns until they are golden brown and puffy, about 30 minutes. Transfer the baking dish to a wire rack and let the buns cool for at least 10 minutes, while you make the sauce.

5 For the caramel sauce: Heat the butter and the brown sugar in a medium saucepan over medium heat, stirring occasionally until the mixture is bubbling and puffy, about

3 minutes. Whisk in the condensed milk. Simmer until the mixture is reduced to a thick saucelike consistency (the mixture should coat the back of a spoon easily). Whisk in the rum and pecans (if using).

6 Using a thin metal spatula, loosen the buns from the sides and turn them out of the dish (but do not separate them yet). Transfer them to a serving platter and spoon half of the caramel sauce evenly over them. Allow the sauce to soak in for about 10 minutes, then serve, pulling the buns apart with your fingers and serving extra caramel sauce on the side.

FOR THE CARAMEL SAUCE

½ cup (1 stick) unsalted butter

1 cup (about 8 ounces) brown sugar, packed

1 (14-ounce) can sweetened condensed milk

1 tablespoon rum (optional)

1 cup (about 4 ounces) chopped toasted pecans (optional)

NOTE The buns can be assembled the night before and placed in the refrigerator after arranging in their baking dish and wrapping with plastic. To bake the next day, allow the buns to rise at warm room temperature for 2 hours before baking as directed.

8 PANCAKE SPOTS WORTH A DETOUR

MAGNOLIA CAFE, AUSTIN, TX

Pancakes are one of the easiest foods to make, yet one of the hardest foods to make just right. What do we look for in pancakes? A thin, crispy exterior that gives way to light and tender insides; but after that, it's up to the gifted pancake-maker to come up with something unique. Here are eight spots around the country that have pancakes truly worth seeking out.

1 MAGNOLIA CAFE
AUSTIN, TX

"Sorry, We're Open," apologizes the sign. But owners Kent Cole and Diana Prechter aren't really sorry—and you won't be, either, after you try the gingerbread pancakes that have attracted a cult following. Both locations of the Magnolia Cafe are open 24 hours, and for the most part, they serve predictable diner food for University of Texas at Austin students, out for post-merrymaking eats. But the gingerbread pancakes will make you feel like it's Christmas, even in the middle of sweaty June. They have all the spicy goodness of a gingerbread cookie in cakelike, fluffy form.

2 AL'S BREAKFAST
MINNEAPOLIS, MN

Served at the justifiably famous Al's near the University of Minnesota, these pancakes have just the right amount of tangy tartness from the buttermilk that goes into them. You'll stand and wait a while to get served, squished with strangers behind the row of stools, but it's worth it. We recommend an order of pancakes with blueberries and corn kernels and all.

3 POLLY'S PANCAKE PARLOR
SUGAR HILL, NH

Great alliteration aside, this is one of the best pancake joints in New Hampshire (and there are many—this is maple syrup country, after all). Attached to an old sugar house where they make their own syrup, Polly's gives you plenty of options for your six-pancake order. Buttermilk oatmeal, cornmeal, plain, buckwheat, or whole wheat, and that's just the batter; for mix-ins, you can have blueberries, walnuts, coconut shreds, or chocolate chips. These pancakes come out three at a time, with the second three waiting until the first are finished, so they never get cold on your table.

BLACKBERRY BLISSCAKES AT M. HENRY, CHICAGO, IL

4 M. HENRY
CHICAGO, IL

They had us at Blackberry Blisscakes. At M. Henry, a sunny, cheery café in Chicago's Andersonville neighborhood, they're our favorite dish on a stellar breakfast menu. The pancakes would be memorably good all on their own—thick yet airy, with a gorgeous brown crust—but layered with smooth vanilla mascarpone and warm blackberries, and finished off with a crunchy-sweet brown sugar and oat streusel, you start to understand why they're called "blisscakes."

5 PAMELA'S DINER
PITTSBURGH, PA

Hotcakes from Pamela's, a cash-only breakfast and lunch joint with six locations in the Pittsburgh area, are somewhere between crepes and pancakes, with all the good qualities of each. Thin and slightly spongy and plenty buttery, they get that brown lacelike design on the surface. But the best part, hands down, are the crispy edges. They're like the crusts of perfectly well-done latkes, all crackly, and you immediately fork-cut them off. The hotcakes come rolled up two to a plate; they're best stuffed with fresh strawberry slices, brown sugar, and tangy sour cream. Pamela's is one of those must-visit institutions in Pittsburgh (there's a framed photo of President Obama near the door from his visit during the 2008 campaign), but the hype is deserved. It's all about the crazy crispy edges.

6 MAIALINO
NEW YORK, NY

One word: ricotta. That's why the pancakes at revered restaurateur Danny Meyer's Roman trattoria in the Gramercy Park Hotel are so ridiculously creamy-tasting and porous—great for syrup fiends, though they're so tasty on their own, they're easy to eat in the nude. And just in case you didn't get enough ricotta in the pancakes, they throw a mountainous dollop on top. Maialino has a gorgeous

RICOTTA PANCAKES AT MAIALINO, NEW YORK, NY

breakfast menu, including many dishes with the most perfectly poached eggs we've ever had, but these pancakes sure are hard to pass up.

7 COFFEE CUP CAFE
SULLY, IA

Even if you're quite a ways from the teeny farm town of Sully, Iowa, the drive to this modest dining room is worth every minute because the light, fluffy pancakes with a crispy exterior are enough to make you moan with pleasure with each bite. They don't use 100 percent maple syrup—they actually make their own "pancake syrup" with two kinds of sugar, two kinds of corn syrup, vanilla, and maple flavoring—but it's tastier than you'd think, smooth and sweet and perfect for pancakes. Time may have aged the Coffee Cup, but the food hasn't suffered in the slightest.

8 MARKET LUNCH
WASHINGTON, DC

Look for Market Lunch's communal table at the end of Eastern Market's long corridor. Though its name may reference another meal, it serves a formidable breakfast. The blueberry-buckwheat pancakes (Blue-Bucks), light, buttery, and juicy-berry-studded, are only sold on Saturdays, when the line starts forming before 8:00 AM. If you're there on a non–Blue-Buck day (that is, a weekday), the "regular" pancakes are a fine substitute.

coffee cup cafe

I used to drive the twenty miles from Grinnell College, my alma mater, to Sully's Coffee Cup Cafe just for a plate of those pancakes (well, and a sticky bun and a slice of pie). Quite an undertaking for a college kid on a weekend—even a food-crazed college kid like myself.

These pancakes are a little Italian, a little dressed up—and man, are they good. With light, almost creamy interiors, the freshness of ricotta, and the slight hint of lemon zest, they don't even need maple syrup. But we won't hold it against you if you pour it on.

lemon ricotta
pancakes

1 Whisk together the flour, baking powder, baking soda, sugar, salt, and lemon zest in a medium bowl. Whisk together the buttermilk, ricotta, melted butter, eggs, and vanilla in a medium bowl. Add the dry ingredients to the wet mixture and whisk until no dry flour remains (mixture should remain lumpy; be careful not to overmix).

2 Heat $1/2$ teaspoon of oil in a 12-inch heavy-bottomed nonstick skillet over medium-high heat (or on an electric griddle) until the oil shimmers. Reduce the heat to medium and wipe out the skillet with a paper towel. Cook the pancakes four at a time using a $1/4$-cup measure to scoop them into the pan. Cook on the first side until bubbles appear and the bottom surface is golden brown, 2 to 3 minutes. Flip the pancakes and cook until the second side is golden brown, about 2 minutes longer. Transfer the pancakes to a plate and cover with a clean kitchen towel while you cook the remaining batches. Serve with maple syrup.

MAKES 12 PANCAKES

1 cup (5 ounces) all-purpose flour

$1/2$ teaspoon baking powder

$1/4$ teaspoon baking soda

2 tablespoons sugar (about $3/4$ ounce)

$1/2$ teaspoon salt

Zest from 1 lemon (about 2 teaspoons)

$1/2$ cup buttermilk

1 cup fresh ricotta cheese, drained (see Note)

2 tablespoons unsalted butter, melted and slightly cooled

2 large eggs

$1/2$ teaspoon vanilla extract

Vegetable oil, for the griddle

Maple syrup, to serve

NOTE For best results, use high-quality fresh ricotta. Check the ingredients list. If it contains anything other than milk, salt, and an acid starter, keep looking. Gum-stabilized brands tend to weep as they cook, resulting in watery pancakes. For best results, spread the ricotta on a plate lined with a triple layer of paper towels, cover with plastic wrap, and allow to drain at room temperature for 30 minutes before using.

egg in toast

An egg fried in the center of a piece of bread. It's a simple preparation of two staple foods, and, perhaps for that reason, it has inspired umpteen nicknames. Egg in Toast is the most common, and certainly the most literal, but we asked Serious Eats readers to tell us what other names they've seen on menus: Popeye, Egg in a Basket, Egg in a Hat, Egg in a Nest, Hen in a Nest, Frog in the Hole, Frog in a Pond, Egg Holes, Moon Egg, Cowboy Egg, One-Eyed Jack, One-Eyed Petes, One-Eyed Pirate, One-Eyed Susie, Bulls-Eye, Gashouse Eggs, Gas Light Eggs, Eggy in Bready, Oeuf en Cage, Huevos con Pan Pegado, Egyptian Egg, Hocus Pocus Egg, Pokes in the Eye.

Most of the flavor in eggs comes from the rich yolks. So how do you make richest, eggiest scrambled eggs? Just up the ratio of yolks to whites. With only salt, pepper, and chives, if you want them, these will be the eggiest scrambled eggs you've ever tasted. Note the absence of cream in the ingredient list—you don't need it.

super-eggy scrambled eggs

SERVES 4

6 large eggs

4 large egg yolks

2 tablespoons unsalted butter

Kosher salt

Freshly cracked black peppercorns

2 tablespoons chopped chives (optional)

Whisk the eggs and egg yolks until they are completely combined and slightly foamy. Melt the butter in a 12-inch heavy-bottomed nonstick skillet over medium heat until it foams. Add the eggs and immediately stir gently with a rubber spatula. Continue stirring, scraping up the cooked egg from the bottom of the pan until the eggs are nearly set (they should still have a wet sheen to them; they will continue to cook as you remove them from the skillet). Season to taste with salt and pepper, stir in chives if desired, and serve immediately.

5 EXTRAORDINARY BREAKFAST SANDWICHES

SMOKED SABLEFISH BREAKFAST SANDWICH AT SEATOWN SEABAR, SEATTLE, WA

1 SEATOWN SEABAR
SEATTLE, WA

We adore the breakfast sandwiches at Tom Douglas's Dahlia Bakery, a breakfast wonderland where brown-sugar sausage patties and English muffins are made from scratch. But Douglas one-upped himself at the Seatown Seabar, at the Pike Place Market, with nearly a dozen different breakfast sandwich creations. Best of all were one with sablefish and cream cheese (buttery, gently smoky fish, cured in-house, with their own whipped cream cheese and fresh watercress) and one called The

Three Little Pigs (porchetta, premium Kassler ham, and whipped lardo—that'd be pure pork fat). You can't talk us out of pork fat in the morning.

2 4505 MEATS
SAN FRANCISCO, CA

While there are a number of contenders for the best Saturday breakfast at San Francisco's Ferry Plaza Farmers' Market (page 335), we wouldn't argue with anyone who voted for the breakfast sandwich at 4505 Meats. Their own maple sausage (indecently juicy, with a red-pepper kick), melted cave-y Gruyère, and an egg cooked to a perfect soft yolk are layered on a soft and buttery roll that soaks up every drippy, fatty bit of commingling meat and egg and gooey cheese. A one-bite cure for a cold waterfront morning.

3 HEWTIN'S DOGS MOBILE
PROVIDENCE, RI

Of course, hot dogs are the focal point at this truck, but don't you dare ignore the sandwiches. The Zephyr Farm Sunnyside Egg sandwich has a perfectly runny egg atop a pile of Blackbird Farm brisket hash, with cheese sauce and pepper relish. Does brisket hash belong in a breakfast sandwich? After trying this, you'll know the answer.

4 SUNRISE BISCUIT KITCHEN
CHAPEL HILL, NC

Drive-through biscuits: now, that's a phrase that makes us happy. Sunrise Biscuit Kitchen is a small drive-though-only joint; you can't miss the line of cars snaking around it. But don't fret, the line moves quickly. The country-perfect biscuits—tall, tender, buttery golden, and still warm—are layered with porky-delicious country ham, sausage, or (our favorite) a well-seasoned piece of expertly fried chicken.

5 NEAL'S DELI
CARRBORO, NC

Just north of Chapel Hill, Matt Neal and his wife, Sheila, quietly rustle up a roster of killer biscuit sandwiches at Neal's Deli. True to his cheffy lineage (his dad, the late Bill Neal, was a founding father of the North Carolina chef scene), Matt uses a combination of made-in-house and carefully sourced foodstuffs to the advantage of the many eaters who stop in. His gently smoked and carefully seasoned pastrami makes a surprising and wonderful filling for a biscuit, but don't think for a moment that the usual suspects of bacon, eggs, ham, sausage, and cheese aren't put to good use—because they are, too.

HAM BISCUIT AT SUNRISE BISCUIT KITCHEN, CHAPEL HILL, NC

Biscuit or toast? Fried or scrambled eggs? Cheddar, Swiss, or American? Everyone has his or her own idea of the perfect breakfast sandwich. So we polled the Serious Eats community to find their favorites. The winner? Pretty classic: bacon, Cheddar, and a fried egg on an English muffin. We fry the eggs and toast the muffin in the rendered bacon fat for extra flavor.

your favorite
egg sandwich

MAKES 4 SANDWICHES

8 slices thick-cut high-quality bacon, cut in half crosswise

4 English muffins, split

4 large eggs

Kosher salt

Freshly cracked black peppercorns

4 slices Cheddar cheese

1 Put an oven rack in the middle position and preheat the oven to 400°F. Arrange the bacon in a single layer in a parchment-lined rimmed baking sheet and bake until crisp, flipping and rotating halfway through cooking, about 15 minutes total. Transfer the bacon to a paper towel–lined plate, reserving the excess rendered fat in a small bowl.

2 Add 1 tablespoon of the reserved bacon fat to a 12-inch heavy-bottomed non-stick skillet. Heat it over medium heat until shimmering, then add two of the English muffins, split sides down, four pieces in all. Toast the English muffins until they are golden brown, about 3 minutes total, and set aside. Repeat with an additional tablespoon of bacon fat and the remaining English muffins.

3 Add another tablespoon of bacon fat to the now-empty skillet and heat over medium heat until shimmering. Break the eggs into the pan and cook them undisturbed for 30 seconds. Use a spatula to coax the white (which should just be beginning to set) into neat, English muffin–size circles. Add 2 tablespoons of water to the pan, cover, and cook until the desired level of doneness is reached, 1 to 4 minutes. Season with salt and pepper.

4 Arrange the English muffin bottoms on a rimmed baking sheet. Place four half-slices of bacon on each English muffin bottom, top with a fried egg and a slice of cheese, then transfer to the oven until the cheese is melted and the sandwich is heated through, about 2 minutes. Close each sandwich, and serve immediately.

in defense of oatmeal

Oatmeal is often the forgotten stepchild of the breakfast menu: the boring, gloppy bowl of virtuous grains that no one really wants to eat. But at Serious Eats, we're crazy about the stuff—particularly when steel-cut oats are involved. When properly cooked, each one has a tendency to pop in the mouth when you bite down.

How do we love oatmeal? Let us count the ways. We love it sweet, like at Iris Café in Brooklyn, where it's topped with cinnamon-caramel apples. We love it smoky, like at Farm on Adderley, also in Brooklyn, where steel-cut oats are cooked down with butternut squash, bacon, and chilies. Yes, we love it savory; at Spread in San Diego, they've been known to cook it with curry and serve it with caramelized sweet onions. (At home, we've tried bacon-cheese oatmeal and soy sauce-scallion.) We even love oatmeal when it's absurdly expensive—at Norma's in Manhattan, the $16 oatmeal brûlée has the same torched sugar crust as crème brûlée.

OATMEAL FROM LOCANDA VERDE, NEW YORK, NY

The best granola is crunchy and clumpy, salty and sweet. The honey and molasses in this recipe help the oats to clump together, with almonds and pepitas (roasted pumpkin seeds) to bulk it up and cayenne, cinnamon, and salt to add a little kick. Perfect for sprinkling on yogurt or snacking by the handful.

granola with
pepitas and cranberries

MAKES ABOUT 1 QUART

3 cups rolled oats

¾ cup pepitas

¾ cup slivered almonds

½ cup dried shredded unsweetened coconut

½ teaspoon ground cinnamon

¼ teaspoon cayenne pepper

1 teaspoon kosher salt

¼ cup sugar

½ cup honey

¼ cup dark molasses

½ cup dried cranberries

1 Adjust your oven rack to the middle position and preheat the oven to 350°F. Combine the oats, pepitas, almonds, coconut, cinnamon, cayenne pepper, and salt in a large bowl and toss to combine. Add the sugar, honey, and molasses, and stir with a rubber spatula until thoroughly combined. Transfer the mixture to a rimmed baking sheet lined with parchment paper or aluminum foil and spread it into an even layer. Bake until it's an even golden brown, stirring every 10 minutes, about 30 minutes total.

2 Remove the pan from the oven and allow the granola to cool thoroughly, at least 15 minutes. It will crisp up as it cools. Transfer the granola to a large bowl and break it into clusters with your fingers. Toss in the dried cranberries, seasoning with more salt if desired. Store the granola in a sealed container at room temperature for up to one month.

If you've only had corned beef hash from a can, you've never had real corned beef hash. Start with good corned beef, add potatoes and poblano peppers, and let the whole thing cook undisturbed until you have a crunchy layer to stir back in. Put down that spatula; it's important to let the cast-iron skillet do its job. Moving things around will prevent you from getting those brown bits—and they're the best part!

corned beef
hash

SERVES 4

4 tablespoons (½ stick) unsalted butter

2 pounds Yukon Gold potatoes, peeled and cut into a ½-inch dice (about 4 cups)

½ pound fully cooked corned beef (about 1 pound raw, simmered for 3 hours until fork-tender), shredded into ½-inch pieces

1 large onion, cut into medium dice (about 1½ cups)

1 poblano chile, cut into medium dice (about ½ cup)

2 tablespoons ketchup or chili sauce (for spicier hash)

1 teaspoon hot sauce (such as Frank's)

Kosher salt

Freshly ground black pepper

4 large eggs

1 Melt the butter in a 12-inch heavy-bottomed nonstick or cast-iron skillet over medium-high heat until the foaming subsides. Add the potatoes and cook, stirring frequently with a rubber spatula or wooden spoon, until they are tender and light golden brown, about 12 minutes total. Add the cooked corned beef, onion, and poblano, and cook, stirring frequently, until the vegetables are beginning to soften, about 4 minutes. Add the ketchup or chili sauce and hot sauce, stir to combine, and season to taste with salt and pepper.

2 Using a rubber spatula or a wooden spoon, gently pack the potatoes and hash into the pan, creating a smooth top. Raise the heat to high and cook undisturbed until the bottom layer is deep brown, about 3 minutes. Using the spatula, lift the browned bits from the bottom of the pan and stir into the upper layers. Repack the skillet and repeat three or four times, until the entire skillet is full of well-browned potatoes, about 10 minutes total. Reduce the heat to low.

3 Make four indentations in the surface of the hash and break an egg into each one. Season with salt and pepper, cover the pan, and cook until the eggs are barely set, about 5 minutes. Bring the skillet to a trivet on the table, and serve immediately.

You can't get much simpler than potatoes and butter. It's the technique that makes the most of these russets. Parboiling them gets them tender and fluffy, while browning them extensively in a skillet and in the oven gets them ultra-crisp and flavorful.

super-crispy
hash browns

SERVES 4

2 pounds russet potatoes, peeled and cut into 1-inch chunks (about 4 cups)

Kosher salt

Freshly cracked black peppercorns

6 tablespoons unsalted butter

1 Place the potatoes and 1 tablespoon of salt in a large saucepan and add water until it is 1 inch above the tops of the potatoes. Bring to a boil over high heat. Reduce to a simmer and cook until the potatoes show only a slight resistance when poked with the tip of a knife, about 10 minutes. Drain the potatoes and spread them evenly on a rimmed baking sheet. Allow them to rest at room temperature uncovered for 10 minutes to dry. They should appear powdery white. Season the potatoes to taste with more salt and black pepper.

2 Adjust the oven rack to the top position and preheat the oven to 400°F. Melt 2 table-spoons of the butter in a 12-inch heavy-bottomed ovenproof non-stick or cast-iron skillet over medium-high heat. Once the foaming subsides, add the pota-toes and press down firmly with a spatula to form an even layer (the potatoes will be partially mashed in the process). Cook without moving until the bottom is a deep golden brown, about 7 minutes. Transfer the potatoes to a medium bowl and toss to incorporate the browned bits. Melt 2 more tablespoons of butter and repeat the browning and mixing steps.

3 Melt the final 2 tablespoons of the butter over medium-high heat, add the potato mixture back to the skillet, transfer to the oven, and cook until the top and bottom are both a crusty golden brown, 10 to 15 minutes. Using a thin flexible metal spatula, release the edges and bottom of the potatoes from the skillet, shaking the skillet until the pota-toes slide around freely. Transfer the potatoes to a serving platter and serve immediately.

NOTE To make the final cooking process shorter, after step 1, the boiled potatoes can be kept in the refrigerator for up to two days.

great names

It's a bold statement, but we're ready to make it: breakfast places have the best names. Some of them, rightfully so, honor the egg: The Egg and I, in Minneapolis; Eggs N Things, in Simi Valley, California; Patty's Eggnest, in Seattle; Good Eggs, in Ephraim, Wisconsin; or Egg, in Brooklyn. Then you have all the pancakeries: Magnolia Pancake Haus, in San Antonio; Pancake Pantry, in Nashville; Polly's Pancake Parlor, in New Hampshire. And we can't forget the waffleries: Ye Olde Waffle Shop, in Chapel Hill, North Carolina; and the Waffle Window, in Portland, Oregon. Other breakfast places sound like children's books: The Friendly Toast, in Portsmouth, New Hampshire (where you can order Green Eggs and Ham); and Kitchen Little, in Mystic, Connecticut. Lunch and dinner just don't seem to have as much fun.

5 BREAKFAST TACO PLACES IN AUSTIN

While other cities in Texas, the Southwest, and beyond may have their own formidable breakfast tacos, there's nowhere with such a tasty concentration as Austin, Texas. Here are five of the most notable locations in our favorite morning-taco city.

1 JUAN IN A MILLION

Here you need one hand for tacos and the other for shaking owner Juan Meza's hand. You'll recognize him in all the framed photos with Texas politicians and local personalities hanging near the register. "I picked the name because Juan and Only was already taken," he said (after giving us bear hugs). His breakfast tacos aren't anything too fancy, but they are satisfying and, as University of Texas Austin students know, very cheap. The Machacado combines chewy shredded beef with eggs, tomatoes, onions, and spicy jalapeño bits that will light up your tongue. The Migas is like a melty, creamy quesadilla but with egg scrambles and pico de gallo. And the Bacon and Potato Taco is happily overstuffed with crisp little bacon bits.

2 IZZOZ TACOS

John Galindo, who started serving tacos out of a trailer in 2008, wants you to try his *non-breakfast* tacos first. (The fried avocado is a town favorite.) We think Galindo doesn't give his breakfast tacos enough credit. The Bac-Spin (pronounced backspin) is made with applewood-smoked bacon, egg scrambles that have soaked up all those bacony juices, and sautéed spinach leaves. The Migas taco, which he learned how to make from his grandmother, has a nice crunch from the broken-up tortilla chips in each cheesy, eggy bite.

3 MI MADRE'S

Whoever's *madre* this was, she did not want you to feel your stomach grumble ever again. These tacos are massive, more like mini breakfast burritos. The first few bites barely make a dent in them. Choose from 19 options—like the #0, the classic bacon-egg-cheese; or the #3, with chorizo made in-house—both of which come in flour or corn tortillas and are spilling with soft, skin-on potato hunks. Take them wrapped in foil to go, or sit out on the back patio, where fans are constantly whirring and the servers will refill your salsa bowl with a syrup pitcher.

4 TACODELI

One of the greatest things about Austin? Fast-casual chains like Tacodeli that are legitimately tasty. The tortillas are from the local El Milagro factory, as close as you can get to making

BREAKFAST TACOS AT JUAN IN A MILLION, AUSTIN, TX

BREAKFAST TACOS AT TACODELI, AUSTIN, TX

them right at the shop, and filled with your choice of beans, ham, sausage, bacon, cage-free eggs, potatoes, chorizo, sirloin, and cheese. They also have special tacos: the Otto has a thick layer of black refried beans at the bottom, topped with curly, crispy bacon, melted Monterey Jack shreds, and big avocado pieces. Or try El Popeye, eggs scrambled with sautéed spinach leaves and topped with queso fresco crumbles. They're even better with a hit of roja or habenero salsa from the fresh salsa bar near the register.

5 LA COCINA DE CONSUELO

Connie (or "Consuelo") is the hair-netted one in the kitchen, wrapping breakfast burritos (she'll also do an open-faced "taco" on double corn tortillas) to order until 11 AM. All of them start with her made-that-morning tortillas—steamy, chewy, and freckled with brown tortilla bubbles—which are good enough to eat straight. All of the $3 burritos are named after customers and friends. We love the Doug: peppery and juicy chorizo folded with scrambled egg and tender potatoes.

the best breakfast taco i ever had

My friend Houston food writer Robb Walsh convened a Houston food bloggers' meeting at Laredo Taqueria, his favorite breakfast taco place. As soon as we walked in, I understood why. A woman at the front of the buffet line was making fresh flour tortillas that would serve as the foundation to what turned out to be my favorite breakfast tacos ever. When your breakfast starts with warm, flaky tortillas this good, the fillings become almost an afterthought. (That may be the first time I've called crispy meat bits an afterthought.) Fatty, spicy chorizo and potato, pork, barbacoa—each was as good as the last.

We're huge fans of spicy breakfasts, and chilaquiles have it all. We fry our own corn tortillas so that they soften but retain their crunch in our tomatillo sauce. A little jalapeño adds heat; creamy sour cream and queso fresco add a cooling tang. To take it really over the top, pair it with fried chorizo or eggs.

chilaquiles
verdes

SERVES 4 TO 6

1 pound tomatillos (about 10 medium), husks and stems removed and split in half

1 poblano chile, halved lengthwise, seeds and stem removed

1 jalapeño pepper, halved lengthwise, seeds and stem removed

1 small onion, peeled and halved from pole to pole

2 garlic cloves

2 tablespoons vegetable oil, plus 1 quart for deep-frying

2 teaspoons kosher salt, plus more for seasoning

Freshly ground black pepper

½ cup fresh cilantro leaves, roughly chopped

1 cup low-sodium chicken broth

10 (6-inch) corn tortillas, cut into quarters

½ pound raw Mexican chorizo (optional; see Note)

½ cup whole milk

1 cup sour cream

6 ounces queso fresco, crumbled (see Note)

1 Preheat the oven to 450°F. Toss the tomatillos, poblano, jalapeño, onion, and garlic in a large bowl with 2 tablespoons of oil and 2 teaspoons of kosher salt. Arrange the tomatillos in an even layer on an aluminum foil–lined baking sheet and roast until they are fully softened and beginning to char, about 15 minutes. Transfer the vegetables to a large saucepan. Add half of the cilantro and all of the chicken broth. Blend with a hand blender (or in a standing blender) until smooth and simmer until slightly reduced over medium heat, about 5 minutes. Season to taste with salt and pepper and set aside.

2 Meanwhile, heat 1 quart of oil in a 5-quart Dutch oven or a large wok to 350°F. as measured on an instant-read or deep-fat frying thermometer. Add about one-third of the tortilla pieces to the oil one piece at a time and fry, stirring and flipping the pieces with a metal spider until light brown and crisp, about 3 minutes total. Transfer the cooked tortilla chips to a large metal bowl lined with paper towels and season immediately with salt to taste. Repeat with the remaining two batches of tortilla chips. Set aside until ready to use.

3 Cook the chorizo in a 10-inch heavy-bottomed skillet over medium heat until it is cooked through, about 4 minutes. Transfer to a paper towel–lined plate and reserve.

4 Combine the milk and sour cream in a small bowl and whisk to combine, seasoning to taste with salt.

why we love chilaquiles

Who can turn down nachos for breakfast? Well, they're not quite nachos, but chilaquiles—fried corn tortillas doused in green or red sauce and topped with queso fresco and sour cream, as well as eggs, or chorizo, or chicken—are still pretty awesome. We love them because they're a great way to use up leftover tortillas, meats, and salsas (and don't repurposed dinner foods make awesome breakfasts?). We also love them because they're spicy and creamy, crunchy, and soft—different textures and tastes coming together in every bite. And, yes, we love them because they're almost like eating tortilla chips for breakfast.

5 Add the tortilla chips to the large saucepan with the sauce and stir with a rubber spatula until the chips are well coated. Transfer the mixture to a 13 × 9-inch baking dish, top with crumbled chorizo, drizzle with sour-cream mixture, sprinkle with the cheese, and bake until bubbly, about 6 minutes. Sprinkle with the remaining cilantro and serve immediately.

NOTE Queso fresco is a Mexican-style fresh cheese; cow's-milk feta can be used in its place. Mexican chorizo is a raw sausage that can be found in some larger supermarkets and Latin specialty stores. If you can't find it, substitute ½ pound ground pork mixed with 1 teaspoon salt, ½ teaspoon black pepper, ½ teaspoon chili powder, ½ teaspoon dried oregano, ¼ teaspoon ground cinnamon, and 1 teaspoon red wine vinegar. Chilaquiles can also be served topped with scrambled or fried eggs.

burgers

at serious eats, WE'RE FILLED WITH LOVE FOR HAMBURGERS.

and cheeseburgers. and onion burgers, GOOBER BURGERS, BUTTER BURGERS, SLUG BURGERS, SLIDERS & MINI HAMBURGERS.

(yes, there's a difference between those last two. we'll get to that later.)

WE LOVE JUST ABOUT EVERY VARIATION, AS LONG AS IT'S DONE RIGHT AND MADE WITH CARE. HECK, WE LOVE THEM SO MUCH WE EVEN HAVE A BLOG ABOUT THEM— AHAMBURGERTODAY.COM.

Hamburgers have a tendency to lurk in your memory long after you've eaten them; don't we all have formative burger memories? My own earliest burger memory—that's easy. I remember going to the Hamburger Express on Central Avenue in Cedarhurst, Long Island, from the time I was eight years old. Why the name? Because the burgers were delivered on Lionel model trains to your seat—the tracks stretching along the counter, which was all of the seating that the Hamburger Express had. And when your burger arrived, the train would whistle.

I remember loving those burgers more than anything else in the world, but I'm sure the delivery system colored my view. What kid *wouldn't* adore a burger delivered via model train? I do remember the burgers there having a great griddled crust, a toasted bun, and oozy, properly melted American

cheese—three of my prerequisites for burger greatness. But I'm prepared to admit that part of the appeal was nostalgia. That's often the case with burgers: the experience is half the fun.

Though not all local burger joints delivered their burgers via model trains, burgers were indeed the province of independently owned mom-and-pop shops until Ray Kroc took over a small-scale local chain from the McDonald brothers in 1961 and expanded it into the worldwide empire it is today. Insta-Burger King in Florida was purchased in 1955—and rebranded as Burger King, McDonald's biggest rival. Local haunts coexisted uneasily with the chains for the next forty years. Some chains earned true loyalty from their customers; In-N-Out Burger in California became a beloved regional institution by using fresh, never frozen meat, and cutting fresh potatoes in full view of the custom-

ers. And by the beginning of the twenty-first century, rapidly growing smaller chains like Five Guys refined their limited menus with better quality fries and meat.

Through much of its history, the hamburger was a food of the people, cheap and fast whether from a local joint or a major chain. But when Judy Rodgers came to the Zuni Café in San Francisco in 1987, she put a burger on her California bistro menu—high-quality beef with fine cheese to top it. Daniel Boulud then took the fancy-pants burger to unimagined levels with his DB Burger, which included shortribs, foie gras, and black truffles. And the chef's approach soon extended down-market. New York restaurateur Danny Meyer introduced a custom-blended burger grind, high-tech burger cooking methods, and frozen custard made with higher quality ingredients when he opened Shake Shack in New York's Madison Square Park in 2004: an affordable take-out burger stand with a chef's sensibility. His inspiration for Shake Shack? His beloved Ted Drewes, the frozen custard and burger stand that he grew up with in St. Louis.

Today it seems that every well-known chef in the country has tackled burgers, including Thomas Keller (of the French Laundry and Per Se), Tom Colicchio (of the Craft restaurants and *Top Chef*), and Food Network star Bobby Flay, who launched Bobby's Burger Palace, a quick-service burger concept, in New Jersey in 2007. How big has burger mania gotten? Hamburger aficionados happily shell out $200 to attend Rachael Ray's annual burger bash, as part of the South Beach Wine & Food Festival or its counterpart in New York.

Still, no matter how high profile the burger has become, people still crave authenticity and the emotional connection they have to local burger joints. That emotional resonance was recognized by author and documentarian George Motz in his *Hamburger America,* both a movie and a book. It's clear that burgers high and low have become an endless source of pleasure and satisfaction for an American public—we don't need to explain the appeal of the hamburger. But if you're still on the fence, keep reading. This chapter will have you jumping down squarely on the cow pasture side.

We've spent years chomping our way around the country and grilling a few thousand burgers of our own, and here you'll find the fruits of that labor: 30 of our favorite burgers in the United States, tips on what to look for in a burger, our guide to perfecting your burger-cooking skills, an introduction to the "Hamburger Fatty Melt," and much more.

sending back your burger

We've all been there. The burger you ordered medium
rare came to the table well done. Do you send it back?
According to a survey on "A Hamburger Today,"
41 percent of readers have no problem sending it back.
Some of those who did cited the fear that the chef
would be angry and do something untoward to the new
burger. But as community member GainesvilleChef
points out, "I have been working in kitchens for a
long time now, and I have never seen anyone spit on a
food re-order. I would much rather a customer
send back something if it's not to their taste!
Just be nice about it."

WHAT MAKES A GREAT BURGER

With so many kinds of burgers out there, "great" depends on context. Still, there are some universal indicators.

beef-to-bun ratio

A burger needs enough beef so its taste comes through, and enough bun to support the meat and juices. And the burger should be the same diameter as the bun. Great burgers are like great sandwiches—all about balance.

bun

It needs to be fresh, appropriately sized, and sturdy enough to support the meat and soak up its juices. But it also needs some give—some softness and squishiness. It's a tough act, balancing tenderness and absorbency so you don't have to resort to a knife and fork to finish.

doneness

Everyone has a preference as to how a burger is cooked; the best burgers are cooked perfectly to one's liking.

burger grind

You want a nice loose-to-medium grind and a patty that is not too densely packed. A fine grind and tight packing makes for a tough, dense burger that starts to resemble a sausage.

cheese

Regardless of what type of cheese you prefer, it should be properly melted, not just perched on top. (Bonus points for two slices of cheese—one below and one on top of the patty.)

fresh ingredients

It should go without saying. But how many burgers have you had with wilted, crunchless lettuce, anemic tomatoes, or stale buns? We've had too many. Get fresh or go home!

BURGER STYLES

The burger is a seemingly simple dish—meat, cheese, bun—but there are more incarnations than a casual eater would suspect. Now that you know what basics to look for in a great burger, here are a few styles to try.

backyard grilled burgers

You know this one. There's almost nothing like a thick juicy burger, charred with dark cross-hatching, that you eat just minutes after pulling it off your grill on a beautiful summer weekend.

pub burgers

These burgers have sizable patties usually no smaller than 8 ounces, often 10 ounces or more. They're typically ovoid in shape, rather than flat, often broiled, and most often seen in pubs (hence the name). It's a style much celebrated in New York City.

fast-food burgers

Do we really need to define this for you? We didn't think so.

fast-food-*style* burgers

The term denotes burgers that seem to take their inspiration from fast-food burgers but are somehow better—in terms of either ingredients or preparation or both. Fast-food-style burgers will be made with fresh, not frozen, beef; use fresh produce; and generally come from a single storefront or, at most, a small, local chain rather than a nationwide chain. Burger Joint and Shake Shack in New York City and Gott's Roadside Tray Gourmet (formerly Taylor's Automatic Refresher) in San Francisco and St. Helena, California, are prime examples.

sliders

Many people think a slider is just a name for a mini burger. Many people are wrong. A slider is something specific: a thin, thin slip of beef, cooked on a griddle with onions and pickles piled atop the patty. The steam from the onions does as much cooking as the griddle. The buns are placed atop the onions, absorbing the pungent aroma and flavor. A slider is at once a hamburger and, yet, something more.

mini hamburgers

Mini burgers encompass every diminutive burger that does not meet the definition of a slider (see above), often because it has been grilled or broiled rather than steam-griddled and almost always because it lacks the bed of pungent onions. There

was an annoying trend, roughly from 2006 through 2008, whereby every chef in the country was putting mini burgers (often misidentifying them as sliders) on his or her bar menu.

steakhouse burgers

The steakhouse burger is defined more by where it's served than by any other unifying characteristic, though there are some general observations one can make. Steakhouse burgers are usually made from the beef trimmings of the various steaks on hand and as such are ground from prime, aged beef. They're almost always massive, hearty burgers on a par with pub-style burgers, and they're often broiled.

kobe/wagyu burgers

A Kobe burger is almost always a bad idea. Most chefs cook these rare to medium rare, so as to not overcook the premium meat, but with so little cooking, the texture inevitably renders as mushy. It's like moist cat food on a bun, with the meat oozing out the sides and back as you try to eat the burger. Kobe burgers are most often seen as mini burgers, as the meat is more affordable in smaller, sharable portions, and the Kobe/Wagyu and the mini burger/slider trends seem to have peaked at the same time.

fancy-pants burgers

Chefs and burgers are a tricky thing: in some cases, high-end chefs work wonders with the humble dish; in others, overthinking can get in the way. Price is a pretty good indication you're eating a fancy-pants burger. But since price varies from city to city, it's difficult to set a hard-and-fast dollar border. Let's just say that if a burger costs double what a McDonald's Quarter Pounder Value Meal does, you're probably in fancy-pants land. If that's not enough of an indication, you know you're heading into rarefied air when one or more of the following is involved:

DOUGHNUT BURGER AT PYT, PHILADELPHIA, PA

» A big-name chef or restaurateur, or a celebrity chef

» Brioche buns

» "House-made" ketchup

» "House-made" anything

» Artisanal or farmstead cheeses

» "Artisanal" anything

» Aioli, remoulade, frisée, microgreens, arugula, etc.

» Designer bacon

» Foie gras

» Dry-aging

» Kobe/Wagyu beef

fusion burgers

Any burger that seeks to inject the flavors of another cuisine. Such mashups may include "Mexican" burgers with jalapeños and spicy cheese; "pizzaburgers" with mozzarella and tomato sauce; or "Korean" burgers topped with bulgogi beef.

megaburgers

Any burger whose sole purpose is to break a record—most often weight, but sometimes price. Typically the result of tired publicity stunts, megaburgers have rapidly increased in number in the last few years, thanks largely to social media— it's almost guaranteed the blogging-Tweeting-Facebooking masses will blab about the three-ton burger you need a forklift to flip.

extreme burgers

Similar to megaburgers, but here the point is less about sheer size than it is caloric overkill—stuffing as much artery-clogging food matter on and about the hamburger sandwich as possible. Examples include our own Hamburger Fatty Melt (page 65) and any variation on the doughnut burger—yes, that's a burger with a doughnut or two as the bun. The first widely recognized specimen was the Luther Burger, at the pub Mulligan's in Decatur, Georgia, in 2005; however, doughnut burgers on the Internet, notably on the blog "Neon Epiphany," date to 2003. Celebrity chef Paula Deen, famous for her love of all things fatty, has made her own version.

stacked burgers

Anything with two or more patties. Popular examples include In-N-Out's Double Double or Wendy's Double. Props to any stacked burger that uses an interstitial bun, like the Big Mac.

deep-fried burgers

Just what it sounds like. The patties of these burgers take a dunk in hot, hot oil. Dyer's Burgers in Memphis is perhaps the most famous deep-fried burger emporium. Variations exist that include entire burgers—bun and all—dipped in batter and deep-fried. They're tasty, but rare.

REGIONAL BURGER STYLES

While some form of the burgers above can be found all over the country, there are many burger styles that represent unique local flavors or philosophies—or that simply sprang up for one reason or another and inspired nearby (but not nationwide) imitation. These are the varied and glorious regional burger styles that represent the ingenuity and brashness for which the United States is known.

smashed burgers

Cooks start with a 4-ounce or so ball of fresh beef, let it cook a bit on a hot, hot griddle, and then give it a good whack with the back of a spatula. The technique leads to a crisp crust with a craggy irregular shape that alternates between crunchy and moist and juicy.

steamed cheeseburgers

Prevalent in a small part of south-central Connecticut, the steamed cheeseburger is prepared in a microwave-size steaming chamber that holds several small trays. Half the trays cradle the beef while the remaining trays contain a molten white Cheddar mixture that is poured onto the patties poststeam. There are a number of steamed cheeseburger joints in that area, notably Ted's Restaurant in Meriden.

cheese-stuffed burgers

Though it probably didn't take a genius to eventually try to stuff cheese *inside* a burger, folks in Minneapolis seem to have perfected the practice. At Matt's Bar, it's called the Jucy Lucy. Variations of the name appear at other Twin Cities bars, like at the 5-8 Club, where it's the Juicy Lucy. But they all follow a similar formula: American cheese stuffed in a pocket within a ground beef patty, all cooked on a flat-top.

green chile cheeseburgers

Indigenous to New Mexico, where the Hatch green chile grows, these burgers are topped with chopped roasted peppers trapped in a gooey, oozy matrix of melted cheese—usually white Cheddar, as happens to be the case at Santa Fe's Bobcat Bite, perhaps the most well-known place that serves them.

chili burgers

You'll find this subset of burgers in Los Angeles, where Original Tommy's is credited with pioneering the style. The generous amount of oozing chili intermingled with the soft beef patty and melted cheese at Tommy's make for an unrivaled flavor combination.

onion burgers

A variation on smashed burgers with a little bit of slider thrown in. The Depression may have been the inspiration for these Oklahoma-based burgers, as throwing half an onion, sliced into rings, into the mix helped the meat go further. The meat is placed on top of the onion and pressed down until they fuse. In the process, the onion becomes almost caramelized as it cooks on a hot, hot griddle. El Reno, Oklahoma, seems to be the focal point of this style, with Johnnie's Grill, Sid's Diner, Robert's Grill, and Jobe's Drive-In.

butter burgers

It's no surprise that butter burgers reach their apotheosis in Wisconsin, the Dairy State. As if a juicy hunk of meat isn't enough juicy fat for you, folks around these parts cook the patties in butter, top them with cheese, and then slather on a hefty dose of the stuff right after it hits the bun.

pimento cheeseburgers

If you're not from the South, it's possible you haven't heard of pimento cheese, much less pimento cheeseburgers. A sort of Southern comfort food that spans all classes and ages, pimento cheese is a mixture of grated cheese—usually Cheddar—plus pimientos, mayo, and spices. Pimento cheese tea sandwiches are often served at high-falutin' functions; it's often spread on celery sticks and served as a hors d'oeuvre. It's not hard to see how this stuff eventually found its way onto a burger.

slugburgers

This is another Southern phenomenon, from a small triangle of an area in northern Alabama, northern Mississippi, and southern Tennessee. In different towns, they are called *slugburgers* or *doughburgers*. Food writer John T. Edge notes in his book *Hamburgers & Fries* that they're also known as *cracker burgers* and *tater burgers*. What they all have in common is a frugality born of the Depression (much like the onion burgers of Oklahoma), when folks in Mississippi learned to use fillers—bread, flour, potatoes, or crackers—to extend their meat supplies.

bean burgers

No, the patty is not made of beans. Native to San Antonio, Texas, they consist of a beef patty topped with canned refried beans, crushed Fritos, and Cheez Whiz.

gooberburgers

Burgers topped with a generous dollop of melted peanut butter. The best-known practitioner is probably the Wheel Inn Drive-In in Sedalia, Missouri, made famous by documentarian George Motz and his burger film and book of the same name, *Hamburger America*.

nut burgers

We're not really sure if this is a true regional style, as it doesn't seem to have made its way that far from its birthplace (Matt's Place Drive-In in Butte, Montana), but it's just crazy enough to merit mention. The nut burger is topped with chopped peanuts mixed with Miracle Whip. Think of it as the "chunky" version of the gooberburger.

pastrami burgers

Popular in much of Utah, the pastrami burger is said to have been invented by Crown Burger, a fast-food joint owned by the Katsanevas family that grew into a family-run local chain. This isn't a "pastrami burger" in the model of a bacon burger, with a few delicate strips of the second meat on top—more than half the sandwich, volumetrically, is pastrami. It's a jaw-unhinger.

THE HAMBURGER FATTY MELT: GRILLED CHEESE, BURGER, GRILLED CHEESE

THE HAMBURGER FATTY MELT

The Hamburger Fatty Melt is a proud creation of "A Hamburger Today" and Serious Eats. From top to bottom, it consists of:

» A grilled cheese sandwich as bun top

» A 4-ounce beef patty

» A grilled cheese sandwich as bun bottom

Got that? It's a burger with two grilled cheese sandwiches as its bun. Wild, huh?

We wish our R&D department here at Serious Eats could claim this as the product of our own grease-addled minds, but we've merely perfected a burger we heard about through a Serious Eats community member, who mentioned the Chubby Melt at the Mossy Creek Cafe in Fishersville, Virginia. It consists of a burger between two grilled cheese sandwiches, smothered with sautéed onions and mushrooms, and topped with Thousand Island.

The Mossy Creek pretty much had it right until it ladled on the toppings. In our opinion, something as glorious as a burger with two grilled-cheese sandwiches as its bun needs little else adorning it.

Once the Fatty Melt hit the Web, it became a viral sensation. But unlike most Web memes, the Fatty Melt concept crossed from the virtual world to the real. You can now order a grilled-cheese–bunned hamburger from coast to coast.

While some seem to execute the concept better than others, we think ours is still the best because we carefully considered the beef-to-"bun" ratio, using just the right bread and amount of cheese.

Though the recipe will work with regular sandwich bread, we recommend thin-sliced bread like Pepperidge Farms Very Thin White Bread to maintain proper beef-to-bun ratio.

hamburger fatty melt

MAKES 2 BURGERS

½ pound freshly ground Basic Burger Blend (page 86)

4 tablespoons plus 1 teaspoon unsalted butter, softened

8 slices sandwich bread, preferably thin-sliced

8 slices yellow American cheese

½ teaspoon vegetable oil

Kosher salt

Freshly ground pepper

Toppings, as desired (we recommend a slice of ripe tomato for each sandwich)

1 Divide the beef blend into two equal parts and shape into square patties ½ inch larger than the bread slices. Set aside.

2 For the grilled sandwiches, butter all eight slices of bread on both sides in a thin, even layer, using ½ tablespoon butter per slice. Place the remaining teaspoon of butter in a 12-inch cast-iron or nonstick skillet over medium heat until the foaming subsides, 2 to 3 minutes.

3 Place two slices of bread in the skillet and cook until the first side is hot but not browned, about 30 seconds. Transfer the slices to a wire rack set in a rimmed baking sheet, hot side up. Top each slice with a slice of cheese. Repeat with the remaining six slices of bread and cheese.

4 Assemble the bread and cheese to form four sandwiches with two slices of cheese in the center of each. Place two sandwiches in the skillet and cook until the first sides are golden brown, about 2 minutes. Flip and cook until they are golden brown on the second side, about 2 minutes longer. Transfer the finished sandwiches to the wire rack and tent with foil to keep them warm while cooking the remaining two sandwiches.

5 Place the skillet over medium-high and heat the oil until it is lightly smoking. Season the patties liberally on both sides with salt and pepper. Place them in the pan and cook without moving for about 3 minutes, until they are well browned. Using a metal spatula, flip the burgers and cook for 1 minute longer, or until the desired doneness is reached. Sandwich each patty between two grilled-cheese sandwiches, adding toppings as desired. Serve immediately.

GOT BUNS, HON?

While there are those who profess to like big buns, we're a little more diverse in our bun appreciation. We like 'em tiny, too (for sliders), or squishy or firm or spongy. It's all about context. As long as the bun in question does its job—supporting the patty, containing its juices, and working with it in harmony—we're happy. Sure, there are purists who say a hamburger can be a hamburger only if it's on a bun. And there's a subset of those folks who insist on a bun of the plain, white variety. We once subscribed to that notion ourselves, but after years of eating hamburgers of all types, we've found that the following bun styles work well, too.

the plain white squishy bun

To be sure, even though we've accepted other buns as legitimate patty-delivery options, the Plain White Squishy remains one of our favorites. Without an assertive flavor of its own, it allows the beef to shine. Its softness is key in giving you what we call a "uniform bite experience": when there's only the slightest variation of bite resistance in the bun and the patty. Your teeth should be able to chomp through the bun and beef with a smooth, continuous motion, with little need to adjust bite pressure. Any textural interest, we believe, should come from the toppings—or from the bits of patty surface that have been seared or charred into crunchiness. The potato roll, another favorite, gives a very similar experience, with just a slight extra sweetness.

the brioche bun

The brioche bun gets a bad rap from purists, who decry its sweetness and butteriness as distractions from the beef. It doesn't help that you see this bun type most often on a chef-driven fancy-pants burger (see page 60). But a careful burger-tailored brioche bun can be a godsend. These rolls tend to be bigger than standard plain white squishies, a necessity on the larger patties you see with this style of burger. And a brioche bun's dense, spongy crumb is especially adept at sopping up the rich, rendered fat of these patties, which are often cooked to a juicy medium-rare as per chef's suggestions. The trick is finding a middle ground between traditionally sweet, rich brioche and a more toned-down bread option.

the english muffin

Sometimes you really need a bready substrate that can stand up to the juice. This is especially true for a burger with beef-to-fat ratios of 75:25 or even 70:30. And for burgers with lots of ooey, gooey melted cheese. Nothing absorbs a burger's liquid gold more efficiently than a moist, spongy English muffin, with its loose crumb and copiously craggy interior.

what doesn't work, or "rustic busts it"

In all our burger-eating endeavors, we have encountered bunnage that no matter how well intentioned, no matter how tasty or juicy the beef, simply kills a good burger. Whenever we see "ciabatta" or "baguette" on the menu, we start looking for the door. These rustic breads—and others like them—are simply too tough and chewy for the ingredients they sandwich. Tough, chewy buns lead to what we call "burger backsliding." That's where the bite pressure you exert to power through the bread is so much that you end up squeezing the patty and its toppings out the back (or sides) of the burger. Add secret sauce to this equation and you're in dangerous territory.

If you see any of these rustic breads bunning the burgers on a given menu, you have our permission to leave the premises immediately and head for a burger establishment that takes its mission more seriously.

we melt when we see a dedicated bun toaster

When we walk into a burger joint with an open kitchen and see in it a bun toaster, we do a greasy little dance of burger joy. That's because you can't go wrong with a toasted bun. In fact, a whopping 85 percent of Serious Eats readers prefer toasted buns (and 58 percent of those bun-toasters prefer buttered, toasted buns).

These machines tell us a couple things: that we're in an establishment that takes its burgers seriously, and that there's enough turnover to warrant an entire machine dedicated to buttering and toasting the buns. That's a good thing. It means your burger will likely be griddled fresh instead of sitting under a warming lamp.

WHERE THE BEEF IS: 30 GREAT BURGERS

1 JOHNNIE'S TAVERN
COLUMBUS, OH

Giant burgers are rarely delicious, and the Super Johnnie Burger at Johnnie's Tavern, a family-run Columbus landmark since the 1940s, is so massive it requires toothpicks to hold it together. But this burger is spectacular, with a careful layering of texture and flavor, molten cheese oozing over the top, and lettuce, tomato, and crisp pickles adding freshness and crunch. The pillow-soft seeded bun does an admirable job of containing the enormous, half-pound-plus patty of fresh ground chuck.

2 TESSARO'S
PITTSBURGH, PA

Many burger joints brag about getting beef delivered daily from a butcher, but how many places actually have a butcher in-house? Tessaro's grinds fresh chuck each morning, and it's formed into patties only moments before it's grilled. The wood-fired grill, getting up to 600° F., puts a serious sear on anything that comes in contact with it, and the burgers are simply superb—crusty, salty, and juicy, perfumed with an intoxicating smokiness. Served on an airy roll, the burger needs nothing more to achieve burger greatness.

3 BOBCAT BITE
SANTA FE, NM

It's the green chile cheeseburger you should order at this much-loved Santa Fe burger shack. But unlike some burgers where flavor-packed toppings compensate for a less-than-great burger, the meat at Bobcat Bite could stand on its own merit. The patties are made from 10-ounce patties of chuck and sirloin, freshly ground—that's a *lot* of beef. They ooze fatty and flavorful juices with each bite, and though the bun isn't quite up to the task of supporting all this delicious sloppy meatiness, it's hard to mind messy fingers with all the beefy flavor.

4 PALACE KITCHEN
SEATTLE, WA

Though the menus rotate often at Tom Douglas's bistro (page 308), the Palace Burger Royale never takes a day off. The juicy patty of wood-grilled Oregon beef is robust in a gamey, aggressively meaty way, and it's served on a fresh bun from

fat makes burgers better

We wish it weren't so, but it is. Fat plays a crucial role in determining a burger's level of deliciousness. It gives a burger much of its flavor and makes a burger juicier—and juicier burgers just flat-out taste better. The ideal meat-to-fat ratio in a perfect burger varies, depending on what cut of meats go into it, but I would say you need a minimum of 20 percent fat to ensure a burger's inherent deliciousness, and 30 percent is not unheard of—even 40 percent, as in Toro (opposite). Be wary of ordering any burger described as lean.

Douglas's Dahlia Bakery. It may be a burger, but it's taken as seriously as anything else on the menu.

 **TORO**
BOSTON, MA

Boston's Toro is an excellent Spanish tapas bar with an equally excellent burger. Made from 100 percent ground shortrib with a fat ratio of nearly 40 percent, this 5-ounce burger comes with an intensely crusty sear imparted by the 900°F. plancha. Ask for it "messy," and chef Jamie Bissonnette will add a massive spoonful of the same finger-licking, garlicky aioli (the Catalan condiment of garlic, oil, and salt), cotija cheese, and espelette pepper mix that they use to coat their famous corn. One of the most deliciously messy creations ever to grease our fingers.

6 PIE 'N BURGER
PASADENA, CA

If you could eat southern California history, it might taste like the perfectly greasy, American dream that is a sloppy Pie 'n Burger burger. Served in the classic drive-in style (paper-wrapped with gobs of toppings), burgers like these are what gave rise to the sandwich's postwar supremacy. You won't have room for a piece of delicious homemade pie, but you may eat it anyway.

 **WHITE ROSE SYSTEM**
LINDEN, NJ

Strange but true: the finest slider joints in the slider-heavy region of northern New Jersey nearly all are named "White." (Blame it on White Castle, the original.) This little Elizabeth Avenue diner dates back to the 1960s and remains untouched, with blue-topped counter stools and a grill that is almost forty years old. Fresh chuck is delivered in 1.7-ounce pucks daily from Jaszt Butcher in nearby Roselle. Each patty is placed on the griddle and receives a spatula smash. Order yours with onions (it improves the sandwich significantly), and they will be placed on top of the patty as it cooks. The finished burger is a classic, the molten cheese and slightly charred onions providing the perfect accompaniment to the tender beef.

8 WHITE MANNA
HACKENSACK, NJ

There's a White Mana (with one *N*) in Jersey City, and a White Manna (with a double *N*) in Hackensack; once operated by the same owner, they've now parted ways, and the double *N* is the way to go. There's generally a line outside the tiny building, but if you're lucky, your wait will be rewarded with a seat at the U-shaped counter and a view of the centrally located griddletop. It is here that the marvel of cheeseburger production unfolds. Balls of beef are placed on a sizzling griddle top, a layer of thinly sliced onions are heaped on top, and the cook then pounds the patty with a spatula until it's flat. Moments later the burgers are flipped and cheese and a potato roll are stacked on top. These are classic sliders at their finest.

in praise of ray's

This is why I love Ray's. I got there at 11:15 AM, put in a burger order, and by 11:30, my food arrived, along with the entire neighborhood: black, white, Asian, Hispanic, army personnel, white-collar executives, construction workers, families, you name it—everyone decided a Ray's hefty, beefy burger was needed. I was told I had to order the Soul Burger Number One, but I was initially skeptical: applewood-smoked bacon, Swiss cheese, and cognac and sherry-sautéed onions sounded like too much going on. Well, I was wrong; this dressed-up burger with a ton of toppings was mighty good. It was cooked medium-rare as ordered, so it was plenty beefy and juicy. Even better was the Mac, which I ordered rare, made with American cheese, tomato, lettuce, pickle, onion, and Ray's Heck sauce, an excellent horseradish-laced creamy condiment.

BURGER AT RAY'S HELL-BURGER, ARLINGTON, VA

9 RAY'S HELL-BURGER
ARLINGTON, VA

A favorite of President Obama and his VP Biden, Ray's Hell-Burger is a D.C. classic—and shows that these elected officials have good burger taste. The first bite into the unadorned meat patty screams success: it's juicy and well seasoned, soft on the inside with a bit of char on the outside, draped in melty cheese and sweet, tender grilled red onions, all sandwiched between halves of a soft sesame seed bun. And while those juices may seep through the bottom bun, it's hard to mind too much—all the more reason to shove this burger into your mouth with due haste.

10 CARL'S DRIVE-IN
BRENTWOOD, MO

We love the crispy edges and browned bits of smashed burgers (page 62), and Carl's Drive-In takes that method to a delicious extreme. Owner Frank Cunetto's classic burger joint has only 16 seats, and if you snag one, you'll have a front-row view of the griddle action: meat smashed on the flat-top and cooked until it's got beautiful lacy edges. They're served as singles, doubles, or triples, and only made better by a slice of melty American cheese—with a house-brewed root beer to wash it all down.

an ode to american cheese

You know, we might as well have called this chapter "Cheeseburgers," since many of the specimens mentioned here have a slice or two of something cheesy melted on 'em. But *what kind* of cheese? We've long favored American.

Shocked? Yeah, it's processed and bright yellow, and it often comes in individual slips of plastic—qualities we don't usually go for. But American cheese is the perfect burger cheese. We couldn't have said it any better than "A Hamburger Today" reader Processed Neon (apt screen name, right?), so we'll paraphrase the reasons he loves it, as they're our reasons, too:

» Its taste—pleasant but not overpowering

» Its versatility across a wide range of burgers styles—griddled, grilled, and broiled

» Its texture and superior melting quality

» It's pure nostalgia (Americans have been melting this cheese on burgers for the better part of a century)

11 COZY INN
SALINA, KS

It may be the aroma that beckons burger lovers both near and far to the Cozy Inn, filling their nostrils and noggins with a healthy dose of nostalgia. This place has been a Salina institution since 1922, but despite an outsize sense of history, the burgers themselves are anything but large—the Cozy specializes in sliders. And though they come with a heaping throw of onions (no exceptions), they absolutely do not come with cheese. Don't even try.

12 BOBO'S DRIVE-IN
TOPEKA, KS

Bobo's is the kind of place where the waitresses call you "Hon" and serve up no-nonsense diner food and amazing burgers. Kansas is a state that knows beef—and knows better than to serve frozen. Expect an irregularly shaped patty of fresh beef with a crisp salty crust and juicy soft interior, topped with a thick slice of oozy American cheese. We suggest ordering a double cheeseburger, which should bring the whole sandwich into proper bun-to-beef alignment.

13 WORKINGMAN'S FRIEND TAVERN
INDIANAPOLIS, IN

This burger shop opened in 1918 as Belmont Lunch—but got the nickname "Workingman's Friend," according to the family that still owns it, since regular customers short on cash could eat on credit until a paycheck came in. Whatever the reason, the name stuck around. And so has the griddle. Fresh-ground chuck is delivered every day, formed by hand into patties, and then smashed down on a grill—producing lacy, crispy edges that many smashed burgers can only aspire to.

14 APPLE PAN
LOS ANGELES, CA

We don't typically go for barbecue sauce on burgers, but here it really works. Apple Pan's burger size is just right, about six or seven bites' worth; the

BURGER AT WORKINGMAN'S FRIEND TAVERN, INDIANAPOLIS, IN

grill imbues it with a savory dark flavor, slightly smoky, which counteracts the hickory sauce's sharpness. An amazing combination of ingredients, simple in arrangement and multifaceted in flavor, and small enough that you'll have room for pie.

15 JOE'S CABLE CAR RESTAURANT
SAN FRANCISCO, CA

Joe's Cable Car is a trek from downtown San Francisco, but you will be greeted by a great burger when you arrive, and by owner Joe Obegi himself, a constant smiling presence. Freshly ground meat carefully cooked on a flat-top griddle is a formula that has benefited burger lovers forever. Longtime Joe's Cable Car aficionados often order the patty melt, and they are on to something; its grilled rye exterior, made golden brown by the combination of butter and the hot griddle, lends a satisfying crunch. The inside is all gooey and juicy from the fresh meat, and the grilled onions and the oozing melted American cheese are the perfect complements to grilled rye bread and the burger patty.

16 UMAMI BURGER
LOS ANGELES, CA

Owner Adam Fleischman uses a secret burger blend (including the super-lean flap-meat beef, from the back of the short loin) that's cooked on a seasoned cast-iron griddle. The cheese on the

burger is made in-house from Gruyère and sherry—through the magic of kitchen science, it's got the nutty tang of Gruyère but the fluid melt of American. Think of it as a high-tech rendition of a totally classic burger.

17 SHAKE SHACK
NEW YORK, NY, AND ELSEWHERE

When Shake Shack opened in 2004 in New York City's Madison Square Park, it marked the beginning of a burger revolution in the Big Apple. Building on the Midwest-style smashed burgers he loved growing up, restaurateur Danny Meyer elevated the genre by carefully selecting a blend of three cuts of beef to produce maximum flavor and juiciness. (We believe it's sirloin, chuck, and brisket, though they'll neither confirm nor deny.) The resulting burgers, with a perfect salty-seared crust, have become the gold standard in the city. It's no wonder people wait in 45-minute lines for them.

18 MOTZ'S BURGERS
DETROIT, MI

All too often, old-school burger joints deliver on aesthetics and nostalgia but fail on flavor. Motz's Burger in southwest Detroit is one of the rare exceptions. Continuously operating as a slider joint since 1929 (it was a White Castle until the mid-1930s), it's about as old school as it gets. Order your burger and the griddle man smashes a hand-balled patty of ground sirloin (ground fresh every morning) onto the ancient, well-seasoned griddle with a handful of thinly sliced onions. As the patty cooks, it picks up the subtle flavor of the decades of patties cooked before it. One flip, a slice of cheese, and a soft steamed bun later, and you have what's in the running for the best slider in the country.

THE SHACK BURGER FROM SHAKE SHACK, NEW YORK, NY

The key to a great patty melt is to get all the ingredients to meld together. We toast the inside of the sliced bread to help the cheese start melting even before the sandwich goes back into the pan. For our onions, we caramelize them in a skillet, then add the collected meat juices from the burger patties for an extra jolt of flavor.

patty melt

MAKES 2 SANDWICHES

6 tablespoons unsalted butter

4 slices rye bread

4 slices American cheese, torn into large pieces

4 slices Swiss cheese, torn into large pieces

Kosher salt

Freshly ground black pepper

½ pound freshly ground chuck, formed into two 4-ounce patties, roughly the size and shape of 1 slice bread

1 large onion, split in half, sliced thin from pole to pole (about 2 cups)

1 Melt 1 tablespoon of butter in a 12-inch heavy-bottomed skillet over medium heat until foaming. Add two slices of bread and swirl them around the pan using your hand or a spatula. Cook, swirling occasionally, until pale golden brown, about 3 minutes. Transfer the bread to a cutting board, cooked side up. Divide the American cheese evenly between the slices, leaving a ¼-inch gap around the edges.

2 Repeat step 1 with the remaining bread slices, additional tablespoon of butter, and the remaining Swiss cheese.

3 Season the hamburger patties on both sides with salt and pepper. Return the skillet to the heat, increase the heat to high, and melt 1 tablespoon of butter in the skillet until it is light brown. Swirl the skillet to coat the bottom with butter, and add both of the burger patties. Cook without moving until a dark brown crust forms on the first side, about 1½ minutes, reducing the heat to medium if the butter begins to burn or smoke excessively. Flip the burgers using a spatula and cook on the second side without moving until a crust develops, 1½ minutes longer.

4 Transfer the burger patties to a plate and reduce the heat to medium. Add the onion, 1 tablespoon of butter, and 2 tablespoons of water to the skillet. Season the onion with salt and pepper. Cook, stirring constantly and scraping up browned bits from the bottom of the skillet, until the water evaporates and the onion starts to fry

and leaves a brown residue on the bottom of the pan. Add another 2 tablespoons of water and continue to cook until the water has evaporated. Repeat two more times, until the onion is soft and a deep golden brown. Add the collected juices from the burger plate to the onion and continue to cook for 30 seconds. Onion should be moist, but not dripping.

5 Divide the onion mixture evenly between the cheese-topped toast slices. Add the burger patties to the slices with American cheese, and close the sandwiches.

6 Add 1 tablespoon of butter to the skillet. Return the skillet to medium heat and cook until the butter melts. Sprinkle the melted butter with salt. Swirl to coat the pan and add the sandwiches. Cook, swirling the sandwiches around the pan frequently, until they are a deep golden brown on the bottom, about 5 minutes.

7 Remove the sandwiches from the skillet, melt the remaining tablespoon of butter in the pan, and sprinkle with salt. Return the sandwiches to the skillet and cook, swirling frequently, until the second side is golden brown and the cheese is melted. Serve immediately.

19 SOLLY'S GRILLE
MILWAUKEE, WI

Solly's Grille, located incongruously next to the Milwaukee Heart Hospital, is famous for the Wisconsin regional delight known as the butter burger. A liberal dollop of Dairy State butter is applied to the burger just after the patty hits the bun. (It's best not to ask how much butter.) But it's not just caloric overkill. By upping the fat, moisture, and salt, the butter plays up all the essential elements of a great burger—and when the totally melted American cheese starts sliding around, too, you know you're in for a drippy-delicious bite.

20 BUD'S BAR
SEDALIA, CO

It's pretty clear who is and who isn't a regular at Bud's, a weathered bar tucked between two train tracks in the town of Sedalia, Colorado—though they've taken measures to get the interlopers up to speed. ("No french fries, dammit," read the waitresses' shirts.) No matter; it's the burger you want. A total classic—griddled chuck patties, melty American cheese—it's one of the most remarkably juicy plain-Jane burgers we've ever eaten. It's made even better by the white squishy bun, placed on top

of the burger while it's still on the griddle, then capped with a lid, so the bun gets steamed right through. Grab a burger at the bar with a $3 beer, strike up a conversation about elk hunting, and you'll see why the regulars seem to never leave.

21 HUDSON'S HAMBURGERS
COEUR D'ALENE, ID

Our friend Tom Douglas, Seattle chef and restaurateur, turned us on to this one. Tom says, "I feel most 'burger joints' have lost their way through a haze of unbridled manipulation and egomaniacal competition of what should be a very simple, straightforward meal. Hudson's Hamburgers is the antithesis of all this crap. Just a beautiful nicely browned beef patty punctuated with a freshly sliced sweet onion and dill pickle then finished with a perfectly toasted squishy bun. Yum!"

22 SERPENTINE
SAN FRANCISCO, CA

This restaurant burger is a smartly composed one: Chef Deepak Kaul puts together a loosely packed puck of well-seasoned, dry-aged beef from local favorite Prather Ranch, griddled to a gorgeous crust, on a fresh, soft, butter-toasted roll from Acme Bread—with house-pickled onions and bread-and-butters, a few sparing leaves of arugula, and fantastically sweet tomatoes. Biting into this burger releases an absolute torrent of savory, funky, just-short-of-bloody meatiness that other

BUTTER BURGER AT SOLLY'S GRILLE, MILWAUKEE, WI

KRAZY JIM'S BLIMPY BURGER, ANN ARBOR, MI

PATTY MELT AT TOP NOTCH BEEFBURGERS, CHICAGO, IL

taurant Jean-Georges before returning to Salt Lake City to open The Copper Onion. While there are a lot of good eats on his menu, the burger might be our favorite. The kitchen grinds meat for a blend that's a whopping 30 percent fat, then cooks the patties precisely to temperature, with a great crust; they're topped with shredded lettuce for a little fresh crunch and red wine–cooked onions that soak up the beefy juices. They're like a French onion soup on your burger.

24 TOP NOTCH BEEFBURGERS
CHICAGO, IL

Top Notch is a good half-hour drive south of Chicago's Loop. But it's easy to find, as the Top Notch Beefburgers sign rises high above a diner that seats more than a hundred eaters. The whole place belongs on the set of *Happy Days*. And luckily, the burgers live up to their name. Made from meat that's ground fresh daily, the burgers get a just-so crust and a juicy interior that soaks into the toasted bun. The burgers are sold by size ranging

burgers can only aspire to. Cheese (Cheddar or Gruyère) melts nicely and adds a little aged flavor and fat, but it's hardly noticeable—the burger's beefiness overwhelms everything, in the best way possible.

23 THE COPPER ONION
SALT LAKE CITY, UT

Utah-born Ryan Lowder trained at the Culinary Institute of America and four-star New York res-

from 1/4 to 3/4 pound; we preferred the two smaller sizes, to preserve the right beef-to-bun ratio. But if you're looking for the ultimate burger and butter and grease experience, order the patty melt: that unbeatable combination of grilled rye bread, American cheese, grilled onions, and fine ground beef.

25 GRAZE
MADISON, WI

Tory Miller, who bought the restaurant L'Etoile from pioneering chef Odessa Piper, opened the more casual Graze next door in 2010. Miller started making a $19 burger for the dinner menu, using meat ground in-house from sirloin, ribeye, and shortribs—but the $10 pub burger, made of pastured Highland beef that arrives already ground from Wisconsin's Fountain Prairie Farms, is a fantastic creation in its own right. The beef was insanely juicy, flavorful, and beefy, served on a housemade English muffin with bacon, Cheddar, and the works. (The perfectly cooked and salted fries are almost as good.)

26 KRAZY JIM'S BLIMPY BURGER
ANN ARBOR, MI

Waiting in the fast-paced, student-filled line, you get an ear for the ordering style here: the grill cooks, who double as cashiers, sling out the attitude as fast as the burgers. It's all quite clearly tongue-in-cheek and easy enough to enjoy. The 1 1/2-ounce balls of chuck (ground in-house daily) are not just pressed into the griddle once; they are smashed and smashed until you can literally see holes in them. What this does is absolutely maximize the surface area browning, giving you far more crispy bits per bite than your average burger—doubly so because each sandwich comes with two patties. Though you'd think that the smashing technique would rob all moisture from the patties, they're deliciously greasy. And adding cheese between each patty only amplifies the goo-factor.

27 TOWN TOPIC
KANSAS CITY, MO

At Town Topic they've been cooking smashed single, double, and triple burgers for decades, and as far as anyone can tell, they haven't changed the formula or the cooking method yet. The counterman puts a wad of ground beef on a ridiculously well-seasoned griddle, smashes it hard, lets it cook for a minute until it forms a crust, salts it, adds the onions if you've ordered them, smashes it again, turns it, adds the cheese, and serves it on a squishy bun. You can order a single, but you really need the double or triple for maximum eating pleasure.

28 EL MAGO DE LAS FRITAS
MIAMI, FL

One bite of the Frita Cubana is all it takes to understand why everyone from local eaters to presidents avail themselves of El Mago de Las Fritas's Cuban style burgers—which may or may not be made with chorizo. (Owner "El Mago," or The Magician, who speaks only Spanish, will smile at you forever without revealing his secrets.) Regulars know to order either the well-seasoned burger topped with super-thin, incredibly crisp matchstick fries, or a burger topped with cheese and a fried egg, which is the ultimate Cuban Miami breakfast sandwich. Just do not order a Frita with cheese without the egg—it apparently is just not done.

29 HOLEMAN & FINCH PUBLIC HOUSE
ATLANTA, GA

Want a burger at Holeman & Finch? Get there before 10:00 PM, and put your order in quick—they only offer 24 burgers each night, from the stroke of 10:00 until they sell out (which, they claim, can be in under a minute). But you don't have to look at your watch: someone will pick up the megaphone and announce that it's burger time. From then on, burgers might as well be the only thing on the menu. It's a well-seasoned, well-crusted double patty you'll get, deliciously juicy even as each one is cooked through, with American cheese that oozes

PATTY MELT AT TOWN TOPIC, KANSAS CITY, MO

between the two patties in the most satisfying of ways. An unsweetened brioche bun and house-made pickles complete the picture. It doesn't get better than this—until you try a super-crisp fry or the deep-fried peach pie for dessert.

30 BLUESTEM
KANSAS CITY, MO

In general, we're not favorably disposed to Kobe beef burgers, finding them mushy and unpleasant. But the Bluestem's Kobe burger has us thinking differently. The patty, delivered already ground from Texas-raised beef, is incredibly juicy, and the coarse enough grind of the meat works perfectly. Add a decent toasted brioche bun, good fries, crispy onions, and Cheddar that's not too sharp, and you have yourself an excellent burger. As we said, it's enough to make us rethink our stance on Kobe beef burgers.

5 GREAT CHEFFY BURGERS

It wasn't too long ago that the phrase "high-end burger" sounded like a contradiction in terms. But over the last few years, some of the country's finest chefs have hopped on board the burger train. While there's a real appeal to the down-and-dirty $3 cheeseburger, there's no denying that pricier restaurants can turn out a mighty fine product. Here are some of our favorite chef burgers across the country.

1 LE PIGEON
PORTLAND, OR

Le Pigeon makes one of the juiciest, meat sponge-iest burgers you may ever eat. James Beard– nominated chef/owner Gabriel Rucker grills a thick ½-pound patty of Cascade Natural Beef, ground in-house, and tops it with Tillamook four-year aged white Cheddar, grilled pickled onions, a hefty mound of crunchy iceberg lettuce slaw, homemade aioli, house-made ketchup, and highly potent housemade Dijon mustard. Although the juices may soak through the soft grilled ciabatta bun, the bread manages to hold up until the last bite. Just make sure you get to Le Pigeon early if you want this burger; they serve only five a night.

2 DAVID BURKE'S PRIMEHOUSE
CHICAGO, IL

The burger patty made of 40-day aged beef has a lineage more exhaustively detailed than most family trees. The beef comes from Primehouse's own line of Black Angus cattle, all the descendants of a single bull named Prime, all with supremely well-marbled beef. That beef, in the restaurant, gets dry-aged for 40 days in a Himalayan salt-tiled aging room; then it's seared at a remarkable 900°F. before it's bunned. But the toppings don't hurt when it comes to making one of the best burgers in the city. A mound of garlic spinach and crispy shallots tops the rich, flavorful patty, and it all comes on a bacon mayonnaise–smeared toasted potato bun. The skin-on fries are a good side, but the asiago-truffle potato skins are even better.

3 CRAIGIE ON MAIN
CAMBRIDGE, MA

In line with the rest of the seriously delicious, funky, thoughtful, and local food at this high-end bistro, Craigie's hamburger is made from three cuts of sustainably raised grass-fed beef (including beef cheek) ground together with bone marrow. A touch of dehydrated miso paste ups the umami factor. Chef Tony Maws slow-cooks the burger to a precise medium-rare in a high-tech steam oven before charring it. Topped with aged Cheddar, crisp fried onion rings, a schmear of sweet, house-made mace-flavored ketchup, red wine vinegar pickles, and watercress dressed with the patty's pan

BURGER AT LE PIGEON, PORTLAND, OR

PRIME STEAK BURGER AT DAVID BURKE'S PRIMEHOUSE, CHICAGO, IL

drippings, it's a composed dish on a house-baked sesame-seed bun.

4 MINETTA TAVERN
NEW YORK, NY

Chefs Lee Hanson and Riad Nasr of Keith McNally's Minetta Tavern tried a dozen different blends from New York's top meat purveyors before deciding on the Black Label blend, from vaunted meat purveyor Pat La Frieda—dry-aged ribeye, along with skirt steak and brisket, sourced from Creekstone Farms in Kentucky. The beef is handled as little as possible, formed into patties, and seared on a plancha with grapeseed oil and clarified butter; it's served with sautéed onions on a buttery, salty brioche bun that's far less sweet than most. The simplicity of the finished burger belies the careful thought and extreme precision involved in bringing it to table.

5 COMME ÇA
WEST HOLLYWOOD, CA

The best cheffy burgers are the product of a combination of competitive urges, endless tinkering, and flat-out burger love. At Comme Ça, they take 8 ounces of high-quality ground beef, salt it, and cook it as many talented chefs cook a steak, on an insanely hot flat-top griddle, until it gets a delicious salted, caramelized exterior. Then they slide it into a 375°F. oven until it's a perfect medium rare, and top it with Cheddar cheese. When you bite into the burger after it's nestled into its soft toasted brioche bun, you might end up wearing it—it's that juicy. The shredded lettuce and special sauce are less important ingredients here; meat, salt, and bun are all you need.

BLACK LABEL BURGER AT MINETTA TAVERN, NEW YORK, NY

5 FAST-FOOD BURGERS WORTH YOUR TIME

Two of the most important determinants of a good burger: fresh beef and an attentive flipper. Two things most fast-food chains lack: fresh beef and an attentive flipper. We'll almost always take a restaurant burger over a fast-food one, but with so many burger chains out there, a few are actually worth a chunk of your burger allowance.

1 IN-N-OUT BURGER

These burgers are grilled to order and made of ground chuck shoulder that's never been frozen. There's a "secret menu" for those in the know to customize their burgers (Animal Style—with extra spread and grilled onions dissolving into the melted cheese; the Flying Dutchman—burger and

DOUBLE-DOUBLE AT IN-N-OUT BURGER

BURGER AT STEAK 'N SHAKE

4 FIVE GUYS

This relative newcomer (founded in 1986) has spread like wildfire within the last few years, from its Virginia base up and down the Eastern Seaboard and beyond. While slightly pricier than your average fast-food burger, a Five Guys burger (or a smaller Little Burger) starts with fresh beef and sits happily between soft, griddled bun halves. The huge barrels of free shell-on peanuts don't hurt, either. And the fries, fresh-cut from sacks of potatoes and crisped in peanut oil, are some of the best fast-food fries out there.

5 BLAKE'S LOTABURGER

Dating back to 1952, Blake's Lotaburger—alternatively abbreviated as either name—has more than 75 locations, but has never moved beyond New Mexico. Grilled fresh from Angus beef and best stacked with Hatch green chiles, Blake's burgers are bold, spicy, and far gutsier than your standard fast-food fare.

cheese, sans bun). The fries are made with fresh potatoes, and if you want, they'll fry them twice. This West Coast burger chain has a cult following; one bite of a Double-Double tells you why.

2 WHITE CASTLE

White Castle seems to be a love-it-or-hate-it proposition, with most of the love coming from people who were introduced to it as kids. The tiny burgers have a flavor that can't be duplicated—oniony to the max and pickle laden. The double cheeseburger is pure chain-burger perfection.

3 STEAK 'N SHAKE

"The Steakburger is a symphony of taste and texture," film critic Roger Ebert once wrote. Since the first Steak 'n Shake opened in 1934 in Normal, Illinois, white-capped griddle guards have been flipping burgers at these diner-style restaurants. A blend of T-bone, sirloin, and strip steak is smashed onto a hot griddle, quickly crusting up before it's scraped and served.

MAKING BURGERS AT HOME

When we posted a thread asking the Serious Eats community where they went for their favorite burger, a number of folks answered, "At home!" Given the number of serious home cooks who visit the site, that was no surprise. But even the most accomplished of burger-makers can pick up some tips, so we've gathered our best intel on DIY burgering here.

Invented in Wichita, Kansas, in 1916 by Walter Anderson (who five years later founded White Castle), sliders were at one time the predominant form of burger on the planet. For these burgers, onions are key—their aromatic steam wafts through and around the beef and buns, which are placed directly on top of the patty as it cooks.

After extensive research, we found that sliders are best when the patty is cooked on top of the onion bed: the cooking is done via steam from the onions. Since they take so long to caramelize, keeping the beef away from the heat during that time ensures that the meat stays moist; the onions perfume both meat and bun all the way through, and have enough time and contact with the griddle to properly soften.

the ultimate
sliders

MAKES 1 DOZEN SLIDERS

2 medium onions, finely minced (about 2 cups)

1 teaspoon kosher salt, plus more for seasoning

1 1/8 pounds freshly ground Basic Burger Blend (page 86)

1 large onion, peeled and grated on the medium holes of a box grater, juices and pulp reserved (about 1 1/2 cups)

Freshly ground black pepper

12 slices American cheese (optional)

16 slider-size buns (2 1/2 to 3 inches across, such as Martin's Famous Dinner Potato rolls)

24 thin dill pickle slices

Condiments, as desired

1 In a medium bowl, toss the minced onion with 1 teaspoon kosher salt. Set aside at room temperature until fragrant, about 10 minutes. Meanwhile, divide the beef into 12 evenly sized balls. Using damp hands, press the balls into patties approximately 1/8 inch thick and 3 1/2 inches wide. Place on a large plastic wrap–lined plate. Patties can be stacked with layers of plastic wrap between each layer. Place in the refrigerator until ready to cook.

2 Add the minced and salted onion to a heavy-bottomed 12-inch skillet, using a spatula to spread into an even layer. Place over medium-low heat and cook without stirring until the bottom of the onion starts turning pale golden brown, 7 to 10 minutes (onion should barely sizzle while cooking—lower the heat if it browns too quickly).

sliders we love

True sliders—not mini-burgers (page 60)—are one of our very favorite ways to eat meat, bread, and cheese. But true sliders, with caramelized onions and steamed buns, are hard to find. Where do we find our favorites? At Motz's Burgers in Detroit, MI (page 73); Shopsins in New York City (page 20); White Manna in Hackensack, NJ (page 70); and a cheese-less version at Cozy Inn in Salina, KS (page 72).

3 Once the onion is golden brown, reduce the heat to low. Add half of the grated onion and the juice to the skillet. Stir the onion with a rubber spatula to release the browned bits from the bottom of the pan and spread into a thin, even layer. Arrange six hamburger patties on top of the onion mixture. Season the tops of the patties generously with salt and pepper. Add six slices of American cheese, if desired. Place the bun bottoms, cut side down, on top of the patties. Place the bun tops, cut side down, on top of the bun bottoms, staggering arrangement to maximize exposure to the steam.

4 Continue cooking over low heat until the burgers are cooked through and the cheese is fully melted, about 3 minutes, adding extra onion juice if the pan runs dry. Reserve at least half of the juice for the second batch of patties. (There should be no sizzling sound, and the mixture should steam constantly—in some cases, substituting water may be necessary if there is insufficient onion juice.) Remove the skillet from the heat.

5 Lift one patty, along with the onion from underneath and both sides of one bun, with the spatula. Pick up the bun top, invert, and place underneath the

spatula (the burger should now be fully assembled, upside down). Slide out the spatula from between the burger and the bun top. Invert, and place on a plate. Repeat with the remaining five burgers. Spoon any remaining onion and melted cheese in the skillet on top of each burger patty, along with two pickles and condiments as desired. Consume immediately, before repeating with the remaining six sliders.

This recipe can also be made by hand. Chop the beef finely with a large knife or cleaver until the desired texture is achieved.

basic
burger blend

MAKES 2 POUNDS

12 ounces boneless beef sirloin, trimmed of gristle, cut into 1-inch cubes

10 ounces beef brisket, trimmed of gristle, cut into 1-inch cubes

10 ounces boneless beef shortrib, trimmed of gristle, cut into 1-inch cubes

USING A MEAT GRINDER

1 Place the feed shaft, blade, and ¼-inch die of the meat grinder in the freezer until well chilled, about 1 hour. Meanwhile, place all the meat chunks on a rimmed baking sheet, leaving space between each piece, and place in the freezer for 10 minutes, until the meat is firm, but not frozen.

2 In a large bowl, combine the chilled meats and toss to mix. Grind the meat, handling as little as possible after it is ground. Use the ground meat immediately, or cover the bowl with plastic wrap and refrigerate until ready to use.

USING A FOOD PROCESSOR

1 Place the bowl and blade of a food processor in the freezer until well chilled, about 1 hour. Meanwhile, place the meat chunks on a rimmed baking sheet, leaving space between each piece, and place in the freezer for 10 minutes, until the meat is firm, but not frozen.

2 In a large bowl, combine the chilled meats and toss to mix. Working in two batches, place the meat cubes in the food processor and pulse until a medium-fine grind is achieved, eight to ten 1-second pulses, scraping down the processor bowl as necessary. Use the ground meat immediately, or cover the bowl with plastic wrap and refrigerate until ready to use.

The quality of the burger meat and its handling are key to the success of a great burger. For best results, use freshly ground beef, and handle as little as possible. These thin patties will remain juicy and moist even when cooked to medium well.

all-american
cheeseburger

1 Spread the meat on a rimmed baking sheet and gather the meat loosely into four even piles. Without picking up the meat, shape the piles into patties approximately 4 inches wide and 1/2 inch thick. When forming these patties, press the meat together very gently, packing as loosely as possible; ragged edges are desirable to allow for a greater surface area, which gives the patty superior browning and crispness. Season generously with salt and pepper. Using a thin metal spatula, flip the patties and season the other side.

2 Add the vegetable oil to a heavy bottomed 12-inch skillet and set over high heat until it just begins to smoke. Using the spatula, transfer the burgers to the skillet and cook without moving until the first side is deep brown with jagged crispy bits, about 2 1/2 minutes. Flip the patties and top each with a slice of cheese. Continue to cook the patties for 1 minute longer, or until desired doneness is reached.

3 Lift each patty, blot the bottom once on a double layer of paper towel, place on the bottom bun, top as desired (or place toppings underneath the patty), cover with the top bun, and serve.

MAKES 4 BURGERS

1 pound freshly ground Basic Burger Blend (opposite)

Kosher salt and freshly ground black pepper

2 teaspoons vegetable oil

4 slices yellow American cheese

4 soft hamburger buns (such as Sunbeam or Arnold), lightly buttered and toasted

Toppings, as desired

In order to achieve the proper crust, these thin burgers need to cook at least to medium. With good-quality freshly ground beef, the burgers should remain moist and juicy. A large griddle can be used to cook more than two burgers at a time. The sweet and tangy special sauce works well on any cheeseburger. (The sauce will keep in the fridge for up to two weeks.)

"smashed" burger

MAKES 2 BURGERS

FOR THE SPECIAL SAUCE

1 tablespoon ketchup

3 tablespoons mayonnaise

$\frac{1}{2}$ teaspoon hot sauce (such as Frank's)

1 teaspoon white vinegar or rice wine vinegar

2 teaspoons sweet pickle relish

$\frac{1}{4}$ teaspoon freshly cracked black peppercorns

$\frac{1}{8}$ teaspoon garlic powder

1 teaspoon granulated sugar

FOR THE BURGERS

10 ounces freshly ground Basic Burger Blend (page 86)

Kosher salt and freshly ground black pepper

$\frac{1}{2}$ teaspoon vegetable oil or nonstick cooking spray

2 slices yellow American cheese

2 soft hamburger buns, preferably potato rolls (such as Martin's brand), lightly buttered and toasted

Toppings, as desired

1 To make the special sauce: In a small bowl, combine all the ingredients and stir until a smooth consistency and even color is reached. Use immediately, or cover and refrigerate.

2 To make the burgers: Form the beef into two tight cylinders, approximately 2 inches wide and 2 inches tall. Season liberally on all sides with salt and black pepper.

3 Add $\frac{1}{4}$ teaspoon oil to a heavy-bottomed 12-inch stainless-steel or cast-iron skillet. Rub the oil into the skillet with a paper towel until the oil is no longer visible. Heat the skillet over high heat until lightly smoking. Reduce the heat to medium-high. Place the beef pucks in the skillet at least 3 inches apart. Rub the bottom of a stiff solid metal spatula with the remaining vegetable oil and press the patties firmly into the skillet until they form approximate 5-inch rounds. Use a second spatula to ensure that the burgers do not stick to the bottom of the first spatula.

4 Cook without moving until a deep brown crust develops, about $2\frac{1}{2}$ minutes. Using the stiff metal spatula, carefully scrape the burgers off of the bottom of the skillet, including as many browned bits as possible. Flip the burgers and top with cheese. Cook for 1 minute longer, until cheese is melted. Transfer the burgers to the bottom buns and top as desired (or place toppings underneath the patties). Spread the inside of the top buns with the special sauce, cover the burgers, and serve.

To cook these burgers over a gas grill, set one burner on high to create a hot zone and leave the remaining burners on low for the cooler zone. Making a slight depression in the center of these large patties helps them maintain their shape during cooking as their edges shrink more than their centers.

big backyard
burgers

1 Divide the beef into four even piles. Form each pile into a patty roughly 4½ inches wide and 1 inch tall. Make a slight depression in the center of each patty with fingers.

2 Ignite a large chimney starter full of charcoal (about 6 quarts or 100 briquettes) and burn until large coals are completely coated in a thin layer of gray ash, about 20 minutes. Spread the coals evenly over one side of the grill bottom. Position the cooking rack above coals and cover until hot, about 5 minutes.

3 Meanwhile, season the patties generously on all sides with salt and pepper. Scrape the grill grates clean with a wire brush. Position the patties directly over the coals, cover, and cook until well browned, about

2 minutes. Flip the burgers, top with cheese (if using), cover, and cook for an additional 2 minutes, or until well browned on the second side. Transfer the patties to the cool side of the grill, cover, and cook until the center of the burger registers 130°F. on an instant-read thermometer for medium-rare (about 1 minute longer), 140°F. for medium (about 2 minutes longer), or 150°F. and above for medium-well to well-done (3 to 5 minutes longer). Transfer the burgers to a cutting board and tent loosely with foil to keep warm.

4 Meanwhile, working with two buns at a time, toast the buns on the hot side of the grill until they are brown and crispy, about 1 minute each. Place the burgers in the buns, top as desired, and serve.

MAKES 4 BURGERS

2 pounds freshly ground Basic Burger Blend (page 86)

Kosher salt and freshly ground black pepper

4 slices yellow American cheese (optional)

4 large hamburger buns (such as Pepperidge Farms or Martin's Big Marty's)

Toppings, as desired

pizza

IT'S DIFFICULT TO EXPLAIN JUST HOW **WE LOVE PIZZA** at serious eats— AND TO ACCOUNT FOR JUST HOW DEEP our love goes.

WE HAVE WRITTEN EXTENSIVELY ABOUT THE CRUSTY, SAUCY, CHEESY STUFF, AND, EVEN THEN, WE HAVE A HARD TIME PUTTING INTO WORDS WHY WE (AND NEARLY EVERYONE, IT SEEMS) CHERISH IT SO.

The nostalgia of childhood might explain some of it. We're introduced to pizza at birthday parties, sleepovers, and post-sport outings, and many of us link it indelibly with memories of our youth. But that seems only part of the story. What about the pies themselves? Is it the seemingly effortless way that bread, tomatoes, and gooey cheese come together?

Above all, a perfect pizza is balanced. None of the three essential elements should overwhelm any of the others. The crust, whether it's New York–style, Chicago deep-dish, or ultra-thin, should sup-port the sauce, cheese, and toppings, but also have a flavor of its own. Good pizza doesn't leave you with a plate of uneaten crusts—as some people call them, "pizza bones."

The ideal sauce is made with high-quality canned tomatoes, with little done to them other than straining, crushing, and seasoning with salt. Added sugar is unnecessary; if the tomatoes are good, they should be sweet enough on their own. There shouldn't be so much sauce that it results in a soggy crust, or so little that all you taste is cheese and bread. (That's what grilled cheese sandwiches

are for.) The sauce should be good enough that you'd want to eat it on its own—or at least sop up any remainder on your plate with those "bones."

There's a lot of cheese variation, but generally a pie should be made with good-quality mozzarella, whether that's a fresh cow's-milk mozzarella (known as *fior di latte*), buffalo mozzarella (made from the milk of water buffalo), or a slightly tangy aged mozzarella (which is what most by-the-slice pizzerias use, and what's most commonly found in grocery stores). In any case, the cheese should be creamy, melty, and distributed in a way that you get some with each bite. It should never be overly greasy or the least bit rubbery.

Toppings, if you go for them, should be chosen with care. The best pizza-makers find high-quality ingredients and prepare them simply so that they shine on their own. Topping combinations should complement not only the "holy trinity" of crust, sauce, and cheese, but also each other, and should become an integral part of the pie—not just roughage or proteins thrown on as an afterthought.

Maybe this is why we love pizza so much—it's a world of variables in the round (or rectangular) whose parts can be tweaked and perfected, giving us limitless options to explore.

Until the 1940s, pizza was an ethnic, working-class food eaten by Italians in the urban areas in which they had settled in the late 1800s. So how did pizza become the mainstream food that it is today?

Soldiers returning from World War II brought home with them a yen for the pizza they had discovered while fighting in Italy. In 1945, WWII vet Ira Nevin combined his pizza-eating knowledge with his experience repairing ovens for his father's business and created the first gas-fueled pizza oven. His Bakers Pride ovens made it possible for anyone with a mixer and some recipes to get into the pizza business. But what really broke pizza far and wide was the birth of the chain pizzeria. Pizza Hut started in Wichita, Kansas, in 1958; Little Caesar's (Garden City, Michigan) sprang up in 1959; and Domino's (Ypsilanti, Michigan) began in 1960. Papa John's, a relative latecomer, opened in the 1980s. For decades to come, these chains would be where most Americans got their pizza.

the history of pizza
THE EUROPEAN YEARS

234 TO 149 B.C.E. Cato the Elder, in his history of Rome, tells of a "flat round of dough dressed with olive oil, herbs, and honey baked on stones."

521 TO 486 B.C.E. The soldiers of Persian emperor Darius the Great are reputed to have baked a flatbread on their shields, covering it with cheese and dates.

79 C.E. Mount Vesuvius erupts and freezes the city of Pompeii in time. In the mid-1800s, Pompeii is excavated and evidence of shops dedicated to the making of flat breads are found—complete with ovens, tools, and layouts that look remarkably like the pizzerias in nearby Naples.

the history of pizza
THE AMERICAN YEARS

1880 TO 1900 Low wages, high taxes, and overcrowding force Italians—predominately southern Italians—to immigrate to the United States. They bring with them their food traditions, including pizza-making.

1912 Joe's Tomato Pies opens in Trenton, New Jersey.

1905 A Italian-born grocer by the name of Gennaro Lombardi applies to the city of New York for the first license in the United States to make and sell pizza. His pizzeria, Lombardi's, still stands today on Manhattan's Spring Street.

1924 Anthony "Totonno" Pero, who had been working at Lombardi's, leaves to open his own pizzeria, Totonno's, in Brooklyn's Coney Island.

1850s Emmanuelle Rocca, in a pamphlet titled "The Customs of Naples," writes, "The most ordinary pizzas, called *coll'aglio e l'oglio*, have for condiments oil, a scattering of salt, oregano, and finely cut up cloves of garlic. Others are covered with grated cheese and seasoned with lard and then some leaves of basil. To the first, tiny fish are often added; to the second, thin slices of mozzarella. Sometimes slices of ham are used or else tomato, mussels, etc."

1889 King Umberto I and his wife, Queen Margherita di Savoia, visit Naples on vacation and ask Raffaele Esposito, reportedly the best pizza-maker in the city, to visit their palace there and make pizza for them. He makes three kinds, one of which is the pizza that would forever bear the queen's name. Topped with tomato sauce, mozzarella cheese, and basil, the pizza Margherita is said to have been inspired by the colors of the Italian flag—green, white, and red.

1929 Another Lombardi's alumnus, John Sasso, leaves the nation's first pizzeria and opens John's Pizzeria in New York City's Greenwich Village.

1943 Deep-dish pizza is born when Ike Sewell opens his Pizzeria Uno in Chicago.

1925 Frank Pepe opens his eponymous pizzeria in New Haven, Connecticut.

1930s Pizzerias open in Boston (Santarpio's, 1933) and San Francisco (Lupo's, which would later become Tommaso's, in 1934). New Jersey sees additional openings with Sciortino's (Perth Amboy, 1934) and the Reservoir Tavern (Boonton, 1936). In 1938, Salvatore "Sally" Consiglio, a nephew of Frank Pepe, opens his own pizzeria, Sally's Apizza, just a few doors down from his uncle's place in New Haven.

THE PIZZA RENAISSANCE: WHERE IT'S HAPPENING AND WHY

In the chain-pizza era of the 1980s and 1990s, when Domino's and Pizza Hut ruled the land, mom-and-pop shops suffered. They simply could not compete on price, and in areas of the country that lacked strong pizza traditions, local, independent pizzerias vanished. It appeared that pizza's flame had gone out.

But it hadn't. The last decade has seen the beginnings of a full-blown pizza renaissance—so many high-caliber pizzerias are opening up across the country that we almost can't keep up. We're constantly hearing of serious chefs moving into the pizza realm or of a rising-star pizza-maker leaving one location to open his or her own shop.

San Francisco is a prime example. Prior to 2004, the options in the Bay Area were slim. Some people would have called it a pizza wasteland. Since then, though, more than a dozen serious pizzerias have opened, each the product of a single person with a laserlike focus on making the best pizza possible. There's A16, Pizzeria Delfina (two locations), Pizzaiolo, Pizzeria Picco, Gialina, Flour + Water, Emilia's Pizzeria, Boot & Shoe Service, Tony's Pizza Napoletana, Zero Zero, and Una Pizza Napoletana. And that's just off the top of our heads. By the time you're reading these words, there will likely be more.

In Chicago, the land of deep-dish and stuffed pizza, a handful of high-profile openings have changed the pizza landscape, with places like Great Lake, Spacca Napoli Pizzeria, and Coalfire offering styles of thin-crust and Neapolitan pizza that were previously all but unavailable. Des Moines, Iowa? Check. San Antonio? There, too. Portland, Oregon. Seattle, the Twin Cities, St. Louis, Kansas City, Pittsburgh. Places we thought had long ago surrendered to the onslaught of the chains have seen good pizza rise like a phoenix from the wood-fired ashes.

pizza renaissance. why now?

There's been a swing toward comfort food in the twenty-first century. Serious chefs have been approaching burgers, macaroni and cheese, fried chicken, and pizza with the kind of focus on ingredients and technique that they had previously brought to bear on high-end dining. And what's more comforting—yet challenging for a chef to perfect—than pizza? As Alice Waters once said to us, "Cooking is easy. Pizza is hard."

Second, we think the rise of high-end pizza has paralleled the rise of the Internet—particularly blogs, bulletin boards, and review sites. These online outposts have made it easier for the public to learn about killer pizza in their cities and even around the country. And for chefs, the unprecedented flow of information about pizza-making itself has helped connect pizzaioli to one another, allowing them to share ideas, recipes, and techniques.

PIZZA STYLE GUIDE

There are all sorts of creations we refer to as pizza. Here's how to tell them all apart.

neapolitan style

Neapolitan pizzas are small (10 to 12 inches in diameter), thin-crust pizzas made in a wood-burning oven. They have a puffy *cornicione* (lip or end crust) and are marked by the use of the freshest ingredients applied sparingly for a careful balance. Besides the Margherita, other traditional variations include the marinara (just sauce and maybe a sprinkling of an aged cheese) or the Napoletana (a marinara pie with anchovies).

new york–neapolitan style (a.k.a. neapolitan-american)

Once Italian immigrants brought their Naples-style pies to the states, their pizza evolved a bit in the Italian neighborhoods of New York to what is known as New York–Neapolitan. This is basically what all the brick-oven pizzerias of New York serve, and they generally serve only by the whole pie. It follows the tenets of Neapolitan style in that it's got a high lip, is cooked in an ultra-hot oven, and uses a judicious amount of cheese (almost always fresh mozzarella) and sauce (typically made from San Marzano tomatoes, as in Naples). It deviates from Neapolitan in that it's typically larger, a tad

NEW YORK–NEAPOLITAN: TOTONNO'S, BROOKLYN, NY

NEW YORK STYLE: JOE'S, NEW YORK, NY

thinner, and more crisp. New York–Neapolitan is rarely found outside New York City. However, we believe this style eventually evolved into . . .

new york style

The round, thin-crust stuff, generally served by the slice, that most people in the United States think of as pizza. We can imagine Chicago deep-dish lovers groaning as they read this, but go ahead and think of a pizza. Almost all of you thought of something round and more on the thin side than the thick side, right? The major chain pizzas, no matter their variations in crust, all essentially resemble this style. A true New York–style pizza ideally has a crust that's at once crisp and chewy. It's generally topped with a blanket of aged mozzarella (rather than fresh) and often has a sauce that's cooked down and more seasoned than the minimalist, just-tomato Neapolitan or New York–Neapolitan sauce. It can be topped with whatever you want, but it's best with only one or two toppings applied (so the crust remains crisp). New Yorkers typically fold it while eating.

sicilian style

These rectangular pizzas usually have a thick crust. Though named for the island of Sicily, you most often see this style in northeastern pizzerias, where it's often served along with the more-often-consumed round pizzas. The cheese may or may not appear beneath the sauce, though it's our understanding that Sicilian-style pizza traditionally featured the cheese under the sauce. It's often marked by the strong presence of garlic, and is also known as a "square slice" because it's cut into squares (or rectangular shapes close enough to square to merit the name).

grandma style (a.k.a. nonna pizza)

This is essentially a thin-crust Sicilian as made at home by Italian grandmothers, hence the name. It has historically been a Long Island phenomenon, but over the past decade it has made inroads into New York City and so-called New York–style pizzerias throughout the country. These pizzas are generally topped by a blizzard of fresh garlic.

roman style

Pizza served in Rome is generally thin and crunchy (but not crackery) and is often oblong or rectangular and cut into squares. It's typically served as pizza *al taglio*, literally "by the cut," or by the slice, which differs from the Neapolitan tradition of serving whole pies only

greek style

Greek pizza is a staple in the New England states. Its dough is heavily oiled, pressed into a pan with a shallow lip, and left to rise just a little bit. The pizzas are then sauced and cheesed with a mixture of provolone, mozzarella, and sometimes Cheddar. The crust becomes very firm and almost fries in the pan owing to the oil. Crusts are spongy, airy, and light.

new haven style

Often cooked in coal ovens, like New York–Neapolitan pizzas, New Haven pies have a very crisp crust that is thin but still typically thicker than New York pizzas. New Haven pizza is marked by a characteristic oblong shape, often served on a sheet of waxed paper atop a metal or plastic cafeteria tray. If you've ever had or heard of a clam-topped

DEEP-DISH PIZZA: UNION JACK PUB, INDIANAPOLIS, IN

pizza, you have New Haven (specifically Frank Pepe's) to thank. The two major players of New Haven pizza are Sally's Apizza and Frank Pepe's, but there are others with their adherents—Modern Apizza, Zuppardi's, Roseland Apizza, and Bar, among them. New Haven partisans often argue that pizza was invented in this Connecticut city.

grilled pizza

Grilled pizza was introduced to Americans in Providence, Rhode Island, by George Germon at Al Forno (where you'll still find the best in this country). Grilled pizza has a thin crust and is cooked quickly—directly on the grate of a grill. It doesn't fall through, instead setting up quickly over the intense heat before being flipped and topped with sauce and thinly sliced toppings. (Toppings must be thin so they heat through in the short cooking time.) Grilled pizza has since moved beyond Providence, and in the last five or so years, we've seen this dish go from obscurity to backyard grills nationwide.

bar pizza

This style is usually very thin-crusted—to leave, we're guessing, plenty of room for beer. It's made with decent, commercial aged mozzarella and comes topped with canned mushrooms, standard pepperoni, and, if you're lucky, house-made sausage. Bar pizza is very similar to something we call . . .

chicago thin crust (a.k.a. midwest-style pizza)

Variations on Chicago thin-crust pizza are found throughout the U.S. heartland, from the Windy City to Ohio to Milwaukee and beyond. The style is round (but can often be oblong), thin, very crisp yet tender-flaky in the crust, and is cut into a grid (known as "party cut" or "tavern cut").

deep-dish pizza

And, of course, you can't mention Chicago without mentioning deep-dish. We don't know if we need to elaborate much, since, like New York–style, you already know what it's about. It's cooked in a deep pan, with a thick, buttery crust and a chunky tomato sauce. There's a lot of cheese and a lot of toppings. The crust is parbaked in the pan before toppings are added; they usually consist of a layer of sliced mozzarella, followed by meats and veggies, then sauce, then grated cheese. Unlike New York–style, it's eaten with a knife and fork. Like Neapolitan-style and New York–style, deep-dish has traveled far from its birthplace. (Although, with a few exceptions, good deep-dish is still hard to find outside Chicago.)

stuffed pizza

It's another Chicago specialty that is often confused with deep-dish because of its similarity. It's assembled and cooked in a similar manner to deep-dish, but it has a top layer of crust and is usually taller and more densely packed with toppings.

trenton tomato pies

In the capital city of New Jersey, "pizza" does not exist. Here, it's known as "tomato pie." As Slice correspondent Rich DeFabritus once wrote, "There is a body of myth and lore attempting to distinguish tomato pie from pizza. The generally accepted explanation is that a tomato pie is built as follows: dough, cheese, toppings, and *then* sauce." Trenton tomato pies would then seem to have much in common with a sauce-last grandma pie or a Detroit-style pizza, but these tomato pies are round.

detroit style

This is similar in form to Sicilian-style pizza; it's square with a thick, satisfyingly greasy pan-baked crust, with the sauce ladled on last. Cheese is applied up to the edges and bakes into a crunchy-chewy coating.

old forge style

Named for the town of Old Forge, Pennsylvania, which is a microclimate for this type of pie, Old Forge style is a medium-thick Sicilian-style pizza. Like pan or Greek pizza, the pan is oiled and the dough acquires an almost-fried effect. The cheese is Wisconsin white Cheddar, rather than the usual mozzarella.

st. louis style

Like Old Forge, this pizza's cheese of choice also sets it apart. Though its thinness might lead you to mistake it for a Chicago thin-crust pie at first, this style's crackerlike crust is unleavened. And it's topped with a special three-cheese blend (provolone, Swiss, white Cheddar) called Provel that's used in place of mozzarella (and sometimes, but not often, in addition to mozzarella). Like Chicago thin-crust, it's usually party-cut. Imo's Pizza is thought to be the originator.

california style

In this style of pizza, the crust is more a vehicle for unique toppings and striking flavor combinations not typically found on other pizza styles—say, goat cheese, or avocado, or egg. Given California's year-round access to fresh produce, vegetables often make an appearance. The late Ed LaDou, who made California pizza famous at Spago in Los Angeles and then later developed the original menu at California Pizza Kitchen, is typically thought of as its inventor.

chicago pizza

Chicagoans of every stripe (including many newspaper columnists) took it personally when I described Chicago deep-dish pizza as "at best, a good casserole." I stand by those words, though I will admit that, at the time, I was not fully aware of the pizza diversity in the city. And I repeat: I love a good casserole.

ALL ABOUT OVENS

Without ovens, obviously, you would have no pizza and no pizza boom. We believe that the best pizzas come from wood-fired and coal-fired ovens. The high heat given off by both wood and anthracite coal can imbue a crust with just the right amount of char, and both fuels can impart a subtle smoky flavor to the pizza. But gas-fired and, in some cases, even electric-powered ovens can get the job done just as well. It ultimately comes down to the heat the oven can obtain and hold—and, of course, the skill of the pizza-maker.

WOOD-BURNING OVEN: TOTALE, NEW YORK, NY

wood-fired ovens

Every few weeks, it seems, in some American city, a story breaks about how a master *pizzaiolo* (that's just a fancy Italian word for pizza-maker) is preparing to open a pizzeria whose defining feature is

WOOD-BURNING OVEN: DELANCEY, SEATTLE, WA

a massive wood-burning oven. Much is made of the high temperatures these ovens can reach and how fast they can cook a pizza, and for good reason.

A Neapolitan pizza cooks via two modes of heat transfer: The bottom of the pizza is cooked by conduction, the direct transfer of energy from the baking surface to the crust. The top of the pizza, on the other hand, is cooked via convection, the transfer of energy via hot air. Conduction is a much more efficient method of heat transfer, which is why, in a professional oven, to cook a pizza properly, the baking stone need only be at around 750°F. or so, while the air above must be significantly hotter—in the 1,000°F. to 1,200°F. range. The temperature difference ensures that both the top and bottom of the pizza cook at the same rate—for Neapolitan-style pizzas, usually less than two minutes. The dome shape of a traditional wood-fired pizza oven

helps create the convection currents and also to reflect heat back down onto the pizza.

coal-fired ovens

The principle behind coal-fired ovens is the same as for wood-fired ovens. But if that's the case, why not just use wood? What's telling is that you'll find coal ovens mostly in the urban centers of the northeast United States, where they're often the legacy of 1800s bakeries that found it easier to procure and store anthracite coal than wood. It was the first of many adaptations Italian immigrant bakers—and eventually pizza-makers—would make in transforming traditional Neapolitan-style pizza into what we call Neapolitan-American pizza: pies with traces of Neapolitan DNA but bigger and crisper, a nod to American tastes.

gas ovens

A gas oven can still make a transcendent pizza—particularly if it's built to cook at the high tempera-tures we've seen are necessary for the endeavor, and if it's outfitted with a stone base. The Wood Stone Corporation in particular makes such ovens. But some of our favorite pizzas are made with the workhorse of the industry: the simple steel-floor "deck oven" that you see at most mom-and-pop pizza joints.

electric ovens

Though much less common in the world of serious pizza—to the point where we had almost dismissed them as not up to the job—an electric oven, in the right hands, can make pizza magic. At Apizza Scholls in Portland, Oregon, *pizzaiolo*-owner Brian Spangler proved the proposition. "I've made pizza with wood-burning ovens, but here's what I've finally decided," Spanger said. "It's all about the BTUs. This oven makes pizza at 700°F., and that's plenty hot enough to bake my pies quickly and thoroughly and get my crust as crisp and airy as I want it."

OUR 30 FAVORITE PIZZERIAS

1 APIZZA SCHOLLS
PORTLAND, OR

For traditional Neapolitan-American pizza made with good ingredients, Brian Spangler's pizza at Apizza Scholls is paradigmatic. The crust has a crunchy exterior that gives way to tender bread dough; the cheese combination (*fior di latte* and aged mozzarella) gives the pie just the right blend of creaminess and tang. The pizza here, made in an electric oven that reaches 700°F., defies what many pizza connoisseurs claim—that good pizza can only come from a coal-, gas-, or wood-fired oven. One bite proves that the type of oven doesn't matter as long as you have oven heat and the skill of a practiced *pizzaiolo*.

2 DI FARA PIZZA
BROOKLYN, NY

One of the most beloved pizzerias in New York— and one of the most bemoaned. This Brooklyn institution, where Dom DeMarco has been plying his trade for more than 50 years, is beloved for the flavor-packed toppings—up to four different kinds of cheese and a savory, thick sauce. It's bemoaned for the wait: just to *order* a pizza can take up to an hour and a half (and that's after you make it out to Midwood, more than an hour from Manhattan). But it's all part of the experience; watching DeMarco slowly snip a bunch of basil over each pizza is half the fun. Take heart that you are watching a slice of Brooklyn pizza history while you wait

hungrily. The pies can at times be a bit too olive-oily, but that aside, they're about as fine an example of the New York slice as you'll find.

3 PIZZERIA MOZZA
LOS ANGELES, CA

Opened as a partnership among Mario Batali, Joe Bastianich, and famed L.A. bread-baker Nancy Silverton (page 312), Mozza serves wood-fired pizzas that are simply a revelation. The crust has a very high lip (what the Neapolitans call the *corni-cione*). As crisp at first bite as it is remarkably tender within, the crust is full of bubbles (on both the outside and inside), what bread-bakers call "hole structure." The toppings are sparse but absolutely delicious—whether they are bacon-and-egg, wild nettles, clam, or pepperoni. There is finally pizza worth traveling for in Los Angeles. It's pizza so good you won't be able to stop eating it.

4 PIZZERIA BIANCO
PHOENIX, AZ

Who would have thought that Phoenix would become a sort of pizza mecca to pieheads from around the country? Pizzeria Bianco, helmed by the soulful poet of pizza, Chris Bianco, has made the city a pizza destination. Respected among fellow pizza-makers and serious pizza fans alike, Bianco's pizzas are life-changing. "I just use the best ingredients possible, don't do too much to

APIZZA SCHOLLS, PORTLAND, OR

DOM DEMARCO AT DI FARA PIZZA, BROOKLYN, NY

THE ROSA FROM PIZZERIA BIANCO, PHOENIX, AZ

them, and let them shine," he says. But that dramatically undersells his talent. Every pizza on the menu is a must-have, but our favorites are the Wiseguy (wood-roasted onion, house-smoked mozzarella, and fennel sausage) and the Rosa (red onion, Parmigiano-Reggiano, rosemary, and Arizona pistachios). Be forewarned: the line is sometimes as long as three hours, but, yes, the pizza is worth it.

5 DOUGH PIZZERIA NAPOLETANA
SAN ANTONIO, TX

We were tipped off to Dough by master pie man Chris Bianco (page 313). That's not an endorsement we would take lightly. Dough's *pizzaiolo*-owner, Doug Horn, is making small, incredibly flavorful Neapolitan-style pizza with careful attention paid to ingredients and how they relate to one another. Horn is more devoted to Neapolitan pizza orthodoxy than Bianco is (Dough has been certified as a VPN pizzeria, page 114), but he knows how to please his meat-loving Texan customers at the same time. His Pork Love pizza tops his wood-fired crust, thinner than you'll find in Naples, with salami, sausage, pancetta, *and* speck—and somehow emerges as a well-balanced (if supremely meaty) pie.

6 BURT'S PLACE
MORTON GROVE, IL

Ponytailed, bearded eccentric Burt Katz is making our favorite deep-dish Chicago pizza in Morton

Grove, a suburb about 15 miles north of the Windy City proper. What makes it so great? A minimal amount of mozzarella, fresh toppings (Katz goes to the market as often as possible to pick up mushrooms, peppers, onions, spinach, and garlic), and—most important—a slightly caramelized, shockingly light and crunchy crust. As is rarely true with deep-dish pies, you'll be able to eat more than just one slice.

7 SALLY'S APIZZA
NEW HAVEN, CT

There's a lot of serious pizza in New Haven—Frank Pepe's, The Spot, Modern Apizza, Sally's. The last has, in our estimation, the superior pizzas, even if the service can be a bit problematic. If you're first in line for the first seating, you will likely see lucky fellows skip the line who have the private reserva-

SALLY'S APIZZA, NEW HAVEN, CT

PENN CORE CLAM PIE AT SERIOUS PIE, SEATTLE, WA

tion phone number. Still, whatever indignities you endure, it's worth it for the pizza. The "plain" pizza is just that—crust, sauce, and a light dusting of Parmesan. But what a great, great pizza. The crust is perfectly baked, crisp-chewy, and flavorful. The sauce is rich and zesty. Order a large for yourself and you can eat it for days.

8 SERIOUS PIE
SEATTLE, WA

The pizzas at Serious Pie are ovals about 12 inches long and 7 inches at their widest; they have an insanely puffy lip, are charred in places, and are dotted with pizza bubbles. The dough is extremely soft, which means that where the crust is topped, the additional ingredients weigh it down enough that there's not much rise in the center. But that same soft elasticity gives those outer edges an airiness the likes of which are matched by only a few pizzerias we've visited. And every topping combination—there's a pizza with clams, pancetta, and lemon thyme, for example—is even more exciting than it sounds on the menu.

9 ZUPPARDI'S APIZZA
WEST HAVEN, CT

The white clam pie, a New Haven specialty, reaches a zenith at Zuppardi's. Be advised to get the *fresh* clam pie, though, for which the shellfish are shucked to order. The clams are tender, briny, perfect, barely heated through, and their clam liqueur leaks and runs out in every direction. This is clam pie prepared by the clam-pizza gods.

fresh clams

I once called to place an order at Zuppardi's and told the third-generation owner that I could pick up the pizza in 30 minutes. He said, "Better make it 35—I've got to shuck the clams for your clam pie." Happy to wait.

DELIVERY PIZZA FROM MOTORINO, NEW YORK, NY

10 COLONY GRILL
STAMFORD, CT

If you're looking for puffy, crisp-chewy pizza crusts, Colony Grill might not be for you. It is, however, the apotheosis of bar pizza, geared toward thinness, absolute crispness, and greasy goodness. It's famous for its hot-oil pizzas (drizzled with chile-infused olive oil), but the real treat is a sausage pizza, topped with porky chunks from De Julio's Sausage Co. just across the street.

11 MOTORINO
MANHATTAN AND BROOKLYN, NY

We wouldn't have predicted that Motorino could become one of our five favorite pizzerias in the country when it opened in Brooklyn in 2008. The man behind it, Belgian-born Mathieu Palombino, had come from stints at high-end Manhattan restaurants—a background that hardly said "pizza pedigree." But in the few years since he's opened in Brooklyn and then in Manhattan, he has racked up praise from all quarters, including us. His

Neapolitan-inspired pizzas have great bready, salty flavor and a crisp-chewy factor that's off the charts. While you can't go wrong with any of the topping combinations, we're partial to the Brussels sprouts and pancetta pizza. It appears in the Serious Eats office with frightening regularity.

12 UNA PIZZA NAPOLETANA
SAN FRANCISCO, CA

No pizza-maker in the United States has done more to advance the notion that pizza can be a minimalist masterpiece than Anthony Mangieri of Una Pizza Napoletana (reflected in the stark aesthetic of his San Francisco storefront, where he and his oven are all the décor of note). That minimalism, however, does not apply to flavor. Using only a palette of buffalo mozzarella, San Marzano tomatoes, garlic, fresh basil leaves, Sicilian sea salt, and fresh halved cherry tomatoes, Mangieri creates a quartet of stunningly good, cloud-light pizzas whose sourdough crusts have perfect hole structure and a fantastic smoky tinge.

surprising toppings we love

There are pizzerias out there, those of the California Pizza Kitchen variety, that will toss Thai salads or slivered duck or anything else onto a crust and call it pizza. While we won't quite say that anything goes, some of our favorite pizzerias in the land top their pies with combinations we had thought unlikely. Until our first bite, that is. (Note: toppings change frequently.)

Our favorites?

GREAT LAKE, CHICAGO, IL
smoked bacon, fresh cream, white corn, Mona (sheep and cow's milk) cheese, chives

PIZZERIA BIANCO, PHOENIX, AZ
The Rosa, with red onion, Parmigiano-Reggiano, rosemary, pistachios

FLOUR + WATER, SAN FRANCISCO, CA
roasted sunchokes, Ruby Crescent potatoes, bagna cauda, gremolata

VARASANO'S, ATLANTA, GA
Emmentaler, caramelized onions

PICCO, BOSTON, MA
Shortrib and Gorgonzola

13 DELANCEY
SEATTLE, WA

Even before this pizzeria in Seattle's Ballard neighborhood opened in 2009, the work of food writer Molly Wizenberg and her chef husband, Brandon Pettit, it was hailed as the single greatest thing ever to happen to Seattle pizza. While it would be nearly impossible for any pizza to live up to those expectations, the pies at Delancey are very fine indeed. Cooked in an enormous wood-burning oven, they're thin-crusted and pliant. Our favorite is the Padrón, where the oven-roasted Padrón peppers bleed their creeping spice all over the blend of fresh and aged mozzarella and grana Padano.

14 PIZZERIA PICCO
LARKSPUR, CA

While San Francisco has any number of fine pizzerias, Bruce Hill's pizzas at Pizzeria Picco are worth the drive over the Golden Gate Bridge to Larkspur. Pies emerge from his wood-burning oven in less than two minutes, with a beautifully elevated crust, remarkably fresh-tasting tomato sauce, and mozzarella that's pulled fresh every day. Many of his pies are seasonal and imaginative, like the Marin ("young organic potato," roasted garlic, mozzarella, and grated grana Padano cheese) and the Cannondale (house-made sausage, roasted red peppers, roasted onions, mozzarella, grana Padano cheese, and basil leaves). But even the Margherita pizza, topped generously with creamy dots of mozzarella, is every bit as memorable. Salty, savory, tangy, and soulful.

15 EMILIA'S PIZZERIA
BERKELEY, CA

Just when it seems like it's all Neapolitan this and artisanal that, Emilia's *pizzaiolo*-owner Keith

DELANCEY, SEATTLE, WA

HEIRLOOM TOMATO PIE AT GREAT LAKE, CHICAGO, IL

Freilich is not trying to knock you out with claims of authenticity, a fancy imported oven, or ultra-chic interior design. Instead, the delicious, down-to-earth pizza speaks for itself amid a tiny store that's more suited for take-out (it has only two three-seat tables). Phone in your order when they start taking them at 4 in the afternoon; otherwise, the wait can get pretty long.

16 GALLERIA UMBERTO
BOSTON, MA

The Sicilian slices at Boston's Galleria Umberto are smothered in blood-red sauce, with a crust that threatens to spill over the pan's edges and with cheese that actually does. Pools of oil quiver in the grooves between slices. If you get a slice to go—packaged in a neat white box and string-tied—the grease will soak right through the cardboard. If that box is in a paper bag, it'll soak through that, too. If that bothers you, this is not your sort of pizza.

17 GREAT LAKE
CHICAGO, IL

Nick Lessins's crust has a beautiful lip, more breadlike than either Anthony Mangieri's at Una Pizza Napoletana or Chris Bianco's pizza at Pizzeria Bianco. It looks and tastes a great deal like Nancy Silverton's pizza at Pizzeria Mozza in Los Angeles—a glorious, light, yeasty crust. His ingredients—like impossibly thin slices of zucchini; tangy, salty Mona cheese; black pepper; and added pepperoni—reveal Lessins's gift for inspired, perfectly proportioned, and wonderfully balanced toppings.

18 PIZZERIA STELLA
PHILADELPHIA, PA

Philadelphia restaurateur Stephen Starr has built a restaurant empire out of his ability to spot the next big thing—food trends with staying power—and then creating a restaurant that executes those trends well. That's just what he did with Pizzeria Stella. He saw the artisanal pizza trend coming straight at him and decided to do something about it. So he and a group of his chefs embarked on a nationwide pizza tour (that's what we call our kind of R&D) and opened Stella shortly thereafter. The wood-burning ovens there produce fine thin-crusted pies with puffy edges that are just chewy and pliant enough.

19 PIZZERIA BASTA
BOULDER, CO

Good pizza turns up in surprising places. In the case of Pizzeria Basta, it's a condominium complex near downtown Boulder. But it's not surprising that such incredible pizza emerges from the oven of Kelly Whitaker. The owner-operator knows his stuff, credentialed on the pizza end (having worked at a pizzeria near Naples) and the chef end (with stints at Michelin-starred L.A. restaurants). Whitaker fires pretty traditional Neapolitan pies in his wood-burning oven, which puts a serious underside char on each pizza. The dough, made with a decades-old starter Whitaker brought over from Italy, rises up into an impressively tall

cornicione—easily two inches, in parts—with an incredibly light, airy interior and a good outside crisp. Toppings are smartly chosen, not strictly orthodox; some imported, some domestic, some local. We loved the Arugula, the house-made smoked mozzarella complementing the smokiness of the charred crust, with La Quercia prosciutto (page 318) and local greens. Puffy edges, flavorful crust, great toppings—absolutely everything we look for in fine pizza.

20 IL PIZZAIOLO
MT. LEBANON, PA

Ron Molinare opened Il Pizzaiolo in the Pittsburgh suburb of Mt. Lebanon in 1996—long before Neapolitan pizza had made inroads across the country. Years later, they're still making classic pies, as certified by the VPN (page 114), with airy-crisp exterior crusts, delightfully soupy centers, and premium toppings like *bufala* mozzarella, prosciutto, and baby arugula. While it's a lovely, civilized restaurant with a full Italian menu, the pizza is still the thing to get.

> *Cornicione*: The edge or lip of a pizza. This is what most Americans refer to as the crust. While this might work for casual conversation, we have to be a little more technical, as we typically use *crust* to refer to the entire bread component of a pie. On 'Slice,' we sometimes call the *cornicione* the *end crust.*

FENNEL SAUSAGE PIZZA AT KEN'S ARTISAN PIZZA, PORTLAND, OR

21 KEN'S ARTISAN PIZZA
PORTLAND, OR

Ken Forkish opened Ken's Artisan Bakery (page 326) in 2001, where his Monday Night Pizza events became the stuff of legend. So, Forkish decided to form Ken's Artisan Pizza, the spin-off wood-fired pizzeria that has become one of the city's best-loved pizzerias. Befitting its bakery roots, Ken's crust is flavorful, crisp, and chewy. His pizza needs no embellishment, though it doesn't hurt to sop up any fallen sauce with the "pizza bones."

22 PIZZAIOLO AND BOOT & SHOE SERVICE
OAKLAND, CA

Charlie Hallowell learned to cook pizza at Alice Waters's famous Chez Panisse (page 313), the influence of which cannot be overstated at his two Oakland pizzerias. Refined technique and respect for Bay Area ingredients run deep. Both locations feature stunning pies made in wood-burning ovens with the creamiest, most buttery mozzarella cheese you have ever tasted.

23 VARASANO'S
ATLANTA, GA

Software developer Jeff Varasano became known to fellow pizza obsessives when he posted a 5,000-word blog detailing his effort to replicate his favorite pizza—a Margherita made at the original Patsy's in New York's East Harlem. He put his pizza paddle where his mouth was and opened a pizzeria in a strip mall in Atlanta's Buckhead neighborhood. Rather than using the coal-fueled method of his beloved Patsy's, Jeff installed high-tech electric Swedish ovens that can maintain the 700°F. heat necessary to produce a superb thin-crusted pizza with plenty of external crunch and internal tenderness. Our two favorite pizzas here are the Nana's House Special, a traditional pie made with mozzarella, tomato sauce, and Italian herbs; and the untraditional but memorably delicious Caramelized Onion with sharp Emmentaler.

on neapolitan and the vera pizza napoletana

In pizza-making today, there is not a small amount of devotion to Old World Neapolitan standards. Most of the pizzerias making big splashes these days stress Neapolitan authenticity as a selling point. The bricks and stone used to build their wood-burning ovens invariably come from the volcanic soil around Mount Vesuvius. The men who build them (and they are all men) are from a handful of families that carry on traditional oven-building work in Naples and, for the right price, around the world. The ingredients used to make the pizzas—the flour, the canned tomatoes, the cheese—are all from Italy, too.

Many pizzerias in this vein apply for accreditation by a group known as the Associazione Verace Pizza Napoletana (whom some call "the Pizza Police"). The association (VPN, for short) certifies that these shops are making authentically Neapolitan pizza as per certain standards regarding ingredients, pizza size and proportions, preparation methods, and the type of equipment used to make it.

Among the pizza cognoscenti, there's a shorthand of abbreviations—VPN, WFO (wood-fired oven), and DOP (Denominazione di Origine Protetta, a designation certifying ingredients as coming from a particular region in Italy or produced to certain standards). It's an alphabet soup that many Neapolitan obsessives sling around, sometimes with a blind faith that it guarantees greatness.

It doesn't.

We've often been skeptical of this strain of pizza authenticity. At best, it can produce amazing pizza; at worst, it inspires petty squabbles about which pizzeria is "most authentic." Simply importing a shipping container of ingredients and checking off boxes on a standards scorecard does not guarantee life-changing or delicious pies.

MARGHERITA PIZZA AT TOTONNO'S, BROOKLYN, NY

24 BELLA MIA COAL-FIRED PIZZA CARY, NC

Fifteen-year-old John Guerra, whose father and two brothers run Bella Mia Coal-Fired Pizza in Cary, North Carolina, tipped us off to their family business by emailing Serious Eats. He wrote, "Your book *Pizza: A Slice of Heaven* changed my entire family's life. It opened our eyes to the world of pizza and what it had to offer." Thus inspired, the Guerras ate their way through many of the nation's best pizzerias and struck out on their own in 2010. And they're making serious pizza indeed: light, puffy crust with just enough char, simple high-quality canned tomatoes for sauce, and creamy mozzarella they make on-site. Return visits confirmed the fact that Bella Mia is not only the best pizzeria in North Carolina, it's one of the best pizza places anywhere. And John Guerra? In hopes to continue the family's newfound pizza tradition, he's already learning to make the pies.

25 TOTONNO'S BROOKLYN, NY

Before the boom in wood-fired pizza swept the nation, pizza geeks held coal-fired pizza in high esteem. We still love the genre and think there isn't another in New York that epitomizes the New York–Neapolitan style as well as Totonno's original location in Brooklyn's Coney Island. A pile of burning coal, creating temperatures of up to 900°F., sits in one corner of the oven, lending smoky flavor to every pie. The crust emerges from the oven charred and blistered, with an outer layer of crispness that gives way to a pliant interior. Topped with just the right balance of fresh-tasting tomato sauce and fresh mozzarella, it's thin and light enough that you may find yourself eating close to a whole pizza on your own. Note: Though there are other Totonno's, we prefer the original location, which is still presided over by the indomitable Cookie Ciminieri.

spotlight on grilled pizza: al forno

If you've ever eaten grilled pizza in this country, you have George Germon to thank. In 1980, he and his wife, Johanne Killeen, opened this now-beloved restaurant in Providence, Rhode Island, where Germon began experimenting with pizza dough, soaking it in olive oil, and then stretching and grilling it. It is sparsely topped pizza that is unique and absolutely wonderful. It's crisp, chewy, and just oily enough—the perfect synergy of flavors and texture.

Because a cup of flour can vary in weight by as much as 25 percent, for best results, it's important to use a digital scale to measure ingredients by weight rather than volume. Italian Tipo "00" flour comes in several varieties. Look for the kind intended for bread baking and pizza. We prefer the Caputo brand in the red paper bag. It's available at specialty Italian grocers or online. Please note that if using table salt, about 1½ teaspoons is equal to .25 ounces.

grilled pizza
margherita

MAKES 4 PIZZAS; SERVES 6 TO 8

½ cup extra-virgin olive oil

4 garlic cloves

1 (14.4-ounce) can whole peeled tomatoes, preferably San Marzano, drained

Bread flour, preferably Italian Tipo "00," for dusting

1 recipe Grilled Pizza Dough (page 120)

Kosher salt

6 ounces mozzarella, fontina, or Jack cheese, shredded

2 ounces Parmigiano-Reggiano or pecorino Romano cheese, finely grated

½ cup finely chopped fresh basil leaves

1 Place the olive oil and garlic in the bowl of a food processor and process until the garlic is finely chopped. (Extra garlic oil can be stored in the refrigerator for up to 10 days.) Place the tomatoes in a fine-mesh strainer set over the sink and squeeze them between your fingers until they have broken into approximate ¼-inch chunks. Allow them to drain for at least 15 minutes.

2 On a heavily floured surface, roll a dough ball into an oval disk about 13 × 9 inches and ¼ inch thick using a rolling pin. Shake off the excess flour and place the dough on a sheet tray lined with parchment paper. Repeat with the remaining dough balls, placing a sheet of parchment between each one.

3 Light a large chimney starter three-quarters full with charcoal and wait until it is fully ignited and the coals are mostly covered in gray ash, about 20 minutes. Arrange the coals under half of the grill grate and place the grate on top. Cover and allow to preheat for 10 minutes.

4 Brush the top of one dough with a thin, even layer of garlic oil and season with kosher salt. Place the dough gently on the hot side of the grill, oiled side down. Immediately brush the top side with a thin layer of oil and season with salt. Cook, checking frequently and moving the dough to encourage even browning, until the bottom is dark brown and charred in spots and the

top is bubbly, 45 to 90 seconds total. Flip using tongs or a large spatula and slide to the cool side of the grill.

5 Apply one-quarter of the mozzarella and the Parmigiano-Reggiano in a thin even layer across the surface of the

pizza. Add the tomato sauce in tablespoon-size dollops across the surface of the pizza (about $1/2$ cup total per pie). Return the pizza to the hot side of the grill and cook until the bottom is cooked and charred in spots, 45 to 90 seconds total.

6 Transfer the pizza to a cutting board with a large spatula or metal pizza peel. Sprinkle with basil and serve immediately. Repeat with the remaining four pies.

Grilling is hands-down our favorite way to cook pizza at home; the grill's intense heat allows pies to cook in less than a minute per side, giving you a crust that's crisp on the edges with a tender, chewy center.

grilled pizza dough

MAKES FOUR 5-OUNCE BALLS OF PIZZA DOUGH

12 ounces bread flour (about 2 cups and 2 tablespoons, preferably Italian Tipo "00"), plus more for dusting

.25 ounces (about 2 teaspoons) kosher salt

.1 ounce (about ½ teaspoon) rapid-rise yeast

Olive oil or nonstick cooking spray, for bowls

1 Combine the flour, salt, and yeast in the bowl of a stand mixer fitted with a dough hook attachment. Whisk to combine. Add 1 cup of water and knead on low speed just until the mixture comes together and no dry flour remains. Allow the mixture to rest for 10 minutes. Knead on low speed for an additional 10 minutes. The mixture should come together into a cohesive mass that barely sticks to the bottom of the bowl as it kneads. Transfer the dough to a 1-gallon zipper-lock bag and refrigerate for at least 8 and up to 72 hours.

2 Transfer the dough to a floured work surface and dust the top with additional flour. Using a bench scraper, divide the dough into four even pieces. Using floured hands, shape each piece into a neat ball by gathering the dough toward the bottom. Coat four small bowls (large cereal bowls work well for this) with olive oil or nonstick cooking spray and add one dough ball to each bowl. Cover tightly with plastic wrap, and allow to rise at room temperature for 2 hours (dough should roughly double in volume).

3 Proceed immediately to make the Grilled Pizza Margherita (page 118).

"GREENPOINTER" AT PAULIE GEE'S, BROOKLYN, NY

26 PICCO RESTAURANT
BOSTON, MA

Some great pizzerias have memorable crusts; others, memorable topping combinations. Picco Restaurant has both. "Our pizzas are cooked well-done," reads the menu, and that's how you want them—the puffy-edged pies, their dough graced with appealing, mellow tang, get deliciously crusty edges that you're tempted to peel off and eat first. But the toppings—sautéed onions, garlic, crème fraîche, bacon, and Gruyère; pumpkin and house-made ricotta—are too enticing. Save room for their excellent homemade ice cream.

27 PAULIE GEE'S
BROOKLYN, NY

Full disclosure: Paul Giannone—that's Paulie Gee, to you and everyone else—was a major player on our pizza blog "Slice," somewhere between an obsessive home pizza chef and a genuine madman.

For years he held occasional pizza tastings at his place in Warren, New Jersey, where he'd built a small wood-fired oven in his yard. But in 2010, he finally decided to quit his job as a software quality-assurance engineer and open a pizzeria of his own. At Paulie Gee's in Greenpoint, Brooklyn, you'll find Neapolitan-inspired pies with imaginative, beautifully presented toppings, like the kale-guanciale (unsmoked Italian bacon) and the Greenpointer (*fior di Latte,* baby arugula, olive oil, fresh lemon juice, and shaved Parmigiano-Reggiano). It's the realization of a lifelong dream—and some of the finest pizza in New York City, to boot.

28 MIA'S PIZZAS
BETHESDA, MD

Pizzaiola-owner Melissa Ballinger learned her craft at Washington, D.C.'s seminal wood-burning oven pizzeria Pizza Paradiso, but based on a recent visit, her pizza-making skills have surpassed those of her mentors. The crusts have plenty of body and character to go along with great hole structure—the hallmark of all great pizza and bread. Every pie we've had at Mia's has been flavorful, crisp, chewy, and well balanced. Even on pizzas like the Salsiccia (sausage, pepperoni, portobello mushrooms, oregano, "spicy sprinkles," mozzarella, and Parm), the crust stayed crisp enough to stand up against the stuff on top. And we love how the Margherita is helped out with shavings of freshly grated Parmesan.

29 TOMATOES APIZZA
FARMINGTON HILLS, MI

"Apizza" to those in the know is shorthand for New Haven–style pizza, derived from the local Connecticut Italian pronunciation. So what's it doing in the middle of Michigan? Owner Mike Weinstein learned the craft from Lou Abate, who learned from Joe Abate, who learned from Sally Consiglio of Sally's (page 106), who learned from the original New Haven pizzaman, Frank Pepe. (Whew. Got that?) The pizza at the Tomatoes' original coal-fired location is a good approximation of the style. To our taste, it's a bit too heavily cheesed, perhaps a nod to its Midwestern audience, but the crust, crisp and satisfyingly chewy, is a dead ringer for its New England forbearers.

30 STOP 50
MICHIANA SHORES, IN

Chicagoans lucky enough to spend a summer weekend in Michiana Shores, Indiana (year-round population, 330), have discovered a great pizza. Chris Bardol's crust is chewy, crisp, and light, thicker in the center than a Neapolitan pie, with lovely charred edges—thanks to a wood-fired oven that climbs to over 900°F. His potato-and-sausage pizza is a thing of beauty, with thinly sliced spuds that pick up a bit of chiplike crispness in that ultra-hot oven. The place is open only from March to November, and just about everything is seasonal.

> "Making pizza is the adult version of playing with Play-Doh, and it tastes a lot better, too." —dhorst

UNION JACK PUB, INDIANAPOLIS, IN

the pizza cognition theory

When I wrote *Pizza: A Slice of Heaven*, I asked my friend and then-editor Sam Sifton (who went on to become the restaurant critic of the *New York Times*) to elaborate on his Pizza Cognition Theory, which postulates that the first pizza a person eats becomes the standard by which that person judges all pizza he or she subsequently eats. According to Sam, "The first slice of pizza a child sees and tastes (and somehow appreciates on something more than a childlike, *mmmgoood*, thanks-mom level), becomes, for him, pizza. He relegates all subsequent slices, if they are different in some manner from that first triangle of dough and cheese and tomato and oil and herbs and spices, to a status that we can characterize as not pizza."

Is this *always* the case? Perhaps not. I believe that people ultimately understand that circumstances beyond their control dictated their initial pizza-eating experiences and preferences—namely, where they lived and where their parents took them for pizza. Furthermore, I believe discernment can be learned once we move away from home. Still, I find that a remarkable number of people find the ultimate expression of pizza to be that which they grew up with, whether thin-crust New York, fluffy-dough Sicilian, or Chicago deep-dish. Home is where the pizza loyalties lie.

WHAT MAKES A GOOD PIE? OR, THE OWNER-OPERATED PIZZERIA

As you've seen, we're not interested in Old World standards for their own sake; we're more interested in pizzerias that are the singular vision of one person. Let's call it the owner-operated pizzeria.

At an owner-operated pizzeria, a single pizza-maker—or a small group of carefully trained and supervised *pizzaioli*—crafts all the pies. The owner-operator takes into account the changing nature of the dough throughout the day. As Roberto Caporuscio, *pizzaiolo* and co-owner of the fine Kesté Pizza & Vino in New York City, says, "Dough is a living thing. It's always changing throughout the night." He, and those like him, will adjust for this changing nature by mixing it a little drier if it's humid, or a little wetter if the weather's dry and hot.

Owner-operators are also keenly aware of how their ovens behave throughout the day, a concept known as oven management. Anthony Mangieri of San Francisco's Una Pizza Napoletana likes to talk about a certain window of time during his pizza-making session when the wood-burning oven's temperature is just right. "You might come in earlier or a little later, and you'll still get a good pizza," he says, "but there's that time of the night when everything's just how I want it, and that's when the best pies happen."

ONE-OF-A-KIND PIZZERIAS

Maybe it's how rooted they are in tradition, maybe it's just how many of them there are, but as restaurants go, pizzerias seem particularly prone to eccentricities. Here are a few close to our hearts.

1 MARIA'S PIZZA
MILWAUKEE, WI

Dangling Christmas lights and Green Bay Packers swag hang from the ceiling. Catholic icons adorn the walls; vinyl tablecloths cloak the tables. It's hard to know what to make of Maria's Pizza when you first walk in—or even after you encounter waitress, heir, and one-woman pizza powerhouse Bonnie Traxel, whose mother opened the pizzeria in 1957. (Bonnie's the one with a towering bouffant.) When a large pizza appears on your table, it's a haphazard slab of a long, unwieldy pie—and with a cracker-thin crust and ample cheese, it's improbably delicious. "We've done it the same way since my mother opened the place," says Bonnie. If it ain't broke, don't fix it.

2 SANTILLO'S BRICK OVEN PIZZA
ELIZABETH, NJ

Third-generation pizza-maker Al Santillo has hit upon a unique way to offer pizza to his clients. Tucked down a passage between two houses, the pizzeria has a menu that reads like a timeline. There's the 1957 (with an extra-thin crust) and the 1964 (with mozzarella, Parmesan, and olive oil), for example—each pizza named for the year in which it was created.

3 MICUCCI'S ITALIAN GROCERIES
PORTLAND, ME

There's something amazing about foodstuffs made and sold in the back of stores, so we were predisposed to like the breadlike pizzas sold at a window tucked into the back of Micucci's, the go-to place for Italian groceries and foodstuffs in Portland. Rick Micucci and his wife, Anna, run the shop that his parents opened more than 60 years ago, and recently added a bakery, serving something like Sicilian pizza. From mid-morning on, you'll find these slices hot from the oven; there's clearly olive oil added to the dough, and it's blanketed with aged mozzarella and a little bit of fresh tomato sauce. Good pizza from a grocery store? Believe it.

SERIOUS HOME PIZZA-MAKING

Up to now we've talked about professional pizza-makers. But that's only part of this crazy, pizza-mad world. While many think of pizza as one of those foods that's tough to make at home, it can be done.

pizza "hacks"

It might start with a simple recipe gleaned from the Internet or a book. (Or one of our recipes.) With that first batch of home-made dough, the seed of a home-pizza freak is planted. Depending on the style of pizza you're trying to achieve, you can make very good pies with a good dough recipe, high-quality ingredients, and some pizza pans.

But a growing number of folks have gone to spectacular lengths to duplicate the pizzas they've eaten in restaurants. It often starts simply with a pizza stone, which gathers and holds heat and can crisp the dough nicely. The problem with trying to cook a pizza on a stone in a regular oven is that the stone gets really hot, and it's hard to get the air temperature above the pizza hot enough to match it—particularly when a home oven goes only to 500°F., or 550°F. at most. The bottom of the pizza dries out and becomes tough or, at worst, burns before the top takes on any color.

At that point, pizza-tinkerers start to go to extremes. There are plans and how-tos on the Internet for stacking firebrick in the oven to re-create an ersatz brick oven, increasing the thermal mass to increase the air temperature above the pizza. The most famous example may be Jeffrey Varasano (page 113), whose attempts to "clone" pizza from Patsy's in East Harlem led him to disable the locking mechanism of his oven's self-clean cycle in an attempt to get more heat from it. (See? It really is all about high temperatures.)

But that's dangerous and can ruin your oven. One of the best ways to get the kind of heat you need to cook both the top and bottom perfectly is using something you already have—your oven's broiler.

> "Getting pizza exactly right is difficult and a thing to be treasured once you finally do get it right. On the other hand, just *trying* to get it right is a lot of fun." —Grumpy Old Man

As noted before, a cup of flour can vary by weight by as much as 25 percent; for best results, it's important to use a digital scale to measure ingredients by weight rather than volume. Italian Tipo "00" flour comes in several varieties. Look for the kind intended for bread-baking and pizza. We prefer the Caputo brand in the red paper bag. It's available at specialty Italian grocers or online. Please note that if using table salt, about 1½ teaspoons is equal to .25 ounces.

basic neapolitan pizza dough

MAKES FOUR 6-OUNCE BALLS OF PIZZA DOUGH

20 ounces bread flour (about 4 cups, preferably Italian Tipo "00"), plus more for working the dough

.3 ounce (about 2¼ teaspoons) kosher salt

.2 ounce (about 1 teaspoon) rapid-rise yeast

.2 ounce (about 2 teaspoons) sugar

Olive oil or nonstick cooking spray

1 Combine the flour, salt, yeast, and sugar in the bowl of a stand mixer fitted with a dough hook attachment. Whisk to combine. Add 1½ cups of water and knead on low speed just until the mixture comes together and no dry flour remains. Allow the mixture to rest for 10 minutes. Knead on low speed for an additional 10 minutes. The mixture should come together into a cohesive mass that barely sticks to the bottom of the bowl as it kneads. Transfer the dough to a 1-gallon zipper-lock bag and refrigerate it for at least 8 and up to 72 hours.

2 Transfer the dough to a floured work surface and dust the top with additional flour. Using a bench scraper, divide the dough into six even pieces, approximately 6 ounces each. Using floured hands, shape each piece into a neat ball by gathering the dough toward the bottom. Coat four small containers (large cereal bowls work well for this) with olive oil or nonstick cooking spray and add one dough ball to each bowl. Cover tightly with plastic wrap, and allow the dough to rise at room temperature for 2 hours (dough should roughly double in volume) before rolling and baking according to specific recipe instructions.

A rolling pin can be used to roll out the pizza dough, but for best results and the highest rising lip, stretch the dough by hand. The traditional tomato of choice for Neapolitan pizza is canned San Marzano plum tomatoes. Look for those with the government-certification (DOP) seal. We prefer real buffalo mozzarella to cow's milk. (Do not use dried or aged mozzarella.) Some electric broilers have built-in safety features that cause them to cycle on and off; make sure that the broiler is on an "on" cycle when you place the pizza under it (the element should be glowing red).

neapolitan pizza **margherita**

MAKES SIX 10-INCH PIZZAS; SERVES 4 TO 6

1 (14-ounce) can whole peeled San Marzano plum tomatoes

½ teaspoon kosher salt, plus more for seasoning

12 ounces mozzarella di bufala (or fresh cow's-milk mozzarella packed in water)

2 cups all-purpose flour, for working the dough

1 recipe Basic Neapolitan Pizza Dough (page 127)

6 tablespoons extra-virgin olive oil

24 fresh basil leaves

1 Drain the tomatoes in a fine-meshed strainer and break them up with your fingers, squeezing out the excess juice. Transfer the tomatoes to a blender, add the kosher salt, and blend until smooth. Transfer to a medium bowl and set aside. Cut the mozzarella into ½-inch chunks and place on a plate on a triple layer of paper towels or a clean kitchen towel. Place another triple layer of paper towels or a clean dish towel on top of the cheese and stack another plate on top. Allow the excess water to blot out for at least 10 minutes.

2 Put the flour into a large bowl. Transfer one ball of dough to the bowl and flip the dough to coat. Lift it and gently pat off the excess flour. Transfer the ball to a floured surface and gently stretch it into a 10-inch circle, leaving the outer 1-inch edge slightly thicker than the center. The best way to do this it to start by gently stretching with your fingertips. Pick up the slightly stretched dough and place it on the opened face of your left hand. Toss it back and forth between your opened hands, rotating it slightly with each toss until it stretches out to around 8 inches in diameter. Return it to the work surface.

With your left hand flat in the center of the round, use your right hand to stretch the edge of the dough out, rotating as needed until it is an even 10 inches in diameter.

3 Have your tomato sauce, drained cheese, pizza dough, olive oil, salt, and basil ready and close to the stovetop. Preheat the broiler to high and arrange the rack so you can just barely fit a 12-inch heavy-bottomed oven-proof cast-iron or stainless-steel skillet between it and the roof of the oven. Heat the skillet over high heat until it is lightly smoking, about 3 minutes. Transfer one dough round to the skillet. It should fill up the entire bottom surface. Working quickly, spread 2 tablespoons of sauce evenly over the dough, leaving the outer 1-inch border unsauced. Top with one-sixth of the cheese chunks. Season with kosher salt. Drizzle with 1 tablespoon of olive oil, and scatter four basil leaves over the surface. Transfer the skillet to the broiler and broil until the pizza is puffed and darkly charred in spots (this can take anywhere between $1\frac{1}{2}$ and 4 minutes, depending on the strength of your broiler). Return the skillet to the stovetop and cook until the bottom is darkly charred in spots, using a thin metal spatula to peek after about 1 minute (depending on the skillet you use, you may skip this step if the pizza is already charred). Transfer the pizza to a cutting board and serve immediately. Repeat steps 2 and 3 to bake the remaining pizzas.

neapolitan pizza
WITH CRISPY SOPRESSATA

The crispy sopressata pizza at New York's Motorino (see photo, right) inspired us to create this variation. Follow the instructions for Neapolitan Pizza Margherita (above), omitting the basil and adding six overlapping slices of thin-sliced sopresatta (about 1 ounce) per pie before baking.

neapolitan pizza
WITH CHARRED KALE AND SWEET ITALIAN SAUSAGE

Remove the stems from a small bunch of curly kale and tear the leaves into rough 2-inch pieces. You should have about 4 cups of loosely packed torn leaves. Toss with ½ teaspoon of table salt and 2 tablespoons of olive oil in a large bowl and allow to sit at room temperature for 15 minutes. Meanwhile, remove the casing from two small sweet Italian sausages (you should have about 8 ounces of meat total). Divide the sausage meat into rough ½-inch chunks and cook in 1 tablespoon of olive oil in a medium skillet over medium heat until the sausage is lightly browned and almost cooked through. Follow the instructions for Neapolitan Pizza Margherita (above), omitting the basil and tomato sauce. Add one-sixth of the sausage chunks and one-sixth of the kale to each pie on top of the cheese before placing under the broiler.

sandwiches, hot dogs & more

sandwiches are IRRESISTIBLY APPEALING.

IN FACT, WE'VE CONCLUDED THAT SANDWICHES HAVE A NEARLY UNIVERSAL DRAW—MORE, WE'D VENTURE TO SAY, THAN ANY OTHER FOOD IN THE NATION. WHY? WELL, WE HAVE A FEW THOUGHTS.

Sandwiches are a food of the people, by the people, for the people. With a few exceptions, they're inexpensive—giving eaters bang for their buck. They're portable; you always have time to grab and carry a sandwich. They're in every corner of this country. And they're always delicious, at breakfast or lunch or dinner or anytime in between.

Sandwiches are as diverse as they are universal. They come out of so many food cultures: Mexican tortas, Italian panini, Chilean chacareros. Regionally or nationally derived, they have a strong sense of tradition attached. You can't think of New Orleans po' boys or New England lobster rolls without recalling the places they're from. And at their

best, they bring nations together. Vietnam meets France in the banh mi. Italy meets the United States in the cold hero. And the Caribbean meets Florida in the Cuban.

The ultimate working-class food, making use of anything and everything edible, sandwiches constitute some of the most innovative foods we know. Great sandwiches are made by everyone from home cooks to lunch-counter owners to highbrow chefs. The greatest sandwich of your life could be lurking around any corner.

But when it comes down to it, what makes a sandwich great is the same—whether it's a tuna melt or a muffuletta or a meatball sub. It's all about balance and ratios and combinations. Balance between flavors and textures; between fillings and breads. The beauty of a sandwich is the number of distinct and delicious sensations you can pack into a single bite, and the way they work together. It's all about architecture.

Not all sandwiches are created equal. So we set out to give you a road map to the best sandwiches we could find anywhere in the country, and that's what you'll find in this chapter. Some of the featured sandwiches have been made the same way for hundreds of years; some have been elevated by chefs we love; others are possible to re-create in your own kitchen.

15 MUST-EAT SANDWICHES

1 TORRISI ITALIAN SPECIALTIES NEW YORK, NY
THE PANAMA

The first time we walked into Torrisi for lunch, we saw acclaimed chef Nate Appleman leaving the restaurant. He called out over his shoulder, "Have you been here yet? Don't overlook the turkey sandwich." And then he was gone. Nate was right. The turkey sandwich is our favorite to hit New York since Leo's Latticini. Called the Panama, Torrisi's sandwich starts with a turkey breast glazed with honey,

garlic, and herbs that's slow-roasted in the oven over a tray of water, so that it's essentially steamed. It's served with spicy sauce, thin red onion, shaved lettuce, mayo, and tomato. It would not be gilding the lily to ask them to put a slice of their terrific house-made mozzarella on the sandwich.

2 THE PIG DURHAM, NC
FRIED BOLOGNA

At The Pig, a super-casual cheffy barbecue joint, owner and young barbecue enthusiast Sam Suchoff uses an electric smoker that produces succulent,

ROAST BEEF AND ONIONS AT BUNK SANDWICHES, PORTLAND, OR

PROSCIUTTO AND GOAT CHEESE AT SALUMI, SEATTLE, WA

smoky barbecue. His brisket is pretty swell, but his bologna sandwich is a thing of porcine beauty. The bologna made from sustainably raised pigs and smoked in-house is finished in a fry pan to get a lovely crisp edge, and comes on a hamburger bun with hot mustard and coleslaw. Bologna tends to get a bad rap as a lunchmeat, but this sandwich elevates it to a starring role.

3 BUNK SANDWICHES PORTLAND, OR
ROAST BEEF, ONIONS, CHEDDAR, HORSERADISH

Before Nick Wood and Tommy Habetz started throwing cold cuts and peppers onto ciabatta rolls, they were working in some serious New York kitchens, including Mario Batali's Po. Now they run a bustling sandwich joint, where there's a line out the door until they close every day at 3 PM. Everything but the bread, which comes from Fleur de Lis bakery and the Vietnamese bakery An Xuyen, is cooked, cured, and made at the store. The roast beef is as melty and thinly sliced as carpaccio, and made even richer with caramelized onions, Tillamook Cheddar, and real horseradish.

4 PHILIPPE'S LOS ANGELES, CA
ROAST LAMB WITH BLUE CHEESE

While many say the classic order is a roast beef French dip (this Los Angeles cafeteria invented the sandwich in 1918), we're partial to the lamb dip. With the same light French roll, a funky blue cheese, and sliced lamb, the whole sandwich is dunked in salty, meaty, gamey lamb jus—all the condiment you need.

5 SALUMI SEATTLE, WA
PROSCIUTTO, GOAT CHEESE, AND FIG

Armandino Batali's best-known product may be his son—this chef named Mario—but Seattle residents know him as the owner of Salumi, one of the finest Italian-style cured meat shops in the nation, now run by daughter Gina Batali and her husband Brian D'Amato (page 329). With both hot and cold sandwiches, most served on bread from Macrina Bakery (page 326), it's hard to order wrong here. We fell in love with the prosciutto, goat cheese, and fig sandwich—the prosciutto soft and tender, the cheese impossibly creamy, and the fig barely sweet but pungent enough to touch every bite.

6 PANE BIANCO PHOENIX, AZ
TUNA, RED ONIONS, OLIVES, ARUGULA

As if owning the nation's finest pizzeria weren't enough (page 104), Chris Bianco keeps a modest sandwich shop a few miles up the road. Almost anything you stuff into his oven-hot rolls would

TUNA AND ARUGULA AT PANE BIANCO, PHOENIX, AZ

one more new-school torta: gallo blanco, phoenix, az

Gallo blanco, meaning "white rooster" (or in Latin slang, "white dude"), refers to chef-owner Doug Robson, who's actually from Mexico City—though most people don't realize that. He makes what he grew up eating, but with ingredients from local Arizona purveyors. The tortas start with a thin, spongy bread that has crisp edges and hugs all sorts of fillings, including *carne asada* (slightly sweet meat shreds topped with charred tomato salsa and cool, creamy avocado) and *cochinita* (slow-braised pork marinated in a punchy mix of achiote, garlic, orange, and guajillo). They're wrapped in butcher paper, and they're the best new-school tortas you'll find in Phoenix.

constitute a memorable sandwich, but his ingredients are smartly sourced and deftly layered—whether you choose a simple tomato and mozzarella or, our favorite, the tuna with red onions, Gaeta olives, and a thick layer of green crunch from the fresh lemon-spritzed arugula. It manages to have the creaminess of the tuna you ate growing up, but without the mayo.

7 XOCO CHICAGO, IL
PEPITO TORTA

Rick Bayless may look every bit the Oklahoma native, but he's spent decades as Chicago's unrivaled master of fine Mexican-inspired cuisine. And his casual operation, Xoco, turns out tortas that we'd call some of the best sandwiches we've ever had. The Pepito—fall-apart, intensely savory short-rib with melted Jack cheese, sweet caramelized onions, black beans, and pickled jalapeños—is an exercise in sandwich mastery, a beautiful marriage of flavors in extraordinary bread that's perfectly crisped.

8 CUTTY'S BOSTON, MA
ROAST BEEF

When we heard that Charles Kelsey and his wife, Rachel Toomey—both alums of the acclaimed magazine *Cook's Illustrated*—were going to turn their obsessive, perfection-bent mind-set into producing the best sandwiches, we knew Boston would get a world-class sandwich joint. They make their own mozzarella for the Spucky sandwich (page 158) and use many breads from first-class local bakery Iggy's. While we'd recommend any one of their sandwiches wholeheartedly, we're partial to the roast beef—ultra-thin sliced beef that's been salt-and-pepper cured and slow-roasted, piled high on a black pepper bun from Iggy's and topped with Cheddar cheese and horseradish-spiked Thousand Island. The kicker is a handful of sweet, oniony, crispy-fried shallots, which elevate the sandwich to modern-classic status. (If you're there on Saturday, don't miss that day's special roast pork sandwich—it might be even better.)

ROAST PORK SANDWICH AT PASEO CARIBBEAN RESTAURANT, SEATTLE, WA

9 CHARLEY THE BUTCHER
WILLIAMSVILLE, NY
BEEF ON WECK

That's short for *Kummelweck*: a bulky salt-and-caraway–topped roll. (*Kummel* is German for "caraway"; *weck*, "roll.") This Buffalo-area specialty is generally made with rare roast beef, with the roll dipped in jus, and freshly grated horseradish on the side. Our favorite is the super-juicy beef at Charley the Butcher out near the Buffalo airport. Owner Charles Roesch was the third-generation owner of meat purveyor Charles E. Roesch and Company, so his butcher pedigree is second to none; his top round is rosy pink and beautifully tender, the roll has just the right caraway-salt balance, and the horseradish is so fresh and delicious you could eat it with a spoon.

10 LA CAMARONERA SEAFOOD JOINT & FISH MARKET
MIAMI, FL
PAN CON MINUTA

To supply the fish for La Camaronera, a fried seafood stand in a tiny strip mall on the outskirts of Little Havana, three generations of the Garcia family have been sending out their own fishing boats before they fry seafood sandwiches better than any others we know. Consider the Original Pan Con Minuta (bread with snapper)—a whole snapper that's been filleted with its tail left on, dredged in cracker crumbs and then again in flour, and fried to the most gorgeous golden brown in super-clean oil. It's then placed on a small, round, perfect Cuban sandwich roll with just the right chew and softness. The result is a fish sandwich that bears no resemblance to a Filet-o-Fish or any bad pub food sandwich you've ever had; if you think you don't like fried fish sandwiches, you have to try this one.

11 BLUESTEM KANSAS CITY, MO
PORK TENDERLOIN

Pork tenderloin sandwiches (page 158) are a Midwestern staple, generally made with pounded-out commodity pork. But at Bluestem, the chef takes designer pork tenderloin left over from a dish they make in the main dining room; dredges it in flour, egg, and Lawry's Seasoned Salt (you've got to love any chef who isn't afraid to use Lawry's); and fries

it in tempura batter. The result is an exceedingly crispy and well-salted Frisbee of fried pork that, in typical pork tenderloin style, spills out the bun's edges in every direction. It's as good as a pork tenderloin can be.

12 STRAIGHT WHARF FISH STORE NANTUCKET, MA
FRESH TUNA

Owner and resident fishmaster Walter Sadowski, with a Red Sox cap and a matching accent, supplies the day's freshest catch to professional and amateur chefs alike on Nantucket Island. But he doesn't just sell by the pound—he'll fry you lunch right there in the shop. A thin tuna steak is flash-seared in a hot cast-iron pan and tossed into a butter-browned soft, squishy roll. Topped with lemon or tartar sauce, if you like, this sandwich is best enjoyed on the dockside tables just outside the door.

13 BAKESALE BETTY OAKLAND, CA
FRIED CHICKEN

Started by Australian chef and Chez Panisse veteran Alison Barakat, Bakesale Betty is rarely without a lunchtime line down the street. Why? The fried chicken sandwich. The bird's the most important part, of course—buttermilk-battered and fried free-range chicken breasts with a seasoned cayenne-spiked crust. But it's made memorable on a torpedo roll from Acme Bread (page 322) and with a generous heaping of slaw, spicy and sharp with jalapeños and parsley. Crunchy and fresh with a subtle afterburn, each bite is immensely satisfying. Just schedule in a while to wait, and put an extra quarter in the meter.

14 PASEO CARIBBEAN RESTAURANT SEATTLE, WA
ROAST PORK

This Seattle institution has something of a devout following, and after one bite of their roast pork sandwich, you'll understand why. The marinated slow-roasted pork, a little sloppy, a little sweet, joins thick rings of caramelized onions on a chewy Macrina Bakery (page 326) roll, spread with a punchy garlicky spread. The result is so much more than the sum of its already appealing parts. How much did we love this sandwich? On a 48-hour fact-finding trip to Seattle, we stopped at Paseo three times—and then flew a sandwich across the country, to the New York office, for the rest of the Serious Eats team to enjoy.

15 THE SENTINEL SAN FRANCISCO, CA
SMOKED AND FRESH SALMON

Sure, plenty of chefs open sandwich shops—but how many of them work the lunch line, day in and day out? Chef Dennis Leary followed up his restaurant Canteen with The Sentinel, a sandwich shop in a former cigar store, where the chef himself makes every sandwich on the menu. It's a rotating list, but the smoked and fresh salmon sandwich is always worth an order. Served on a slightly eggy, puffy roll with crisp fennel-apple slaw and the kind of fresh mayo that makes everything taste better, it's about as good as lunch gets.

PO' BOYS

The New York area has heroes; much of the mid-Atlantic has hoagies; New England has grinders. But in and around New Orleans, it's the poor boy (or po' boy) you'll find. These Louisiana French bread–clad sandwiches, their long loaves both crusty and airy, come stuffed with fried seafood, roast beef, french fries, sausage, ham—or just about anything else you can imagine. They're best fully "dressed," in local parlance, with lettuce, tomatoes, mayo, and pickles. The variations are endless.

At Domilise's, a cheery yellow-painted outfit in the residential Garden District that's equal parts bar, sandwich shop, and family rec room, po' boys are perfect exercises in proportion. Fat-bellied oysters, flour-dusted and dropped in the fryer only once you place an order, are piled on thin-crusted loaves from the esteemed Leidenheimer Baking Company; mayo and ketchup commingle into a sweet, creamy dressing that binds the crusty seafood to the bread. Grip down on that bread and the oysters start to fall apart, fusing their delicious sweet brine into the sandwich innards. If it's an overstuffed sandwich you prefer, you might favor the hefty po' boys from Dooky Chase—with better-seasoned breading than many shops, the fried seafood (we love the oysters) stacks to fill a mayo-spread crusty roll to capacity. And at Crabby Jack's in Jefferson and R&O up near Lake Ponchartrain, the rolls can't even pretend to corral the crunchy fried shrimp that inevitably tumble out into the wrapping.

But even better might be the roast beef po' boy. Forget about chilly, pink-centered cold cuts; in New Orleans, roast beef means sloppy, gravy-drenched meat in thick slices that threaten to fall apart altogether. At R&O, the beef is bathed in a dark, intensely salty gravy that soaks into the seeded roll; it's pulled back from the brink of too savory by the mayonnaise and pickles that tame the gravy's essential meatiness. (Some of us are partial to the R&O's Special, the same roast beef topped with a layer of grill-seared sliced ham.) But at Parasol's (whose kitchen has relocated to Tracey's Bar around the corner), the beef is cooked until it disintegrates, almost like a pulled pork, until it's something neither solid nor liquid—the line between meat and gravy blurs into a glorious fatty suspension, cradled in crusty Leidenheimer bread. They advertise the best roast beef in New Orleans—and we can't say they're wrong.

ROAST BEEF PO' BOY AT TRACEY'S BAR AND RESTAURANT, NEW ORLEANS, LA

> **"How on earth can one choose among the wonderfulnesses of sandwiches? I keep obsessing over one I never tasted, only saw on menus in a phone book on Long Island: Egg and Potato Heroes. I keep thinking about that, especially if the potatoes were cooked with some onions."** —lemons

ROAST BEEF SANDWICH AT BUNK SANDWICHES, PORTLAND, OR

TORTA FROM XOCO, CHICAGO, IL

THE ARTISANAL SANDWICH MOVEMENT

The sandwich is a food of the people: historically cheap, filling, and governed by tradition—the stuff of walk-up stands and blue-collar lunch counters. But over the last few decades, we've seen upscale chefs reinterpreting the classics with an eye toward technique, ingredient sourcing, and careful refinement. Purists may scoff at these pricey acts of heresy; critics may sneer at the romanticization of the humble lunch. We're just happy to see more great sandwiches in the world.

THE ARISTA AT PAESANO'S, PHILADELPHIA, PA

ROAST PORK SANDWICHES

OLD SCHOOL
JOHN'S ROAST PORK, PHILADELPHIA, PA

It may be known for a certain Whiz-topped steak creation, but we're of the opinion that Philadelphia's real sandwich trump card is the roast pork: a regional favorite often served with provolone and spinach or broccoli rabe. And while naming a best one is tough, we'd have to point you to the sandwich at John's Roast Pork—a seeded roll from Carangi Bakery, soaking in pork juice, heaped with pork, best with provolone and spinach.

NEW SCHOOL
PAESANO'S, PHILADELPHIA, PA

Walk in the door, take one of the few stools at the lunch counter, and you might fall for the Philadelphia spot's scrappy lunch-counter aesthetic. Until you look at the menu, that is, which boasts chickpea fritters, house-made condiments, and suckling pig. It's that last sandwich, called the Arista, that we can't stop thinking about. Imagine the very essence of a baby pig—suckling pig cooked until so tender you could eat it with a spoon, studded with crispy bits of skin and drowned in its own jus—piled into a seeded roll, with bracingly bitter, just-cooked broccoli rabe and shreds of provolone so sharp as to act like a condiment. Too drippy to order to go, it's best sucked down at the counter, where the guys will drop Wet Nap after Wet Nap beside you. They know how it is.

on the cheesesteak

If we have time for one sandwich in Philly, it won't be a cheesesteak—it'll be a roast pork. But that's not to say we're not fans of the cheesesteak, too: thinly shaved ribeye or top round, cooked through on a griddle, often chopped up with cooked onions and peppers, and topped with provolone or Cheez Whiz. Purists will claim that the only proper bread for a cheesesteak is a long roll from Amoroso's Baking Company—long and crusty but soft enough to soak up the meat juices. Our favorite cheesesteak? Right back at John's. It may be called John's Roast Pork, but let's face it: in Philadelphia, no sandwich shop could reign supreme without making a worthy cheesesteak.

There is no shortage of recipes for the cold lobster roll. So we'd rather give you a recipe for the lesser known but equally alluring hot lobster roll. Here's the equation that we came up with: just-cooked lobster meat plus hot butter plus a toasted, buttered roll equals deliciousness.

hot buttered
lobster rolls

MAKES 4 LOBSTER ROLLS

2 live lobsters, about 2 pounds each

Kosher salt

6 tablespoons unsalted butter

4 top-split hot dog buns

1 Kill the lobsters by plunging the tip of a large chef's knife into the carapace of each one, $1\frac{1}{2}$ inches behind the eyes, until the point of the knife hits the cutting board. Bring the blade down between the lobster's eyes to split the head in half. Grasp the tail with a kitchen towel and twist and pull it to remove it from the body. Twist and remove both claws. Discard the lobster body, or reserve it for stock.

2 Add 5 quarts of water and $\frac{1}{2}$ cup of salt to a large stockpot. Set the pot over high heat, cover, and bring to a rolling boil. Have a large bowl filled with ice water ready for chilling the cooked lobsters. Place the lobster tails in the pot, cover, and cook for 1 minute. Add the claws to the pot, cover, and cook for 2 more minutes. Using a large strainer basket or tongs, remove the lobster tails and claws, and immediately plunge in the ice water. Allow them to chill completely, about 5 minutes.

3 Using a lobster cracker or the back of a heavy knife, crack each lobster's shell and remove the meat. Discard the empty shells. Roughly chop the lobster meat into $\frac{1}{2}$-inch pieces (parts of the lobster may still appear translucent). At this stage, the lobster can be refrigerated for up to 1 day before completing the recipe.

LOBSTER ROLL AT PEARL OYSTER BAR, NEW YORK, NY

4 Melt 2 tablespoons of butter in a medium skillet over medium heat. Toast the hot dog buns in butter until both cut sides are golden brown and crispy, about 5 minutes, lowering the heat if the butter begins to burn. Place the buns on a large plate and tent with foil while you heat the lobster.

5 Add the remaining butter to the skillet along with the lobster meat. Cook over medium heat, stirring constantly, until the butter is melted and the lobster meat is cooked through, about 4 minutes. Season to taste with salt. Mound the lobster meat into the four hot dog buns, and serve immediately with potato chips.

LOBSTER ROLLS

OLD SCHOOL
RED'S EATS, WISCASSET, ME

You might feel like a lobster roll–addicted lemming when you join the long line at Red's on any summer's day. But 45 minutes later, after you sample said lobster roll, made with almost a half pound of Maine lobster meat, you realize that maybe the lemmings are on to something. That much lobster tucked into a buttered and heated hot dog bun with either melted drawn butter or mayo on the side (you want the drawn butter) makes up one mighty fine sandwich.

NEW SCHOOL
NEPTUNE OYSTER BAR, BOSTON, MA

Just about anything on the menu makes us happy at this sleek, narrow fish bar in Boston's North End. But it's the hot lobster roll we keep coming back for: enormous chunks of fresh, sweet lobster tossed in warm butter and served in a split-top buttered bun. The pile of supremely tender, crispy brown fries doesn't hurt, either.

MUFFULETTA

OLD SCHOOL
CENTRAL GROCERY, NEW ORLEANS, LA

If you ask for a muffuletta recommendation in New Orleans, you'll probably be pointed to the Central Grocery—a place that'll make you fall in love with the sandwich at first bite. Layer upon layer of Italian-American cold cuts, sharp Provolone, and amazing olive salad are piled inside a hunk of bread that's just a little greasy on its own—and much greasier after all the meaty, olive oil-y juices soak in. It's easy to see how this is a classic.

NEW SCHOOL
COCHON BUTCHER, NEW ORLEANS, LA

How can a rookie in the New Orleans sandwich game claim the title of the best muffuletta in the city? When that rookie is fine Nola chef Donald Link, and his shop is Cochon Butcher, equal parts meat market, lunch stop, and wine bar. It's not just the giardiniera olive relish Link makes in-house; the thinly sliced ham, the mortadella, and the Genoa salami are all made and cured on the premises, too. Perfect each ingredient, and you have the perfect sandwich.

MUFFULETTA AT COCHON BUTCHER, NEW ORLEANS, LA

If you can find muffuletta bread at a Sicilian bakery, use it. Otherwise, a large (12 × 8-inch) loaf of focaccia or ciabatta will work. Giardiniera is an Italian-American pickled vegetable mix consisting of cauliflower, carrots, celery, and red peppers. It can be found in Italian specialty stores or in jars in the international section of the supermarket.

muffuletta

1 Place the olives, giardiniera, peperoncini, capers, and garlic in the bowl of a food processor. Pulse until roughly chopped, about six 1-second pulses. Transfer to a medium bowl and stir in the olive oil. Allow to marinate at room temperature for 30 minutes.

2 Cut the bread in half horizontally. Spread a half cup of the olive mix evenly over the bottom half of the bread, along with enough olive oil to completely coat the surface. Spread the remaining olive salad over the top half of the bread.

3 Spread the capicola in an even layer over the top half of the bread. Repeat with the mortadella, sopressata, and provolone. Close the sandwich by lifting the bottom bun and inverting it over the top bun and fillings (the sandwich will be upside down). Wrap the sandwich tightly in plastic wrap and invert it. Refrigerate for at least 1 hour to let the olive salad flavor penetrate the meat and bread. Cut the sandwich into quarters, and serve.

MAKES 1 LARGE SANDWICH; SERVES 2 TO 4

1 cup mixed pitted Italian olives (about ¾ pound)

1 cup giardiniera

4 jarred pickled peperoncini, stems removed

2 tablespoons capers, drained and roughly chopped

1 medium garlic clove, finely minced (about 1 teaspoon)

½ cup extra virgin olive oil

1 loaf muffuletta bread (or focaccia or ciabatta)

⅓ pound sliced hot capicola

⅓ pound sliced mortadella

⅓ pound sliced sweet sopressata

⅓ pound sliced provolone cheese

THE BEST GRILLED CHEESE (RECIPE OPPOSITE)

GRILLED CHEESE WE LOVE

BOUCHON BAKERY
LAS VEGAS, NV; YOUNTVILLE, CA; AND NEW YORK, NY

It's easy to make a tasty grilled cheese; it's not easy to make a grilled cheese that bests every other you've had. But chef Thomas Keller maintains the same impossibly high standards in sandwich-making at his Bouchon Bakery as he does in the kitchen at his exalted restaurants, Per Se and the French Laundry. The secrets? Fontina and Gruyère, melting into a single tangy, creamy core, hugged by white bread lovingly coated in French butter and fried to a beautiful golden burnish.

GRILLED CHEESE AT BOUCHON BAKERY

While fine grilled cheeses can be make from fontina and Gruyère, as at Bouchon Bakery (opposite), we wanted to perfect the all-American, less fancy grilled cheese sandwich for your home kitchen. For best results, use sliced Cheddar cheese from the deli and Kraft Deli Deluxe slices, which come packaged but not individually wrapped. The combination of sharp Cheddar and American provides both flavor and the necessary "ooze" factor.

the best grilled cheese

MAKES 2 SANDWICHES

3 tablespoons unsalted butter

4 slices high-quality white sandwich bread

2 slices American cheese

2 slices sharp Cheddar cheese

Salt

1 Melt ½ tablespoon butter in a large heavy-bottomed skillet over medium-high heat. Place two slices of bread in the skillet and swirl until all the butter is absorbed. Toast until very light golden brown, about 1 minute. Transfer to a cutting board and place 1 slice of American cheese on the toasted side of the bread. Add another ½ tablespoon of butter to the skillet and repeat with the two remaining slices of bread, topping them with Cheddar cheese.

2 Assemble the sandwiches so that each one has two cheese slices in the center with the untoasted sides facing outward. Melt 1 tablespoon of butter in the now-empty skillet over medium-low heat. Sprinkle the skillet with ½ teaspoon of salt and add the sandwiches, swirling them around the pan with a spatula until all the butter is absorbed. Toast until the first side is a deep golden brown, about 3 minutes, reducing the heat if the butter begins to burn. Remove the sandwiches, melt the remaining 1 tablespoon of butter, sprinkle the pan with another ½ teaspoon of salt, then return the sandwiches, untoasted side down, and swirl until the butter is absorbed. Toast until the second side is a deep golden brown and the cheese is thoroughly melted, about 3 minutes.

3 Cut the sandwiches on the diagonal and serve immediately.

Bacon may not be among the most traditional banh mi fillings, but boy does it work in this recipe. Mixed deli meats such as ham and bologna can be substituted for the bacon. But since high-quality thick-cut bacon is so widely available, we recommend you stick to it. An inexpensive Japanese mandoline will make short work of the carrot and daikon julienne, but they can also be done by hand. The large holes of a box grater will also provide acceptable results. For best results, use Vietnamese-style rice-flour baguettes. Avoid French baguettes, which are too chewy for these sandwiches. The best substitute is a high-quality hero roll.

bacon
banh mi

MAKES 4 SANDWICHES

1 large carrot, cut into 2-inch matchsticks ⅛ inch thick (about 2 cups)

1 small daikon radish, cut into 2-inch matchsticks ⅛ inch thick (about 2 cups)

¾ cup plus 2 teaspoons sugar

Kosher salt

½ cup white vinegar

16 slices thick-cut bacon

4 Vietnamese baguettes or high-quality hero rolls

1 teaspoon Vietnamese or Thai fish sauce

1 teaspoon Maggi seasoning sauce

1 teaspoon soy sauce

4 tablespoons mayonnaise

1 cucumber, peeled, seeded, and cut lengthwise into 8 strips

1 jalapeño pepper, stemmed, seeded, and cut lengthwise into matchsticks

1 bunch fresh cilantro (about 16 sprigs)

Freshly ground black pepper

1 Place the carrot, daikon, ¼ cup of sugar, and 1 tablespoon of salt in a medium mixing bowl. Using your hands, massage the salt and sugar into the vegetables until they begin to soften and exude liquid. Set the bowl aside at room temperature for 30 minutes, then drain the vegetables. Meanwhile, combine the vinegar, ½ cup of sugar, and ½ cup of water in a small bowl or Tupperware container and mix until the sugar is dissolved. Pour the vinegar mixture over the drained vegetables, and refrigerate until ready to use, at least 1 hour. (The vegetables should last at least 10 days, and will get better with time.)

2 Adjust the oven rack to the middle position, and preheat the oven to 400°F. Line a rimmed baking sheet with aluminum foil and spread the bacon over it. Bake the bacon until crispy, about 15 minutes, then drain on a plate lined with two layers of paper towels.

3 Remove the foil from the baking sheet and discard it, then place the four baguettes on the now-empty baking sheet. Toast for 3 minutes until the exterior is crispy. Meanwhile, in a small bowl, combine the fish sauce, Maggi seasoning sauce, soy sauce, and the remaining 2 teaspoons of sugar.

4 With a bread knife, slit the baguettes lengthwise, leaving a hinge to keep the two halves connected. Spread 1 tablespoon of mayonnaise evenly inside each baguette. Stuff the baguettes with four slices of bacon, two cucumber strips, a few slices of jalapeño, and four sprigs of cilantro. Drizzle with the fish sauce mixture and season with salt and pepper. Close the sandwiches and serve.

BANH MI

Think of the banh mi as Vietnam's answer to the hoagie. The cross-cultural love child of France and native Vietnam, it's a sandwich built from a wheat- and rice-flour baguette, nearly always with pickled carrots and daikon, cucumber, mayo, and cilantro, very often with pork liver pâté, and any number of meat or vegetable fillings: roasted pork, grilled pork, sausage, ham, chicken, tofu. Done right, it's a playground of flavors and textures, a sandwich that's crispy, soft, meaty, salty, sweet, fresh, sour, and spicy all at once. While banh mi has made major national inroads as of late, most of the best are still served in cities with large Vietnamese communities, notably in California, Massachusetts, Florida, Louisiana, and Texas.

5 OF THE BEST DELIS ACROSS AMERICA

1 KATZ'S
NEW YORK, NY

Sure, it's a tourist destination, but this hundred-year-old deli still has the magic. Katz's serves a pastrami sandwich to die for. The pastrami is juicy, well seasoned, and explodes with flavor. Best of all, it's hand-cut by a brigade of expert multicultural slicers who will give you a taste of the meat as your sandwich is made. Grab that drippy piece of pastrami with your fingers, plop it in your mouth, and you'll understand the decades and decades of happy sandwich customers.

2 LANGER'S
LOS ANGELES, CA

The Langer family has been serving up a truly great pastrami sandwich since 1947 in a neighborhood that no one would describe as quaint. What makes a Langer's pastrami sandwich truly great? The pastrami is a little smokier and a little pepperier than Katz's—but it's the double-baked rye bread that really makes a difference. Norm Langer and his band of deli men purchase their bread almost fully baked, but then finish it off in their own oven, so it's hot and crusty and steamy within. What a difference a second bake makes.

3 ZINGERMAN'S
ANN ARBOR, MI

Zingerman's was started by two students at the University of Michigan, Ari Weinzweig and Paul Saginaw. Notice anything strange? Neither of them is named Zingerman. Ari and Paul just thought the name sounded Jewish and had lots of energy. Their deli, too, has lots of energy, though it goes way beyond Jewish deli food in its purview. But since you have to start somewhere on Zingerman's huge menu, we recommend the Reuben. They bake the rye in-house, cure their own sauerkraut, import aged Swiss from Switzerland, and win medals for their house-cured Black Angus corned beef. Really, they've found a way to improve upon every element of the classic Reuben.

4 KENNY AND ZUKE'S
PORTLAND, OR

Ken Gordon and Nick Zukin have a similar approach to Zingerman's, but ratchet up the do-it-yourself component even more. Their pastrami, cured and smoked in-house, is absolutely killer; they claim it's the best in the world. (You know what? It's got a shot.) It's aggressively seasoned with coriander, garlic, and pepper. How can you eat pastrami here? Let us count the ways. Pastrami cheese fries, pastrami eggs benedict, pastrami burgers, and of course the classic pastrami

PASTRAMI SANDWICH AT KENNY AND ZUKE'S, PORTLAND, OR

PASTRAMI SANDWICH AT JAKE'S, MILWAUKEE, WI

sandwich on their fresh-baked, strongly flavored, caraway seed–studded dark rye.

5 JAKE'S
MILWAUKEE, WI

What was once a great kosher-style deli in a Jewish neighborhood has now become a soulful sandwich provider to Milwaukee's substantial African-American population, as the neighborhood has shifted demographically over the decades. But no matter their background, everyone still comes to Jake's for the same reason: amazing sandwiches made with house-cured, hand-cut corned beef that has loads of fat and meat-laden nooks and crannies. The Vienna Beef pastrami, also hand-cut, is also phenomenal, if not *quite* up to the impossibly high corned beef standards. Jane and Michael Stern (of *Roadfood*) claim that Milwaukee is the greatest corned beef town in America, and based on Jake's, it's hard to disagree.

High-quality store-bought corned beef can be used in place of the homemade corned beef here. But in the course of developing this recipe, we discovered how simple it is to make your own corned beef—and just how moist and delicious it turns out.

reuben

MAKES 4 SANDWICHES

2 pounds Corned Beef Brisket (page 156), cut into ¼-inch slices

8 ounces sauerkraut

8 thick-cut slices Jewish rye or pumpernickel bread

½ cup Russian Dressing (opposite)

8 slices Swiss cheese

4 tablespoons unsalted butter, softened

1 Adjust the oven rack to the middle position and preheat the oven to 350°F. Spread the corned beef slices in a foil-lined rimmed baking sheet. Pour ½ cup of water over the beef, cover tightly with aluminum foil, and place in the oven. Steam in the oven for 10 minutes, until hot. Meanwhile, place the sauerkraut and its juices in a small heavy-bottomed skillet. Cook over medium heat, stirring constantly, until heated through, about 2 minutes.

2 Place four slices of bread on a cutting board. Top each slice with a quarter of the beef followed by a quarter of the sauerkraut, a quarter of the Russian dressing, and two slices of Swiss cheese. Top each sandwich with a second slice of bread. Spread the top of each sandwich with ½ tablespoon butter.

3 Place two large heavy-bottomed skillets over medium heat. Divide the remaining butter evenly between them, 1 tablespoon per pan. Heat the pans until the butter stops foaming. Swirl the pans to coat the bottom, then add the sandwiches, buttered side up. Cook, moving the sandwiches around the pan occasionally, until the sandwich bottoms are golden brown and crisp, about 5 minutes. Using a metal spatula, carefully flip the sandwiches and cook on the second side, moving them around the pan occasionally, until crisped on the second side. (If you don't own two large skillets, the sandwiches can be made in two batches. Keep the first two sandwiches warm on a wire rack set in a rimmed baking sheet in a 200°F. oven tented with foil while you cook the second two sandwiches.)

4 Remove the sandwiches to a cutting board, flipping them so the cheese is at the top. Cut in half and serve.

russian
dressing

Mix all the ingredients in a small bowl. Use immediately, or cover and refrigerate until needed. The dressing will keep in the refrigerator for up to one week in a sealed container.

MAKES ½ CUP

¼ cup mayonnaise

2 tablespoons ketchup

2 teaspoons prepared horseradish

1 teaspoon white vinegar

1 teaspoon sugar

2 teaspoons sweet pickle relish

1 teaspoon Worcestershire sauce

½ teaspoon hot sauce (such as Frank's Red Hot)

½ teaspoon freshly ground black pepper

Look for well-marbled beef. The point (or deckel) cut of the beef brisket, a triangular cut with a good amount of fat, will produce the best results, but flat (or first-cut) brisket, of a uniform thickness, is also acceptable. The finished product will not be bright pink in the manner of commercial corned beef.

corned beef
brisket

MAKES ABOUT 2 POUNDS

1 cup kosher salt

2 tablespoons whole black peppercorns

1 tablespoon fennel seeds

1 tablespoon coriander seeds

8 allspice berries

8 juniper berries

4 bay leaves

1 medium onion, roughly chopped (about 1 cup)

1 medium carrot, roughly chopped (about ¾ cup)

2 celery stalks, roughly chopped (about 1 cup)

1 point-cut fresh beef brisket (3 to 4 pounds; see note above)

1 Combine the salt, peppercorns, fennel seeds, coriander seeds, allspice, juniper, bay leaves, onion, carrot, celery, and 2 quarts of water in a medium saucepot. Place the pot over high heat. As soon as it comes to a boil, shut off the burner and allow the liquid to cool completely.

2 Place the beef in a 2-gallon zipper-lock bag. Pour the brine over the beef, squeeze as much air as possible out of the bag, and seal it. Place the bag flat in the refrigerator inside a container just large enough to hold it. Allow the beef to pickle for at least three days, and up to one week, flipping the bag once a day.

3 Fill a large stockpot with a tight-fitting lid with 1½ inches of water and place a steamer basket in the bottom. Place the pot over high heat until the water comes to a boil. Reduce the heat to maintain a gentle simmer. Place the beef in the steamer basket with the fat cap facing up. Put the lid on the pot and steam until the beef offers no resistance when pierced with a fork, 3½ to 4 hours, topping up the water as necessary.

4 Transfer the beef to a container that just fits it, pour any liquid left in the pot over the beef, cover it with foil, and allow the meat to cool completely before slicing.

PULLED PORK SANDWICH FROM ED MITCHELL'S THE PIT,
AT THE BIG APPLE BARBECUE BLOCK PARTY, NEW YORK, NY

BARBECUE SANDWICHES

lexington sandwich nirvana

I love my barbecue sandwiches, and there may be nowhere better than Lexington Barbecue in Lexington, North Carolina, for a chopped pork sandwich. Order a coarsely chopped barbecue sandwich with meat cut from the outside of the pig and topped with a piece of skin, and served with the ever-present chopped coleslaw. You'll get crunch, creaminess, tenderness, smokiness, sweetness, and just a hint of acidity in every perfect bite. You might just order another one.

What makes a great barbecue sandwich? *Great barbecue.* Fact is, you could put perfectly smoked meat between slices of month-old Wonder Bread and still end up with something pretty tasty. In fact, a lot of these sandwiches come on white bread or another simple delivery vehicle. While not every barbecue joint will deign to mask their low-and-slow meat in bread, the ones that do make some of the greatest sandwiches we know: the hickory-smoked, vinegar-laced chopped pork at Chapel Hill's Allen & Son (page 202); the indecently juicy beef sausage at Southside Market in Elgin, Texas (page 194); the pulled pork, smoked for more than 18 hours, at Big Bob Gibson's Bar-B-Q in Decatur, Alabama (page 201); and the barbecue brisket at Smitty's Market in Lockhart, Texas (page 194), where both fatty and lean brisket are piled into one happy heap. (For more great barbecue, see the chapter beginning on page 173.)

SUPER-REGIONAL SANDWICHES

While some sandwiches show up on menus all over the country, others hardly register outside their native cities. Here are some of our favorite little-known sandwiches from across America.

SPUCKY
BOSTON, MA

You've heard of subs, of hoagies, even of grinders, but what about the Spucky? Unique to Boston and the surrounding area, it's an increasingly rare term for a classic sub sandwich.

HOT BROWN
LOUISVILLE, KY

Chef Fred Schmidt conceived of the Hot Brown sandwich at the Brown Hotel in Louisville in the 1920s, in the attempt to create an indulgent, satisfying late-night meal for partygoers, according to food writer John T. Edge. His creation became a quick Kentucky favorite. It's an open-face roasted turkey sandwich topped with mornay sauce, garnished with bacon—we'd want one after a long night out, too.

HORSESHOE
SPRINGFIELD, IL

Invented at the Leland Hotel in 1928, the Horseshoe is an open-faced meat sandwich (generally ham) crowned with creamy cheese sauce and either fries or hash browns, all perched on a foundation of thick-sliced toast. Diner food at its finest—and about six meals in one.

SPIEDIES
WESTERN NEW YORK

This is a sandwich so beloved, it has an annual festival in its honor. Native to the Triple Cities area around Binghamton, New York, the Spiedie is a sandwich that derives from *spiedo,* the Italian word for "spit." The sandwich originally was skewered cubes of marinated lamb that were grilled to a crisp and pulled off the spit using the slice of Italian bread that you ended up eating it with. Today, chicken and pork are a bit more popular, served on either soft Italian bread or an Italian hoagie roll.

PORK TENDERLOIN
PRIMARILY INDIANA AND IOWA

Take pork loin, bread it, deep-fry it, and plop it on a bun. It's basically a play on *Wiener schnitzel,* swapping pork for veal. It's also pounded so thin the meat can reach comically large dimensions, sometimes engulfing a whole plate. The bun can end up looking woefully inadequate for the job. But who are we to complain about an excess of fried pork?

STEAMED
KNOXVILLE, TN

Yep, steamed. A specialty of Knoxville, Tennessee, though occasionally found in other parts of the country, these meat-and-cheese subs are heated in a steamer, melting them all hot and gooey before they're topped with cold veggies and condiments.

ITALIAN BEEF
CHICAGO, IL

The Italian beef sandwich is a Chicago staple, a thick roll filled with roasted thinly sliced beef marinated in spices like garlic and oregano. You can get it "dipped," when the whole sandwich gets dunked in the roasting gravy, or "dry"; "sweet" gets you sweet green peppers; "hot," a spicy giardinara. Even get it as a "combo": in addition to the beef, they add a fat link of Italian sausage. Meat on meat: we'll take it.

DUTCH CRUNCH
BAY AREA, CA

Dutch Crunch is a dense, doughy bread with a moist crumb that you can find at any number of bakeries in the Bay Area. What sets it apart is the crackly top—with crunchy little bits growing from the paler crust underneath. The bread is coated with a wash of rice flour, butter, sugar, and yeast; in the oven, the top crust splits and browns, giving it a distinctive streaked or spotted crust. (Needless to say, the crunch is the best part.) Any sandwich tastes better on Dutch Crunch, but sliced turkey and avocado is about as northern Californian as it gets

JIBARITO
CHICAGO, IL

Is it a sandwich if it's not bookended by bread? Perhaps not, but the Jibarito, a Chicago–Puerto Rican creation with fried plantains as the "bun," surely deserves a mention. Introduced to Chicago by Juan Figueroa of the Puerto Rican Borinquen Restaurant, the sandwiches are offered with many fillings, but the best may be steak: tender and juicy, with the sauce that results from steak drippings, mayonnaise, and garlic oil dissolving into a beautiful mess—one that actually needs the study, starchy plantain to hold it together. Despite its Puerto Rican bent, it's an Illinois invention.

the medianoche

When I was eating my way through Miami in search of book-worthy victuals, I was armed with recommendations from chefs, bloggers, and food writers. Chef-restaurateur Michelle Bernstein (Michy's and Sra. Martinez) sent us to La Esquina del Lechon, a pork and steak house in the Doral neighborhood. The pig logo told us we were in the right place; so did the two pigs we saw roasting right next to our outdoor table. The Cuban sandwich we bought was solid, tasty, satisfying—confirming my long-held theory that Cuban sandwiches are always at least *pretty* good. But the Medianoche, the Cuban sandwich's first cousin, made with softer pan dulce (it would have been a Spanish brioche if they used butter) and the same layers of ham, roast pork, and Swiss cheese, was crazy good. Dipped into the green sauce that came with our sandwiches, the Medianoche made a bid for entrance to the Serious Eats' Sandwich Hall of Fame.

We've replaced the traditional roasted pork in this sandwich with a quicker cooking cut, blade-end pork chops. There is still plenty of fat to keep the sandwiches moist and flavorful. If you can get good Cuban rolls, use them. Otherwise, high-quality hero rolls or small loaves of ciabatta will work.

cubano **mixto**

MAKES 4 SANDWICHES

⅓ cup olive oil

1 small onion, finely diced (about ¾ cup)

2 garlic cloves, finely sliced

2 teaspoons dried oregano

½ cup juice from 1 orange

Kosher salt and black pepper

1 pound blade-end pork chops, bones removed (about three 1-inch-thick chops)

1 tablespoon vegetable or canola oil

4 loaves Cuban bread, high-quality hero rolls, or small ciabatta

2 tablespoons yellow mustard

4 kosher dill pickles, thinly sliced lengthwise

⅔ pound sliced cooked ham

½ pound Swiss cheese slices (about 8 slices)

2 tablespoons unsalted butter

1 Heat the olive oil in a small heavy-bottomed skillet over medium heat until it shimmers. Add the onion, garlic, and oregano. Cook, stirring frequently, until the vegetables are soft but not brown, about 5 minutes. Add the orange juice and simmer until slightly reduced, about 2 minutes. Season to taste with salt and pepper. Transfer half of the mixture to a medium bowl and reserve the remainder at room temperature. Add the pork chops to the bowl and rub the marinade all over them with your hands. Cover the bowl and place it in the fridge for at least 30 minutes and up to 8 hours.

2 Heat the vegetable oil in a large heavy-bottomed skillet over high heat until shimmering. Remove the pork chops from the marinade and pat them dry with a paper towel. Add the pork chops to the skillet and cook without moving until well browned, about 2 minutes. Flip the chops, reduce the heat to medium, and continue to cook until the chops register 140°F. on an instant-read thermometer, about 4 minutes longer. Transfer the chops to a cutting board, and allow to rest at least 5 minutes.

cuban sandwiches

I have a theory about Cuban sandwiches, born of tasting hundreds from all over the country: Cuban sandwiches are always at least quite good; sometimes they're very, very good, but even so, there isn't much difference between any of them. Boiled ham, roast pork, Swiss cheese, pickle, and mojo (garlic sauce) put on Cuban-style bread and in a sandwich press: How could any such sandwich not be delicious?

There is one Cuban sandwich that towers over all others, the one April Bloomfield makes at the Spotted Pig in New York City. Purists scoff at this notion, put off by Bloomfield's use of prosciutto in the sandwich (as well as its $17 price tag), but I say it doesn't matter when a sandwich tastes this good.

3 Preheat the oven to 250°F. Split the rolls in half. Spoon the reserved marinade over the cut side of the rolls and spread it around with the back of the spoon. Divide the mustard evenly among the rolls, and add a layer of pickles. Slice the pork thinly on a bias and lay the pork slices on top of the pickles. Layer on the ham and cheese and close the sandwiches.

4 Melt the butter over medium-low heat in a large heavy-bottomed skillet until the foaming subsides. Add two sandwiches and press down firmly with a second skillet. Cook until the bottom bun is crisp, about 5 minutes. Flip the sandwiches, press again, and continue to cook until the second side is crisp and the fillings are heated through, about 5 minutes longer.

5 Wrap the sandwiches in foil and transfer to the oven to keep warm while heating the other two sandwiches. Serve immediately.

CRAZY SANDWICHES (THAT WE ACTUALLY LIKE)

Great sandwiches aren't about size: just because a sandwich has a pound of meat in it doesn't mean it's delicious. Still, sandwiches do lend themselves to excess. (There's an awful lot you can stuff between two pieces of bread!) And while these wacky sandwiches don't necessarily make our Top 15, they're crazy concoctions we eat, enjoy, and even love.

SANDWICHES WITH FRIES
PRIMANTI BROS.
PITTSBURGH, PA

Why serve fries and slaw *with* your sandwich when you could toss them right on top? Originally a wooden lunch stand for Depression-era truckers pulling up to the loading docks across the street, Primanti's came up with the idea of layering a sandwich's usual sides right onto the sandwich itself, for a one-handed lunch on the go. Though there are now almost two dozen locations, it's best to head "dahntahn," in Pittsburghese, for the original.

THE MACHINE GUN
BRUGES
SALT LAKE CITY, UT

It sounds like a novelty stunt, or a Primanti's knockoff—Belgian frites and fried merguez sausage and tons of sauce in a bun, served at Bruges, Belgium, native Pierre Vandamme's fries-and-waffles shop. But it's a classic *friterie* sandwich called a Mitraillette, directly translated to "machine gun"—and a far more refined sandwich than the description lets on. The merguez is snappy and hauntingly spicy, made by acclaimed Utah lamb producer Morgan Valley Lamb; the frites, Bruges's specialty, are crispy and creamy and delicious outside a sandwich or within. And the tangy, mildly spicy andalouse sauce brings it all together.

FRENCH-BREAD PIZZA SUBS
HOT TRUCK
ITHACA, NY

No one appreciates sloppy sandwiches like college students late on Saturday nights. The Hot Truck has been serving French-bread pizza subs to Cornell students since 1960, and they claim to have invented this sandwich. Light, airy Ithaca Bakery French bread is halved horizontally, spread with a generous amount of pizza sauce and mozzarella, baked open-face until the bread is satisfyingly crisp, and then folded over to make the whole thing easily portable. The sloppiest is known as a Sui (short for "suicide"—garlic French bread loaded with sauce, mushrooms, sausage, pepperoni, and mozzarella).

FAT DARRELL
"GREASE TRUCKS"
NEW BRUNSWICK, NJ

What the Hot Truck is to Cornell, the Grease Trucks are to Rutgers University in New Brunswick. Here, you'll find "fat sandwiches"—essentially hoagies stuffed with french fries, chicken tenders, and all other manner of fried foods. The Fat Cat is the original fat sandwich, stuffed with burger patties and fries, but it's the Fat Darrell that's really jaw-dropping: chicken fingers, mozzarella sticks, french fries, and marinara sauce all piled into a hoagie roll.

THE BOMB
SAL, KRIS, AND CHARLIE'S DELI
ASTORIA, NY

What's on The Bomb at Sal, Kris, and Charlie's Deli in Astoria? Like the sign behind the counter says, everything. No, seriously. *Everything,* layered on really great hero bread with a shatteringly crisp exterior and airy crumb (from Corona's Bakery Boys of New York). If you ask one of the deli guys for specifics, you'd better have time for the answer because they will rattle off a list as long as your arm. Ham, turkey, salami, pepperoni, and mortadella. And three kinds of cheese: American, Swiss, and provolone. And lettuce, tomato, onion, and roasted peppers. And dressing, mustard, and mayo. And we're probably still leaving something out.

WHOLEY'S WHALER
ROBERT WHOLEY & CO.
PITTSBURGH, PA

The Whaler is aptly named (in terms of size, not in terms of the meat it contains), but that name still doesn't quite prepare you for the massive sandwich you're served. Almost embarrassingly large, really. Five massive fried fish fillets, each more than half a foot long, piled on bread that's served more as an accessory than a real sandwich roll, encasing less than a third of the fish. With creamy house-made tartar sauce and a pleasantly soft roll from Mancini's Bakery next door, it's more than worth the considerable (if enjoyable) effort to eat.

DUTCH CRUNCH
LITTLE LUCCA
SOUTH SAN FRANCISCO, CA

What's more northern Californian than a sandwich on Dutch Crunch? A sandwich on Dutch Crunch slathered with garlic sauce and jalapeño relish. Their sandwiches are enormous—your arms will get tired holding one—and all of them, unless you request otherwise, are served with that crazy garlic-heat combination, which will have you breathing a particularly pungent fire all day. With roast beef and melted cheese, it's a little over the top, but impossible to stop eating.

the best hot dogs you can buy

To make a great hot dog at home—whether smothered in chili, sidled with pickles, or squiggled with ketchup—you have to start with a great tube of meat. Here are six of our favorites that you can purchase in stores (or order online) and cook at home.

» Boar's Head Natural Casing Beef Frankfurters

» Papaya King Hot Dog

» Sabrett All Beef Natural Casing Frankfurters

» Vienna Beef Natural Casing Hot Dogs

» Hoffy Hollywood's Original Natural Casing Beef Frankfurters

» Usinger's Natural Casing Pork and Beef Frankfurters

15 HOT DOGS WE LOVE

1 PAPAYA KING
NEW YORK, NY

The Papaya King hot dogs, an all-beef, natural-casing Sabrett hot dog with one supposedly secret ingredient that we've never been able to identify, are beefy, juicy, and have that snap. One of the best things to order is a combination slaw and sauerkraut dog with pickles and their spicy hallmark mustard. It's sweet, salty, spicy, and meaty at the same time. What could be better?

2 WALTER'S HOT DOG STAND
MAMARONECK, NY

What makes this hot dog stand better than any other? (Besides the roadside Asian pagoda it's housed in?) The Walter's dog itself, its recipe devised by the original Walter. Made of pork, beef, and veal, it's grilled, split open, brushed with a buttery sauce, and grilled again split side down—maximizing the heat-to-meat action, leaving each dog with plenty of golden brown crust. And since they're split in half, they stack nicely, so you can get a single dog, two, or even three to a single soft, squishy bun.

3 JIMMY BUFF'S ITALIAN HOT DOGS
EAST HANOVER, NJ

New Jersey may have the most varied and diverse hot dog culture in the country, and mailman John Fox, who goes by the handle "hotdoglover" at Serious Eats, has made it his life's work to sample every hot dog in the Garden State. So when he informed us that "the finest all-beef natural-casing dog in Jersey" is served at Jimmy Buff's in East Hanover—first fried in oil in the tilted steel pan used to make Italian hot dogs, then finished off on a charcoal grill, put on a toasted bun, and topped with Admiration deli mustard—we hightailed it to East Hanover. He's right. It's a great hot dog.

4 HOT DOUG'S
CHICAGO, IL

Hot Doug's owner Doug Sohn may be the Bono of the hot dog world. When we invited him to New York to serve his hot dogs and duck-fat fries at a Serious Eats event in New York, tickets sold out in an hour. With good reason. He served what could only be described as his greatest hits: a perfect classic Chicago hot dog, a hot dog topped with foie gras, and french fries cooked in duck fat (which he serves only on Fridays and Saturdays) at his self-described sausage superstore and encased-meat emporium. Doug serves his Chicago dogs either steamed or grilled and also adds caramelized onions. Caramelized onions, of course, make just about any food taste better.

5 SUPERDAWG
CHICAGO, IL

As Serious Eats contributor Nick Kindelsperger once pointed out to me, Superdawg violates every cardinal rule of Chicago hot dogs and still serves one of the country's great tube steaks: (1) Superdawg serves a skinless all-beef hot dog (2) that isn't made by Vienna Beef and (3) uses a wedge of pickled green tomato instead of a fresh tomato slice. Yet instead of these three hot dog faux pas resulting in a strikeout, Superdawg serves up a hot dog home run—incredibly beefy, juicy, and smoky.

6 GENE AND JUDE'S
CHICAGO, IL

At Gene and Jude's, they have more trouble with punctuation than they do with their hot dogs—apostrophe placement and proper plural spellings confound them. (You'll find one sign saying "Gene and Jude's"; another, "Gene's and Jude's.") But when you get to Gene and Jude's you are not there to test their grammar or spelling—you're there for one of the best hot dogs in the country. You'll find aluminum bun warmers so that your bun is properly warmed, ceramic crocks for heating your natural-casing Vienna beef hot dog, and a guy slicing up potatoes for the fries. Ask for a single with your fries well done. One of the fellows on the assembly line will take one of the perfectly steamed buns, place one of the hot dogs in it, and top it with french fries, sport peppers (medium-hot, brined peppers), onions, relish, and mustard, and then salt the entire creation. One bite and you'll understand why Chicago is such an unbeatable hot dog town.

7 BEN'S CHILI BOWL
WASHINGTON, DC

Is the Ben's Chili Bowl half-smoke technically a hot dog? Who knows—and when something is this delicious, who cares? A quarter-pound, half-pork, half-beef smoked sausage is served on a warm steamed bun and topped with mustard, onions, and homemade chili sauce; Ben's half-smoke is a unique gustatory experience that hits the spot any time of the day or night. If you want a little extra crunch and snap in your half-smoke, have it split and grilled on request.

8 PINK'S
LOS ANGELES, CA

A Pink's chili dog is nearly perfect in every way: a steamed and then grilled natural-casing all-beef Hoffy brand hot dog, meaty chili, mustard, and raw onions. Pink's serves its hot dogs many different ways, and they offer hamburgers, too, but the quintessential Pink's meal is two chili dogs.

ed on hot dogs

I love hot dogs. And why not? At their best they're meaty, juicy, garlicky, and have a lovely snap. Of course, aficionados will read that description and rightfully conclude that I have a bias toward all-beef kosher-style hot dogs with natural casings. Kosher-style hot dogs—not kosher proper, which can no longer be made with natural casings, as the rabbis forbid that some years ago—always have a fair amount of garlic in them, and their natural casings give the dogs that snap. Such dogs are best griddled or char-grilled, and the hot dog buns are best toasted, or at the very least, heated.

Of course, my bias means that many hot dog styles are going to be left off my list of favorites. Fans of deep-fried Jersey hot dogs are going to be disappointed by my not including Rutt's Hut. Georgians will note that the Varsity and the Nu-Way weiners out of Macon are nowhere to be found. There are no Lucky Dogs from New Orleans, no franks from Connecticut (Swanky Franks, Rawley's, Super-Duper Weenie), Maine (Red's Eats), Alabama (Pete's Famous), or Detroit (All American and Lafayette Coney Island). They're all worthy and estimable examples of tasty wieners—but they're just not the hot dogs I dream about.

9 LET'S BE FRANK DOGS
SAN FRANCISCO AND LOS ANGELES, CA

A politically correct hot doggery started by Sue Moore, a former meat forager at Chez Panisse, Let's Be Frank serves a solid hot dog—natural-casing, uncured but smoked, all-beef. They're taut and delicious beauties tucked into griddled buns and served, if you wish, with grilled onions, organic sauerkraut, and an occasional mystery condiment whose ingredients Moore refuses to divulge.

10 BIKER JIM'S GOURMET DOGS
DENVER, CO

Truth be told, Biker Jim Pettinger's creations probably fall more into the sausage category than the hot dog one, but, like the half-smokes at Ben's Chili Bowl, we can overlook such a distinction thanks to the sheer deliciousness of these things. Biker Jim, a former repo man, excels in the field of wild-game sausage, with choices like the Alaskan reindeer sausage, buffalo, rattlesnake, elk jalapeño Cheddar, and "whatever else I feel like." He serves them from carts in downtown Denver, where they're split, cooked flame-grilled, and served to long lines of regular customers. Be sure to ask about any off-menu specials.

11 TOP DOG
OAKLAND AND BERKELEY, CA

There are four locations of Top Dog around Oakland and Berkeley, and Top Dog #4 is tucked into the entryway of a CVS pharmacy, as strange a place for a hot dog stand as we've ever seen. The Top Dog frankfurter is cradled in an oversized bun, like the type of roll you'd get with a Philly cheesesteak—but even though it seems like the wienie-to-wheat ratio would be all off, it isn't. That airy, perfectly toasted bun compresses perfectly around the dog, which we're told is a special blend made for the mini chain by Vienna Beef (natural-casing,

all-beef). And the additional bun space allows you to add a liberal helping of condiments from one of the most generous self-serve toppings bar we've ever seen.

12 BACON DOG CARTS
SAN FRANCISCO, CA

The late-night bacon dog carts of San Francisco's Mission District are an oasis and a mirage all at once. They provide after-midnight sustenance to legions of famished barhoppers, but like a desert vision, they always seem to be just on the horizon. It might take several attempts to find one on Mission Street, where they often appear between 16th and 24th Streets. Bacon-wrapped and then griddled on a portable flat-top cooker, the dogs are loaded with jalapeños, onions, ketchup, mustard, and mayo. They definitely hit the spot for the inebriated hipsters queued around the cart.

13 MONSTER DOGS
SEATTLE, WA

A caulking gun may not seem like it has any place among the accoutrements of a serious hot dog stand, but when it's filled with cream cheese it makes sense. How else are you supposed to apply this viscous condiment to a hot dog? That's right, it's a condiment—one that defines a Seattle-style hot dog. And it works. The mild sweetness of the cheese complements the smoky flavor of the

SHACK-CAGO DOG FROM SHAKE SHACK, NEW YORK, NY

flame-grilled beef franks. Try it as-is first, and then add a little barbecue sauce and hot mustard for full effect.

14 OKI DOG
LOS ANGELES, CA

Like the bacon dog carts in San Francisco, the Oki Dog is a study in excess that seems best suited for consumption after a bender, just before passing out. Oki Dog, which takes its name from owner Sakai "Jimmy" Sueyoshi's Okinawan heritage, became popular in its original location on Santa Monica Boulevard in the 1970s because it stayed open late. Folks leaving Hollywood's various night-clubs would stop in for one of its signature dogs before heading home. It's notable on this list for being the only hot dog that's not served in a bun. Instead, the Oki Dog comprises two franks wrapped in a tortilla, along with pastrami and chili cheese.

15 AQUI CON EL NENE
TUCSON, AZ

It's high noon and the sun beats down on a dusty gravel parking lot in north Tucson, Arizona. The temperature doesn't phase Tucsonans in the know, however, who line up at the little trailer where owner Salvador Gastelum and his crew dish out the finest example of the Sonoran dog that we've ever had. The Sonoran dog reportedly got its start in Mexico's Ciudad Obrégon, where *dogueros* began wrapping hot dogs in bacon and then cooking them on flat-top griddles. Served in a modified Mexican bolillo roll (small and soft), the meat is topped with freshly chopped onion, tomatoes, pinto beans, mayo, ketchup, and mustard—though topping bars often offer even more variety you can ladle on yourself. Gastelum opened his stand in 2004 after having worked at two of Tucson's celebrated Sonoran dog spots, BK Carne Asada and El Güero Canelo, which are good, too. But at Aqui con el Nene, the balance of all the ingredients is just right.

HOT DOG WITH MUSTARD AND ONIONS FROM CHARLIE'S FASHION HOT DOGS, NEW YORK, NY

sandwich exploration in new orleans

OYSTER PO' BOY AT DOMILISE'S, NEW ORLEANS, LA

A po' boy mission: fly to New Orleans, try 24 po' boys, fly out—all in under 10 hours. We'd had many of these sandwiches before, of course, even in the last year, but we wanted to experience them all in one fell swoop. Impossible? Nope. Just pure Serious Eats madness. It was a long, hot day, choreographed by Ed and our own Carey Jones and chauffeured by Pableaux Johnson, a freelance writer and photographer who had written the definitive New Orleans food guidebook that had the

DOMILISE'S, NEW ORLEANS, LA

horrible misfortune to be published the month before Hurricane Katrina struck. Poor timing aside, he's as good a tour guide as we've ever encountered.

Zimmer's Seafood was first: a beautifully classic shrimp po' boy on bread from Gendusa Bakery next door; fish po' boys we regarded just as highly. Dooky Chase, in Treme, had shrimp and oyster po' boys perfectly seasoned and fried (along with Creole gumbo that was downright transcendent) and Mr. Chase himself was there to charm us. Tracey's was next, the kitchen formerly at bar and po' boy shop Parasol's, with a phenomenal roast beef po' boy with pickles and mayo. Mahony's, on Magazine Street, is a sandwich shop with a hint of cheffiness, though owner Ben

Wicks's grandmother was right there in the shop with him, doing the sandwich running. Our favorite sandwich was a grilled shrimp and fried green tomatoes with remoulade—a downright inspired idea for a po' boy. (Best enjoyed with fries topped with beef-laden gravy.)

Domilise's classic po' boys blew us away—everything about the place seemed right; it wasn't faux funky, but real New Orleans funky, with Abita beer served by the bottle and the shop's sign perilously propped on the yellow walls outside. And we wrapped up the day at R&O's, enthusiastically endorsed by *New Orleans Times-Picayune*'s Brett Anderson. We dined at a park right on nearby Lake Pontchartrain—right near where one of the levees broke during Hurricane Katrina. The three sandwiches were sublime: the sesame-seeded po' boy rolls were a nice, unique touch; the roast beef was insanely beefy, salty, and gravy-laden; and the fried shrimp po' boy was deftly fried with a lovely crunch. It had already been a 20-plus po' boy day, so we had room for only a bite or two; we gave the rest of the sandwiches to a lone fisherman, who was thrilled to receive them.

Somehow it seemed right, eating our last po' boy on the shore of Lake Pontchartrain, five years after Katrina—R&O's was back, just feet from the water; Dooky Chase was back, in a flooded-out neighborhood; and though New Orleans took the greatest punch any hurricane ever delivered, it felt like the city was on its way back, too.

barbecue

I HAVE NO IDEA WHY THE PURSUIT OF **barbecue has loomed** SO LARGE IN MY LIFE FOR MUCH OF THE LAST 40 YEARS, but thoughts of barbecue BURN IN MY PSYCHE, low and slow, JUST AS A PORK SHOULDER SMOKES.

I DIDN'T GROW UP WITH THE STUFF.

As a New Yorker who grew up in a city suburb, my "barbecue" was the cured and smoked beef known as pastrami. And I certainly didn't have what writer Calvin Trillin says his father received from a rabbi in Joplin, Missouri—a barbecue easement that allowed him to consume copious amounts of pork ribs without violating Jewish dietary laws. (Though we did consume a fair amount of pork at our own nonkosher home.)

When I arrived for college at Grinnell, Iowa, in the fall of 1969, I started going to blues clubs in Chicago—many of which were on the South Side of the city, home to many of Chicago's best barbecue joints. That includes the venerable Lem's (page 200), which became my go-to place for ribs, rib tips, and links. When I would visit my brother and his wife in southern California, I would make a beeline for Gadberry's, a terrific Texas-inspired barbecue joint located in south-central Los Angeles. I also spent the summer of 1971 in San Francisco, and much of what I remember about that summer (besides going to a single concert featuring the Rolling Stones, Stevie Wonder, and Ike and Tina Turner, and losing the car door of my beloved robin's egg–blue Datsun when I opened it into a passing bus) was taking the money I won bowling and spending it on local barbecue.

Many of those who lived in the barbecue belts of this country always knew they had a good thing going—but when did the rest of the nation start to really embrace our meat culture as the treasure it is? In 1974, Calvin Trillin, a Missouri native, forever changed the barbecue landscape in this country when he wrote in *Playboy* (which of course we all read for the articles on food) that Arthur Bryant's, a Kansas City barbecue joint, was possibly "the single best restaurant in the world." I was enthralled by the very idea of Trillin's declaring that in such a humorous and elegantly written piece. In so doing he was not only calling national attention to Arthur Bryant's and according it proper respect—he in fact legitimized the passion of barbecue aficionados across the land.

Urban barbecue does exist in pockets outside the South and Midwest; when I returned to New York, one of the jazz musicians I worked with turned me on to Singleton's in Harlem, a South Carolina–style barbecue joint where you shoved your money under a bulletproof window to pay for some pretty good 'cue. But for the most part, my revelatory barbecue moments occurred on jaunts outside the city. My own first visit to Arthur Bryant's was in 1986, when I was in Kansas City on business—I told the executives that I'd be happy to bring dinner to the research facility for the focus group I was leading. They knew little of my master plan: picking up barbecue from Arthur Bryant's and twists from LaMar's Doughnuts. Need I add that those focus groups were a smashing success?

In recent years, even in regions without an indigenous barbecue culture, the entire nation has gone hog-wild for barbecue. Classically trained chefs and restaurateurs in big cities have traveled the nation sampling regional barbecue styles before opening restaurants that tried to replicate what they had found. Virgil's, Daisy Mae's, and Blue Smoke in New York; Memphis Minnie's in San Francisco; Redbones in Somerville, Massachusetts, outside Boston; and Red, White, and Blues in Washington, D.C., are just a few examples.

There are barbecue festivals and rib cook-offs all over the United States—in both big cities and small towns, attended by working folk and college-

RIBS AT RACK AND SOUL, NEW YORK, NY

fresh enthusiasts. More than a quarter-million barbecue-obsessed folks attend Memphis in May for the World Champion Barbecue Cooking Contest; hundreds of competition barbecue teams vie for $100,000 in prizes and supreme bragging rights. In the previously barbecue-starved New York City, several hundred thousand folks attend the Big Apple Barbecue Block Party every June to sample the food of some of the great pitmasters in America. And in Kansas City, there's the American Royal Barbecue Competition, called the "World Series of Barbecue." Barbecue is no longer a strictly local enterprise, confined by the traditions of a very particular region: it's an art and a craft we've all come to enjoy.

There's so much to love about barbecue culture. It's honest regional food cooked by larger-than-life characters, often equal parts pitmaster, yarn-spinner, and cultural wiseman. I'm thinking of Mike Mills, Ed Mitchell, as well as the late great Ray Robinson, Arthur Bryant, J.C. Hardaway—characters who appear through this chapter. Their food is real, it's emotionally resonant, it's connected to the place it's made, and it's seriously delicious.

So grab a beer and come along on a barbecue adventure: find out where we eat our favorite ribs and brisket, meet some of the great pitmasters of our time, and even learn how to replicate barbecue's greatest hits in your own kitchen or backyard.

WHAT IS BARBECUE?

This is a question with as many answers as folks who venture to ask it. First, the word can be used in many ways. We love long, warm evenings eating hot dogs, hamburgers, vegetables, even pizza, cooked on a gas or charcoal-fired grill outside—a cookout that can be called a barbecue. Some people would say that the act of grilling meat can be described as barbecuing. We won't venture an argument on whether the use of the word *barbecue* for a Weber-grill cookout is appropriate.

What we call barbecue throughout the book, however, refers to meat—usually pork, beef, chicken, or lamb—cooked slowly at a low temperature using a combination of direct and indirect heat in a smoker, pit, or covered grill. The heat source is ideally wood that's burned down to charcoal, but other people use some combination of gas, electricity, and wood chips with varying degrees of success.

Even once you've met those parameters, you'll find argument. Is meat slow-cooked by electricity or gas real "barbecue"? Or does the meat have to be smoked over wood or charcoal? Different people will give different answers—and, of course, you'll find regionalists all over the nation claiming that only western North Carolina chopped shoulder or Texas brisket is *true* barbecue; that all true barbecue has a vinegar sauce, or a mustard sauce, or a tomato sauce, or no sauce at all.

But at Serious Eats, we're equal-opportunity barbecue fans.

more on barbecue

I love one of Lolis Eric Elie's barbecue definitions in his book *Smokestack Lightning*: "Whenever pork and people come together, it's a safe assumption that the rich people will end up with the ribs, lips, foots, and chitterlings. Barbecue is largely the art of turning the bony, less desirable portions of the pig into something worth chewing the gristle for."

And Mike Mills, of 17th Street Bar & Grill (page 201), says, "Real barbecue is about smoke, seasoning, patience, and perseverance—along with a few secrets, of course. And maybe some tall tales and outright lies."

BARBECUE ACROSS THE COUNTRY

Many parts of America have strong indigenous barbecue cultures, but their similarities end there—some use the pig, some lamb, some cow; some use vinegar in the sauce, some mustard, some tomato; some cook a whole hog, some cook just a particular part of an animal.

Meat, sauce, and sides all distinguish one part of the barbecue world from another. How to make sense of all these different traditions? Here's our style guide.

ALLEN & SON, CHAPEL HILL, NC

north carolina

There are two major traditions in North Carolina barbecue, separated by Route 1, extending north and south from Raleigh. East of that Barbecue Divide, you'll find the Down East style, which is characterized by a vinegar-pepper sauce and cooking the whole hog. The pig is cooked low and slow over hickory before the meat is roughly chopped and served as a sandwich or on a plate or cardboard trays.

In western North Carolina, it's generally the Lexington style you're eating—just the pork shoulder (or its smaller first cousin, a Boston butt), pulled and then chopped up, with sauce based on tomato as well as vinegar. It's often topped with slaw and served on a bun.

south carolina

It's best known for whole-hog barbecue with mustard sauce, but South Carolina has three other sauce traditions, each in a different part of the state: tomato, ketchup, and vinegar-pepper. Sweatman's (page 200) in Holly Hill serves mustard sauce; Scott's Bar-B-Que (page 201) in Hemingway serves a vinegar-pepper sauce. Whole-hog barbecue in the state is often served in a cafeteria-style line, where you can ask for the various cuts:

"Despite differences over the definition of a word, it's all about who you're with, where you are, etc. It's all about sharing good times and good food with people we love. It's kinda like potato salad. Everyone's got their own take on it." —RossS

inside and outside meat, skin, or ribs, in whatever combination. At both Sweatman's and Scott's, and many other places, it's only served on weekends.

kentucky

Lamb or mutton is Kentucky's contribution to our barbecue conversation; it's generally served with burgoo, a spicy stew made with a form of pork or mutton and some combination of lima beans, corn, okra, and potatoes.

texas

In East Texas, barbecue is derived from Southern African-American and soul-food traditions—ribs and pork are prominently featured, but they also serve brisket, often heavily sauced and simmered after being smoked, until it falls apart like pot roast.

The central Texas traditions, on the other hand, are derived from Czech and German butchers and meat markets. Beef is king, here. You'll find brisket in all forms—both the leaner, dryer "first cut," or top half of the brisket, and the whole brisket, which includes a layer of fat between the two layers of meat. You'll also see clod (the shoulder of the cow), Flintstonian-size beef ribs, and sausage served with Saltines or white bread, plus pickles and raw onions. Sauce is irrelevant, unnecessary, and unbecoming of real central Texas barbecue. In fact, sauce is not even available at places like Kreuz Market (page 194) or Smitty's Market (page 194).

tennessee

In Memphis you'll find everything from two styles of ribs (dry and wet) to sliced or chopped pork sandwiches, to anomalies like barbecue spaghetti and barbecue bologna. Dry ribs are coated with a spice rub before they're cooked; wet ribs have been sauced before smoking.

Ribs can either be whole spare ribs, St. Louis–cut ribs (the spare ribs minus the rib tips), or even baby backs, which some barbecue purists scoff at (as they're leaner, with less delicious fat). We cer-tainly don't scoff, not after having Mike Mills's transcendent baby backs.

Dry rub involves a spice mixture crust that invariably includes paprika, salt, cayenne pepper, cumin, and garlic powder; wet ribs are all about the sauce. You'll also find sliced pork shoulder sandwiches in Tennessee, among other subspecialties. In central and western Tennessee, it's the whole hog plate or the pork sandwich. And just like in South Carolina, you'll find many weekend-only establishments. The Serious Eaters love B.E. Scott's in Lexington, Tennessee (page 201).

missouri

Kansas City is one of the capitals of American barbecue, and ribs, brisket, and burnt ends are its currency. Barbecue sauce really matters here—it's not just a way to add flavor to less delicious meat, it's integral to the experience of barbecue itself. Sides of choice? Beans with shards of meat and killer skin-on fries. Sides figure heavily in Kansas City barbecue culture. The Serious Eaters recommend LC's, Big T's, and Oklahoma Joe's.

St. Louis has a regional barbecue style all its own, with St. Louis pork ribs and barbecued pig snouts. Yep, the snouts. "Crispy snoots" are barbecued cartilaginous nostrils, which are usually cooked over an open grill until crisp and then smothered in sauce.

illinois

Chicago, particularly the South Side, has its own tradition of urban barbecue. Here, spicy sausages called hot links, ribs, and the fattier shortrib pieces called rib tips are cooked in what's known as an aquarium-style smoker. Meats are cooked over wood within long, rectangular boxes, with glass doors that open. That's how barbecue joints can create a smoky environment to cook the meat while smack in the middle of a major city. Rib tips are 2-inch square strips of chewy pork that have been cut from the lower end of the spareribs when St. Louis ribs are being cut. The Serious Eaters love Honey 1 BBQ, Uncle John's, and Lem's.

KANSAS CITY BBQ RIBS (SEE RECIPE, PAGE 190)

HOW DOES IT BURN?

Barbecue fans talk about the heat source used to make slow-smoked meat the same way pizza fans discuss the merits of coal, gas, and wood-fired ovens. Many, if not all, of the pitmasters we mention in this book are traditionalists who cook only with wood. Keith Allen of Allen & Son (page 202) in Chapel Hill, North Carolina; and Rodney Scott of Scott's Bar-B-Que (page 201) in Hemingway, South Carolina, even chop the wood themselves.

While we'll concur that wood that burns down into charcoal produces the best-tasting barbecue, we've also had plenty of mighty tasty 'cue cooked in gas-powered smokers flavored with wood chips, gas-and-wood combo smokers, electric smokers, and everything in between. It's said 'cue as good as the best of the wood-only pitmasters? No, it isn't, but it can definitely do the trick if you find yourself in a city or a part of the country that discourages the use of wood-only cooking.

new york barbecue

For the longest time New York was a barbecue wilderness, a place where 'cue freaks could hardly get a decent barbecue sandwich or plate of ribs. What happened to change this sorry situation? Restaurateur and barbecue lover Danny Meyer and one of his chefs, Kenny Callaghan, went on a cross-country barbecue tour in search of inspiration. Virgil's and Blue Smoke opened the New York barbecue floodgates. Now there seems to be a barbecue joint on every other corner of New York, including Daisy Mae's BBQ USA, opened by classically trained chef Adam Perry Lang; Hill Country; Dinosaur Bar-B-Que; and a list of places too long to mention. I enjoy eating at every one of these urban barbecue joints, but what's interesting is that each seems to be able to truly master only one kind of barbecue. At Daisy Mae's it's Lang's shortribs, at Dinosaur Bar-B-Que it's the spareribs, at Blue Smoke it's the beef ribs, and at Hill Country it's the moist brisket.

New York has even gotten into the barbecue festival act. The Big Apple Barbecue Block Party, hosted by the good folks at Blue Smoke, is a genuine New York happening. Every year 100,000 people come to

BURNT ENDS FROM RUB BBQ, NEW YORK, NY

BIG APPLE BARBECUE BLOCK PARTY, NEW YORK, NY

Madison Square Park and its surrounding streets and queue up for hours to sample the barbecue of some of America's greatest pitmasters, including Mike Mills (page 201), Chris Lilly (page 201), and the great Ed Mitchell, who cooks fifty whole hogs over wood on the streets of New York. Those hogs go into what is surely the best whole-hog barbecue sandwich that has ever been served up in New York City. Ed has a solid barbecue joint in Raleigh, North Carolina, called The Pit, but to sample the best of what Ed has to offer barbecue-wise, you're going to have to brave the lines at the Big Apple Barbecue Block Party, because that's where he works the whole-hog magic. He mixes some shoulder, belly, and loin, and—if you ask nicely—some crunchy skin into each sandwich. It's a barbecue buffet on a bun.

Normally we like our pulled pork plucked straight from a full-on smoker, but here we've hit on a way to make delicious pulled pork sandwiches using a covered charcoal grill. Do take the time to try the coleslaw. It really makes the sandwich.

pulled pork sandwiches
with coleslaw

MAKES 4 TO 5 POUNDS COOKED PORK; SERVES 8 TO 10

FOR THE PULLED PORK

3 tablespoons light brown sugar

3 tablespoons paprika

2 tablespoons chili powder

1 teaspoon garlic powder

2 teaspoons freshly ground black pepper

2 teaspoons ground coriander

1 tablespoon kosher salt

2 large slabs (about 7 pounds) rib-on, skin-on pork belly, 2 inches thick (see Note)

5 to 6 cups wood chips, soaked in water for at least 30 minutes

FOR THE SAUCE

1 cup cider vinegar

¼ cup light brown sugar, packed

2 tablespoons red pepper flakes

2 tablespoons hot sauce (such as Frank's)

2 teaspoons kosher salt

1 For the pulled pork: Mix the brown sugar, paprika, chili powder, garlic powder, black pepper, coriander, and salt in a small bowl. Set the spice mixture aside. Place both slabs of the belly on a cutting board rind side down and rub them evenly with one-fourth of the mixture on each slab. Pick up one slab and place it rind side up on the other slab to create a single 4-inch-thick slab of belly, with rind on both the top and the bottom. Using butcher's twine, secure the slabs tightly in this position. Rub the remaining spice rub on the exterior of the tied pork belly. (At this point, belly can be stored in refrigerator, uncovered, for up to 24 hours.)

2 Place a disposable aluminum baking sheet on the rack underneath one half of a charcoal grill. Ignite a large chimney starter half full with charcoal (about 50 coals). When the coals are mostly covered with gray ash, empty them onto the other half of the grill and arrange them into an even layer. Add 2 cups of soaked wood chips directly on top of coals. Set the cooking rack in place and cover the grill with the vents fully open until the wood begins to smoke heavily, about 5 minutes. Add the pork belly to the cool side of the grill, keeping it as far from the live coals as possible. Cover the grill.

3 Every hour, for 6 to 8 hours total, flip and rotate the belly, and add 12 coals and ½ cup of wood chips. Cook until the belly is tender enough to shred with a fork (the rind will be hard and crusty—check the sides of the belly for doneness). Remove it from the grill, tent with foil, and allow to rest for 30 minutes. While the pork is cooking, make the sauce and the coleslaw.

4 For the sauce: Combine the vinegar, brown sugar, red pepper flakes, hot sauce, and salt in a medium bowl. Whisk until the sugar is dissolved.

5 For the coleslaw: Combine the cabbage, onion, carrot, salt, vinegar, mustard, mayonnaise, sugar, and ground pepper in a large bowl and toss to combine. Allow the slaw to rest for at least 1 hour, covered in the refrigerator, then toss again. Adjust salt, pepper, and sugar to taste.

6 When the pork is done resting, use heatproof gloves or two forks to shred the meat into 1-inch pieces, discarding the bones, fat, and rind, if desired. Toss the pulled pork with the sauce to season to taste. Serve immediately on soft buns topped with coleslaw.

FOR THE COLESLAW

1 head green cabbage, cored and finely sliced or chopped (about 8 cups chopped)

1 medium red onion, finely sliced (about 1 cup)

1 large carrot, grated on large holes of box grater (about 1 cup)

1 tablespoon table salt, plus more to taste

6 tablespoons cider vinegar

1 tablespoon Dijon mustard

¾ cup mayonnaise

2 tablespoons granulated sugar

2 teaspoons freshly ground black pepper, plus more to taste

TO SERVE

8 to 10 soft buns

NOTE Look for two large slabs of pork belly with the rib bones and rind still attached. Pork shoulder can be substituted for the belly. Pork shoulder is often labeled "Boston butt" or "pork butt." Look for bone-in, skin-on shoulders, if using.

This is a south-of-the-border variation on the previous recipe. It's traditional to double up on corn tortillas when serving—wrap the pork, sauce, and condiments with a stack of two tortillas.

mexican-style pulled pork tinga

MAKES 4 TO 5 POUNDS COOKED PORK; SERVES 8 TO 10

FOR THE PULLED PORK

2 tablespoons dried oregano

3 tablespoons chili powder

1 tablespoon garlic powder

1 tablespoon cinnamon

2 tablespoons paprika

2 large slabs (about 7 pounds) rib-on, skin-on pork belly, 2 inches thick (see Note, page 183)

5 to 6 cups wood chips, soaked in water for at least 30 minutes

1 For the pulled pork: Mix the oregano, chili powder, garlic powder, cinnamon, and paprika in a small bowl. Reserve 2 tablespoons of the spice mixture. Place both slabs of the belly on a cutting board rind side down and rub them evenly with one-fourth of the remaining spice mixture on each slab. Pick up one slab and place it rind side up on the other slab to create a single 4-inch-thick slab of belly, with rind on both the top and the bottom. Using butcher's twine, secure the slabs tightly in this position. Rub the remaining spice rub on the exterior of the tied pork belly. (At this point, the belly can be stored in refrigerator, uncovered, for up to 24 hours.)

2 Place a disposable aluminum baking sheet on the coal rack underneath one half of a charcoal grill. Ignite a large chimney starter half full with charcoal (about 50 coals). When the coals are mostly covered with gray ash, empty them onto the other half of the grill and arrange them into an even layer. Add 2 cups of soaked wood chips directly on top of coals. Set the cooking rack in place and cover the grill with the vents fully open until the wood begins to smoke heavily, about 5 minutes. Add the pork belly to the cool side of the grill, keeping it as far from the live coals as possible. Cover the grill.

3 Every hour, for 6 to 8 hours total, flip and rotate the belly, and add 12 coals and ½ cup of wood chips. Cook until the belly is tender enough to shred with a fork (the rind will be hard and crusty—check the sides of the belly for doneness). Remove it from the grill, tent with foil, and allow to rest for 30 minutes. While the pork is cooking, make the sauce.

4 For the sauce: Heat the olive oil in a 10-inch stainless-steel skillet over medium-high heat until it shimmers, about 2 minutes. Sauté the diced onion and the chopped garlic until lightly browned, about 6 minutes. Add the chipotle chiles en adobo, tomato paste, chicken broth, red wine vinegar, and the 2 tablespoons of reserved spice mix. Cook, stirring often, until the sauce is reduced to 1 cup.

5 When the pork is done resting, use heatproof gloves or two forks to shred the meat into

1-inch pieces, discarding the bones, fat, and rind if desired. Toss the pulled pork with the sauce to season to taste.

6 To serve: Heat the tortillas. Preheat an 8-inch nonstick skillet over medium-high heat until hot. Working with one tortilla at a time, dip each tortilla in a medium bowl filled with water. Transfer the tortilla to the hot skillet and cook it until the water evaporates from the first side, and the tortilla is browned in spots, about 30 seconds. Flip the tortilla and cook until it is dry, about 15 seconds longer. Transfer the tortilla to a tortilla warmer, or wrap it in a clean dish towel. Repeat with the remaining tortillas.

7 Serve pulled pork immediately with warmed tortillas, any remaining sauce, chopped cilantro and onions, Mexican-style sour cream, and lime wedges on the side.

FOR THE SAUCE

2 tablespoons olive oil

1 medium onion, diced (1 cup)

3 garlic cloves, chopped

¼ cup canned chipotle chiles en adobo, chopped

¼ cup tomato paste

1 cup low-sodium chicken broth

2 tablespoons red wine vinegar

TO SERVE

30 to 40 corn tortillas

2 cups cilantro leaves, roughly chopped

2 large onions, finely diced (about 3 cups)

1 cup Mexican-style sour cream

6 to 8 limes, cut into wedges

the cuts

BEEF

BRISKET (WHOLE)
A cut of meat from the lower chest of an animal (in the barbecue world, when you hear about brisket, it'll almost always be beef). Used to make corned beef and pastrami, or smoked in Texas-style barbecue.

POINT CUT
Brisket can be divided into two parts; the richly marbled, fatty triangular section is called the deckle or the point cut.

FLAT CUT
The leaner section of the brisket, called the flat cut or the first cut.

BURNT ENDS
A specialty of Kansas City barbecue, burnt ends are irregularly cubed small cuts from the point half of the brisket, charred on at least one side.

CLOD
A cut of beef from the shoulder region, used in Texas barbecue.

BEEF RIBS
Flintstone-sized bones with lots of connective tissue attached. The chewy meat on them demands gnawing.

SHORTRIBS
The beef equivalent of spareribs; in the hands of a skilled pitmaster, they become irresistibly tender and juicy.

PORK

SPARERIBS Ribs taken from the side of the rib cage, spareribs are generally fattier than baby backs.

BABY BACK RIBS Taken from the top of the rib cage, between the spine and spareribs, baby backs are generally leaner than spareribs.

ST. LOUIS RIBS Slabs of spare ribs with the rib tips removed.

RIB TIPS Irregular strips cut from the lower ends of the spare ribs, with small sections of meat clinging to sections of cartilage.

SAUSAGES

HOT LINKS Coarse, spicy pork sausages typical of Chicago barbecue. Serious Eats writer Michael Nagrant once called them "sputtering sizzling red pepper–flecked garlicky smoked sausages"—that should give you an idea.

HOT GUTS A nickname for Elgin Hot Sausages, from Elgin, Texas; beef and pork sausages with red pepper and sage—so called because they tend to burst open at first bite.

THE 25 'CUE JOINTS WE CAN'T LIVE WITHOUT

1 OKLAHOMA JOE'S
KANSAS CITY, MO

Oklahoma Joe's occupies a building that was once a filling station—in fact, you can still get gas right next to the Oklahoma Joe's parking lot. Ignore the name. This is a Kansas City barbecue joint, though the ribs and brisket actually take a backseat to the barbecue chicken, which has gently smoked, succulent chicken meat that is surprisingly moist (even the white meat). Next to Big Bob Gibson's (page 201), it might have been the best barbecue chicken we've ever had. The spicy coleslaw is also great at Oklahoma Joe's (way better than the frozen seasoned fries—blasphemy, as far as we're concerned). And the onion rings are killer.

2 L.C.'S BAR-B-Q
KANSAS CITY, MO

While they have some problems with spelling, grammar, and punctuation at L.C.—"All orders Does Not include french fries or any side order," the sign says; "All Sandwich's come with fries"—they really know what they're doing when it comes to barbecue. The burnt ends at L.C.'s blew away any others we've ever had, within Kansas City or out. They're smoky, succulent, and supremely beefy, with a perfect meat-to-fat ratio and a wonderfully charred crust. If you want to know what a burnt

RIBS AT OKLAHOMA JOE'S, KANSAS CITY, MO

end is supposed to taste like, go to L.C.'s. The ribs are also excellent, again with the right meat-to-fat ratio and a seriously smoky flavor.

3 LOUIE MUELLER BARBECUE
TAYLOR, TX

Here's the drill at Louie Mueller's, as it's been done since 1949, when the first of three generations of Muellers (that would be Louie) opened his doors. When you get to the front of the line you are given a

big t's bbq

After a few stops on my Kansas City barbecue tour, I smelled like smoke, my rental car smelled like smoke, and I didn't care. I kept going, heading to Big T's—a recommendation from the valet at my hotel, Dave, who'd seen the barbecue leftovers in my trunk and laughed, "That's my kind of air freshener." I immediately trusted anything he had to say.

At Big T's, I saw a fire truck parked in front and a drive-through window; the entire parking lot was perfumed with smoke. Per Dave's instructions, I ordered the rib tips—along with a half rack of long side ribs, a beef sandwich, and some burnt ends.

While I was waiting for my food, I started talking about KC barbecue with a friendly couple—and boy, did they have opinions. "You never heard of Big T's? Damn, man, Big T's is the real deal. We like it better than L.C.'s, where the portions are small and the prices are too high. Arthur Bryant's is where all the movie stars and dignitaries go, and it's okay, but it's nothing compared to Big T's."

I told them how excited I was to be at Big T's, that I had come all the way from New York to try its 'cue. Another fellow waiting for his food chimed in: "All the way from New York? Well, that's good. Because now you in Kansas City, where a man can make a living working with his hands not working for the man. You can't do that in New York, can you? I don't think so. I moved here from Chicago, and I know you can't do it in Chicago."

It turns out that all my newfound KC friends—the couple, the handyman, and Dave the valet parker—were right. Big T's rib tips were amazing: equal parts crunchy crust, tender pork with just enough chew, and blissfully tasty pork fat. Its ribs and burnt ends were even smokier than L.C.'s (though they may have been too smoky). And Big T's sweet, gently spicy sauce made its sliced beef sandwich extremely tasty. Thanks, Dave—it's a trip I'm glad I made.

Kansas City is our favorite rib town, so we had to come up with a killer KC-style ribs recipe that could save us the time and the airfare a trip to Kansas City requires. These ribs have just the right combination of chew and tenderness.

kansas city
bbq ribs

**MAKES 2 FULL RACKS;
SERVES 4 TO 6**

FOR THE RIBS

¼ cup dark brown sugar, packed

3 tablespoons paprika

½ teaspoon cayenne pepper

2 teaspoons garlic powder

1 tablespoon freshly ground black
   pepper

1 tablespoon kosher salt

2 full racks pork spareribs
   (preferably St. Louis cut),
   trimmed of excess fat,
   membrane removed

2 cups apple cider vinegar

1 cup apple juice

3 cups wood chips, soaked in water
   for at least 30 minutes

1 For the ribs: Combine the brown sugar, paprika, cayenne pepper, garlic powder, black pepper, and kosher salt in a small bowl. Set aside 2 tablespoons of the mixture. Rub the remainder evenly over the ribs, working it into the meat with your hands. Combine the cider and apple juice in a 1-quart liquid measure.

2 Place a disposable aluminum baking sheet on the coal rack underneath one half of a charcoal grill. Ignite a large chimney starter half full with charcoal (about 50 coals). When the coals are mostly covered with gray ash, empty them onto the other half of the grill and arrange them into an even layer. Add 2 cups of soaked wood chips directly on top of the coals. Set the cooking rack in place and cover the grill with the vents fully open until the wood begins to smoke heavily, about 5 minutes. Add the ribs to the cool side of the grill, staggering them so that they are slightly overlapped. Cover the grill and cook, brushing the ribs with the apple cider mixture every 30 minutes. Every hour, for about 4 to 5 hours total, flip and rotate the ribs and add 12 coals. 2 hours into cooking, add the remaining cup of wood chips to the coals. Cook until the ribs are tender enough to pierce with a fork with little resistance, but are not quite falling off the bone.

3 For the sauce: Meanwhile, combine all the sauce ingredients in a medium saucepan along with the 2 tablespoons of reserved spice rub. Bring to a boil over high heat, reduce to a simmer, and cook until thickened and reduced to about 3 cups.

4 Brush the top side of the ribs with the sauce and return to hot side of the grill, sauced side down. Cook for

2 minutes. Meanwhile, brush the second side with the sauce. Flip the ribs and cook for a further 2 minutes. Repeat the saucing and flipping steps a total of three times until a thick layer of sauce is built up on the ribs. Remove the ribs, tent with foil, and allow to rest for 20 minutes. Paint with more sauce, and serve immediately, passing extra sauce tableside.

FOR THE SAUCE

2 cups low-sodium chicken broth

1 cup ketchup

¼ cup dark molasses

1 medium onion, grated on the large holes of a box grater (1 cup)

¼ cup Worcestershire sauce

1 tablespoon brown mustard

3 tablespoons dark brown sugar

¼ cup apple cider vinegar

⅓ cup tomato paste

2 teaspoons hot sauce (like Frank's)

We've never met an Asian spare rib we didn't love, so we had to include at least one version of an Asian-style rib. Five spices (star anise, fennel seed, cloves, cinnamon, and Sichuan peppercorns) plus a ginger glaze gives these ribs just the right balance of spice and sweet.

bbq spareribs
with five-spice rub and sticky ginger glaze

MAKES 2 FULL RACKS; SERVES 4 TO 6

FOR THE RIBS

3 tablespoons brown sugar

4 star anise

2 tablespoons fennel seeds

1 teaspoon whole cloves

1 tablespoon Sichuan peppercorns

1 cinnamon stick

2 full racks pork spareribs (preferably St. Louis cut), trimmed of excess fat, membrane removed

2 cups rice wine vinegar

3 cups wood chips, soaked in water for at least 30 minutes

1 For the ribs: In a spice grinder, grind together the brown sugar, star anise, fennel seeds, cloves, Sichuan peppercorns, and cinnamon until they are finely ground. Transfer to a small bowl. Set aside 1 tablespoon of the mixture. Rub the remainder evenly over the ribs, working it into the meat with your hands. Combine the rice wine vinegar and 1 cup of water in a 1-quart liquid measure.

2 Place a disposable aluminum baking sheet on the coal rack underneath one half of a charcoal grill. Ignite a large chimney starter half full with charcoal (about 50 coals). When the coals are mostly covered with gray ash, empty them onto the other half of the grill and arrange them into an even layer. Add 2 cups of soaked wood chips directly on top of the coals. Set the cooking rack in place and cover the grill with the vents fully open until the wood begins to smoke heavily, about 5 minutes. Add the ribs to the cool side of the grill, staggering them so that they are slightly overlapped. Cover the grill and cook, brushing the ribs with the rice wine vinegar mixture every 30 minutes. Every hour, for about 4 to 5 hours total, flip and rotate the ribs and add 12 coals. Two hours into cooking, add the remaining cup of wood chips to the coals. Cook until the ribs are tender enough to pierce with a fork with little resistance, but are not quite falling off the bone.

3 For the sauce: Combine all the sauce ingredients in a medium saucepan along with the 1 tablespoon of reserved spice rub. Bring to a boil over high heat, reduce to a simmer, and cook until thickened and reduced to about 3 cups.

4 Brush the top side of the ribs with the sauce and return to the hot side of the grill, sauced side down. Cook for 2 minutes. Meanwhile, brush the second side with the sauce. Flip the ribs and cook for a further 2 minutes. Repeat the saucing and flipping steps a total of three times, until a thick layer of sauce is built up on the ribs. Remove the ribs, tent with foil, and allow to rest for 20 minutes. Paint with more sauce, and serve immediately, passing extra sauce tableside.

FOR THE SAUCE

1 tablespoon grated fresh ginger

2 shallots, finely chopped

4 garlic cloves, finely chopped

1 cup low-sodium chicken broth

$\frac{1}{4}$ cup soy sauce

$\frac{1}{2}$ cup tomato paste

$\frac{1}{2}$ cup light brown sugar, packed

$\frac{1}{4}$ cup sherry

$\frac{1}{4}$ cup honey

$\frac{1}{2}$ cup hoisin sauce

$\frac{1}{2}$ cup ketchup

taste of brisket; you will be blown away. Order a quarter-pound of moist brisket, from the fattier, more tender end; watch as they grab it from the indoor pit (do not try this at home) and slice it. You should get a fine house-made beef sausage, made with beef, beef tallow (fat), and a natural casing—plus a slice or two of clod (beef shoulder) and maybe a beef rib. All of this glorious smoked meat will be served on a tray with white butcher paper. Sides are fine but unnecessary, except maybe a pickle or two; sauce is definitely superfluous.

4 SMITTY'S MARKET
LOCKHART, TX

The saga of Smitty's and Kreuz Market is complicated: "Kreuz Market" opened in 1900 and was purchased in 1948 by Edgar "Smitty" Schmidt; in 1999, Smitty's sons wanted to expand, but his daughter, who owned the building, stayed put. So now there's a new, bigger Kreuz Market elsewhere in Lockhart, while the original has been renamed Smitty's. But this just means there are now two phenomenal barbecue joints in Lockhart. Smitty's is smaller and feels much more personal, like a discovery. The brisket and clod just might be better than those at Louie Mueller's—which is really saying something.

5 KREUZ MARKET
LOCKHART, TX

In a new and much larger location, Kreuz Market could probably hold 400 barbecue lovers at any one time—but the barbecue doesn't seem to have suffered as a result. The moist brisket, the clod, and the sausage are all spot-on; the moist brisket, in particular, may be juicier here than at Smitty's, and their sausage is even better.

6 SOUTHSIDE MARKET
ELGIN, TX

You don't eat a Southside Market sausage so much as wear it—that's why old-time barbecue fanatics call them "Elgin hot guts." The fat that explodes when you bite into a sausage creates a new pattern on whatever shirt you're wearing. But it's hard to

mind, since the sausage—made with beef trimmings, beef tallow, salt, and cayenne pepper—is that good. Southside Market has been making Elgin hot guts since 1886. Ernest Bracewell Sr. bought the business in 1968, and now Bryan Bracewell, of the third generation, is carrying on the family barbecue tradition. He churns out 1 million pounds of sausage every month and serves some serious brisket and other pit-smoked meats at the restaurant and sausage-making facility they opened in 1992.

7 CITY MARKET
LULING, TX

While in much of Texas you're eating beef barbecue, the pork ribs at City Market are dynamite, pork ribs for the ages—crunchy on the outside, tender on the inside, with just the right amount of chew. And their sausages, while not as juicy as Southside Market's, are plenty flavorful and coarsely ground, just the way barbecue sausage should be.

8 SNOW'S
LEXINGTON, TX

Ever since *Texas Monthly* named Snow's the best brisket in Texas, we knew we had to make it out to Lexington. Of course, Snow's doesn't make it easy on 'cue lovers. They're only open one day a week, on Saturday, from 8:00 AM until the meat runs out. So we resorted to FedEx for our first and second (and third . . .) tastes of Snow's brisket. And even their mail-ordered brisket was everything we could hope for: well-marbled, juicy, and just smoky enough. It's also so salty you'll find yourself reaching for the water bottle, but as far as we're concerned, that just makes it tastier.

9 PIERSON & COMPANY BAR-B-QUE
HOUSTON, TX

The draw at Pierson & Company is that of East Texas African-American barbecue ribs by way of southwest Louisiana, which is where owner-pitmaster Clarence Pierson hails from. Ribs were meaty and porky, with just enough chew and just

To make a serious barbecue brisket in your own back-yard, use the fattier, more marbled pork cut of brisket, which essentially bastes the meat as it smokes.

barbecue **brisket**

1 For the brisket: Rub the meat evenly on all sides with salt, pepper, and sugar. Place the brisket on a rack set in a rimmed baking sheet and refrigerate, uncovered, for at least 1 hour and up to overnight.

2 Place a disposable aluminum baking sheet on the coal rack underneath one half of a charcoal grill. Ignite a large chimney starter two-thirds full with charcoal (about 65 coals). When the coals are mostly covered with gray ash, empty them onto the other half of the grill and arrange them into an even layer. Add 2 cups of soaked wood chips directly on top of the coals. Set the cooking rack in place and cover the grill with the vents fully open until the wood begins to smoke heavily, about 5 minutes. Add the brisket to the cool side of the grill, fat side up. Tent the brisket with foil and cook, adding 20 coals and 1/2 cup wood

chips every hour. Remove the foil tent after 4 hours. Continue cooking until the brisket shreds easily with a fork, 6 to 7 hours total. Transfer to a cutting board, tent with foil, and allow to rest 30 minutes.

3 For the sauce: Melt the butter in a medium saucepot over medium-high heat until the foaming subsides. Add the onion, garlic, and chili powder and cook, stirring constantly, until the onion is softened but not brown, about 3 minutes. Add the tomato sauce, Worcestershire sauce, brown mustard, dark molasses, cider vinegar, hot sauce, and cayenne to taste. Simmer for 10 minutes, until the sauce is slightly reduced. Set aside.

4 To serve: Slice the brisket using a carving knife into long, thin slices across the grain. Serve immediately with white bread, pickles, and sauce.

FOR THE BRISKET

1 whole point-cut brisket, 5 to 6 pounds (see Note)

2 tablespoons kosher salt

1 tablespoon freshly ground black pepper

1 tablespoon sugar

6 cups wood chips, soaked for at least 30 minutes

FOR THE SAUCE

2 tablespoons unsalted butter

1 medium onion, finely diced (1 cup)

3 garlic cloves, finely chopped

2 tablespoons chili powder

1 (14.4-ounce) can tomato sauce

2 tablespoons Worcestershire sauce

2 tablespoons brown mustard

1/4 cup dark molasses

3/4 cup cider vinegar

1/4 cup hot sauce

Cayenne pepper to taste

TO SERVE

High-quality sliced white bread

Pickles

NOTE We prefer the fattier point cut of brisket, but if using a flat cut, reduce the cooking time by about 2 hours.

RIBS AT HONEY 1 BBQ, CHICAGO, IL

enough fat; the juice-oozing beef links are equally good, perfect for those who want their sausage without spice. But whatever meat you're ordering up, be sure to partake of the brilliant invention that is the smooth, creamy mashed potato salad.

10 THELMA'S
HOUSTON, TX

Everyone loves to eat at Thelma's, from cops to carefully coiffed folks in suits and ties to neighborhood denizens who know what a treasure they have. Thelma herself is a grinning force of nature at the bunkerlike barbecue joint and soul-food restaurant. She cooks, takes orders, and presides over the dining room with supreme authority. My local expert, Texas food man Robb Walsh, told us to order both inner and outer brisket—while the inner meat was a little more moist, the outer meat had an excellent crunch, and together, the two made a most satisfying plate of food. Thelma's thin-crusted fried catfish was a revelation, almost good enough to distract us from the barbecue.

on barbecue and domestic harmony

My dear wife, Vicky, likes barbecue well enough, but doesn't share my boundless enthusiasm for it. Yet she succeeded in using my passion to meet her own cultural needs—when we embarked on a South Carolina barbecue and historic homes and gardens tour. Never heard of such a thing? Well, we developed the itinerary together, based on one fundamental tenet: every barbecue joint I dragged her to had to be offset by a visit to a historic home or garden. I'm sure Vicky remembers Middleton Place Plantation and Garden rather fondly. Me, I can't forget the 'cue, hash, and ribs we had from the buffet line at Duke's in Summerville.

HOT LINKS AT LEM'S BAR-B-Q, CHICAGO, IL

UNCLE JOHN'S BARBECUE, CHICAGO, IL

11 FRANKLIN BARBECUE
AUSTIN, TX

Generally, the best barbecue tends to come from the old guard—institutions that have been revered for decades. But Aaron Franklin's barbecue breaks all the rules. It's in Austin proper, not out in small-town Texas; it only opened a storefront in 2011; its owner is under 35; it's making brisket so good that fifty-person lines form an hour before it even opens. (The brisket is so tender and fatty that we call it "barbecue confit.") Franklin learned to cook barbecue from his grandfather and, after working at John Mueller's in Austin, purchased that restaurant's smoker to start his own business. After a year selling out of a trailer, he opened Franklin Barbecue, where he reigns behind the counter, slicing up remarkably juicy sausage, smoked turkey on some occasions, and his renowned brisket: as tender as that cut can get, with a melty, supple fat layer that tastes of pure meat and smoke in a way that can only be achieved with classic low and slow heat.

12 HONEY 1 BBQ
CHICAGO, IL

As you approach Honey 1, the smoke hits you while you're still a few blocks away. (There's nothing like a preview of coming attractions.) "The smoke is no joke" is their motto, and they're not kidding. All the meats are cooked in an aquarium smoker (page 178) and they emerge as juicy and smoky as any first-class barbecue we know. The ribs keep a little bit of chew and a spectacular crust, cooked until a little bit soft but still clinging to the bone; everything comes with sweet, piquant but gently spicy barbecue sauce on top. Honey 1 is not on the South Side, but it's of the South Side, and it's as soulful as any barbecue joint we know.

13 UNCLE JOHN'S BARBECUE
CHICAGO, IL

Mack Sevier is the pitmaster at Uncle John's on Chicago's South Side, and though his ribs and rib tips are transcendent, it is his hot links that have made him famous. Serious Eats contributor Michael Nagrant once described Sevier's links as "the bastard love child of a kielbasa and a pepperoni stick." There's nowhere to eat it, but no one will look twice if you use the hood of your car for the purpose.

on the pitmaster

Pitmasters are the good folks who actually care for your barbecue as it's cooking, hour after hour. Some own their own joints, of course, but others toil in the background—the unsung heroes of barbecue, with less ink, less adulation. They stay up all night tending the fire and the flesh, and it's diligence that gives us the miraculous fusion of smoke and meat that we eat when we go to a great barbecue joint.

There are legendary pitmasters, like the late Arthur Bryant, who became justifiably famous in their lifetime—and then there were pitmasters like Memphis's J.C. Hardaway, who plied their craft in the shadows, in modest joints and restaurants and bars where only the locals went. Hardaway cooked for years at Hawkins Grill in Memphis before it was sold, and then spent his last barbecue cooking days around the corner at the Big S Grill, which is where *Smokestack Lightning* author Lolis Eric Elie took me one sultry October day.

I remember walking back into the kitchen and ordering our barbecue sandwiches from Mr. Hardaway. His already smoked pork shoulder was sitting on the grill wrapped in tin foil. I was not overly optimistic that anything resembling barbecue greatness could come from that pork wrapped in tin foil—but one bite and all my doubts disappeared. Lolis describes what we found:

"As Al Green or Albert King or Frankie Beverly played on the jukebox, J.C. cut a few slices and set them to warm on the grill. On the same grill, he toasted the hamburger buns. While the meat cooked, he splashed them with barbecue sauce from an old Palmolive dish-detergent bottle. The meat was then placed on a worn chopping board, chopped with a dull clever, placed on the toasted bun, topped with a mayonnaise-based coleslaw, cut in half, stuck with a toothpick, and served. J.C.'s hot sauce is hot, but there is flavor beneath the pepper and the overall experience brings a smile to the tongue. It is the sort of sandwich that makes you begin debating halfway through it, whether you should order a second so that it will be ready the moment you finish the first. In J.C. Hardaway, the shoulder sandwich has discovered its Stradivarius."

Next time you go to the Skylight Inn in Ayden, North Carolina, ask if you can meet James Henry Howell; shake his hand and tell him you're a fan. Do the same at whatever joint you visit. They'll appreciate the acknowledgment—and you may appreciate the barbecue even more.

RIBS AT LEM'S BAR-B-Q, CHICAGO, IL

14 LEM'S BAR-B-Q
CHICAGO, IL

Strictly take-out, Lem's is of those places where you slide your money under a bulletproof window to pay, but the vibe is always loose and friendly. Rib tips here are the thing to get, but the ribs (cut all the way to the bone) and the links are also worth an order—though those links are a bit more variable. They perk up quite a bit with the sauce; it's more vinegary than sweet, and even the mild carries quite a kick.

15 SWEATMAN'S BBQ
HOLLY HILL, SC

Step up to Sweatman's and you'll take part in a whole hog buffet featuring hash, slaw, cracklins, ribs, and every kind of pig part you can imagine. The hogs are cooked over oak, hickory, and pecan wood, imbuing the flesh with smoky flavor. They separate the pork into light and dark portions, tender inner portions of the hog, or greasy, slightly chewy meat from the edges. Sweatman's is so good you will contemplate paying for a second meal just to go through the buffet line again.

16 MARTIN'S BAR-B-QUE JOINT
NASHVILLE, TN

One of the single greatest bites of food you can possibly put in your mouth is the pork belly Patrick Martin plucks from his pigs—which might well be cooking for more than 17 hours. It's barbecue crack, plain and simple. Patrick Martin is a throwback: he has great passion for real barbecue and the entire culture thereof. He is a firm believer in the power of combining smoke, wood, and meat to create magic. And even more important, the man can cook—as one bite of that pork belly, his pulled pork, or his ribs will show you.

17 SCOTT'S BAR-B-QUE
HEMINGWAY, SC

Scott's is a family affair. From Monday to Wednesday, it's a country grocery store; on Thursday, Friday, and Saturday, it becomes a truly extraordinary barbecue joint. Rodney Scott slow cooks whole pigs on hardwood charcoal that's been burned down from wood that Rodney and company collect from all over his neck of the woods. The menu is really simple—pig, all parts—but it's perfectly seasoned and smoked and made into something absolutely unforgettable, thanks in no small part to the sauce. Serious Eats barbecue correspondent James Boo described it as "a mighty two-step of pepper, then vinegar; in a region where vinegar, then pepper is the norm. It was the perfect complement that sauce should be, introducing a forward tang with a hefty pitch of heat behind it."

18 B.E. SCOTT'S BARBECUE
LEXINGTON, TN

"Ricky Parker hasn't had a good night's sleep since 1989," food writer John T. Edge once wrote about the pitmaster at B.E. Scott's. That's because he tends to the whole hogs that cook in his two pits all night. But that sleep deprivation is the only way to produce this kind of pig, giving you a pork sandwich that's simultaneously crunchy, tender, sweet, and just smoky enough. Get some sleep, Ricky—you deserve it.

19 COZY CORNER BBQ
MEMPHIS, TN

In his book *Smokestack Lightning,* Lolis quotes Memphis singer Ruby Wilson on Cozy Corner: "Now, they can sweat you some meat over there." Yes they can, Ruby. Though other Memphis barbecue joints are more famous than Cozy Corner, it's the one place we have to visit in the city. Ray Robinson Sr. put barbecue Cornish game hens on the map in the barbecue world. They're so tasty you'll think they deserve a place in the barbecue pantheon alongside pulled pork, brisket, and hot links. They'll even serve you a barbecued bologna sandwich, or truly excellent rib tips. Robinson's son tends the joint now, but it's just as good as ever.

20 BIG BOB GIBSON BAR-B-Q
DECATUR, AL

Chris Lilly has become a rockstar pitmaster. He's hosted barbecue television shows and is asked for autographs everywhere he goes—but the fame is well deserved. His championship pork shoulder, which is injected with a blend of mystery spices and liquids before it's cooked, is the pulled pork sandwich all others should be judged by. The exterior meat has a crunchy, blackened crust, while the interior flushes a smoke-tinged reddish pink. Big Bob Gibson also makes extraordinary barbecue chicken—with skin that's miraculously tasty and crisp, and breast meat that's succulent and well smoked, it's the rare barbecue chicken that can hold its own against the other meats. The coup de grace is the ridiculously tasty mayonnaise-based white barbecue sauce, which tastes like the best "white sauce" you would ever order on a gyro or souvlaki sandwich.

21 17TH STREET BAR & GRILL
MURPHYSBORO, IL

Mike Mills, of 17th Street Bar & Grill, is such a great yarn-spinner and barbecue raconteur that he could make a good living on the lecture circuit if he ever got tired of making barbecue. But we're grateful that he's still making serious 'cue. Though Mills has a way with slow-cooked meats of every variety, baby back ribs are his thing. Some barbecue purists deride baby backs as not fatty and porky enough, but in Mills's hands, they develop a lovely outer crust suffused with flavor from his paprika-spiked magic dust dry rub, and that crust has just enough chew to let you appreciate the tender inside bites even more.

allen & son

Barbecue snobs are always talking up the Allen & Son in Chapel Hill and talking trash about the Pittsboro, North Carolina, barbecue joint of the same name. But the Pittsboro location is the original Allen & Son. Keith Allen then sold that location to a longtime employee and pitmaster when he opened the Chapel Hill joint in the following years. At Pittsboro, they use an electric smoker to cook shoulders with some direct heat for a surprisingly short amount of time. It's a troubling description for a barbecue purist, but the barbecue sure is good—as are the hush puppies and the coleslaw. Keith Allen stays true to his traditionalist roots at Chapel Hill. In the end, Chapel Hill is a better barbecue joint, but I will tell you that Pittsboro isn't bad at all.

What's the future of endeavors like the Chapel Hill joint? I worry about that. Last time I was at Allen & Son I asked my friendly, fresh-faced server if Keith Allen still chops his own wood and makes everything from scratch. "He still does," the server answered. "I can tell you that I wouldn't do it." We hope that when Allen steps down, somebody else will step up!

22 ALLEN & SON
CHAPEL HILL, NC

Keith Allen is a barbecue purist of the highest order. He still uses wood to cook his barbecue, he still splits his own logs to fire the smoker, and he still makes all his side dishes and desserts from scratch—everything from french fries to banana pudding to vanilla ice cream. And the food that results is outstanding. Allen takes whole pork

shoulders, cooks them in back of his restaurant for hours and hours, using wood that burns down to charcoal. His barbecue is so juicy, so porky, so flavorful it soaks through the oversized bun it's usually served on. What you get on your plate is the luck of the draw here, since you can't specify or request outside meat or coarsely chopped or skin when you order—but have faith because every part of the pig is astoundingly good. And it's okay if you ask nicely for a piece of crunchy pig skin; they do sell it by the piece, so they will grant that request.

23 SKYLIGHT INN
AYDEN, NC

The late, great pitmaster Pete Jones, who opened the Skylight Inn in 1948, put a rather funky rendition of the U.S. Capitol dome on the roof of the joint when *National Geographic* declared it the barbecue capital of the world in 1984. Pete died in 2006, but his nephew Jeff and his son Bruce still uphold the same standards they learned from Pete, and pitmaster James Henry Howell cooks whole hogs all night over hickory and oak. Each cardboard tray you're served holds a transcendent array of pig, with plenty of creamy, succulent inside tenderloin meat, crispy outer meat, and little bits of crispy skin. It's all topped by a finely chopped, just vinegary enough coleslaw, and accompanied by an old-fashioned piece of flat cornbread made with pork drippings. There is a peppery vinegar sauce available as a condiment at Skylight, but a sandwich here needs none of it.

24 LEXINGTON BARBECUE NO. 1
LEXINGTON, NC

There's a lot to make sense of at Lexington Barbecue. That's the name on the menu and on the huge sign outside; but the natives call it either Lexingon Barbecue 1 (there used to be a Lexington Barbecue 2 run by founder Wayne Monk's brother, but it's long gone) or HoneyMonk's (because Wayne Monk was apparently quite the ladies' man in high school). So if you get lost trying to find Lexington

PORK SANDWICH AT ALLEN & SON, CHAPEL HILL, NC

the wilber's sandwich run

A few years ago my wife and I were invited down to a pig picking—a celebratory feast built around slow-cooking a whole pig, and picking the meat right off the animal—in Willow Springs, a tiny town a few miles east of Raleigh, North Carolina. Our hosts, the wonderful mystery writer Margaret Maron and her husband, Joe, thought I was more than a little nuts when at 11 AM I asked Joe if he wanted to drive to Wilber's Barbecue—*while* we waited for his two-hundred-pound pig to be smoked. Being an extraordinarily gracious fellow, he came along, and we soon found ourselves eating one of the best barbecue sandwiches I'd ever had. We got another one for the road—on our way back to his place to consume a lot more barbecue.

Barbecue (and you will), ask for either Lexington Barbecue 1 or Honeymonk's. Then, once you're actually there, what you should order can't be found on the menu. It's the outside meat you'll want to try, which comes from the exterior of the smoked and slow-cooked pork shoulders, which have spent up to nine hours over coals of hickory and oak. Throw in coleslaw and a big slice of skin and you'll have a barbecue meal to rival any.

25 WILBER'S BARBECUE GOLDSBORO, NC

Wilber Shirley and his current pitmaster (heir to the late, great Ike Green) cooks whole hogs in back of his restaurant, over wood that his pitmaster burns down to charcoal. Put those chopped-up hogs on a bun, and you'll have one of the best barbecue sandwiches in the land. Because Wilber's sandwiches are made with the whole hog, each bite has just the right combination of crunch and tenderness.

street food

IT FITS PERFECTLY INTO THE **serious eats ethos:** OUR DESIRE TO FIND TASTY, ACCESSIBLE, SOULFUL FOOD at every turn, FOR EVERYONE TO ENJOY.

STREET FOOD IS PARTICULARLY NEAR AND DEAR TO OUR HEARTS AT SERIOUS EATS—FOR MANY REASONS.

At its best, street food is delicious, relatively inexpensive, and the product of one person's endless dedication. And though street food has become terribly trendy in some parts of America of late, with crowds in New York and Los Angeles following vendors on Twitter and lining up for lunch, I have long felt an intense personal connection to it. In fact, street food runs in my family. My grandmother made ends meet in the 1920s and '30s on New York's Lower East Side by selling pickles out of a wooden barrel. In the dead of winter, that couldn't have been an easy way to make a living. I have always thought that pickle brine courses through my veins—no wonder I have such a soft spot in my heart (and stomach) for street fare.

Even now, in the twenty-first century, street food is still largely the province of immigrants selling the foods of their homeland to recent arrivals—as well as to others, who are attracted to the appealing sights and scents, the reasonable prices, and the romance of eating on the street. But it is no longer exclusively so. Street food has gone mainstream and upscale—way beyond pickles, hot dogs, and tacos. Immigrants now share the sidewalks with both young entrepreneurially minded chefs and other young upstarts, drawn by the relative ease of taking their food dreams to the streets.

And from that start, many street vendors did graduate from street vending to renting a storefront—like Joel Russ, the founder of the great appetizer and smoked fish store Russ & Daughters, in New York's Lower East Side. And this progression is still taking place a hundred years later, with carts like Calexico in New York and the Kogi BBQ truck in Los Angeles opening storefronts.

Where did street food go from the pickle barrel? Ice cream trucks, hot dog and pretzel carts, and coffee and danish carts immediately come to mind. Ice cream trucks, both Good Humor and the independents, began to crop up on the streets of New York and elsewhere in the late 1940s and '50s. On the street where I grew up, in the shadow of

TACOS FROM MARINATION MOBILE, SEATTLE, WA

Kennedy Airport, two trucks would appear, though never simultaneously. Our go-to on Adele Road, though, was an independent ice cream truck driven by Smitty, a World War II vet who seemed to genuinely love his job. Smitty was awesome. He extended us mini lines of credit when we needed it—that's major when you're ten years old. Also, he was willing to split Popsicles and sell half for a nickel. (No wonder we were so loyal to Smitty.)

In the 1970s, when I started working for the New York City Parks Department, the street food vendors were my go-to lunch option. I ate hundreds of all-beef Sabrett franks, and my friend Bob and I

managed to find carts that grilled hot dogs instead of having them sit in that pool of dirty water. We soon found carts serving chicken with rice plates, manned by Bangladeshi and Pakistani immigrants.

Mister Softee soft ice cream trucks have long been peddling their drippy wares across the Northeast—but in the twenty-first century, you'll find even *those* a little more dressed up. Doug Quint founded New York's Big Gay Ice Cream Truck in 2009, from which he sells Mister Softee soft-serve with creative toppings like toasted curried coconut and young ginger syrup and wasabi pea dust. Doug has no food background—he's a classical bassoonist

> "How else can you eat three meals a day for $10?—not even Rachael Ray can manage that." —femmebot

and a candidate for a doctorate of musical arts degree from the CUNY graduate center. But in his off hours, he started the Big Gay Ice Cream Truck with his partner, Bryan Petroff, for some of the same reasons my grandmother started selling pickles—to make a living that allows you to be your own boss. In Doug and Bryan's case, there's the added appeal of gaining an outlet for creativity.

Today, immigrants still run many food carts and trucks, but these days the immigrants come from so many other countries—Pakistan, Egypt, Mexico, Puerto Rico, the Dominican Republic, Senegal, Ecuador, China—and they're still working insanely hard. As one of my favorite street chefs, Mohammed Rahman of New York's Kwik Meal, told me, "Here I get to make my food the way I want it, sell it at half the price I'd have to sell it for in a restaurant, nobody yells at me, and I get to spend my evenings at home with my family. God bless America."

And while enterprising upstarts may still be selling on the streets, these days you are just as likely to find your food truck manned by trained chefs. In the pre-celebrity chef days, long before Food Network, chefs toiled in an arduous, structured, hierarchical work environment, slowly working their way up the ranks while frequently enduring verbal abuse. Only after putting in many years could they perhaps strike out on their own.

Naturally, many talented chefs bridled at this system, like Roy Choi. Choi left his kitchen job at an upscale restaurant in southern California and decided to jump off the restaurant circuit; he took whatever savings he had and started a food truck in Los Angeles, making and selling his own unique fusion of Mexican and Korean cuisines. He quickly became a culinary phenomenon with a burgeoning empire that includes four trucks and a casual restaurant. He's inspired line cooks all over the country to follow suit—much to the delight of eaters everywhere.

Street food now garners major media attention: terrific blogs like Zach Brooks's "Midtown Lunch" (covering New York, Philadelphia, and Los Angeles) are devoted almost entirely to street food, and there's even an annual award ceremony—the Vendy Awards, in New York, Philadelphia, and Los Angeles—honoring the best in the business. Today, it's easy to eat well on the street and, thanks to the recipes in this chapter, to replicate those good eats at home.

20 FAVORITE STREET-FOOD STOPS

MARINATION MOBILE, SEATTLE, WA

We're supporters of street food everywhere—but not all carts are created equal. Here are some of our favorites from across the nation.

1 NONG'S KHAO MAN GAI
PORTLAND, OR

In Thai, *khao* means "rice" and *gai* means "chicken." The cart's namesake chicken and rice dish is the only thing they serve (though you can get additions like chicken liver and fried chicken skin). It comes bundled in white butcher paper along with

BIRYANI CART, NEW YORK, NY

a cup of broth, cilantro leaves, cucumber coins, and a small tub of brown sauce (which packs a wallop of ginger, garlic, vinegar, and chile). Though simple, the dome of still-steamy white rice and the pile of poached chicken with all the fixins are the perfect harmony of healthy, homey Asian flavors. The Bangkok-born proprietress, nicknamed Nong, ate a lot of this popular street food in her native Thailand before bringing it to Portland.

2 MARINATION MOBILE
SEATTLE, WA

Since Kamala Saxton and Roz Edison sent their cheery truck out into Seattle's lunchtime streets in 2009, they've gained quite a following for their Hawaiian-inflected, Asian-meets-Mexican fusion fare—like Spam sliders and miso-ginger chicken tacos. Anything you order will be fresh and tasty and nicely spiced, but if there's one thing you shouldn't miss, it's the kimchi fried rice bowl: a healthy scoop of rice absolutely laden with crunchy, fiery kimchi, big chunks of cabbage and spice permeating every bite, with a jiggly fried egg on top. It's even better with a meat topping, like the kalbi beef you can pile on top.

3 BIRYANI CART
NEW YORK, NY

Opened in 2004 by Meru Sikder, a former banquet chef for a New Jersey Hilton, the Biryani Cart started off as a standard Midtown Manhattan

with gyro meat or spicy chicken tikka marinated in yogurt and spices. Now his cart is covered with media clippings and two nominations from the Vendy Awards, the city's street-food Oscars, and he's opened a second cart right next to the first that sells the kati rolls until the wee hours.

4 THE BIG EGG
PORTLAND, OR

You don't expect a breakfast wrap to be this good—but at this yolk-colored cart run by Gail Buchanan and Elizabeth Morehea, at the Mississippi Marketplace pod (one of many street-food lots in Portland), they're good enough to eat every morning. Unwrap the foil to unleash a steamy, just-grilled tortilla filled with grilled portabello mushrooms, perfectly seasoned and crispy potato chunks, scrambled eggs, roasted red peppers, creamy fontina cheese, poblano salsa, and a refreshing drizzle of yogurt-lime sauce, the magic stuff that ties it all together.

5 BUTTERMILK TRUCK
LOS ANGELES, CA

There's something really lovable about this breakfast and late-night truck, which scoots its way around Los Angeles. First off, owner and French Culinary Institute grad Gigi Pascual is not afraid to use buttermilk. It's part of what makes her red-velvet silver-dollar pancakes so scarfable. The other part is the cream-cheese maple butter—essentially frosting—to complete this excuse to eat pancake-shaped cupcakes for breakfast. The buttermilk love extends to her biscuits, which are baked fresh inside the truck daily, then griddled to get those golden-buttered edges. Those biscuits sandwich a fried egg, cheese, and your choice of applewood-smoked bacon, chicken-apple sausage, or tocino, the Filipino version of lardons.

6 TÁBOR
PORTLAND, OR

It's tough to wrap your mouth around the Schnitzelwich, a Frisbee-size, super-crispy breaded pork cutlet that dwarfs the ciabatta sandwiching it. (The

WRAP FROM THE BIG EGG, PORTLAND, OR

chicken-and-rice cart—with a small twist. Whereas most carts serve only chicken with creamy and hot sauces and rice, Sikder would always have one Indian dish as a special—alternating between chicken tikka masala and chicken biryani. He built up a loyal lunchtime fan club, but business really exploded in 2007 when he started serving kati rolls, something like an Indian burrito. The rolled-up chapati, a chewy unleavened flatbread, gets filled

r.i.p. bloop: on the transience of street carts

Since we started researching this book, one of our very favorite finds—Bloop, an all-oatmeal cart in Portland, Oregon—has, unfortunately, left the streets; the lease on the truck they shared with fellow food operator Sonny Bowl ran out in February 2011.

But we still couldn't help but tell you about it. The technical definition of *bloop,* according to the cart's founder Kat Clark, is the sound oatmeal makes. (Her niece coined the term.) The morning-only cart went through 25 pounds of rolled oats a week, usually sourced from Portland local company Bob Red Mill. That's a lot of blooping!

It breaks our hearts that Bloop is no longer open in the mornings, selling delicious oatmeal to the people of Portland—but transience is just part of the magic of street carts. It's a bittersweet thing: one day, they're selling you a sandwich; the next, they've closed up and rolled away. Every day they appear is a day to be thankful for.

the vendy awards in nyc (and beyond)

Street food has come a long way since 2001, when Sean Basinski, a Georgetown law grad and Fulbright fellow, founded the Street Vendor Project in New York City as a way to provide legal representation and advocacy to immigrant vendors. Over the years, those vendors have become more tech-savvy and arguably more imaginative. Basinski organized the first Vendy Awards, the Oscars of street food, in 2004. The delicious competition brings together the best vendors from all over the five boroughs; nominees are chosen through an online voting system, and

the winner is selected by Vendys attendees and a team of "celebrity judges." "Vendors are traditionally immigrants and outsiders and underdogs," Basinski said. "I have always been inspired by how hard they work and struggle, asking for nothing more than the right to carry out a small business in public space." The Vendys fervor has spread to Los Angeles, which held its inaugural competition in 2010, and to Philadelphia in 2011.

SANDWICH FROM TABOR, PORTLAND, OR

BURGER FROM SKILLET STREET FOOD, SEATTLE, WA

same goes for the chicken cutlet and fried porto-bello alternatives.) And all of them squirt bright crimson ajvar (an eastern European paprika spread), sour creamy horseradish, and caramelized onions everywhere. Monika and Karel Vitek, both originally from the cart's namesake town in the Czech Republic, also serve goulash—heavy on the herbs, with caraway seeds and Hungarian paprika swimming in there; big doughy spaetzle lumps sit on top for soaking. Look for the "Czech out the Czech food" sign on this red hut and listen for the Bohemian polkalike beats.

7 GARDEN STATE
PORTLAND, OR

Over 2,500 miles from his New Jersey homeland, Kevin Sandri makes his mom's old-school Sicilian food using ingredients from Oregon's Willamette Valley, such as the grass-fed beef he uses to make his mama's meatballs, which come piled in a Philly-style hoagie roll with homemade marinara and melted provolone. ("I wanted the bread to be big and cheap, not artisanal," he told us.) It's satisfying in the same way a huge, cheesy slice of lasagne is. It's not the daintiest thing to eat—and neither is the delicious chickpea fritter sandwich he serves on aioli-swiped bread from Portland's Fleur de Lis bakery, with a bright crunch from the zucchini and carrots on top.

8 SKILLET STREET FOOD
SEATTLE, WA

Doesn't lunch just taste better when it's served from an Airstream trailer? Skillet's burger—grass-fed beef griddled up still juicy, topped with arugula, cambozola, and a bacon jam so good you're tempted to just ask for it smeared on bread—is one of the best we've ever had from a truck. And the hand-cut fries might be even better. That's not to say you shouldn't go for a seasonally inspired special instead, but man, is it hard to pass up that burger.

9 NINA'S FOOD
LOS ANGELES, CA

Nina's is really the heart and soul of Los Angeles street food: authentic Mexico City–style eats, including Nina Garcia's must-order Pambazo—a torta-like sandwich that's dipped in red guajillo pepper sauce, filled with potatoes and chorizo bits, and grilled. You have to top it (or the quesadillas, or whatever else you order) with her dry salsa: a mix of sesame seeds, pumpkin seeds, peanuts, and chopped-up dried chiles. Look for Nina on bustling Breed Street at dinnertime, where she's attracted even more out-of-towners since winning a Vendy Award in 2010—the first year Los Angeles held the street-food Oscars.

BIG GAY ICE CREAM TRUCK, NEW YORK, NY

10 BIG GAY ICE CREAM TRUCK
NEW YORK, NY

This isn't your average Mister Softee ice cream truck, and classically trained bassoonist Doug Quint isn't your average ice cream man. He enlivens otherwise uninteresting vanilla and chocolate soft-serve with toppings like cayenne dust, saba, olive oil, and sea salt. The legendary (but intermittently available) Choinkwich, a chocolate-cookie ice cream sandwich wrapped with bacon, is as fun to say as it is to eat. And who doesn't love pumpkin butter? The Gobbler, a Thanksgiving nod served all summer long, layers pumpkin butter with vanilla soft-serve and graham cracker crumbles. Look for his truck, painted with a cheery rainbow cone, near Manhattan's Union Square between April and October.

> " I would love to have my own cart. I'd take a lead from the street vendors of India and start one of the chaats cart that are found all over the country. Or maybe a noodle cart like in Hong Kong? Ah . . . the possibilities are endless! " —shazza

5 reasons portland is the street-food mecca

You may be thinking, why are so many of your favorite street carts in Portland, Oregon? Because it's the greatest street-food city we know. While other spots in America certainly have their own local favorites, there's nowhere with an on-the-go food culture quite like Portland's. Why do we love it so?

1 There are more than 500 vendors lining the streets.

2 Think of almost any type of food, and Portland has it covered—from Thai (Nong's Khao Man Gai) to jambalaya (The Swamp Shack) to Scottish (The Frying Scotsman) to Bosnian (Ziba's Pitas) to the biggest sandwiches you'll ever shove into your mouth (Big-A** Sandwiches).

3 The blog "Food Carts Portland," written by Brett Burmeister and Lizzy Caston, has been profiling carts on an almost daily basis since 2007—so there's an index to the madness.

4 Pods! That's what they call the food court–like clusters of carts (usually between two and ten) in parking lots, gravel-paved open spaces, and parks throughout the city. Some cater to downtown office lunchers, while others don't get going until after dark for the late-night crew. (Those usually involve a deep fryer.)

5 For $5 to $7, you can get an affordable, quick, and filling meal.

11 PEKING DUCK STAND
FLUSHING, NY

While street food in general almost always delivers bang for the buck, the man and woman working the Peking Duck window on a street corner in Flushing's Chinatown dispense the single greatest bargain bite we've ever seen—a perfectly conceived and executed mini Peking Duck bun for one buck. Here's what happens when you order one (or, well, ten). The woman prepares the bun with hoisin sauce and carefully shredded scallion, and then her partner slices one or two pieces of duck with gorgeously burnished crispy skin (with just about all of the fat properly rendered) and places them in the bun. You can bring home a Peking duck dinner for two that costs five dollars a head. This is insane.

12 HAPA RAMEN
SAN FRANCISCO, CA

Richie Nakano, sous chef at acclaimed San Francisco restaurant Nopa, loved good ramen so much he decided to start a stand at the Ferry Plaza

DOLLAR DUCK BUN FROM PEKING DUCK STAND, FLUSHING, NY

In Midtown Manhattan, you'll see (and smell!) chicken and rice carts on almost every city street. Office lunchers and late-night eaters alike love the chicken-and-rice platters (which rarely cost more than $5) as hearty and spicy meals on the go; we've replicated those Styrofoam-packaged meals here.

halal cart–style chicken and rice with white sauce

SERVES 4 TO 6

FOR THE CHICKEN

2 tablespoons lemon juice

1 tablespoon chopped fresh oregano

½ teaspoon ground coriander

3 garlic cloves, roughly chopped (about 1½ tablespoons)

¼ cup light olive oil

Kosher salt and freshly ground black pepper

2 pounds boneless, skinless chicken thighs, trimmed of excess fat (6 to 8 thighs)

1 tablespoon vegetable or canola oil

FOR THE RICE

2 tablespoons unsalted butter

½ teaspoon turmeric

¼ teaspoon ground cumin

1½ cups long-grain or Basmati rice

2½ cups chicken broth

Kosher salt and freshly ground black pepper

1 For the chicken: Combine the lemon juice, oregano, coriander, garlic, and olive oil in a blender. Blend until smooth. Season the marinade to taste with kosher salt and black pepper. Place the chicken in a 1-gallon zipper-lock bag and add half of the marinade (reserve the remaining marinade in the refrigerator). Turn the chicken to coat, seal the bag, and marinate the chicken in the refrigerator for at least 1 hour and up to 4 hours, turning occasionally to redistribute the marinade (see Note).

2 Remove the chicken from the bag and pat it dry with paper towels. Season with kosher salt and pepper, going heavy on the pepper. Heat the oil in a 12-inch heavy-bottomed cast-iron or stainless-steel skillet over medium-high heat until it is lightly smoking. Add the chicken pieces and cook without disturbing until they are lightly browned on the first side, about 4 minutes. Using tongs, flip the chicken. Reduce the heat to medium and cook until the chicken is cooked through and the center of each thigh registers 165°F. on an instant-read thermometer, about 6 minutes longer. Transfer the chicken to a cutting board and allow to cool for 5 minutes.

3 Using a chef's knife, roughly chop the chicken into ½- to ¼-inch chunks. Transfer to a medium bowl, add the remaining marinade, cover loosely with plastic, and refrigerate while you cook the rice and prepare the sauce.

4 For the rice: Melt the butter over medium heat in a large Dutch oven. Add the turmeric and cumin and cook until fragrant but not browned, about 1 minute. Add the rice and stir to coat. Cook, stirring frequently, until the rice is lightly toasted, about 4 minutes. Add the chicken broth. Season to taste with salt and pepper. Raise the heat to high and bring to a boil. Cover, reduce to a simmer, and cook for 15 minutes without disturbing. Remove from the heat and allow to rest until the water is completely absorbed and the rice is tender, about 15 minutes.

5 For the sauce: In a small bowl, combine the mayonnaise, yogurt, sugar, vinegar, lemon juice, parsley, and 2 teaspoons black pepper. Whisk to combine. Season to taste with salt.

6 To serve: Return the entire contents of the chicken bowl (chicken, marinade, and all juices) to the skillet. Cook over medium-high heat, stirring occasionally, until heated through. To serve, divide the rice, lettuce, tomato, and toasted pita bread evenly among four to six plates. Pile the chicken on top of the rice. Top with the white sauce and hot sauce. Serve immediately, passing extra sauce at the table.

FOR THE SAUCE

½ cup mayonnaise

½ cup Greek yogurt

1 tablespoon sugar

2 tablespoons white vinegar

1 teaspoon lemon juice

¼ cup chopped fresh parsley

Kosher salt and freshly ground
   black pepper

TO SERVE

1 head iceberg lettuce, shredded

1 large tomato, cut into wedges

Fluffy pocketless pita bread,
   brushed in butter, lightly
   toasted, and cut into 1 × 3-inch
   strips

Harissa-style hot sauce

NOTE Do not marinate the chicken longer than 4 hours or it'll get a mushy texture. If you must delay cooking the chicken for any reason, remove it from the marinade, pat it dry with paper towels, and refrigerate until ready to cook.

Market—bringing a chef's perspective to the Japanese noodles with fine, fine results. The fabulous broth is rich and porky, made from pork bones and bonito, and in it swim Nakano's own noodles, slippery pork belly that falls apart at a chopstick poke and melts gloriously on the tongue, and an egg slow-cooked *sous vide* so that its soft-set yolk holds its shape just so. Next to NYC's Ippudo, it's our favorite ramen in the country.

13 RED HOOK LOBSTER POUND
WASHINGTON, DC

Red Hook isn't in D.C.—it's in Brooklyn. That's where this truck got its start, selling Maine-fresh lobster to urbanites after driving it down on a weekly basis. Now the truck offshot is run by business partners of the company's co-founder, Susan Povich. You have your choice between Maine style (chilled lobster, with mayonnaise) and Connecticut style (warm, with butter). At $15 a roll, it's a pricey five or so bites, but the butter-toasted white J.J. Nissen roll is spilling with chunks of the sweet, fresh lobster meat. For a cheaper thrill, try the shrimp roll: the plump Maine crustaceans get splashed with tarragon mayo.

14 REBEL HEROES
ARLINGTON, VA

Tan Nguyen sells all kinds of heroes from her Arlington truck, just outside of D.C.: banh mi, Cuban sandwiches, meatball subs, and "eggs de resistance" (a breakfast 'wich served all day). Her signature sandwich (with help from her Vietnamese mother Ninh Ta, who co-owns the truck) has to be the roast pork banh mi: thin slices of pork, bright cilantro, jalapeño, and pickled stuff (carrots and daikon radish) on a fresh-baked, crunchy and airy baguette. Most of the heroes also get a slather of mayo: lime mayo, chipotle mayo, or if you can handle it, the Rebel Mayo spiked with sriracha. And if you realize you can't handle it a little too late, save your tongue with one of their iced Vietnamese coffees.

hapa ramen

I read about Hapa Ramen on my last day on a trip to San Francisco, so I thought I was foiled until I realized that I was going to be arriving back in the city six days later—albeit on Saturday *night*, not Saturday morning, when the ramen was sold at the Ferry Plaza Market across the street. That's when I hatched an insidiously ingenius plan: e-mail Jason Stone, the general manager of the hotel I always stay at in San Francisco, ask him to buy a bowl of ramen for himself and one for me at the Ferry Plaza Market, and then I would have it when I got to the hotel from the airport. Not only did he have it ready and waiting for me, he had the fine Japanese restaurant in the hotel, Ozawa, heat it up. And how was it? Every bit as good as I'd dreamed.

15 FREDDY, THE KING OF FALAFEL AND SHAWARMA
ASTORIA, NY

Freddy Zeidaies, the self-proclaimed king of this chickpea fritter kingdom on 30th Street and Broadway in Astoria, grew up eating a style of falafel that's egg-shaped; according to Freddy's falafel geometry, a regular ol' ball doesn't offer the same perfect ratio of crunchy outsides to soft insides. Every platter (falafel, kefta, or chicken kebab) also comes with magenta, freshly pickled turnip rods and pickles shipped in from the West Bank. You know your falafel vendor is serious when he imports pickles from 6,000 miles away.

16 ODD DUCK FARM TO TRAILER AUSTIN, TX

You can smell the wood grill even before this trailer officially opens for dinner at 5:30 PM. Bryce Gilmore opened the Odd Duck in 2009 after having worked in a hotel kitchen in Aspen. He shops at the Austin farmers' market on the weekends for his ingredients. The house-cured (trailer-cured?) pork belly in his napkin-required slider is from Richardson Farms near Rockdale, Texas, and sits on a squishy brioche bun from Austin's Moonlight Bakery, with pickled peppers and eggplant grilled in the trailer. Sit at the benches in the gravelly parking lot where they're stationed and the Odd Duck staff will bring your order to you—now that's street-food service!

ODD DUCK FARM TO TRAILER, AUSTIN, TX

Hot, satisfying, and deliciously deep-fried, falafel is just about the perfect fast food. Here, we toast the chickpeas to remove much of the moisture before making the falafel so that each ball is light, not mushy, inside. Our favorite falafel comes from Taïm in New York City (page 242); we used parsley, mint, and cilantro, just as they do, for a fresh blast of flavor.

falafel

SERVES 2 TO 3

FOR THE TAHINI SAUCE

¼ cup tahini

½ cup Greek yogurt

1 tablespoon lemon juice

Kosher salt

FOR THE ISRAELI SALAD

1 medium cucumber, peeled, seeded, and cut into ½-inch chunks

1 small red onion, cut into ¼-inch dice

1 tablespoon lemon juice

1 medium tomato, seeded, cut into ¼-inch dice

Kosher salt and freshly cracked black peppercorns

3 tablespoons parsley leaves

3 tablespoons cilantro leaves

2 tablespoons fresh mint leaves

1 Adjust the oven rack to the center position and preheat the oven to 300°F.

2 For the tahini sauce: Combine the tahini, yogurt, and 1 tablespoon of lemon juice in a small bowl. Whisk until smooth and season to taste with the kosher salt. Set aside.

3 For the Israeli salad: Combine the cucumber, onion, lemon juice, and tomato in a medium bowl. Toss the salad with ½ tablespoon of kosher salt and transfer it to a strainer. Set the strainer in the bowl and allow it to drain for at least 30 minutes at room temperature. Discard the juices, and transfer the vegetables to the bowl. Add the parsley, cilantro, and mint and toss to combine. Season to taste with salt and pepper.

4 While the salad is draining, make the falafel: Toss the drained chickpeas and the olive oil in a large bowl and spread them on a rimmed baking sheet. Toast in the oven, shaking every 10 minutes, until they are slightly dried, about 25 minutes total. Set them aside and reduce the oven temperature to 200°F.

5 Combine the cumin and coriander in a small, heavy-bottomed stainless-steel skillet. Toast the spices over high heat, stirring constantly, until fragrant, about 30 seconds. Transfer the spices, garlic, red pepper flakes, baking powder, flour, onion, parsley, cilantro, and mint to the bowl of a food processor. Pulse until a rough paste is formed, scraping down the sides of the processor as necessary, about 12 one-second pulses. Add the reserved chickpeas, stir with a spatula to combine, and pulse until the mixture is cohesive but still very chunky, eight to ten 1-second pulses. Transfer the mixture to a large bowl and season to taste with salt and pepper. Form the mixture into 24 balls about 1¼ inches in diameter, pressing the balls just until they hold together.

6 Heat the peanut oil to 400°F. in a large Dutch oven or wok. Carefully add half of the falafel to the hot oil and fry until golden brown and crisp, about 3 minutes, agitating the falafel occasionally with a spider or slotted spoon. Transfer the falafel to a paper towel–lined rimmed baking sheet to drain and season immediately with salt. Keep the cooked falafel warm in the oven while you cook the remaining falafel. Repeat with the remaining falafel. Serve immediately in pita bread with the salad and tahini sauce.

FOR THE FALAFEL

1 (14.4-ounce) can cooked chickpeas (garbanzo beans), drained

2 tablespoons extra-virgin olive oil

½ teaspoon ground cumin

½ teaspoon ground coriander

1 garlic clove, finely grated

1 teaspoon red pepper flakes

1 teaspoon baking powder

1 tablespoon flour

½ small red onion, cut into ¼-inch dice

3 tablespoons parsley leaves

3 tablespoons cilantro leaves

2 tablespoons fresh mint leaves

Kosher salt and freshly cracked black pepper

1½ quarts peanut oil or vegetable shortening

Pita bread, for serving

17 GOURDOUGH'S
AUSTIN, TX

The mustachioed doughnut mascot on this shiny Airstream trailer has a smile on his face—he knows how tasty he is. Made fresh to order, these deep-fried guys are topped with all sorts of fruits, nuts, and even fried chicken (the Mother Clucker). They're so big—about a 6-inch radius!—that eating them is a fork-and-knife job, though most of the late-nighters (they close around 3 AM on weekends) just stuff them down. The centers are white and fluffy; the outsides, perfectly crisp. The Naughty & Nice is unfussy and as perfect as fried dough dusted with cinnamon and sugar gets, or try the Funky Monkey: fried with grilled bananas and iced with cream cheese and brown sugar.

18 TRUCKIN' GOOD FOOD
PHOENIX, AZ

You know a man is serious about his Nutella when he has a tattoo of it on his forearm. Jeff Kraus fell in love with the hazelnut paste on a trip to France

SELECTIONS FROM GOURDOUGH'S, AUSTIN, TX

with his wife, Erin, in 2009, and now even mixes it with maltodextrin to create a Nutella powder for his eclairs filled with roasted banana cream. It's one of the desserts on his prix-fixe menu (ever heard of a truck with a prix-fixe menu?). The idea for the truck formed on that French trip, too. "I've always wanted to own a simple and small cafe, and the Parisian style made sense for my menu and personality," said Kraus. "Plus my fashion sense, beard and messy hair and fitted clothes, is French-like." He works with Arizona farms, like Big Happy Farms and Superstition Farms in Mesa, and Crow's Dairy in Buckeye. A French-inspired, locally driven, Arizona food truck? You gotta love it.

19 CRÈME BRÛLÉE CART
SAN FRANCISCO, CA

There are some street-food concepts—like the idea of buying a crème brûlée from a guy on a bike—that seem destined to take off whether the food's good or not. How wonderful, then, that Curtis Kimball's silky, crunchy-sugar-topped crème brûlées are so tasty—custards of Honey Vanilla or Mexican Chocolate or Lavender, sprinkled with sugar and torched to order. We're particularly fond of the Dulce de Loco, a goat-milk dulce de leche that's exactly the right balance of sweet, funky, and goaty.

20 CHOW TRUCK
SALT LAKE CITY, UT

Asian tacos are all the rage in street food (thanks to the Kogi Truck's Roy Choi, page 232), but few do them as well as the Chow Truck, a partnership between Salt Lake restaurateur SuAn Chow and chef Rosanne Ruiz. Their spice-dusted calamari is breaded and fried to order, shatter-crispy tentacles with fried lemons and cilantro and a chipotle aioli dipping sauce; the spicy beef in the tacos is super-tender and intensely savory, brightened by a crunchy Asian slaw. It's fast food made by people who know food—and flavor.

5 questions you've always wanted to ask a food-truck vendor

Food blogger Marvin Gapultos started the Manila Machine in order to bring his native Filipino fare to the people of Los Angeles. We chatted with him about the life of a food truck entrepreneur.

Q How much does it cost to start up a food-truck business?

A Start-up costs for food trucks vary greatly—anywhere from $15,000 to $80,000. It all depends on whether you lease or buy your truck, and what kind of food you'll be serving. Money aside, the cost in time and sanity alone is ginormous. I've aged five years in the last three months, and I'm also now completely nuts.

Q How did you conceptualize your menu?

A The Filipino menu is the result of two food bloggers (myself and my business partner, Nastassia) brainstorming and cooking, and brainstorming and cooking. Many of the savory dishes—everything from the lumpia, to the pork belly adobo, to the sisig, to the beef tapa—originated from my own recipes that have appeared on my food blog. Nastassia is on dessert duty—she makes a mean leche flan. We exchange ideas and taste-test every concept before serving it on the truck.

Q Are you making a good living, or just getting by?

A You have to take into consideration all the food costs, the labor costs, and the truck lease and maintenance costs, and then factor in that you have to split your profits with however many business partners you have. Yes, if all goes well, the pay can be good, but you shouldn't get into the food-trucking business for money alone.

Q Where do you go to the bathroom?

A I don't. At least not during a shift. Things are so hot and hectic on a food truck, there's little time to even think about visiting the little boy's room. And remember, I'm in an enclosed box standing in front of a sizzling griddle, a bubbling fryer, and a steamy steam table—I do a lot of sweating, thus reducing the need for a bathroom break.

Q If I were to start a food truck of my own, could you give me a few words of wisdom?

A This is perhaps the question I get asked the most. My answer, and the answer everyone told me at first: Don't do it. Don't start another food truck. The work is too hard. Keep your life and enjoy what you have. But, if you're like me and want to go against that sage advice, understand that this will be the hardest thing you ever attempt. You will have nightmares about prepping meat, angry customers, random ingredients, and anything else involved with your new venture. You will have some bad days, and not see your family as much. Don't start a food-truck business expecting to make a million, or to meet Tyler Florence. Believe in your concept, and have faith that people will enjoy your food. There really and truly is something special about feeding people and putting smiles on their faces. You will have some good days.

5 TACO TRUCKS WE LOVE

A made-right-there taco for a buck or two is about as satisfying as it gets. Taco trucks serve some of the freshest, cheapest, most honest food for lunchtimers and late-night revelers alike. Bring on the pico de gallo!

1 HONEST TOM'S TACOS AND COFFEE PHILADELPHIA, PA

Tom McCusker, a.k.a. "Honest Tom," keeps the Drexel University students taco-satiated. "Me, I'm not that honest of a man, but my ingredients are. They're in season and local, mostly purchased from the Clark Park farmers' market. And we don't skimp." After seeing the taco truck light in Texas, he came back and started this tie-dyed–looking truck in 2009. His breakfast tacos are filled with roasted potatoes, fresh guacamole (which he learned how to make at a Drexel cooking class), bits of hot jalapeño, eggs, and melted cheese. Some breakfast tacos are sadly mushy inside, but these potatoes get that great golden-brown crust. He also gets potato points for his sweet-potato tacos. Grilled inside the truck, the potatoes get a nice charred outside while staying creamy inside.

BREAKFAST TACOS FROM IZZOZ TACOS, AUSTIN, TX

2 IZZOZ TACOS
AUSTIN, TX

After owning his own steakhouse for years, John Galindo bought a trailer off of Craigslist and outfitted it with burners for slow-cooking the carne guisada in his Escobar tacos. The stewed meat, a central Texas tradition, cooks in a big pot for four hours in the morning. The machaca in his Slow-rider tacos braises for even longer (eight hours). He's also made up a few new traditions of his own, like the tempura-battered avocado taco: crispy but not greasy, lightly dressed with his chipotle-sherry vinaigrette and topped with fresh arugula and cotijo cheese crumbles. The breakfast tacos (opposite) are some of the best in the city. Eat them outside on the Fisher Price plastic furniture and octopus merry-go-round (they also have big-kid picnic tables).

3 MARISCO'S GERMAN TACO
TRUCK SAN DIEGO, CA

Seafood from a truck can seem risky, but this is some of the best ceviche you'll find, served in a generous pile on a crunchy corn shell tostada. The lime-marinated octopus, tilapia, and shrimp pieces in the ceviche mixte are fresh (purchased from San Diego that morning) and bright-tasting, mixed with avocado slices, red onion, and cilantro flecks, and drizzled with a bright-red hot sauce. Fish tacos are also a big hit here (grilled or fried), but the best taco is the Gobernator. Good luck trying to fold this one—it's piled with grilled shrimp, sautéed onions, peppers, and celery. Most people transform the hood of their car into a dining room table.

4 COUNTRY BOYS
BROOKLYN, NY

Fernando Martinez and his wife, Yolanda, spend their summer weekends wedged between other trucks on this corner facing the Red Hook ballfields in Brooklyn. Families playing soccer all afternoon, as well as outsiders on a huarache pilgrimage, come for the oblong piles of Mexican goodness. The

COUNTRY BOYS, BROOKLYN, NY

sandal-shaped fried masa is layered with refried bean mash, lettuce, tomato, guacamole, and your choice of meat (beef, chicken, or pork). They need to be wrapped in double paper plates to prevent drippage, which, let's face it, is pretty inevitable.

5 TACOS GARCIA
YOUNTVILLE, CA

Less than a hundred paces from the French Laundry (arguably America's finest restaurant) is a rare affordable Napa Valley lunch option. Stationed in the parking lot of Yountville dive bar Pancha's, this truck serves tacos in a double wrap of soft, fresh corn tortillas with just enough onion and cilantro, and your choice of a dozen meat options. The chorizo-like longaniza has crispy, salty browned edges; lengua is so tender, the tongue meat dissolves in your mouth. Or you can get the cabeza, the fried carnitas, the super-seasoned pastor, the tender beef suadero, and—well, you get the idea. Grab three tacos, perch on the rickety table setup behind Pancha's, and you'll be well-fed for less than $5.

The taco is such classic street food—cheap, simple, and utterly delicious. We're especially fond of those with porky, fatty, crispy-edged carnitas. While the pork usually stews in gallons of hot lard, for the purposes of home cooking we pack it in tightly so that it cooks in its own fat and a little bit of vegetable oil, low and slow, making the carnitas every bit as tasty. For the best tacos, get the freshest corn tortillas you can find.

carnitas tacos with salsa verde

SERVES 4 TO 6

2 medium onions

½ cup chopped cilantro

3 pounds boneless pork butt (shoulder), rind removed, cut into 2-inch cubes

1 tablespoon kosher salt, plus more for seasoning

1 medium orange

6 garlic cloves, split in half

2 bay leaves

1 cinnamon stick, broken into 3 or 4 pieces

¼ cup vegetable oil

6 medium tomatillos (about 1½ pounds), husked and split in half

2 jalapeño peppers, split in half lengthwise, stem removed

24 corn tortillas

1 cup crumbled queso fresco or feta cheese

3 limes, cut into wedges, to serve

1 Adjust the oven rack to the middle position and preheat the oven to 275°F. Cut one onion into a fine dice and combine it with the cilantro in a small bowl. Cover with plastic wrap and refrigerate until needed. Split the remaining onion into quarters and set it aside. Season the pork chunks with 1 tablespoon of salt and place the pork in a 9 × 13-inch glass casserole dish. The pork should fill the dish with no spaces. Split the orange into quarters and squeeze the juice over the pork. Nestle the squeezed orange pieces into the casserole dish, in with the pork. Add two onion quarters, four garlic cloves, the bay leaves, and the cinnamon stick to the cas-serole. Spread the entire contents of the dish into an even layer. Pour the vegetable oil over the surface. Cover the dish tightly with aluminum foil and place in the oven. Cook until the pork is fork-tender, about 3½ hours.

2 Set a large fine-meshed strainer over a 1-quart liquid measure or bowl. Using tongs, remove the orange pieces, onion, garlic, cinnamon stick, and bay leaves from the pork. Transfer the pork and the liquid to the strainer. Let them drain for 10 minutes. Transfer the pork back to the casserole dish. You should end up with about ½ cup of liquid and ½ cup of fat. Using a flat spoon or de-fatter, skim the fat from the surface of the liquid and add the de-fatted juices back to the pork. Shred the pork into large chunks with your fingers or two forks. Season the pork to taste with salt. Refrigerate it until ready to serve. Transfer the remaining liquid to a medium saucepot.

3 To make the salsa verde, add the tomatillos, the remaining two onion quarters, the remaining two garlic cloves, and the jalapeños to the saucepot with the strained pork liquid. Add water until it is about 1 inch below the top of the vegetables. Bring to a boil over high heat, reduce to a simmer, and cook until all the vegetables are completely tender, about 10 minutes. Blend the salsa with a hand blender or in a stand-up blender until smooth. Season it to taste

with salt. Allow to cool and refrigerate it until ready to use.

4 Preheat the oven on its broiler setting. Place the casserole dish with the pork 4 inches under a high broiler and broil until it is brown and crisp on the surface, about 6 minutes. Remove the pork, stir with a spoon to expose new bits to the heat, and broil again for 6 more minutes, or until crisp. Tent the dish with foil to keep warm.

5 As the pork is broiling, heat the tortillas. Preheat an 8-inch nonstick skillet over medium-high heat until it is hot. Working one tortilla at a time, dip a tortilla in a medium bowl filled with water. Transfer to the hot skillet and cook until the water evaporates from the first side and the tortilla is browned

in spots, about 30 seconds. Flip and cook until it is dry, about 15 seconds longer. Transfer the tortilla to a tortilla warmer, or wrap in a clean dish towel. Repeat with the remaining tortillas.

6 To eat, stack two tortillas on top of each other. Add 2 to 3 tablespoons of the carnitas mixture to the center. Top with the salsa verde, chopped onions and cilantro, and queso fresco. Serve with lime wedges.

kogi's korean taco-loving cult following

Los Angeles–based truck Kogi BBQ started parking outside nightclubs in 2008 with the intention of feeding the hungry late-night masses with Korean-inspired tacos, burritos, and sliders. Within months, the truck garnered lines of hundreds willing to wait up to two hours for Korean-Mexican dishes—such as tacos filled with spicy pork, spicy barbecue chicken, or shortribs—created by chef Roy Choi. Before making Korean tacos one of the hottest food trends, and since then spawning many copycat trucks across the country, Choi spent his culinary school externship in the kitchen of four-star Le Bernardin in Manhattan. "It was a disaster," he recalls, and admits being ejected from famed French chef Eric Ripert's kitchen six times. Part classically trained chef, part kitchen rebel, Roy Choi is a flavor-fusion visionary who's responsible for a new cuisine on a McDonald's budget. "When you eat it, it tells the story about a city," Choi says.

Kogi BBQ dramatically popularized the kimchi quesadilla, a delicious Korean-Mexican hybrid using kimchi (Korean fermented cabbage) for spice and crunch. In our version, we cook the kimchi first to prevent excess moisture from getting the tortillas too soggy.

kimchi
quesadillas

MAKES 4 QUESADILLAS

2 tablespoons unsalted butter

1½ cups cabbage kimchi, roughly chopped into approximate ¼-inch shreds

2 pickled jalapeño peppers, minced (about 2 tablespoons)

2 cups shredded Cheddar cheese

½ cup cilantro leaves

2 tablespoons toasted sesame seeds

4 (8-inch) flour tortillas

2 tablespoons canola oil

Kosher salt

1 Heat the butter in a 10-inch heavy-bottomed stainless-steel or cast-iron skillet over medium heat until the foaming subsides and the butter starts to brown slightly, about 2 minutes. Add the kimchi and cook, stirring occasionally, until the kimchi is well browned. Transfer the kimchi to a large bowl and allow it to cool for 5 minutes. Add the jalapeños, cheese, cilantro, and sesame seeds, and toss to combine.

2 Spread one-fourth of the mixture evenly over half of one tortilla, leaving a ½-inch border around the edge. Fold the tortilla in half and flatten firmly. Repeat with the remaining three tortillas. Heat ½ tablespoon of canola oil in the skillet and set over medium heat until the oil shimmers, about 1 minute. Add two quesadillas to the skillet. Brush the tops with an additional ½ tablespoon oil. Sprinkle with kosher salt. Cook until crisp, blistered, and brown on the first side, about 2 minutes. Flip the quesadillas, season the tops with salt, and cook until the second sides are crisp and brown, about 2 minutes longer. Transfer to a cutting board, allow to cool slightly, cut into thirds, and serve immediately.

FRIED BRUSSELS SPROUT SALAD FROM
EAST SIDE KING, AUSTIN, TX

CHEFFY TRUCKS

1 LUDOTRUCK
LOS ANGELES, CA

French-trained chef Ludo Lefebvre, whom you may recognize from *Top Chef Masters*, pretty much had to start this fried-chicken–centric truck after people tried his "chicken ball" (it sounds much classier in French, *provençal pepite*) and were

obsessed at first bite. The dark thigh meat orbs are deep-fried to order, then sprinkled with herbs de Provence. You bite into it, releasing all that moist chicken steam, as the dark brown, crispy shell comes apart. It's easy to inhale in just a few bites. If you have any left to dip, try Lefebvre's sauces, especially the tongue-awakening and slightly fruity piquillo pepper.

2 EAST SIDE KING
AUSTIN, TX

More dive bars should have food carts run by three chefs whose other night job is at an incredible restaurant (in this case, Uchi). Sous-chef Paul Qui and sushi chefs Moto Utsonomaya and Ek Timrek opened this psychedelic-looking cart covered in monster designs in the backyard of the dive bar Liberty Bar. The vaguely Asian-eclectic menu combines things you recognize, but rarely experience together. Deep-fried beets with kewpie mayo? Get them. The root veggies are first roasted to bring out their natural sweetness, then fried in a thin cornstarch coating and salted. Dunk them in the big plop of kewpie mayo sprinkled with shichimi tougarashi, a semi-spicy Japanese spice blend. Or try the Fried Brussels Sprout Salad—how Brussels sprouts were meant to be eaten.

MOBILE GOES BRICK AND MORTAR

So we've seen chefs turning to street carts—what about street carts that have turned into restaurants?

1 POK POK
PORTLAND, OR

Pok Pok started as a take-out shack outside of chef-owner Andy Ricker's house. Once the lines for his Southeast Asian street food, especially the garlic-and-lemongrass-scented game hen, started snaking down the street, he added seating in his living room and bought more grilling rigs. The house-party vibe of his now two-story restaurant—you can also sit outside under a canopy of straw umbrellas and holiday lights—is part of the fun. Ricker, who isn't Thai but spent years traveling and learning to cook in northern Thailand, serves food that's a sour-spicy-salty-umami revelation. He presses his own coconut juice, which shines in khao soi kai—a soup with house-made curry paste, chicken on the bone, mustard greens, shallots, dried shrimp, yellow noodles, and chili paste.

2 DESSERT TRUCK
NEW YORK, NY

The Dessert Truck, quite possibly the first haute confectionery on wheels, started parking outside an NYU dorm in the fall of 2007. Co-owner Jerome Chang, a French Culinary Institute graduate who worked in Le Cirque's pastry kitchen, sells crème brûlée, chocolate bread pudding, and cream-stuffed bomboloni from a retrofitted postal truck. In 2010, Chang opened a Lower East Side store-front called Dessert Truck Works, so you don't have to chase them for their confections anymore.

POK POK, PORTLAND, OR

hallo berlin

Since 1981, the late, great Rolf Babiel was dispensing sizzling, juicy wursts from a New York cart parked outside the University Club on 54th Street, west of Fifth Avenue. He had no chef's pedigree; he was just a guy who found his calling selling mighty tasty sausages on the street of New York. Rolf died in 2008, far too young, but his legacy and his sausages live on in a beer garden and a storefront, Hallo Berlin express in Manhattan—as well as at a cart manned by his brother just outside the University Club. All street eaters should raise a stein to Rolf, who helped put serious street food on the map.

stweet vendors—
the power of twitter

One of the more interesting uses of Twitter, the microblogging service that allows people to beam out real-time updates, is to relay information to street-food customers. Vendors use their BlackBerries, iPhones, and other mobile devices to update fans on changing locations, menu specials, customer feedback, or just plain silliness. "The Twitter culture blows my mind. It's crazy to think that something that contains fewer than 140 characters is so powerful," said Jeff Kraus of Truckin' Good Food in Arizona. In Orange County, Dan Quickel, of Dan Dan BBQ, tweets every day. He has to. The truck relocates daily, and he says he wouldn't have a business without sharing locale info through this avenue. Doug Quint, of New York's Big Gay Ice Cream Truck, tweets more than 25 times each day. In August 2010, when Proposition 8 (on the subject of gay marriage) was repealed in California, he used Twitter to offer a special deal: "Order by saying 'Prop 8 can suck it,' and you get a rainbow (DUH!) sprinkle cone for $1—then merrily skip on your way. Exact change."

4 MOBILE PIZZA OVENS

Pizza made on the go? It sounds unlikely—given how hot ovens have to get for first-class pizza—but these four mobile outfits show us how it's done.

1 MOTO BENE
ATLANTA, GA

French Culinary Institute grad Dan Latham was working for Mario Batali before he started towing this portable pizza oven to Atlanta-area farmers' markets. After firing it up, he shops around the market for toppings like onions and sausage. The cheese, which comes from a local family-owned dairy called Johnston Family Farm, is creamy and generously applied, and the sauce is made from San Marzano tomatoes. Latham turns out some perfectly baked crusts with a nice char and good hole structure.

2 WY'EAST PIZZA
PORTLAND, OR

Pizza from a corrugated-side Brady Bunch–era camper? It may be one of the coolest street-food vehicles you've seen. Husband-and-wife owners Squish and Red make only 22 balls of dough a night, so if you're looking for a pie, you have to get there early. All dough is made by hand in the Wy'east camper. The pre-ferment starts the night before and goes 12 hours, then the final dough is mixed and ferments for another 6, for a total of 18 hours. The pizza, which comes from a teeny oven that can turn out only one at a time, is more of a thin-crust New York style than a Neapolitan style (page 98). But the crust is crisp-chewy and nicely browned, and the toppings and sauce are top-notch.

3 VERACI
SEATTLE, WA

Marshall Jett and Errin Byrd have been plying their craft from portable pizza carts since 2004. They started showing up at farmers' markets in the Ballard neighborhood of Seattle, cooking pizzas with fresh toppings bought right there from the stands. They eventually expanded to three portable ovens, which they've designed and built themselves using a special refractory clay mixture that can withstand temperatures up to 1300°F. Not that they *cook* pizza at that crazy heat—it would quickly become charred beyond recognition, so they normally cook it between 900°F. and 1100°F. for less than two minutes, which gives it a crispy, chewy thin crust.

4 PIZZA MOTO
BROOKLYN, NY

Dave Sclarow debuted Pizza Moto at the Brooklyn Flea, a weekend flea market in the Fort Greene neighborhood of Brooklyn, in 2008. The mobile trailer–mounted oven cranks out Neapolitan-style, wood-fired pies that are adequately crisp-chewy with a fairly airy hole structure. They're topped with sauce made from San Marzano tomatoes and creamy, fresh mozzarella from Aiello's in nearby Carroll Gardens. Straight from the oven, they get a liberal dusting of grated grana Padano cheese and a pour of very fragrant extra-virgin olive oil.

fried foods

LET'S FACE IT.
everyone loves
FRIED FOOD.

IF I'M FACED WITH THE CHOICE OF FRENCH FRIES OR A BAKED POTATO, I'LL CHOOSE THE FRIED SPUDS EVERY TIME.

Ditto for Chinese dumplings: steamed or pan-fried? No contest. Roasted or fried chicken? Who are we kidding? I do love a perfectly roasted chicken with crisp skin and moist and juicy meat, but a perfect piece of fried chicken trumps that every time.

Freshly shucked raw oysters and clams may be tasty, but I'd still rather be eating a fried-clam roll in Ipswich. The whole idea of baking instead of frying falafel is a crime against nature. And I know I shouldn't admit this, but fried okra and fried zucchini blossoms are my favorite vegetables.

What else is compelling about fried food? It crosses all cultural, racial, and class divides. America's Southerners, both black and white, certainly can claim a leadership position in the fried-chicken universe, but the Koreans and the Chinese and the Latinos hold their own. So do the Russians, and those from the other Georgia. Great Jewish delis serve excellent thick-cut french fries—but so do French bistros and brasseries. The Japanese fry pork cutlets, *tonkatsu*, better than just about anybody. (They have entire restaurants focused on them.) When you walk around Naples you realize that the Neapolitans love their *frittura* (fry shops) as much as they love pizza. We shouldn't forget that Sicilians love their *panella*, or chickpea fritters. And in southern France, in Nice, they know how to make killer chickpea pancakes, called *socca*. Back on this side of the Atlantic, at many state fairs like those in Wisconsin and Minnesota, they'll fry just about anything, from macaroni and cheese to spaghetti and meatballs.

In Milwaukee and in parts of upstate New York, you'll find fish fries, but Minnesotans have their beloved fried pike or walleye. And on any shoreline in America—seaside or lakeside—you're likely to find some fantastic fried seafood.

So we're going to introduce you to our favorite fried-food spots around the country. We won't go so far as to call this list definitive—after all, any corner store with a deep-fryer could be turning out something remarkable. But you'll find fine fried bites at every joint in this chapter. And if you don't feel like getting on a plane and heading to Memphis for some of Gus's (justifiably) World Famous fried chicken—a stance we will grudgingly accept—we have recipes to keep you satisfied. We hope they'll help you get over what I've had for many years in my kitchen, a fear of frying.

FRIED SMELT, CALUMET FISHERIES, CHICAGO, IL

FRIED CLAMS, PEARL OYSTER BAR, NEW YORK, NY

DOUGHNUTS, DAILY DOZEN DOUGHNUT COMPANY, SEATTLE, WA

"Favorite fried food? I'm going to have to go with calamari. NO, fried green tomatoes. NO, clams. NO, onion rings. NO, definitely, fried mac 'n' cheese. NO . . . I can't make that decision. Sorry." —izatryt

15 FRIED BITES WE LOVE

FRIED BEETS AT EAST SIDE KING, AUSTIN, TX

1 TAÏM NEW YORK, NY
FALAFEL

Taïm means "tasty" in Hebrew, but that's about the biggest understatement imaginable. The falafel at this tiny West Village storefront is our favorite in New York City (and we've methodically tried nearly 100); we haven't come across better anywhere in the States. They serve red, yellow, and green falafel, but we're partial to the green: fresh from the fryer, each falafel ball is improbably light on the inside, with a burnished brown, crispy shell. Parsley, mint, and cilantro add a bright freshness, but herbs aren't all you taste; the nuttiness of the chickpeas still comes through, too. Although best ensconced in fluffy white pita with the shop's ethereally creamy hummus and fresh Israeli salad, the falafel balls are more than good enough to crunch through all on their own.

2 RANCHO DE CHIMAYO CHIMAYO, NM
SOPAPILLAS

Double the fat, double the fun. Most New Mexican meals begin with a basket of freshly fried sopapillas—leavened and fried bread treats served with honey on the side. But they're not just fried in fat—they're lard-based, too. Proper sopapillas should be fluffy and light, with a crispy and golden surface that tears into shards of flaky dough. While some restaurants prefer somewhat oilier renditions, we're fans of the lighter sopapillas at the famous Rancho de Chimayo restaurant. Breaking each sopapilla releases a rush of hot air from the interior—hot, doughy, lard-laced air.

3 EAST SIDE KING AUSTIN, TX
FRIED BEETS

East Side King's beet fries make you wonder why we use potatoes so often. Though beets tend to inspire love-or-hate sentiments, these fries might even turn on the haters. They're first roasted, then get a light coating of cornstarch and a deep-fry inside this teeny food stand in the backyard of an Austin dive bar. Dunk the wedges, naturally sweet and lightly salted, in the Kewpie mayo spiked with shichimi tougarashi—a zesty, semi-spicy mix of ground-up peppers, sesame seeds, ginger, and orange peel. Who knew beets could be so enticing?

FALAFEL AT TAÏM, NEW YORK, NY

In coming up with a catfish recipe, we wanted to replicate that magical catfish at Taylor Grocery (page 244) as closely as possible—to transport you to Taylor Grocery upon first bite. We think we've succeeded.

crispy fried
catfish

SERVES 4

4 catfish fillets, 6 to 8 ounces each

1½ teaspoons kosher salt, plus more for seasoning

Freshly ground black pepper

1 cup all-purpose flour

¼ cup whole milk

2 large eggs

½ cup yellow cornmeal

¼ teaspoon cayenne pepper

2 cups vegetable oil, for frying

1 lemon, cut into 8 wedges

1 Pat the catfish fillets dry with paper towels, season with salt and pepper, and set aside. In a shallow bowl or pie plate, combine ½ cup of the flour and ½ teaspoon salt. In a second bowl or pie plate, whisk together the milk and eggs. In a third bowl or pie plate, combine the remaining ½ cup flour, the cornmeal, cayenne pepper, and 1 teaspoon salt.

2 Adjust an oven rack to the middle position and preheat the oven to 200°F. Dip one catfish fillet in the flour mixture, then shake off the excess. Dip the fillet in the egg mixture, turn to coat it well, and let the excess moisture drip off. Transfer to the cornmeal mixture, turn to coat, then transfer to a wire rack set in a rimmed baking sheet. Repeat with the remaining three fillets.

3 Heat the oil in a heavy-bottomed 12-inch skillet to 400°F. Carefully slide two coated fillets into the oil and cook until the first side is golden brown, about 2 minutes. Carefully flip the fillets with two spatulas and cook until the second side is golden brown, about 2 minutes longer. Transfer the cooked fish to a wire rack in a rimmed baking sheet and set in the warm oven while you fry the remaining two fillets. Serve immediately, passing the lemon wedges at the table.

FRIED CHEESE CURDS AT NORTHPOINT CUSTARD,
MILWAUKEE, WI

4 TAYLOR GROCERY OXFORD, MS
FRIED CATFISH

Why does fried catfish taste better at Taylor
Grocery than anywhere else? Sure, it's crisp,
greaseless, and perfectly fried, but that doesn't
quite account for the magic. Perhaps part of it is
the place itself. Taylor Grocery is, in fact, an old
wooden-floored grocery store; drinks and appe-
tizers are served in a corrugated-steel garage next
door. It's as stripped down as it gets—and don't
those well-worn places usually know how to fry?

5 CALUMET FISHERIES CHICAGO, IL
FRIED SMELT

How might you encounter Calumet Fisheries, a
seafood shack on the barren, industrial far South
Side of Chicago? If you're lost on the way to Indiana,
less than a mile away; or if you're waiting at the
95th Street drawbridge for half an hour as a 300-
foot tanker passes through. (Or you're *looking* for
that drawbridge—the one the Blues Brothers drove
right over in the 1980 film.) However you stumble
upon Calumet, it's imperative you stop inside. They
smoke their own shrimp and fish on the premises,
but their fried offerings are worth a try, too. It's
only when you place your order that the breaded
smelt are tossed in the fryer, so every white-boxed
order is super-crunchy and piping hot. There's no
seating at Calumet, so grab some fried and smoked

calumet fisheries
I've never seen anywhere quite like Calumet
Fisheries (below). Sure, I'm used to ramshackle
seafood shacks on the shores of lakes or on
the New England coast, but not in a rusted-out
stretch of the far South Side of Chicago, over-
looking a barge-trafficked waterway and a
grim industrial landscape. So I was dumb-
founded (and delighted) when I tasted their
offerings: crisp-fried smelt and shrimp, sure,
but also smoked shrimp that were, far and
away, the most memorable bites I had on a
whirlwind eating tour of Chicago. Smoked
right behind the storefront in a worn wooden
smoker, they're plump and sweet and delectably smoky—like smoked salmon without the
oiliness, or smoked trout without the dryness.
But really, they're not like anything else. You
just have to try them.

seafood, plop down on the grass outside, and tuck
into an improbable industrial picnic.

6 NORTHPOINT CUSTARD MILWAUKEE, WI
FRIED CHEESE CURDS

The rest of the country may have mozzarella sticks,
grilled cheese sandwiches, quesadillas, or any
number of other ways to satisfy their need for something crunchy, melty, and cheesy, but Wisconsin,
the Dairy State, has them all beat with fried cheese
curds. At NorthPoint Custard, chef Joe Bartolotta's
seasonal burger-and-custard shack right on the
shore of Lake Michigan, the white Cheddar curds
are super-crispy and well seasoned, the cheese
oozing slowly from each one on first bite.

7 THE FRY BREAD HOUSE
PHOENIX, AZ
FRY BREAD

Fry bread is a specialty of Native Americans throughout the states, and Cecilia Miller learned how to stretch hers by hand, growing up on the Tohono O'Odham Reservation, before she opened the Fry Bread House in Phoenix. Not unlike a state-fair fried dough, the breads are thick, leavened doughs that puff up pillowy and soft in the deep fryer. Like crepes, they're wrapped around fillings both sweet and savory; the red chile beef is the order not to miss.

8 DUCKFAT PORTLAND, ME
DUCK FAT FRIES

Of course, a sandwich shop named Duckfat turns out killer fries. Amply ducky, with a beautiful sprinkle of salt, they're among the best things that have ever happened to potatoes. And if that's not *quite* enough duck for you, they can also be served with a Duck Fat gravy dipping sauce. Duck Fat squared? A little much. But we'll take it.

9 LOS BARRIOS
SAN ANTONIO, TX
FRIED TACOS

You've had hard-shelled tacos, you've had soft tacos, but once you try Diana Barrios Treviño's

JOE'S SUPERETTE, BROOKLYN, NY

puffy tacos, you may be willing to forsake all other forms. The puffy taco is a San Antonio specialty, and while her family's Los Barrios restaurants didn't invent it, there's no question it's their signature dish. A round of corn dough made from fresh masa is quickly deep-fried and folded with two spatulas to form a taco shell that's super-crisp on the outside but soft within—it's surprisingly light for fried dough, not doughy or heavy in the slightest, just airy and corn-y inside. They're filled with beef, chicken, or beans, and can be topped with guacamole and lettuce and tomato and all the usual fixin's, but the crisp, pliant puffy shell is what you'll end up dreaming about.

10 FLANDERS FISH MARKET & RESTAURANT
EAST LYME, CT
FISH AND CHIPS

The menu at Flanders Fish Market & Restaurant, a few miles inland from the Connecticut shoreline, is a little overwhelming. It's divided by seafood and landfood, and under the seafood section, you'll see the word *fried* an awful lot. But you can't go wrong with the fish 'n chips, where the fish is white, moist but not-greasy pollock. It flakes apart like an accordion, and the thin fried jacket (a simple flour and spices base) clings to the fish, just how we like it.

11 4505 MEATS
SAN FRANCISCO, CA
CHICHARRONES

Imagine biting into a crunchy Cheeto—and suddenly finding your mouth filled with supple, slippery porkiness, speckled with sugar, sea salt, and chile. That's what eating the chicharrones at chef Ryan Farr's 4505 Meats is like. They're cooked in rice-bran oil, which helps create their ethereal lightness—a lightness that dissolves into the essence of pig on first crunch. You'll find no pork rinds better than these.

12 GALLERIA UMBERTO
BOSTON, MA
ARANCINI

Neither its unadorned storefront nor its sign ("Galleria Umberto Rosticceria") hints at the fantastic pizza and calzone waiting within. But the Sicilian slices (page 99) can't be beat—nor can the fist-size arancini—fried balls of rice, golden brown but not a bit greasy. Each bite yields still-firm rice, oozing sharp cheese and a ground-beef center as meaty as any proper ragu you've ever had. Galleria Umberto serves the kind of food that's only good fresh from the kitchen—but with limited hours and a line inevitably stretching out the door, there's so much turnover that the food is always fresh.

13 CASAMENTO'S RESTAURANT
NEW ORLEANS, LA
FRIED OYSTERS

If there were a church of fried seafood in this country, it would have to be Casamento's. The restaurant was founded in 1919 by Joe Casamento; Joe's grandson C.J. Gerdes and his wife, Linda, still make sure the oysters are fried the same way Joe did, dredging them in cornmeal and frying them in lard in cast-iron pans. The only question to ponder at Casamento's: whether to have a fried oyster plate or an oyster loaf (the fried guys stuffed into a halved Texas Toast–like pan bread). Note: Call or check the Casamento's website before you go; Casamento's closes in the summer.

14 WIENER AND STILL CHAMPION
EVANSTON, IL
CORN DOG

They fry all sorts of strange and improbable things at the old-school dog stand Wiener and Still Champion: pickles, bacon, gyro meat. But it's the corn dog, surprisingly, that shows good taste and restraint: their Dippin' Dogs, which start with classic all-beef Vienna dogs, are neither too greasy nor too much like corn pudding; they've got a pleasantly airy, genuinely cornbread-like coating with just the light crisp of the deep fryer. We're not surprised that a great corn dog comes from a great hot dog town.

15 DUFF'S
AMHERST, NY
BUFFALO WINGS

The spicy, deep-fried chicken wing is as much a quintessential part of the American eating experience as hot dogs and hamburgers. Though they were first served at the Anchor Bar in Buffalo, New York, in 1964 (and Anchor is still frying some crispy, juicy specimens), we prefer the messier versions at Duff's just north in Amherst, where the sauce seeps into the chicken and comes in minutely graduated hotness levels from mild to mild medium and right on up to "Death" and "Armageddon"—which really will burn your face off, if that's your thing.

---

casamento's

This is how much I love Casamento's: I've almost missed many a flight out of New Orleans when I've convinced a taxi driver to swing me by on the way to the airport. (Even though it's not really on the way.) In fact, I can't even count how many oyster loaves and oyster plates I've scarfed down in the backseat of a cab—or even tried to carry onto the plane. That said, though I'm a fan of the drive-by, Casamento's gorgeous, completely tiled, inside and out, restaurant is worthy of a proper sit-down eating experience. You'll think you're eating at the bottom of a gorgeous, old-fashioned swimming pool.

For best flavor, use fresh-shucked oysters. Canned oysters can be used if fresh are not available. Homemade tartar sauce is worth every second of the (minimal) extra effort; while the bottled stuff can be too sweet and gummy-tasting, this version gets a better vinegary kick from the capers and pickle. For a sweeter, tangier tartar sauce, replace the cornichon with 2 tablespoons of sweet pickle relish.

fried oysters
with tartar sauce

SERVES 3 TO 4

FOR THE TARTAR SAUCE

$\frac{1}{2}$ cup mayonnaise

1 medium shallot, minced (about 2 tablespoons)

$\frac{1}{4}$ cup drained capers, minced

$\frac{1}{4}$ cup finely minced cornichons (about 8)

1 teaspoon fresh lemon juice

$\frac{1}{2}$ teaspoon Worcestershire sauce

2 tablespoons chopped Italian parsley

$\frac{3}{4}$ teaspoon freshly cracked black peppercorns

FOR THE OYSTERS

2 large eggs

$1\frac{1}{4}$ cups all-purpose flour

$\frac{1}{2}$ cup cornmeal

1 teaspoon freshly cracked black peppercorns

2 teaspoons kosher salt, plus more for seasoning

1 teaspoon paprika

2 quarts peanut oil

2 dozen freshly shucked oysters, drained

1 For the tartar sauce: Combine the mayonnaise, shallot, capers, pickles, lemon juice, Worcestershire sauce, parsley, and black pepper in a small bowl and stir to combine. Set aside.

2 For the oysters: Whisk together the eggs and 3 tablespoons of the flour in a medium bowl. The mixture should have the consistency of thick pancake batter. Add up to 1 additional tablespoon of flour to thicken, if necessary. In a separate medium bowl, whisk together the remaining 1 cup flour, the cornmeal, black pepper, 2 teaspoons salt, and the paprika. Heat the oil in a Dutch oven or wok to 350°F.

3 Add the drained oysters to the egg mixture and turn to thoroughly coat them. Allow the excess batter to drip back into the bowl before the next step. Hold the bowl with the flour mixture in one hand, and, tossing the contents constantly, add the oysters to the flour one at a time with your other hand. The oysters should remain separated inside the bowl with the flour mixture.

4 Carefully add the oysters to the oil one at a time and fry, agitating constantly, until they are light golden brown and crisp, about 1 minute. Transfer to a paper towel–lined plate to drain, and season immediately with salt. Serve immediately with the tartar sauce.

FRIES YOU MIGHT NOT HAVE MET

Ah, the french fry—despite its name suggesting other national loyalties, is any food more beloved in America? Piled up next to burgers, hanging out with sandwiches, and turning up at fast-food joints and classy urban bistros and restaurants of all kinds, they're the ultimate culinary butterflies, sneaking their way onto plates all across the land. You may know the crispy-edged, creamy-middled Belgian fries, with their many delicious dipping sauces; classic, skinny, beautifully golden french *frites*; super-seasoned curly fries. But what about the fry's many other faces?

jojo potatoes

In parts of the Pacific Northwest, Montana, and elsewhere in pockets across the country, fried potato wedges are known as JoJo potatoes (or JoJos, for short). Cut lengthwise and generally covered in a spicy, salty seasoning, they're the stuff of barrooms and convenience stores and summer camps, belly-filling and satisfying.

duck fat fries

Just what they sound like—potatoes deep-fried in rendered duck fat, which lends them an elusive depth and duckiness that you have to taste to understand. Generally, though not always, the stuff of higher-end restaurants.

garlic fries

Garlic and potatoes are hardly strangers, but northern California has a particular penchant for garlic fries: roughly chopped raw garlic and parsley tossed with skin-on fries. The first bite, with still-crisp fries and the bright bite of garlic, is a wonderful thing. While the fries soon grow soggy, the garlic juices seep into the soft potato interior, and the extra oil blends in with the garlic bits, leaving you with a deliciously pungent puddle of potato that's every bit as tasty. Warning: Your fingers won't smell quite right for days.

disco fries

A heap of thick-cut french fries with gravy and cheese sauce, most often found in the greater New York and New Jersey area. It's total diner food. And a close cousin of . . .

poutine

A Canadian specialty of gravy and cheese curds, piled on fries, a dish that's becoming more popular on menus across the United States. The fries quickly soften under the salty, meaty gravy, and the cheese curds start to melt, leaving you with lovely, stringy cheese strands and some curds that still squeak under your teeth. A pile of sloppy deliciousness.

french fry sandwiches

That'd be fries *in* your sandwich, not just on the side. In New Orleans, the french-fry po' boy is everywhere—yep, fries as the *filling* in a barely crusty roll, generally doused in gravy. And at the famed Primanti Bros. in Pittsburgh (page 162), they throw fries right into every sandwich, whether ham or cheese or pastrami, before crowning it with the top slice of bread. It's a mighty mouthful.

and with the fries, fry sauce

Where you find fries in Utah, you're likely to find fry sauce, too. A blend of ketchup, mayonnaise, and occasionally other spices, it's such a regional staple that McDonald's served fry sauce in its Utah locations until 1997.

Just a few minutes in a boiling vinegar bath removes excess starch from the potatoes; the vinegar also prevents the fries from disintegrating by strengthening the pectin that holds its cells together. The fries are fried twice, giving you extra-crisp fries with a dry, fluffy interior—our favorite kind.

thin and crispy french fries

SERVES 2 TO 4

2 pounds russet potatoes (about 4 large), peeled and cut into $\frac{1}{4}$-inch-thick matchsticks (put in a bowl of water)

2 tablespoons white vinegar

2 tablespoons kosher salt, plus more for seasoning

2 quarts peanut oil

Kosher salt

1 Place the potatoes and vinegar in a large saucepan and add 2 quarts of water and 2 tablespoons of salt. Bring to a boil over high heat. Boil for 10 minutes. The potatoes should be fully tender, but not falling apart. Drain and spread on a paper towel–lined rimmed baking sheet. Allow to dry for 5 minutes.

2 Meanwhile, heat the oil in a 5-quart Dutch oven or large wok over high heat to 400°F., as registered on an instant-read thermometer. Add one-third of the fries to the oil (oil temperature should drop to around 360°F.). Cook for 50 seconds, agitating occasionally with a wire-mesh spider, then remove the potatoes and let drain on a second paper towel–lined rimmed baking sheet. Repeat with the remaining potatoes (working in two more batches),

allowing the oil to return to 400°F. after each addition. Let the potatoes cool to room temperature, about 30 minutes. (For best results, freeze potatoes at least overnight, or up to 2 months.)

3 Just before serving, remove the fries from the freezer, if they have been frozen. (Thawing them is not necessary.) Return the oil to 400°F. over high heat. Fry half of the potatoes until crisp and light golden brown, about $3\frac{1}{2}$ minutes, adjusting the heat to maintain at around 360°F. Drain them in a bowl lined with paper towels and season immediately with kosher salt. Cooked fries can be kept hot and crisp on a wire rack set on a sheet tray in a 200°F. oven while the second batch is cooked. Serve immediately.

FRIED CHICKEN: 12 OF OUR FAVORITE SPOTS

No book on American food would be complete without a mention of—or, heck, a chapter on—fried chicken. And these days, you see fried chicken everywhere, from national chains to high-end restaurants. But we're generally partial to the sorts of age-old, un-cheffy chicken joints that have been around for decades.

1 BARBECUE INN
HOUSTON, TX

Barbecue Inn is a misnomer if ever there were one because these folks fry like you wouldn't believe. The fried chicken leaves their barbecue in the dust. Imagine a fried chicken breast that is so juicy it squirts you in the eye when you take a bite: that's what happens at Barbecue Inn. The crust and skin

WILLIE MAE'S SCOTCH HOUSE, NEW ORLEANS, LA

fuse beautifully; they're so crunchy you can hear each bite three tables away. And they salt this bird just as much as you could hope for. All the chicken is fried to order, so you'll never find yourself stuck with the warming tray rejects.

2 CHARLES' COUNTRY PAN FRIED CHICKEN
NEW YORK, NY

The legendary Charles Gabriel is perhaps New York's greatest fried-chicken cook. Over the years, he's run fried-chicken trucks, partnered with New York restaurateurs, and more; in recent years, he's returned to Harlem, having reopened his much-loved bare-bones soul-food restaurant there. Charles learned his craft near Charlotte, North Carolina; he cooks the chicken in huge, black cast-iron skillets, the way many purists insist it be cooked. Crisp and crunchy on the outside, Charles's chicken comes out of those pans miraculously free of grease. Even the breasts are tender and juicy. His constant attention to the frying chicken ensures that it's always fried just right. Note: One of Charles's current outposts, Rack and Soul, in the shadow of Columbia University, will serve you fried chicken that is not fried to order. Resist the tempta-

tion for instant fried-chicken gratification and tell them you want your chicken fried to order—they'll happily oblige.

3 WILLIE MAE'S SCOTCH HOUSE
NEW ORLEANS, LA

What can the finest fried chicken inspire others to do? Willie Mae Seaton's shotgun shack of a restaurant was destroyed in Hurricane Katrina—the Treme neighborhood in which it stands was flooded for weeks. But the Southern Foodways Alliance, an organization documenting Southern food history, rallied fans and supporters from across the country to come and physically rebuild Willie Mae's Scotch House—fueled by one meal of fried chicken each day. The restaurant reopened in 2007. It's now run by Willie Mae's granddaughter, Kerry Seaton, who's still using her grandmother's methods—wet batter, salt, and pepper—to miraculous effect.

4 GUS'S WORLD FAMOUS FRIED CHICKEN
MASON AND MEMPHIS, TN

The Gus's location in Memphis is one wide juke joint of a room, barely lit and decorated with unlit Christmas lights strung on the beams. If you're told your chicken will take 20 minutes, it'll probably be more like 45. But that's okay: this is fried chicken as God meant it to be, with a gorgeous burnished brown, lacquered crunchy exterior that achieves that mystical, cosmic oneness between skin and crust and juicy, moist chicken flesh within. It's all perfectly seasoned with salt and pepper and just enough cayenne pepper to let you know it's there.

5 FRENCHY'S CHICKEN
HOUSTON, TX

Though Percy "Frenchy" Creuzot Jr. (one of the great food names of all time) died in 2010, his fried chicken lives on. The man had a most excellent fried-chicken pedigree; Frenchy came to Houston from New Orleans, where he was an old family friend of the late, great, New Orleans fried-chicken master Austin Leslie. There are always long lines

willie mae's

In 2005, I was onstage at the James Beard Awards, the Oscars of the culinary world, co-presenting Ms. Seaton her "America's Classic" Award (along with friend and fellow fried-chicken connoisseur, food writer, and historian John T. Edge), in recognition of Willie Mae's part in American food culture and the extraordinary rebuilding of her restaurant. By the time she arrived onstage to pick up her medal, all three of us were crying—and as I looked out into the audience, we were not alone.

FRIED CHICKEN AT IZOLA'S, CHICAGO, IL

at Frenchy's, which is actually good news for fans of fried chicken—the longer the line, the greater your odds of getting chicken that's fresh from the deep fryer. Served up hot, Frenchy's Creole-style chicken (seasoned with garlic and cayenne) is juicy, salty, and just spicy enough. Frenchy's is a mini-chain, but prolific Texas food writer Robb Walsh, who knows more about Texan food than any other person on the planet, swears by the original Scott Street location.

6 PRICE'S CHICKEN COOP
CHARLOTTE, NC

Joining the ranks in the deep-fried corner of our fried-chicken pantheon is Price's Chicken Coop, a pleasingly chaotic chicken shack that's been around since 1952, when Charlotte was a very different place. Be ready with your order—in this South End stop, a more savvy patron might fight to get his in first—but know that it's worth the hassle to fight the good fight. A properly deep-fried crust is a thing of beauty: thick, crunchy, and so good you'd want a mouthful even without all that chicken underneath. Price's accomplishes all that, but with supremely moist chicken that's just as tasty as its fried shell. There's no place to sit (or

price's

I was standing in the parking lot in back of Price's Chicken Coop about to dig into my box of chicken when my friend Kathleen Purvis exclaimed, "I don't know why anyone orders anything at Price's but thighs and gizzards." When she said that I was digging into my reasonably juicy breast that was part of my mixed half chicken order. I stopped eating it mid-bite and switched to the thigh in my box. Damn, that Kathleen knows her Price's—no surprise as she's been living, eating, and writing about Charlotte food for more than 20 years. The thigh at Price's is mindblowingly good, so crisp, so juicy, so salty, I wanted to go back and order a couple of thighs for the road. The gizzards were really good, too—and I am not usually a gizzards man. These gizzards were pop-in-your-mouth addictive, with an organ meat flavor kicker that delights and surprises.

IZOLA'S, CHICAGO, IL

izola's

Here's what I love about Izola's. It's not just the history—the place was (and, to some extent, still is) a living room of sorts for black Chicago political figures, and many of their photos still hang on the walls. It's not just the comfortable, lived-in feel, food made with no pretense and a lot of soul. It's just how simple the philosophy is: make fried chicken that's delicious. After sending our compliments to the kitchen, the chef, Shirley, came out to greet us, clearly delighted that we'd enjoyed our meal. "Do you brine the chicken?" we asked. "Do you soak it in buttermilk? What's the secret?" She shrugged. "I dunk it in beaten egg and milk. I dip it in flour seasoned with salt and pepper and garlic powder. Then I deep-fry it 'til it's done." The woman just knows what good chicken is. And she ought to—she's been cooking it, first learning from her mother, since she was ten years old.

even, really, to stand) at Price's, so head out to the hood of your car.

7 IZOLA'S
CHICAGO, IL

To say that Izola's on Chicago's South Side is stuck in a time warp is something of an understatement. "Minimum in the dining room: $2.20," reads the menu. "Your wife a bum cook? Eat at IZOLA'S!" entreats a sign behind the bar. Only the 10-foot Obama photo gives you any sense of what decade it is. But no matter—they make some of the finest fried chicken we've ever had. The deep brown crust crackles under the teeth, a highly seasoned, unbelievably tasty prelude to the super-moist meat. We can't vouch for much else on the menu (we really didn't try much else, though the chicken and pea soup is mighty tasty), but we'd drive from anywhere in Chicago for this fried chicken.

8 McHARDY'S CHICKEN & FIXIN'
NEW ORLEANS, LA

We first tried McHardy's chicken on an insanely long but tightly scripted day of New Orleans eating, almost all of it of the po' boy persuasion (page 140). We thought we wouldn't have a moment for any unplanned discoveries—but thankfully, we were wrong. In the neatly decorated, modest storefront of McHardy's, there were wire bins overflowing with breasts, wings, drumsticks, and thighs; in the back of the bins were metal frying troughs that allow chicken pieces to be fried in large quantities, utilizing a process best described as halfway between pan-frying and deep-frying in a Fryolator.

One bite into a drumstick and we knew we'd found something remarkable. The crust was thin and applied so artfully we couldn't distinguish between it and the skin. The bird was perfectly seasoned with salt, pepper, and just a little garlic. No cayenne needed, thank you very much. Even the white meat, always a tricky proposition, was juicy and tender. We asked the owner where she learned to cook chicken like that. "From my mother, of course," she said with a smile.

MCHARDY'S CHICKEN & FIXIN', NEW ORLEANS, LA

9 STROUD'S
KANSAS CITY, MO

Stroud's fried chicken is paradigmatic: crunchy-crusted, the fat underneath the skin almost completely rendered, and dark meat that was explosively juicy and moist. We've found that some Kansas City locals speak poorly of Stroud's, but we're wondering if the naysayers are just trying to convince others that KC had moved beyond fried chicken and barbecue. Both are still fantastic. The moist but not-too-sticky cinnamon buns make a most excellent dessert.

mothers and daughters

Based on my extensive fried-chicken research, I'm willing to go on record as saying that mothers and daughters tend to produce better fried chicken than fathers and sons.

10 BAILEY AND CATO
NASHVILLE, TN

When we drove up to Bailey and Cato, we loved everything about the place—the little wooden house it was tucked into, the unpretentious, understated signage. But we got there 15 minutes before it opened, and while we were walking around, checking out the hairstylist next door, we noticed the small parking lot was filling up fast. So we hurried back to be the first through the door. We ordered the fried chicken and were told it would be a while. When it finally hit our table, just seconds out of the fryer, the chicken had the kind of spicy, cracklingly crisp skin we dream about. Moral of the story? Good fried chicken comes to those who wait.

11 THE COLONNADE
ATLANTA, GA

Around since 1927, The Colonnade is best experienced on Sunday afternoons, when the after-church crowd is putting back the fried chicken. Don't fill up on the tender yeast rolls, delicious as they may be—far better to save room for the well-seasoned, super moist chicken with a perfectly crunchy crust. As always, don't mind the slow service if it means your chicken is that much closer to the fryer.

12 BABE'S CHICKEN DINNER HOUSE
ROANOKE, TX

At Babe's Chicken Dinner House, a cavernous old hardware store-turned-restaurant near Fort Worth in the tiny town of Roanoke, the only choice involved in ordering your meal is whether you have chicken-fried steak or fried chicken. While that's kind of a great choice, and Babe's chicken-fried steak is swell, there's a reason it's called Babe's Chicken House. This is fine fried chicken, as juicy-crunchy as a chicken lover could hope for. Iceberg lettuce, creamed corn, biscuits, and mashed potatoes appear at your table, along with cream gravy that you won't feel compelled to use. "We work so hard at keeping it fresh," Mary Beth Vinyard (a.k.a.

cheffy fried chicken

In the last 20 years, many seriously talented chefs have tried their hand at fried chicken. How did this trend get started? I remember top-notch Atlanta chef Scott Peacock teaming up with legendary Southern cookbook author Edna Lewis to write *The Gift of Southern Cooking*. On Tuesday nights, Peacock served fried chicken from a recipe the two devised at his restaurant Watershed; it sold out every week. Inspired, perhaps, by Lewis and Peacock, chefs all over the country began to tackle the magical brown bird. We've had spectacular fried chicken from David Chang's New York restaurant Momofuku Noodle Bar, at Holeman & Finch Public House in Atlanta, at Suzanne Tracht's Jar in Los Angeles, and at Robert Stehling's Hominy Grill in Charleston. We certainly don't object to chefs getting into the fried-chicken game. The bar is already set pretty high by the 12 establishments included in this section, and so many others like them; but anytime chefs try to raise the standards of deliciousness, we're in favor.

Babe), who owns the restaurant (and several others of the same name) with her husband, told one journalist. "It tastes just like it came out of your grandmother's kitchen. That's really our goal—to make you feel like you're eating in your grandmother's home."

Our fried chicken recipe went through many iterations before we hit upon perfection. First and foremost, we like our chicken to achieve that "cosmic oneness" between skin and crust. But that's not enough. The chicken flesh itself has to be moist and juicy within its dark brown crispy jacket. This Southern fried chicken achieves all of the above.

southern fried **chicken**

SERVES 4

1 cup buttermilk

1 tablespoon and 2 teaspoons kosher salt, plus more for seasoning

1 whole 4-pound chicken, cut into 10 parts, or 3½ pounds bone-in, skin-on breast, legs, drumsticks, or wings

1½ cups all-purpose flour

½ cup cornstarch

1 tablespoon baking powder

¼ teaspoon cayenne pepper

½ teaspoon garlic powder

1 tablespoon paprika

1 tablespoon freshly ground black pepper

1 quart peanut oil

1 Whisk the buttermilk and 1 tablespoon salt in a medium bowl. Add the chicken pieces and toss them to coat. Transfer the chicken and buttermilk to a 1-gallon zipper-lock bag and refrigerate for at least 1 hour and up to overnight, flipping the bag occasionally to redistribute the contents and evenly coat the chicken. Remove the chicken from the bag, rinse the chicken under cold running water, and pat the pieces dry with paper towels.

2 Whisk together the flour, cornstarch, baking powder, cayenne pepper, garlic powder, paprika, black pepper, and 2 teaspoons salt in a large bowl. Working a few pieces at a time, dredge the chicken in the flour mixture, pressing the flour to each piece until it firmly adheres. Transfer the coated chicken to a fine-meshed strainer and shake to remove the excess flour. Transfer to a wire rack set in a rimmed baking sheet. Allow the chicken to rest at room temperature for 30 minutes.

3 At the end of the resting period, heat the oil in a 12-inch straight-sided sauté pan or a cast-iron skillet over medium-high heat to 375°F., about 5 minutes. Place the chicken in the pan, skin side down. The temperature should drop to around 275°F. Adjust the heat to maintain the temperature at 275°F. for the duration of cooking. Cook the chicken until it is a deep golden brown, about 6 minutes. Carefully flip the chicken pieces and continue to cook them until the second side is golden brown, the thickest part of the breasts registers 155°F. on an instant-read thermometer, and the legs register 175°F., 6 to 8 minutes longer.

4 Remove each chicken piece as it finishes cooking. Transfer the chicken to a rimmed baking sheet lined with paper towels, season with salt, and let rest for 5 minutes before serving.

Flour contains proteins that can cause a crust to turn a little leathery or tough. Cornstarch, on the other hand, is a pure starch, so chicken dipped in cornstarch stays super-light and crisp—it's the key to the texture of Korean fried chicken. Just as we do in our french fry recipe, we fry the chicken twice. The first time is to help it cook all the way through; the second is to crisp up the crust just before serving.

korean fried
chicken

SERVES 4

3 pounds mixed chicken pieces (thighs, drumsticks, sectioned wings, or breast halves split in half; see Note)

1 cup cornstarch

2 teaspoons kosher salt

1 teaspoon grated fresh ginger

2 tablespoons soy sauce

1½ tablespoons rice vinegar

1 tablespoon Asian sesame oil

3 tablespoons honey

2 tablespoons Chinese chili-garlic paste

2 quarts peanut oil

2 scallions, greens and whites, finely sliced

NOTE We prefer the moisture and flavor of chicken thighs, drumsticks, or wings, but breast meat can be used as well. For the best texture, be sure not to cook the breast meat past 160°F., as registered on an instant-read thermometer.

1 Pat the chicken pieces dry with paper towels and toss in a large bowl with ¼ cup cornstarch and 1 teaspoon salt until it's well coated. Spread on a wire cooling rack set in a rimmed baking sheet. Set aside at room temperature while you make the sauce.

2 Combine the ginger, soy sauce, vinegar, sesame oil, honey, and chili-garlic paste in a small saucepan. Bring the mixture to a boil over medium-high heat and simmer until syrupy, about 4 minutes. Transfer the sauce to a large mixing bowl and set it aside.

3 Heat the peanut oil in a large wok or Dutch oven to 350°F. In a large bowl, combine the remaining ¾ cup cornstarch with remaining 1 teaspoon salt and ¾ cup water. Stir with a fork until a smooth slurry is formed. Working in two batches, dip the chicken pieces in the cornstarch slurry with tongs, allowing the excess to drip back into the bowl; then carefully add the chicken to the hot oil. Fry, agitating constantly with a wire-mesh spider, until the chicken is light golden brown, about 5 minutes. Return to the wire rack and repeat with the second batch of chicken.

4 When ready to serve, reheat the oil to 400°F. Return the chicken to the oil in a single batch and cook, agitating constantly with the wire-mesh spider, until the chicken is deep golden brown and the center of the largest piece registers 160°F. on an instant-read thermometer, 5 to 8 minutes.

5 Transfer the chicken to a paper-towel–lined bowl to drain the excess oil. Transfer to the bowl with the sauce. Add the scallions and toss the chicken to coat. Serve immediately.

why we love
korean fried chicken

If you're a fan of anything super-crispy, Korean fried chicken might be the chicken for you. It's not breaded, exactly, but dipped in cornstarch before it's fried twice—leaving you with totally rendered fat and a thick, incredibly tasty shell that soaks up the beautifully melded flavors of ginger and honey and soy. Sweet and spicy, crunchy and juicy, it's just about the perfect bite. The Korean chain Bon Chan Chicken, which has opened a number of U.S. locations, is where the Serious Eaters head when we need a Korean fried-chicken fix.

the clam belt

Here's the thing about fried clams: they're either really good (sweet, nutty, crisp, and greaselessly fried with no breading other than flour) or they're not. And good clams can go bad faster than you think. My tip for maximum enjoyment: ask that the clams be put on a plate, instead of one of those impossibly cute cardboard clam boxes, so the clams stay crisp and crunchy. Those boxes are a dastardly form of clamicide because the fried clams end up steamed and soggy when they're piled on top of each other. Avoid the clam heap at all costs.

There are fried clams to be had all up and down the New England shores, and on Long Island and coastal New York—the stretch we like to call the Clam Belt. Some of our favorites? Bigelow's, in Rockville Centre, the quintessential Long Island clam shack that's just one long horseshoe-shaped counter. In Connecticut, at the Sea Swirl, about a seven-minute detour off I-95 in Mystic, the clams are delicious and the onion rings are the side of choice. Save room for excellent soft ice cream.

Everyone rhapsodizes about the Clam Box in Ipswich, Massachusetts; their clams are delicious, and lines stretch into the hours, but the seafood is a touch too battered for our taste. For crisper clams, head to J.T. Farnham's, which overlooks the Essex Salt Marsh—where live many of the clams that end up in fryers. Just down the road at Essex Seafood Restaurant and Fish Market, clams are fried a little longer, so they end up a lovely dark brown color.

On the islands off Cape Cod, there's The Bite on Martha's Vineyard, where the clams are excellent (though they do come in the dreaded box). There's also its less-celebrated neighbor Sandy's Fish and Chips, where the clams are mighty fine and the scallops and fried fish, caught right off the Cape, are just as tasty.

While Maine is not known for its fried clams, Bob's Clam Hut in Kittery is actually a swell fried-clam shack. Plump and crunchy, soft and salty within, the regular fried clams are top-notch, and served with house-made tartar sauce.

And of course, where there are good clams, there are chefs who know what to do with them at local fine restaurants. In Boston, Neptune Oyster fries Ipswich clams to a salty, shatter-prone crisp, and they're just as good at B&G Oysters across town; in New York, at Mary's Fish Camp, the clams are excellent, crunchy and clammy and delicious.

A HALF-DOZEN DOUGHNUTS WE LOVE

Is it *doughnut* or *donut*? Merriam-Webster still lists *doughnut* as its main entry, and we're inclined toward the old-fashioned spelling. But when we asked the Serious Eats community, user Thebookpolice had this to say: "Donuts are too awesome to be accompanied by an 'ugh.'"

1 DOUGHNUT PLANT
NEW YORK, NY

Please don't ask us to name the best offering at doughnut visionary Mark Isreal's ambitious shop. We really can't. But here are some favorites, depending on your doughnut personality. For traditionalists, the Vanilla Bean doughnut, which resembles the typical glazed doughnut, but has the added depth of high-quality vanilla; for chocoholics, the Blackout doughnut, downright fudgy with a cake-crumb coating; for PB&J addicts, the Peanut Butter and Jelly doughnut, where the jelly actually tastes like fruit; and for any sweet tooth, Tres Leches.

DOUGHNUT PLANT, NEW YORK, NY

DAILY DOZEN, SEATTLE, WA

3 SPALDING'S BAKERY
LEXINGTON, KY

With designer doughnut shops opening in cities across the country, it's kind of refreshing to hit a doughnut shop that still makes old-fashioned yeasty glazed doughnuts without pedigree. For more than 80 years, the Spalding's doughnuts have been so light and golden brown and delicious we find ourselves shipping boxes of them across the country. The best doughnuts are the freshest doughnuts—but a Spalding's doughnut eaten a thousand miles away is still better than most doughnuts out there.

2 DAILY DOZEN DOUGHNUT COMPANY
SEATTLE, WA

While much of Seattle may have a soft spot for Top Pot Doughnuts, with locations all over the city, we prefer this little Pike Place Market stall. Sure, you can get fresh doughnuts at plenty of shops—but at Daily Dozen, mini doughnuts are actually plucked from the Donut Robot II conveyer belt. (That may mean a *little* more oil, but we won't complain.) Tossed into a brown paper bag with sugar, sprinkles, or cinnamon, they're handed over the counter. They're so hot that when you bite one open, steam pours from its interior. Moist, squishy, crunchy with sugar—the little guys tend to disappear before you've even walked to the next stall. (Skip the frosted ones. Straight-up sugar is where it's at.)

4 SHIPLEY DO-NUTS
TEXAS, LOUISIANA, OKLAHOMA, NEW MEXICO

The platonic ideal of a doughnut may be served at the original location of Shipley Do-Nuts, where they fry your doughnuts to order. That's right. Where else fries doughnuts *to order*? Buy an extra dozen because the first dozen won't make it to their intended location intact. Also, resist the urge to eat them immediately or you might be dealing with some serious tongue burns. Shipley has more than 220 locations serving reliably good yeast doughnuts, but if you want to be guaranteed life-changing, fried-to-order doughnuts, go to the Shipley on 3410 Ella Boulevard in Houston.

5 MORNING CALL COFFEE STAND
METAIRIE, LA

Café du Monde may be listed in every New Orleans
guidebook, and their beignets sure are tasty—but
bite for bite, we prefer the super-fluffy fritters at
Morning Call in suburban Metairie. They're fried
to a uniform honey hue, with the slightest deliciously oil-crisped crust encasing a pillowy, almost
airy dough within, as light as the clouds of pow-
dered sugar you'll shake on top. Those who seek out
Café du Monde for its charm (or chicory coffee),
don't worry—Morning Call has both in spades.

6 BANBURY CROSS
SALT LAKE CITY, UT

The problem with doughnuts is often the way you
feel *after* eating them—surprisingly weighed down,
given how airy the things look. Not at Banbury
Cross, where the raised doughnuts are almost
cloudlike in the lightness of their stretchy, yeasty
dough. With just the thinnest outside crust, they're
best with a classic, not-too-sweet glaze or the
cinnamon sugar, happily heavier on the former
than on the latter. They're some of the best traditional doughnuts we've ever had.

MORNING CALL COFFEE STAND, METAIRIE, LA

"Growing up, my grandpa was the
donut man at a local gas station. I
spent many graveyard shifts with
him in the back whipping up all
kinds. The best was a plain cake
donut fresh out of the grease and
way too hot to eat. God, I miss him
and those donuts." —kerque

apple fritters at old fashioned donuts

Old Fashioned Donuts in Chicago is just that—a bakery lost in a time warp, where you can watch the doughnuts being made in windows right in front of the store as you walk in. You will be confronted by trays of doughnuts in the display case, and you might consider getting a dozen assorted—but you'd be mistaken in doing so. What you want is just one apple fritter, which will easily feed four doughnut-crazed eaters. The thing is enormous—almost the size of your head—and not exactly light fare. But it's astoundingly tasty, a little greasy, a lot cinnamon-y, with big chunks of apple all encased by an appropriately sweet glaze. If all this sounds like it's too much for you, the glazed doughnuts are almost as good.

REGIONAL FRIED FOODS

French fries, fried chicken, onion rings—sure, you'll find those offerings just about anywhere in the United States. But some corners of the country have fried foods all their own.

TOASTED RAVIOLI
ST. LOUIS, MO

Toasted? Not quite. While their exact origins are disputed, "toasted" ravioli—that is, ravioli that have been breaded and deep-fried—were popularized in The Hill, the Italian neighborhood of St. Louis. Whether they're cheese-stuffed or meat-filled, the pasta shells get a slightly dry, crispy veneer, thus the name. They're often served with marinara for dipping.

CHEESE CURDS
WISCONSIN

You'll find cheese curds—fresh, irregular clumps of young, unaged cheese—all over Wisconsin. They're sold by the bag, in mild rubbery chunks that squeak between the teeth. And where you find cheese curds, you'll also find them fried. They're breaded or battered before they're deep-fried, leaving you with salty, crispy nuggets of slowly oozing cheese. Delicious.

FRIED BISCUITS
INDIANA

In parts of southern Indiana, some biscuits aren't baked—they're fried, the butter- or lard-based biscuit dough dropped straight into the deep-fryer. Made right, they're greaseless and golden brown, airy and steamy within, so delicious that they need none of the butter they're invariably served with. But a swipe of apple butter, the other sidekick? Never a bad thing. According to Serious Eats contributor Nick Kindelsperger, the Nashville House

oxford creamery

My wife and I often stop off to see friends in Mattapoisett, Massachusetts, and when we do, I feel compelled to bring lunch. Luckily for me, Mattapoisett is the home of a classic seasonal fried seafood and ice cream spot, the Oxford Creamery. The charming blue-and-white shack serves fish and chips as a whole fillet (most often cod) that's been dipped in an eggy batter that fries up crispy and puffy and light all at the same time. Fried scallops have a much tighter crust, so you really taste the sweet nuttiness of the scallops. Fried clams are every bit as delicious. But the onion rings here are even better. Great onion rings fall into two camps: wispy shards of lightly battered onion with a dimpled crust; or slightly puffy, thicker but still light. The Oxford Creamery makes a paradigmatic puffy onion ring, with minimal puff and maximum crunch. (For dessert, grab a scoop of Richardson's Grape Nut ice cream—so good you'll be tempted to take home a quart for breakfast.)

FRIED TURKEY

closely associated with the fish fry as Wisconsin—where just about every restaurant in the state seems to serve fried fish on Fridays, a tradition that's no longer confined to Catholics. You'll generally get cod, perch, or walleye along with fries and slaw. (Speaking of walleye, Minnesota's home and restaurant cooks fry up a mean walleye fillet.) And in Buffalo, Rochester, and Syracuse, you'll find Friday fish fries, too.

PEANUTS
NORTH CAROLINA

"Eat Shell-N-All!" is the tagline of Jerry's Nut Company, one of North Carolina's leading fried-peanut sellers. That's right: the little guys are fried right in the shell. It's a curious sensation the first time you bite into one—they're just a *little* tougher than anything you're used to eating—but the fibers crunch away one crackly, oily, incredibly salty chew at a time. Strange but delicious.

STATE FAIR FOODS
ACROSS AMERICA

Fried Oreos. Fried cookie dough. Fried *beer*. These are the famed foods of American state fairs, where the mentality seems to be "If you fry it, they will come." A few crazy examples? Chocolate Smooches, which are deep-fried and battered Hershey's Kisses at the Arkansas State Fair; "deep-fried Coke," or deep-fried Coke-flavored batter nuggets topped with Coke syrup and whipped cream, at the State Fair of Texas; and battered, deep-fried Hostess chocolate cupcakes at the Iowa State Fair.

Restaurant, at Nashville, Indiana's Brown County Inn, makes killer fried biscuits.

TURKEY
MUCH OF THE SOUTH AND BEYOND

If you're accustomed to roasting your Thanksgiving bird, the notion of fried turkey might surprise you. But if you're willing to brave it—that is, if you're willing to plunge a whole skinned animal into a violently frothing cauldron of oil—you'll be rewarded with a golden, crispy bird way more exciting than your average roasted turkey. Don't worry, your oven won't get lonely: you'll still heat it up for the stuffing.

FISH FRIES
WISCONSIN, UPSTATE NEW YORK, AND BEYOND

In many predominantly Catholic regions of the country, you'll find fish on the menu during Lent and on Fridays, when religious tradition used to forbid the eating of red meat. But nowhere is so

sweets &
bakeries

a single piece
OF CHOCOLATE,
THE SMALLEST
oatmeal-raisin cookie,
OR EVEN A TINY PIECE OF PIE
CAN BRING SUCH UNPARALLELED PLEASURE.

THERE'S NEVER BEEN A BETTER TIME TO HAVE A SWEET TOOTH IN AMERICA—AND THAT'S PARTICULARLY GOOD FOR THE SERIOUS EATS TEAM BECAUSE WE DO LOVE DESSERT.

Why are sweets better now than ever before? A confluence of things old and new.

The old: the classic labors of love, multigeneration family businesses—the bakers and ice cream makers and chocolatiers whose skills have been honed over decades, who still care very deeply about everything they sell. The new: the current generation of artisanal sweet-makers and pastry chefs, who have brought with them the knowledge they gained from culinary school and the experience they gained from working in terrific restaurants—enterprises that required them to look to both America and beyond for borrowed inspiration and techniques. Added to that are the high-quality, locally grown fruits bakers and pastry chefs are sourcing for their creations. This formidable combination of forces has been brought to bear in just about every sweet thing out there.

Let's take ice cream. Fifty years ago the ice cream landscape consisted of national supermarket brands of varying quality; beloved local and regional brands like Blue Bell (Texas), Brigham's (Boston), and Gifford's (Maine); and a few old-fashioned, emotionally resonant ice cream parlors (Margie's Candies in Chicago, C.C. Brown's in Los Angeles, Jahn's and Schrafft's in New York); and

BOUCHONS FROM BOUCHON BAKERY, NEW YORK, NY

small-batch local favorites sold mostly in their own shops, like Bassetts in Philadelphia, Graeter's in Cincinatti, and Bud's Ice Cream in San Francisco. What changed the world of ice cream? In 1960, Herman Mattus introduced Häagen-Dazs, a high-butterfat, super-premium ice cream. Outside of Boston in 1973, Steve Herrell had introduced the concept of mix-ins to ice cream (what vanilla isn't improved by M&M's, Reese's Pieces, and chunks of Heath Bar smashed in?). In the late sixties and early seventies, pastry chefs like Nancy Silverton at Spago and Lindsey Shere at Chez Panisse started making their own ice cream in small batches, out of locally grown fruit, high-end French chocolate and butter, and whole vanilla beans. Silverton and Shere inspired the next generation of pastry chef-turned-ice cream-makers to open their own shops to explore their seemingly unlimited palette of ice cream flavors. That's how we lucky ice cream lovers came to have the likes of Jeni's Splendid Ice Creams (Columbus, Ohio), Humphry Slocombe and Bi-Rite Creamery (San Francisco), and The Bent Spoon (Princeton, New Jersey) in our midst.

Chocolate-chip cookies underwent a similar transformation. While they started as a home-baked treat, made in kitchens all across the country, those cookies begot Chips Ahoy and other huge national brands—as many people stopped having the time and inclination to bake. Famous Amos and Mrs. Fields came along in the 1970s, selling higher-end chocolate chip cookies in freestanding stores. And what's more, pastry chefs started getting into the act, experimenting with better ingredients (Scharffen Berger chocolate chips, high-quality butter), looking to leave their own mark on the cookie universe while maintaining the timeless and ageless qualities we love. And because chefs love to mix savory elements into their sweets, sea salt started making its way into chocolate-chip cookie recipes, too (page 282).

Hot chocolate, occasion cakes, chocolate bars, frozen custard, gelato, pie—they've all evolved in similar fashion, as you are about to find out in this chapter. So come along and explore the ever-evolving world of sweets in America.

A DOZEN SWEET BITES

ICE CREAM SANDWICH FROM IT'S-IT, SAN FRANCISCO, CA

There are delicious sweets in every corner of the country—picking a top dozen is quite the difficult task. But what you have here is Serious Eats' Sweet Honor Roll: some of the desserts that haunt our dreams long, long after the very first bite. We can't promise we've tasted every sweet out there. But we can ensure that every one of these treats will leave your sweet tooth deliriously happy.

1 IT'S-IT SAN FRANCISCO, CA
ICE CREAM SANDWICH

These ice cream sandwiches were first hand-dipped at the San Francisco amusement park Playland-at-the-Beach, where they had a four-decade run. When the park was razed, they moved to a factory a few towns south, in Burlingame, and they're still sold all over the Bay Area and beyond. Rich ice cream, chewy oatmeal cookies, and a crisp dark chocolate shell—what's not to love?

2 MODERN PASTRY BOSTON, MA
CANNOLI

If you're a fan of cannoli in the North End, Boston's Italian district, odds are you're a Mike's Pastry fan or a Modern Pastry fan—a rivalry as intractable as the Yankees and the Red Sox. But we'll take the lighter, crisper, filled-to-order cannoli at Modern, with a delicate ricotta filling that's not too sweet, any day of the week.

3 TED DREWES ST. LOUIS, MO
CONCRETE

We think there's better frozen custard in our great country than Ted Drewes. But we still love their concretes: an ultra-thick interpretation of a milkshake, made with vanilla frozen custard and rounded out with optional mix-ins like nuts, candy, fruit, and other sundae-style fixings. The concrete is so thick that the servers make a show out of holding the "drink" upside down with the spoon suspended in the mix, without any danger of it falling out. The Dutchman Delight—vanilla custard blended with butterscotch, chocolate, and pecans—is wobbly-knees good.

4 TARTINE BAKERY SAN FRANCISCO, CA
BRIOCHE BREAD PUDDING

Here's the really neat trick Tartine's Elisabeth Prueitt pulls off in her absurdly good brioche bread pudding: she manages to make it obscenely rich and cloud-light at the same time. And in such a sizable portion, you can spend a blissful half-hour with it, one sweet spoonful at a time. It's topped with the finest gift nature has to offer: seasonal fruits from northern California.

5 BOUCHON BAKERY YOUNTVILLE, CA; NEW YORK, NY; LAS VEGAS, NV
BOUCHONS

Thomas Keller's incomparable bakery has never handed us a sweet we didn't like. But again and again, we find ourselves returning to their signature bouchons: dense, chocolatey, brownie-like cakes with the depth of fine French Valrhona chocolate and the sweetness of high-quality butter. Though they're not much bigger than your thumb, they're more than rich enough to satisfy.

6 TEAISM WASHINGTON, DC
SALTY OATS

Does salt belong on a cookie? In this case, absolutely—just a pinch on top. The large, coarse crystals really make the spices and plump oatiness sing. The idea for these cookies came to their creator Terri Horn, who collaborated with D.C. shop Teaism, while she was sea-kayaking off the coast of Maine. But as much as the Salty Oat fanbase has begged, they won't reveal the secret recipe.

7 TWO LITTLE RED HENS NEW YORK, NY
CHEESECAKE

Sure, big names like Junior's and S&S are bound to come up when you talk about New York's best cheesecake. But after tasting dozens, we're still devoted to the cheesecake from Upper East Side

CHEESECAKE FROM TWO LITTLE RED HENS, NEW YORK, NY

DEATHCAKE ROYALE FROM CUPCAKE ROYALE, SEATTLE, WA

bakery Two Little Red Hens: dense but not leaden, creamy and vanilla-touched, with a gorgeous dark graham cracker crust. Simple, elegant, perfect.

8 CUPCAKE ROYALE SEATTLE, WA
DEATHCAKE ROYALE

You think you like chocolate? You don't know chocolate. Smaller than your fist, with delicate chocolate curls on top, this little cake couldn't look less threatening. Think again. Available only around Valentine's Day, this is the most decadence you can shove into a little square—a layer of the bakery's classic chocolate cake topped with ganache made with Stumptown espresso and a fudgy layer of Theo Chocolate, all dipped in dark chocolate ganache. One tiny forkful and you're already beaten. Continue at your own risk.

9 LOUISE'S OLD FASHIONED BAKED GOODS CARRBORO, NC
POUND CAKE

At the Carrboro Farmers' Market (page 333) we found a lot of cheffy artisanal bakers selling rosemary this and sea salt that, but our favorite sweets were the homey, old-school baked goods made by Louise Parrish. Her pound cakes are so moist, buttery, and light, not leaden in the stomach; we can even forgive Louise for using lemon flavoring in her lemon cake rather than fresh lemon juice. It's still incredible. (Her mini pecan and sweet potato pie tarts are equally pleasure-inducing.)

HOT CHOCOLATE AT HOT CHOCOLATE, CHICAGO, IL

10 BI-RITE CREAMERY
SAN FRANCISCO, CA
AFTERNOON SNACK

Most sundaes leave you full enough to collapse on the table, groaning and clutching your belly; this one will have you fighting through the pain and ordering seconds. Bi-Rite Creamery's already exemplary ice cream (the intensely full-flavored roasted banana is used here) is topped with homemade graham crackers, lush whipped cream, and a deep, almost smoky caramel sauce.

11 HOT CHOCOLATE
CHICAGO, IL
HOT CHOCOLATE

Mindy Segal actually serves a lot more than hot chocolate at her restaurant in Chicago; we've had great burgers there, and all kinds of other delicious savory and sweet things. But she named her restau-

rant Hot Chocolate for a reason. It comes in many forms, of which we love the black and tan ($1/3$ hot fudge and $2/3$ medium hot chocolate) and the affogato ($2/3$ medium hot chocolate, $1/3$ dark, with a scoop of coffee cocoa nib ice cream). The latter isn't exactly the traditional Italian gelato-and-espresso treat, but when something is this good, who cares?

12 MOZZA2GO
LOS ANGELES, CA
BUTTERSCOTCH BUDINO

We love pudding at Serious Eats, and this butterscotch *budino* (the Italian term for pudding) made by Dahlia Narvaez at Mozza2Go, is just about as good as pudding gets—crazy creamy, intensely butterscotchy, just salty enough, and mercifully not too sweet, even with the caramel sauce poured on top. Narvaez is a protégé of Mozza co-owner Nancy Silverton, and she's learned her lessons well. This butterscotch is a perfectly balanced sweet, and balance is a hallmark of Silverton's food.

jugos y lechon

All right, we promised you a healthy dessert—but why not precede that course with some pig, when you're at El Palacio de Los Jugos? Put in time in the fast-moving pig line and you'll find what could be our favorite chicharrones anywhere (the kind with pig meat attached, not just the fried skin), with a perfect ratio of crunchy skin and tender pig meat and fat, along with a side order of pig-flavored yucca and rice and beans.

favorite healthy sweets: fresh juices

El Palacio de Los Jugos in Miami is half a huge open-air juice bar, and half a *lechoneria* (pig emporium)—a pretty unbeatable combination. Start with some cold coconut water sipped from a fresh coconut that's been sliced open to order; or with a quart of insanely delicious, ice-cold fresh pineapple juice, which bears no resemblance to the thick, syrupy pineapple juice out of a can. If you're lucky, as we were, you will get a glimpse of owner Polly, a force of nature who presides over this little bit of Havana in Miami with enormous grace, energy, and good cheer.

GROWN-UP CANDY: SUGAR DONE RIGHT

There are candy bar conglomerates and haughty Swiss chocolatiers, but there's also an awful lot of candy in between. With close attention to ingredient sourcing, a sense of whimsy, and a sparing hand with the sugar, these sweetmakers are turning out some of the most adult candies we know.

1 FRAN'S CHOCOLATES SEATTLE, WA
SALTED CARAMELS

Salted caramels are so ubiquitous these days, we wouldn't be surprised to see Kraft start making them. But if you love chocolate-covered salted caramels as much as we do, you want to give credit where credit is due. In the 1980s, Fran Bigelow, inspired by candy she had in France, began selling her paradigmatic dark-chocolate–covered, smooth-and-oh-so-buttery caramels topped with a few grains of *fleur de sel* (French sea salt) at her shop in Seattle. That's not to say that there aren't many other fine caramels made with good chocolate and *fleur de sel*. But we haven't come across a better one.

2 GARRISON CONFECTIONS CENTRAL FALLS, RI
PRETZEL BALLS

Garrison, where do we begin with you? We'd be happy with a box of your peanut butter patties, or chocolate tablets, or brittle squares, or anything else. But of them all, the most addictive award goes to the Pretzel Balls. Like the chocolate and yogurt-covered pretzels sold in bulk bins, these little guys have that great salty-sweet balance, and a light crunch that makes them even more poppable.

3 L.A. BURDICK CAMBRIDGE, MA
CHOCOLATE MICE

These tiny mouse-shaped chocolates, each with filled bellies, almond ears, and a tail of silk, are almost too adorable to contemplate eating. But one nibble and you'll silence your qualms about sending them to an early grave in your stomach. Larry Burdick's dark-chocolate mouse has a dark chocolate and orange filling; the milk chocolate mouse has a mocha interior; his white chocolate mouse is filled with dark chocolate and cinnamon. For variety, Burdick sells penguins, too.

4 RECCHIUTI CONFECTIONS SAN FRANCISCO, CA
S'MORES

There's no doubt that we all have a soft spot in our hearts for that universal campfire treat, the s'more. But chocolatier Michael Recchiuti has taken our obsession with that childhood treat to another level. For the do-it-yourselfers, he has created a s'mores kit with house-baked graham crackers, house-made vanilla marshmallows, and a bar of fine bittersweet chocolate. And for those eaters who don't want to bother with the fire, Recchiuti also makes s'mores bites, ready to be devoured.

5 SAHAGUN CHOCOLATES PORTLAND, OR
KA-POW! CHOCOLATE BAR

Sahagun Chocolates owner Elizabeth Montes is one of these young, quiet next-generation chocolate

larry burdick

The first time I sought out Larry Burdick's little chocolate mice in the late 1980s, he was still shaping them from his tenement apartment on New York's Upper East Side. When I asked if I could buy a few for a New Year's party, Burdick said: "Well, I'm all sold out of the mice I made today, but I still have some of yesterday's mice. They're day-old mice, so I wouldn't feel right about selling them. But take as many as you can carry." That's what I call a commitment to freshness.

obsessives who has raised the level of candymaking in the country quite a few notches—not only making refined chocolates but also coming up with new ones altogether. Case in point? The KA-POW! chocolate bar, which essentially swaps out roasted single-origin coffee beans (from roasters including Portland's Stumptown) for the cocoa beans, so that you get a bar that you'll think is chocolate, until you bite in and get the coffee shock of a strong espresso. Not recommended as a midnight snack.

6 ASKINOSIE CHOCOLATES
SPRINGFIELD, MO
CHOCOLATE HAZELNUT SPREAD

It's easy to love Nutella, but if you start examining Nutella too closely you'll find that it doesn't taste very chocolatey—and it *really* doesn't taste very hazelnutty. There are wonderful, crazy expensive imported Italian chocolate-hazelnut spreads,

CHOCOLATE MICE FROM L.A. BURDICK, CAMBRIDGE, MA

PIG CANDY FROM RONI-SUE'S CHOCOLATES, NEW YORK, NY

but it's hard to justify spending thirty dollars on a jar. That's why we were thrilled to discover the chocolate-hazelnut spread of Askinoisie Chocolates, the pride of Springfield, Missouri; made with Washington hazelnuts crushed into nut butter and slow-mixed with roasted cocoa nibs and cocoa powder. It's cheap enough to eat a spoonful every day, but if you can stop after one spoonful of this nutty chocolate, you're stronger than we are.

7 POCO DOLCE SAN FRANCISCO, CA CHOCOLATE TILES

We've always thought of tiles in terms of Scrabble and such, but Poco Dolce owner Kathy Wiley has shown us the ways of candy tiles—flattish chocolates about two inches square. Her Sesame tile features crisp, toasted sesame seed toffee, bittersweet chocolate, and gray sea salt. It's a model of understated, elegant, nutty candy perfection. The Burnt Caramel Almond tile gives you refreshingly unsweet burnt caramel toffee, roasted slivered almonds, and bittersweet chocolate.

liddabit sweets

Roni-Sue doesn't just create memorable chocolates; she inspires others to do the same. Case in point: Liddabit Sweets, founded by Liz Gutman (an assistant chocolatier at Roni-Sue) and Jen King. They figured out how to put three of our favorite tastes into one irresistible snack: beer, caramel, and pretzels. They use two local brews, Brooklyn Brewery's Brown Ale and East India Pale Ale, that are reduced and stirred into their caramel along with crunchy pretzel chunks from a great Pennsylvanian Amish pretzel maker, Martin's. When you bite into one, an elusive whiff of beer only deepens the smoky toffee taste, saved from the brink of richness by the salty pretzel crunch.

8 RONI-SUE'S CHOCOLATES
NEW YORK, NY
PIG CANDY

Everybody's making chocolate bars filled or topped or studded with bacon these days. But only Rhonda Kave has the brilliant audacity to take whole slices of good (but nondesigner) bacon, cook them until they're done but still pliant, and coat them entirely in either dark or milk chocolate. It's a stroke of piggy, chocolatey genius. Roni-Sue's also makes terrific butter crunch candy rolled in bacon and chocolate.

9 TCHO CHOCOLATE
SAN FRANCISCO, CA
DARK CHOCOLATE

When one of our favorite pastry chefs, Karen DeMasco (page 32), told us that TCHO chocolate might be the best chocolate she has ever tasted and cooked with, our ears and our taste buds perked up. And the day we received two enormous packages of TCHO in the mail was one of the happiest days the office has ever had—like a chocolate-lover's Christmas morning. Their four kinds of dark chocolate—Madagascar with "citrus" notes, the Ghanian chocolate with "chocolatey" notes, the Ecuadorian with "nutty" notes, and the Peruvian with "fruity"—have distinct characters and all the hallmarks of great chocolate: complex, clean-tasting, layers of flavor, with a creaminess that doesn't leave a residue on your tongue.

CHOCOLATE SQUARES FROM TCHO, SAN FRANCISCO, CA

Brownies are a particular obsession at Serious Eats' World Headquarters; every few weeks, one of our contributors saunters into the office armed with a batch of brownies that he or she claims are the best. For this recipe, we have borrowed something from all of them, and by doing so we might just have created the best brownies yet. These are serious brownies, halfway between cakey and fudgy, insanely chocolatey, not too sweet, and touched with just the right amount of salt. Bring them into your office and you just might get that promotion you've been after. At the very least, you'll make a bunch of new friends.

MAKES SIXTEEN 2-INCH BROWNIES

2 tablespoons softened butter, for coating the pan

2 tablespoons cocoa powder, for dusting the pan

12 tablespoons (1½ sticks) unsalted butter, room temperature, cut into cubes

2 (4-ounce) bars high-quality milk chocolate, coarsely chopped

2 (4-ounce) bars high-quality dark chocolate, coarsely chopped

¾ cup (5.25 ounces) granulated sugar

¾ cup (5.25 ounces) light brown sugar, packed

2 tablespoons vanilla extract

4 large eggs, room temperature

½ cup (2.5 ounces) all-purpose flour, sifted

1 teaspoon *fleur de sel* or sea salt

1 tablespoon instant espresso powder

1 (4-ounce) bar high-quality bittersweet chocolate, coarsely chopped (optional)

triple-chocolate adult brownies

1 Position a baking rack in the lower third of the oven and preheat to 325°F. Cut a piece of parchment paper into a 8 × 12-inch rectangle. Use it to line the bottom and sides of an 8-inch square cake pan, the parchment extending up and over the edges. Use the softened butter to grease the top of the parchment, and dust with cocoa powder.

2 Place the cubed butter and the milk chocolate and dark chocolate in a medium microwave-proof bowl and microwave at 15-second intervals, stirring between each phase, until the butter and the chocolates are completely melted and smooth, about 1½ minutes total. Alternatively, melt the butter and the chocolates in a bowl set over a double boiler until smooth.

3 Allow the chocolate mixture to cool at room temperature for 10 minutes, then add both the granulated and the brown sugars and the vanilla, beating the mixture with a wooden spoon until incorporated. Add one egg at a time, beating until the batter becomes completely homogenous between additions. Add the flour, salt, and espresso powder, and mix vigorously until the batter is glossy and pulls away from the sides of the bowl, about 3 minutes. Fold in the bittersweet chocolate, if desired.

4 Pour the mixture into the prepared pan and rap the pan firmly against the counter a few times to even out the top and get rid of any air bubbles. Bake until a wooden skewer inserted into the center of the pan comes out moist but clean, about 45 minutes, rotating the pan twice during cooking.

5 Place the pan on a cooling rack and allow it to cool for 15 minutes. Remove the brownies using the parchment sling, and place them directly on the rack. Allow them to cool completely before cutting and serving.

Everyone at Serious Eats has strong feelings about chocolate-chip cookies—which makes sense, given how many we've tasted in our search for the best. So when it came to developing our own recipe, there was no shortage of opinions to be dealt with. In the end, we all agreed that our recipe had to produce chocolate-chip cookies that were crunchy on the outside and soft and chewy on the inside, have the right chocolate-to-dough ratio, have a distinct but not overwhelming buttery flavor, and taste almost as good six hours later as they did right out of the oven. And just like the brownies, they had to have a little salty kick. These cookies deliver on all counts.

chocolate-chip
cookies

MAKES TWENTY-FOUR 4-INCH COOKIES

3½ cups (17.5 ounces) all-purpose flour

1½ teaspoons baking powder

1¼ teaspoons baking soda

1½ teaspoons coarse sea salt, plus additional salt for sprinkling lightly on cookies

1½ cups (2½ sticks) unsalted butter, room temperature

1⅔ cups (11.5 ounces) light brown sugar, packed

1 cup (7 ounces) granulated sugar

2 large eggs

1 teaspoon vanilla extract

5 (4-ounce) bars high-quality bittersweet chocolate, still in their wrappers

Coarse flaky sea salt

1 Whisk the flour, baking powder, baking soda, and coarse sea salt together in a large bowl. Set aside.

2 In the bowl of a stand mixer, combine the butter and the sugars. Beat on medium speed with the paddle attachment until light and airy, about 4 minutes. Add the eggs one at a time, beating for 30 seconds after each addition to incorporate, and scraping down the sides of the bowl with a rubber spatula as necessary. Add the vanilla and whip for 30 more seconds to combine.

3 Add the flour mixture to the butter mixture and mix at low speed until just combined, about 30 seconds.

4 Using a heavy rolling pin or small skillet, whack the chocolate bars (still in their wrappers) one at a time repeatedly until they are broken into small chunks no larger than ½ inch. Unwrap the broken bars and add the broken chocolate, including smaller pieces and crumbs, to the dough bowl. When all five bars have been added to the bowl, mix on low speed until just combined, about 1 minute.

The dough should end up looking light brown with larger chunks of chocolate dispersed throughout it.

5 Cover the dough and refrigerate until cold, at least 1 hour and up to overnight.

6 To bake the cookies, adjust two oven racks to the upper middle and lower middle positions and preheat the oven to 350°F. Roll half of the dough into twelve $1\frac{3}{4}$-inch balls, approximately 3 tablespoons of dough in each. Place the balls 3 inches apart on two parchment-lined cookie sheets, six cookies per sheet.

7 Bake the cookies for 8 minutes, until they are completely spread out. Remove them from the oven and sprinkle each cookie with sea salt.

8 Return the pans to the oven, rotating them from front to back and top to bottom. Continue baking until the cookies are golden around the edges but still soft in the center, a further 6 to 8 minutes.

9 Allow the cookies to cool for 3 minutes, then slide the parchment, along with the cookies, onto two cooling racks while you cook the remaining 12 cookies. To store the cookies, allow them to completely cool, then place in a covered container at room temperature for up to three days.

THE COLD STUFF: ICE CREAM, GELATO, AND FROZEN CUSTARD

Some people are ice cream fans, or gelato connoisseurs, or frozen custard loyalists, but we'll take anything chilled and scoopable. Here are our frozen favorites from across the land. While some of these shops stick to classics like chocolate and vanilla, and others churn up flavors as wildly experimental as prosciutto or honey-blue cheese, all of them turn out fine, creamy, full-flavored frozen concoctions we love.

ICE CREAM AT THE BENT SPOON, PRINCETON, NJ

10 ICE CREAM SPOTS WE LOVE

1 THE BENT SPOON
PRINCETON, NJ

Whatever you do in this colorful artisan ice cream shop, don't insult New Jersey. Because Gabrielle Carbone and Matt Errico, the good folks at The Bent Spoon, are beyond devoted to the Garden State; their intensely flavorful ice creams and sorbets are inspired by the state's seasonal bounty. But "seasonality" doesn't quite capture the philosophy. It's not "Where can I get the best ingredients for this ice cream?" It's "This is what I want to be eating right now. Let's make an ice cream out of it!" That explains the sorbets of summer corn and heirloom tomato, autumn sweet potato ice cream and pumpkin mascarpone.

2 TOSCANINI'S
CAMBRIDGE, MA

It's an oft-cited fact on both sides of the Charles River that Bostonians eat more ice cream than anyone else in the country; visit Toscanini's and it's easy to see why. Gus Rancatore opened Toscanini's between Harvard and MIT in 1981, gaining a following so devoted his patrons once raised over $30,000 to pay off a tax bill that left the shop in jeopardy. The Burnt Caramel might explain this loyalty. Silky but not too sweet, it tastes exactly like the sugar left on the stove for just a second too long,

or like the darkest parts of a crème brûlée. It's the tail end of caramel, just shy of bitter, and while after an initial dark, smoky lick you expect the acrid taste of scorched sugar to kick in, it doesn't. It stops just short. It's genius.

3 JENI'S SPLENDID ICE CREAM
COLUMBUS, OH

It's a good thing the counterfolk will let you sample your way through their offerings before you commit to an order; frankly, we couldn't help you decide between them. It's not enough that Jeni's Splendid Ice Cream scoops an incredibly high-quality product, with cream from family-owned Ohio dairy Snowville Creamery going "from cow to kitchen" in under 48 hours. It's not enough that their classic flavors, the tongue-tingling, cinnamon-laced Queen City Cayenne and the not-too-sweet Salty Caramel, are almost impossible to pass up. No, Jeni's has to offer a dizzying roster of seasonally rotating flavors, unusual creations from Goat Cheese Red Cherry to Strawberry Buttermilk to Wildberry Lavender. Your best bet for maximum tasting (without a bellyache)? A "study" of four half-scoops.

4 HUMPHRY SLOCOMBE
SAN FRANCISCO, CA

Any shop scooping flavors of Jesus Juice (Côtes du Rhone red wine and Coca-Cola) and Prosciutto (just what it sounds like) will get our attention. What's so improbable about pastry chef-turned-ice-cream-wizard Jake Godby is that his flavors *work*. While the options behind the counter change often, the constants are balanced salt and focused flavors. The Balsamic Caramel brings out the deep, striking sweetness of aged balsamic; the Vietnamese Blue Bottle Coffee carries all the depth and roast of fine beans. And the Secret Breakfast, a superlatively creamy milk ice cream, cornflake bits, and bourbon, will unseat rum raisin as our boozy ice cream of choice.

what am i scooping?

Ice cream, frozen custard, and gelato are all cold and sweet and creamy and deliciously lickable, but the similarities end there. Here's how to tell them apart.

ICE CREAM The dairy-based dessert you know and love, sometimes made with a base of just milk and cream, sometimes made from a base that includes egg yolk.

GELATO This Italian-style frozen dessert has a lower fat content than ice cream, less sugar, and less air, giving it more intense flavor than standard ice cream as well as its characteristic smooth, almost elastic texture.

FROZEN CUSTARD True frozen custard must have egg yolk (at least 1.4 percent) in the base; it's made in a particular machine, which chills the custard and extrudes it in long ribbons of creamy deliciousness. The machine keeps overrun (that's the amount of air incorporated into the dessert) much lower than most ice cream. It's neither frozen nor held at subzero temperatures, so it's served much warmer than ice cream usually is. Between the custard composition, the low overrun, and the higher serving temperature, frozen custard is distinctively thick and smooth, with flavors that tend to come through clearly.

5 SWEET REPUBLIC
SCOTTSDALE, AZ

In the summer of 2008, Le Cordon Bleu–trained chef Helen Yung and her partner Jan Wichayanuparp opened Sweet Republic to almost immediate acclaim. Their ice cream, all hand-crafted in small batches, runs from the perfectly made classics (super-minty Mint Chip) to the more inventive (Medjool Date, Sweet Corn) to the downright wacky. Warning: if you order the I Love Bacon or the Honey Blue Cheese, get ready—they taste just like they sound.

6 MALLARD ICE CREAM
BELLINGHAM, WA

When we once asked the folks at Mallard Ice Cream to send us a few pints, their response was, "We can't choose just a few flavors. We'll send eighteen!" All their ice cream starts with a custom custard base created by Oregon's Lochmead Dairy that's then hand-processed with as many fresh, locally sourced, organic ingredients as possible, and slow-churned using an ice-and-salt method that results in a creamier ice cream. We're partial to the Exotic Grains of Paradise (sweet on first bite, cut by a fiery West African pepper) and the cookie-loaded Cookies and Kremlin.

7 AMY'S ICE CREAMS
AUSTIN, HOUSTON, AND SAN ANTONIO, TX

Amy Miller never intended to be an ice cream entrepreneur; but slinging scoops at Boston's legendary Steve's Ice Cream, while she was a pre-med student at Tufts, changed her mind. She opened Amy's Ice Cream in Austin in 1984, and since then, they've grown into a locally beloved mini chain of insanely creamy flavors, premium ingredients, and scoopers who love to toss your ice cream around before it finally lands in your cone. Don't leave without trying the malty Shiner Bock flavor—beer ice cream may sound unlikely, but even non–beer fans will appreciate its sweet tang.

8 GRAY'S ICE CREAM
TIVERTON AND BRISTOL, RI

In the tiny state of Rhode Island, food loyalties are strong and last for generations. Such is the case at Gray's, which has been serving home-made ice cream to locals for more than 80 years. Patrons drive from across the state (in fairness, it's never really that far) for a heaping portion of the New England classic, Grape-Nut Ice Cream, which tastes exactly like the delicious milk left over after a bowl of mostly devoured cereal.

9 SWEET ROSE CREAMERY
BRENTWOOD, CA

When Zoe Nathan and her husband, Josh Loeb, of Huckleberry (page 27) open an ice cream shop, they don't mess around. Nathan hired fellow Tartine (page 25) alum Shiho Yoshikawa, whom they had already lured to southern California to bake bread at Huckleberry, and anointed her "Ice Cream Chef." Unlike most other high-end ice cream artisans, Yoshikawa doesn't use a single base for the different flavors. Every flavor is made separately from scratch. The result: each ice cream has a slightly different texture and incredibly distinct flavor. Yoshikawa's vanilla is eggy and custardy and intensely rich; it tasted like a crème brûlée without the brittle top. Caffe Luxxe Coffee offers deep coffee flavor that's just sweet enough with a serious caffeine jolt.

10 24 CROWS
FLINT HILL, VA

An innkeeper in northern Virginia directed us without hesitation to 24 Crows—an art gallery, coffee, and gift shop, featuring local artists and, it turns out, killer house-made ice cream. Flavors like Apricot, Cappuccino, and Caramel with Majorcan Sea Salt and Roasted Almonds were creamy, smooth, and vividly flavored. Co-owner Heidi Morf started making ice cream more than 30 years ago at the Inn at Little Washington, and she's been making simply great ice cream out of eggs, cream, milk, and sugar ever since.

5 GELATO SPOTS WE LOVE

Capogiro in Philadelphia—"may" find, because many of their flavors are seasonal and made with local ingredients. Since opening their first location in 2002, owners Stephanie and John Reitano have offered more than 370 flavors of their dense, creamy gelati and smooth, intensely flavored sorbetti made fresh every morning.

2 DOLCEZZA
WASHINGTON, DC

Even when it's not peak fruit season, Robb Duncan, owner of Dolcezza (that's "sweetness" in Italian), thinks up whimsically complex gelato flavors. He uses spices, chocolates, citrus, and nut blends for his Argentine-style gelato. The Argentine part means Duncan and his co-owner Violeta Edelman (also his wife; they met in the Amazon jungle before moving to D.C.) use more cream than Italian gelato does, and no eggs. The Pistachio is earthy,

1 CAPOGIRO GELATO ARTISANS
PHILADELPHIA, PA

Thai Coconut Milk, Chocolate Ginger, and Lime with Cilantro are just a few of the flavors you may find at the four locations of artisanal gelateria

GELATO AT CAPOGIRO, PHILADELPHIA, PA

GELATO AT GROM, NEW YORK, NY

4 GROM
NEW YORK, NY; MALIBU, CA; AND ABROAD

Yes, Grom is a chain, but an Italian-based one, and the home of some of the finest gelato in this country. (When it opened in New York in 2007, there were lines that stretched for a full city block.) With absurd attention to ingredients (some chocolate comes from Colombia, some Venezuela, depending on what's best for the flavor) and focused but exciting flavors that rotate constantly, it's pricey but, in our opinion, worth every penny or euro-cent. Their Pistachio tastes like fresh-roasted nuts whipped into silky creaminess; the Grapefruit is like biting into the sweetest, juiciest, coldest grapefruit ever. Their gelato somehow makes every flavor taste more like itself.

5 PITANGO GELATO
BALTIMORE, MD

Ice cream may often follow a full meal, but a first swirl of Pitango's Caffe Espresso ice cream is enough to reawaken your palate and have you swooning with delight—it's creamy, surprisingly light, and full of intense, vivid coffee flavor. The chocolate gelato is equally powerful, with an ultra-chocolatey base and the tiniest of chocolate chips. Even better might be the sorbetti, which are often made with fruit from local farms: Strawberry, Pear, and Rhubarb are three full-flavored options worthy of serious consideration.

the Dulce de Leche is as good as any in Argentina, and when it is fruit season, go with anything berry-studded.

3 ANGELO BROCATO
NEW ORLEANS, LA

We'll be honest: when we walk into an old-fashioned parlor that would fit right into any city's Little Italy, we're not too optimistic about the gelato. But Angelo Brocato's in New Orleans still paddles out silky, beautifully complex flavors more than 100 years after the shop opened. The original Brocato learned his craft in Sicily, as an apprentice at a Palermo ice cream parlor, and his descendants still run the shop. The cannoli, their crispy cinnamon-spiked shells filled to order, are just as good as the gelato.

5 FROZEN CUSTARD SPOTS WE LOVE

custard is creamy, eggy, not too sweet, and downright silky—and that's just what you'll find at this Milwaukee institution. It's never stored at subzero temperatures, so it manages to stay light on the tongue despite its incredible richness. Even the plainest of Kopp's flavors, the vanilla, is tasty, thanks to Neilson Massey vanilla extract, but the chocolate might top it—truly chocolatey (rather than cocoa-powdery) and delectably creamy and smashingly good.

2 LEON'S FROZEN CUSTARD
MILWAUKEE, WI

Yep, two picks from Milwaukee, a town that'll have you know it's the custard capital of the world. Locals tend to swear allegiance to either Kopp's or Leon's, but we have no problem pointing you to both. Leon's is a throwback of a dessert stand— neon signs, employees decked out in little hats— and the prices look like they haven't budged since the '50s. But even without all the nostalgia, it'd be worth a visit for the remarkable custard that

1 KOPP'S FROZEN CUSTARD
MILWAUKEE, WI

You can't talk about frozen custard without talking about Kopp's, founded in 1950. Our ideal frozen

FROZEN CUSTARD AT KOPP'S, MILWAUKEE, WI

FROZEN CUSTARD AT LEON'S, MILWAUKEE, WI

slowly churns out from the large metal machines. Superbly creamy, thick enough to resist quick melt, it's delicious even in the simple vanilla form, though it's hard to pass up the butter pecan or the other special flavors.

3 SCOOTER'S FROZEN CUSTARD
CHICAGO, IL

This self-described mom-and-pop frozen custard shop is only open seasonally—so at least half the year, Chicago residents can get the good stuff. Scooter's vanilla custard is creamy, smooth, and filled with vanilla flavor. Nothing artisanal, just delicious. The shakes and concretes (custard blended with various add-ins) won't let you down, either. They do custard so right, you can save yourself a trip to Milwaukee.

4 SHAKE SHACK
NEW YORK, NY, AND BEYOND

Danny Meyer, the restaurant emperor of New York, opened the fast-food-style burger joint Shake

Shack (page 73) in 2004. But as good as his burgers are, they may be equaled by the fresh, silky custards and concretes he modeled after those at Ted Drewes (page 272) of his native St. Louis. And bite for bite, his custard is better—you can clearly taste the egg yolks and the real vanilla. Special flavors of custards and concretes change each month, but we'll always love the salted caramel and the seasonal pumpkin pie mix-in.

5 OLD-SCHOOL FROZEN CUSTARD
SEATTLE, WA

Dense and silky, the standard flavors from this Capitol Hill custard shop taste like real vanilla and real chocolate, not extract and cocoa powder. While each day brings a new special flavor, and there are endless options for sundaes and mix-ins, the naked vanilla custard is the best way to appreciate the buttery-smooth, gently eggy custard in its purest form.

SHAVE ICE AT WAIOLA, HONOLULU, HI

...AND MORE FROZEN FUN

FROZEN YOGURT
CULTURE ORGANIC FROZEN YOGURT, PALO ALTO, CA

By the end of the 2000s, cities all over the nation were swept by a wave of tart frozen yogurt shops like Pinkberry and Red Mango, selling frozen yogurt that actually tasted like, well, yogurt. And though they've spawned knock-offs and imitators by the dozens, we've never found any as good as Culture in Palo Alto (a city where health-minded yuppies and dessert-crazed college kids collide to forge a perfect fro-yo storm). Made with milk from the highly acclaimed organic Straus Family Creamery, the tart yogurt is silky-creamy with a lovely mellow tang; special flavors like Summer Blueberry-Pomegranate or Fall Pumpkin are worth a try, too. But what really sets Culture apart are its toppings: honey-sweetened pumpkin seed brittle, homemade marshmallow and fudge sauces, and even a different fruit crisp each day. Scoop it on top, and it's like dessert à la mode—but backwards.

SOFT-SERVE
XOCO, CHICAGO, IL

Rick Bayless's Mexican-inspired casual spot may be known for its tortas (page 137), but even after trying half a dozen, we dove into their vanilla soft-serve with glee. Sound dull? Not when it's this creamy—and topped with maple-pecan-bacon-streusel, all doused in a salted caramel sauce that tasted just shy of burnt in the very best way possible. While bacon in sweets isn't a trend we're always happy with, the bacon here added just the right salty crunch, without turning the whole thing into a pigfest. We licked the cup clean.

SHAVE ICE
WAIOLA, HONOLULU, HI

Shave ice—like a mountain-size version of the finest snow cone you've ever eaten, drowned in syrup and covered in toppings—is a staple of Hawaiian life. And while Waiola is one of the better known, it's also, in our opinion, the finest. In more than one sense: the ice is shaved so finely it's like snow that dissolves on the tongue. Syrups range from green tea to passionfruit to lychee, and toppings include condensed milk, custard, azuki beans, and mochi. Not enough excitement? Get ice cream on top.

SAVORY DESSERTS
MOLLY MOON'S HANDMADE ICE CREAM SHOP, SEATTLE, WA

How savory can desserts get and still be desserts? That's a question that comes to mind at ice cream shop Molly Moon's in Seattle, where you might find a sweet corn ice cream served with browned butter, Parmesan cheese, and cayenne—or a rich chocolate ice cream (made from Seattle's Theo Chocolate) with bergamot-infused olive oil and sea salt. Both stop just short of overkill—the corn ice cream has only the sweetness of the natural kernels, giving the sundae a summer freshness; the depth of the chocolate ice cream counters the olive oil and salt that grace its top, never letting them take over. And while not quite savory, and perhaps not to everyone's taste, the spicy ginger ice cream is magnificent.

SALT, OIL, HEAT, AND SWEETS

Sea salt. Olive oil. Cayenne pepper. These are hardly ingredients that bring desserts to mind. But when used judiciously, we find that savory ingredients can really strut their stuff in desserts. A few flakes of sea salt can make any sweet flavor pop, whether caramels, chocolate-chip cookies, fudgy brownies, or even ice cream. The fruity, grassy notes of olive oil come out beautifully in cakes or muffins or even gelato. And the fiery heat of red pepper spices up hot chocolate beautifully. Trust us. One note of warning: beware of overdoing it. A little bit of salt or heat is magical; but a lot, we wouldn't wish upon anyone.

SUNDAE AT MOLLY MOON'S, SEATTLE, WA

The best olive oil gelato we've ever tasted was our first experience with this magical frozen concoction, at Mario Batali's pizzeria Otto. There, pastry chef Meredith Kurtzman served us our first scoop—exotic but familiar, superbly creamy, with just enough fruity, buttery olive oil. Well, it tasted like heaven. We didn't want to ask Meredith for her recipe (she is justifiably reluctant about giving it to others), so we set out to develop our own.

extra-virgin olive oil **gelato**

MAKES ABOUT 1½ QUARTS

3 cups whole milk

1 cup heavy cream

½ teaspoon vanilla extract

8 large egg yolks

1 cup (7 ounces) sugar

1 teaspoon kosher salt

¾ cup best-quality extra-virgin olive oil

Coarse sea salt and additional extra-virgin olive oil, for serving

1 In a large, heavy-bottomed saucepan, bring ¼ cup water to a simmer over medium heat and cook until it has almost completely evaporated. Add the milk, cream, and vanilla to the pan and bring to a simmer, stirring frequently to ensure that the mixture doesn't stick to the bottom and burn. Remove the pan from the heat.

2 Combine the egg yolks, sugar, and salt in the bowl of a stand mixer fitted with the whisk attachment and whisk at medium speed until the mixture lightens in color and falls away from the whisk in thick ribbons, about 5 minutes. With the mixer running on low, slowly drizzle in the olive oil. Continue whisking while you slowly add the milk mixture.

3 Return the ice cream base to the saucepan and cook over medium-low heat, stirring constantly, until the mixture registers 180°F. on an instant-read thermometer. Immediately strain the custard through a fine-mesh strainer into a heat-proof bowl. Chill over an ice bath, stirring occasionally, until it is completely cold, about 15 minutes (or simply store the warm mixture in the refrigerator overnight).

4 Freeze the custard in an ice cream maker according to the manufacturer's instructions. Freeze for at least 1 additional hour before serving. If you plan on serving the gelato later than 1 hour after freezing, allow it to soften in the refrigerator for 30 minutes before serving. The gelato is best when slightly softened. Drizzle with additional olive oil and sprinkle with sea salt before serving, if desired.

TRIPLE COCONUT CREAM PIE AT DAHLIA BAKERY, SEATTLE, WA

11 PIES WE LOVE FROM COAST TO COAST

1 DAHLIA BAKERY AND PALACE KITCHEN SEATTLE, WA
COCONUT CREAM PIE

Seattle superstar chef-restaurateur Tom Douglas has made quite a name for his triple coconut cream pie, baked at his Dahlia Bakery and served for dessert at his Palace Kitchen restaurant. And why not? Silky, coconutty custard is mounded with clouds of vanilla whipped cream, all crowned with crunchy coconut, in a fall-apart flaky pie crust that cradles it all.

2 HOOSIER MAMA CHICAGO, IL
RASPBERRY PIE

Chicago is a great food town, but Indiana has it licked when it comes to pie. Lucky for Chicagoans,

BLUEBERRY PIE AT HOOSIER MAMA, CHICAGO, IL

then, that Hoosier (Indiana native) Paula Haney set up shop in the city. We're partial to her double-crusted fruit pies—particularly her fresh raspberry pie, with a balance of sweet and tart that seems to echo the world's most perfectly ripe raspberry. But it's hard to overlook the banana cream pie: quivering vanilla-speckled banana cream topped with thin banana slices and house-made vanilla wafers and white chocolate shavings, all in a supremely light, flaky crust. As Serious Eats contributor Michael Nagrant once said, "It's a pie worth burning in the firey hells of fatness for."

3 STEVE'S AUTHENTIC KEY LIME PIES BROOKLYN, NY
THE SWINGLE

We've braved wind, weather, and a trek to the remote Brooklyn neighborhood of Red Hook for a

the best breakfast i ever had

I am ready to nominate Hoosier Mama proprietor and pie-ologist Paula Haney for a MacArthur genius award. That's how delicious her pies are. Her double-crusted fruit pies have gorgeous all-butter crusts made with just right amount of salt and sugar, and her fruit fillings always taste like the essence of whatever fruit is in them, nothing more and nothing less.

Recently, Serious Eats editors Carey Jones and Robyn Lee (page 9) and two of our Chicago correspondents descended on Hoosier Mama for my all-time favorite specialty meal—the all-pie breakfast. I was first introduced to the all-pie breakfast by the Magnolia Grill's incredibly gifted pastry chef and co-owner Karen Barker (page 309); she completely blew my mind with an array of pies eaten on one fine morning in 2007, and I've been wanting to replicate the experience ever since. That's why we ordered one slice of every pie on Hoosier Mama's menu.

Her raspberry pie was sweet, tart, and just acidic enough; her apple pie is just as good, the cinnamony apples hitting the sweet spot between soft and firm. Her cream and custard pies are just as inspired. The blueberry may have formed a bit of a puddle, but it was the best pie-filling puddle I've ever dipped a spoon into. Key lime pie had a spicy lime flavor with gingersnap crust, the pear raspberry had fruit that kept a bit of a bite, and the apple crumb pie had just a little bit of custard to make it all come together.

Banana cream pie, with white chocolate ribbons, was remarkably banana-y without being cloyingly sweet. The chocolate cream pie was paradigmatic, intensely chocolatey with no insipid cocoa powder flavor; the coconut custard pie was an equally perfect representation of the form. It's not to be confused with the coconut cream pie, which surprised me with its balanced coconut flavor and the toasted coconut topping that lent a little much-needed crunch. And a Hoosier Maple Sugar Cream Pie, with a rich light brown custard, was ridiculously smooth and showed off the flavor of sugar, not just the toothaching sweetness. (Concerned about our nutritional intake during this pie bacchanalia? We also had a savory pie, with in-season corn and tomatoes—surprisingly light and oh-so delicious.)

Is it any wonder that that was the best breakfast I ever had?

taste of the Swingle (a chocolate-dipped Key limer on a stick) at Steve's Authentic Key Lime Pies. And it's worth it every time: the spicy tartness of the Key lime pie filling, the crunch of the graham-cracker crust, and the perfectly balanced bitter-sweet chocolate, all coming together perfectly on the little wooden Popsicle stick.

4 DUARTE'S TAVERN PESCADERO, CA
OLALLIEBERRY PIE

Pronounced *oh-La-leh*, the olallieberry is a cross between the loganberry and the youngberry—the former of which is a blackberry-raspberry cross and the latter, a blackberry-dewberry cross. (Whew.) Complicated genealogy aside, the olallie-berry at Duarte's Tavern in the northern California oceanside village of Pescadero has just the right balance of tart and sweet, so tasty you don't mind that the seeds get stuck in your teeth. The browner than golden crust may look quite thick, but it's so flaky it falls apart at the slide of a fork—and after one forkful, you realize it's so good, light and salty and sweet, that you're *glad* it's so thick. More crust to eat.

5 SCRATCH BAKERY DURHAM, NC
LEMON CHESS PIE

Scratch Bakery owner Phoebe Lawless thinks more like a chef than a pastry chef. That's because she worked for eight years for one of the country's

LEMON CHESS PIE AT SCRATCH BAKERY, DURHAM, NC

more pies from phoebe lawless

I can't say enough about Phoebe Lawless, in my estimation one of the finest pie-bakers in America. The lemon chess pie may be one of my favorites, but others are just as sensational: her almost demure chocolate tart with sea salt, the barely sweetened intense chocolate drawn out by the sea salt, and both ingredients find-ing a fitting home in a buttery crust that is the other foundation of her pastry-making great-ness. Two other pies are must-tries at Scratch: a brown butter pecan pie that tastes like fantas-tic butter pecan ice cream in pie form; and her sugar pie, which delivers just as much tart and creamy flavor as it does sweet, thanks to the buttermilk Lawless uses in the recipe.

finest chefs (who happens to be a baker), Karen Barker of the Magnolia Grill in Durham, North Carolina, where Scratch is located. Is this a dis-tinction without a difference? I don't think so. Lawless understands how to integrate savory ingredients into sweets in a way that draws out flavor in surprising but logical ways. Take her lemon chess pie. Lawless uses whole paper-thin slices of lemon, so that when you bite into the pie you get all these surprising bursts of flavor and texture; it's sweet and just acidic enough, like any great-tasting citrus thing.

BLUEBERRY PIE AT YURA ON MADISON, NEW YORK, NY

6 GRAND TRAVERSE PIE COMPANY TRAVERSE CITY, MI
CHERRY PIE

Traverse City calls itself the "Cherry Capital of the World," and Michigan grows more cherries than any other state—so where better to go for cherry pie? At this pie shop, every last crust is still hand-rolled and shaped. The cherry crumb, cherry peach crumb, and raspberry-cherry are all worth a bite, too.

7 HOMEMADE ICE CREAM & PIE KITCHEN LOUISVILLE, KY
CHESS PIE

Imagine pecan pie without the pecans, and you'll get a sense of the delicious sugary suspension that is the filling of a chess pie. At Louisville institution Homemade Ice Cream & Pie Kitchen, the chess pie stops just short of too sweet, helped by a crumbly, salty crust and the brown-sugar depth of the custard filling. (Though if you're sugar-shy, some of their other pies may make your teeth recoil in fear.)

8 YURA ON MADISON NEW YORK, NY
BLUEBERRY PIE

All right. We love Maine's wild blueberries—smaller, sweeter, and more intensely flavored than their cultivated counterparts. We love Maine blueberry pie. But we've never had a blueberry pie that rivaled the one from Yura's on Manhattan's Upper East Side. It's loosely packed with tiny, still intact wild Maine blueberries splashed with lemon juice, held together by a loose syrup that tastes just as strongly of blueberry, cradled by a flaky, buttery, salty-sweet crust so good we've been known to break off the edges and eat them first.

9 TED'S BAKERY HONOLULU, HI
CHOCOLATE HAUPIA PIE

Start with haupia, a firm and intensely flavored Hawaiian coconut pudding, in a tender, flaky pie shell. Top with a looser chocolate pudding, dollop with whipped cream, and you have a beautiful marriage of chocolate, coconut, and cream in each bite. And despite its richness, it's light and cool enough to eat even in shaved-ice weather.

10 COFFEE CUP CAFE SULLY, IA
DOUBLE-CRUSTED RHUBARB PIE

You'd think farm cafes in small towns serving great pie would be ubiquitous in Iowa, but unfortunately that's not the case. That's why the Coffee Cup Cafe is such a find, a place where world-class pies are still coming out of the oven. A recent visit had us weeping tears of pleasure as we dug into a piece of rhubarb pie. The rhubarb was appropriately tart, the crust was flaky as all get out, and the ratio of filling to crust was just perfect.

11 MRS. BLAKE'S PIES VINEYARD HAVEN, MA
STRAWBERRY-RHUBARB PIE

There are a million reasons to fall in love with picturesque Martha's Vineyard, but Mrs. Blake's pies are what did it for us. The late Eileen Blake started baking pies in her family's double-wide trailer and selling them by the side of the road years ago, and pie lovers have been flocking to her dirt driveway ever since. Her daughter took over the pie-baking responsibilities after Mrs. Blake died, and we're happy to tell you the pies are as good as ever. Her double-crusted strawberry-rhubarb pies are a model of pie-baking consistency. The thin crusts are always flaky, the appropriately sweet and tart fruit not too goopy, and the bottom crust is always baked all the way through. In other words, pie perfection. But if you need another, you can't go wrong with the lemon chess pie, which Mrs. Blake started making when Former President Clinton told her it was his favorite.

baked goods at state road restaurant

Other than Mrs. Blake's pies, it was hard to find a seriously delicious baked good on Martha's Vineyard until the restaurant-bakery-cafe State Road opened a few years ago. The restaurant is solid, but the baked goods made by pastry chef Rose Sarja and sold in the cafe in the morning are insanely good. Her caramel-pecan sticky buns are exemplary: light, moist, loaded with cinnamon flavor, and somehow, miraculously, not too sweet. Her chocolate-chip and her kitchen-sink cookies are buttery miniature masterpieces. Both cookies are more pliant than crunchy, and both pack an insane flavor punch.

And as long as we're talking about baked goods on islands off Cape Cod, we'll point you to a few good ones on Nantucket, too: the soak-through-the-bag buttery, crisp, and pliant chocolate-chip cookies at Something Natural; the fine cinnamon-sugar morning buns and other breakfast pastries at Daily Breads; the homey and delicious cake doughnuts at Downyflake Restaurant; and the macarons, yeast doughnuts, and elephant-ear cookies at Nantucket Bake Shop.

We had Mrs. Blake's and the Coffee Cup Cafe's crust in mind when we set out to develop this apple pie recipe, and we have to say we succeeded beyond our wildest imaginations. The keys to making this pie work: using both butter and shortening in the crust, and packing the apples into the crust to keep them firm.

classic
apple pie

MAKES 1 PIE

FOR THE CRUST

2½ cups (12.5 ounces) all-purpose flour

2½ teaspoons kosher salt

3 tablespoons sugar (1¼ ounces)

12 tablespoons (1½ sticks) unsalted butter, cut into ½-inch chunks, and refrigerated until chilled

½ cup cold vegetable shortening

1 For the crust: Place the flour, salt, and sugar in a food processor and pulse with four 1-second pulses to combine. Remove half of the flour mixture to a small bowl and set aside. Add the butter chunks to the food processor, then add the shortening, breaking it into small pieces with your fingers and dropping them into the processor bowl. Shake the processor bowl until the shortening and butter are well coated with flour.

2 Process with eight 1-second pulses until the mixture just starts to collect in clumps. Add the reserved flour mixture to the processor and distribute everything evenly in the bowl with a rubber spatula. Process with four or five quick pulses, until the mixture is broken up and well mixed. Empty the mixture into a large mixing bowl.

3 Sprinkle ⅓ cup of ice-cold water evenly over the mixture. Using a rubber spatula, fold the dough together until it forms a shaggy ball. If necessary, add additional cold water a teaspoon at a time until the dough holds together. Press the dough into a uniform mass with your hands, then divide it into two even balls. Flatten the balls into 4-inch disks and wrap tightly with plastic wrap. Refrigerate for at least 45 minutes or up to three days in advance. Allow the dough to sit at room temperature for 15 minutes before rolling.

4 For the filling: Toss the apples, sugars, salt, lemon juice, cinnamon, and cornstarch together in a large bowl.

5 Roll out one disk of dough on a generously floured work surface into a 12-inch circle about ⅛ inch thick. Transfer the crust to a 9½-inch pie plate by rolling it loosely around the rolling pin and unrolling it into the plate. Carefully work the dough into the corners of the plate by lifting the edges with one hand, and gently pushing into place with the other. Leave the edges overhanging and place the dough in the refrigerator until completely chilled, at least 30 minutes. Meanwhile, adjust an oven rack to the lowest position and on it place two rimmed baking sheets stacked on top of each other. Preheat the oven to 425°F.

6 Add the apple mixture to the pie shell, smoothing out the top with a rubber spatula. Roll out the second disk of dough and transfer to the top of the pie, allowing the edges to overhang. Use kitchen shears to trim the edges of both the top and bottom crusts until only ½ inch is left hanging over the edge. Working around the pie plate, carefully fold the dough edges underneath themselves until the dough is even with the rim of the pit plate. Use scissors, a fork, or your thumb and forefingers to flute the edges of the crust and seal it.

7 Brush the crust evenly with beaten egg white and sprinkle it with about 1 tablespoon of granulated sugar. Cut five slits in the top of the dough radially to allow ventilation.

8 Place the pie on the preheated baking sheets and bake for 20 minutes, until the top is beginning to brown. Rotate the pie, reduce the oven temperature to 375°F., and continue baking until the crust is a deep golden brown and crisp, about 30 minutes longer. Transfer the pie to a wire rack and allow to cool for at least 2 hours before serving.

FOR THE FILLING

4½ pounds (8 or 9 medium) sweet-tart apples, such as Fuji, Golden Delicious, or Royal Gala, peeled, cored, and cut into ¼-inch slices (about 8 cups)

¼ cup (1.75 ounces) granulated sugar

½ cup (3.5 ounces) light brown sugar, packed

¾ teaspoon kosher salt

1 tablespoon juice from 1 lemon

¼ teaspoon ground cinnamon

2 tablespoons cornstarch

1 egg white, lightly beaten

Granulated sugar, for sprinkling

Serious Eats editor Robyn Lee is the macaron connoisseur in the office (the woman worships at the altar of French pastry chef-god Pierre Hermé), so we knew we'd have to get a recipe up to her exacting standards. After much experimentation and many failed batches, we finally arrived at a recipe that received the Robyn Lee seal of approval. We think they'll receive yours as well.

vanilla
macarons

MAKES ABOUT 24 COOKIES

FOR THE COOKIES

2½ cups (12 ounces) almond flour, placed in freezer for at least 30 minutes

2½ cups (10 ounces) confectioners' sugar

4 large egg whites, room temperature

1½ tablespoons granulated sugar (¾ ounce)

Pinch of cream of tartar

1 teaspoon vanilla extract

1 For the cookies: Place 1¼ cups of the almond flour and 1¼ cups of the confectioners' sugar in a blender and blend until completely pulverized, about 45 seconds, stopping and stirring with a rubber spatula as necessary. Transfer to a medium bowl. Repeat with the remaining almond flour and confectioners' sugar. Sift the almond flour mixture or shake through a fine-mesh strainer to remove any larger chunks.

2 In a stand mixer fitted with a whisk attachment, whip the egg whites on high speed until soft peaks form. Add the granulated sugar, cream of tartar, and vanilla and continue whipping until the eggs hold stiff peaks. Remove the bowl from the mixer. Add the almond flour mixture to the meringue in four stages, gently folding with a rubber spatula between stages,

until completely homogenous. The resulting mixture should slowly flow like lava when the bowl is tilted, and any peaks should slowly flatten themselves out within 30 seconds. Transfer the mixture to a pastry bag fitted with a ½-inch plain tip (or use a zipper-lock bag with the corner cut off).

3 Adjust two oven racks to the upper and lower middle positions and preheat the oven to 325°F. Line two cookie sheets with parchment paper. Pipe twelve 1½-inch circles of the mixture onto each parchment sheet, leaving a 1-inch space between each cookie. You should use half of the batter to form 24 circles. Bake until the cookies are an even light golden brown and still soft to the touch, about 18 minutes total, rotating the pans halfway through cooking. Transfer the parchment sheets to cooling racks, reline the baking sheets, and repeat with the remaining batter. Allow the cookies to cool completely.

4 To make the buttercream: While the cookies are cooling, combine the granulated sugar and $\frac{1}{4}$ cup water in a small saucepan and cook over medium-high heat until simmering. Brush the sides of the pan with a moist brush to remove any sugar crystals and cook until the sugar registers 248°F. on an instant-read thermometer, brushing the pot with water occasionally as it cooks to prevent crystallization. Take off the heat and set aside, proceeding immediately to the next step before syrup cools completely.

5 In a stand mixer fitted with the whisk attachment, whisk the eggs on high speed until pale yellow and thickened, about 2 minutes. Reduce the speed to medium low and carefully pour the hot syrup into the eggs. Continue whisking on medium speed until the mixture cools to room temperature, about 5 minutes. Add the vanilla and butter, a few cubes at a time, allowing each addition to be incorporated before adding the next. The mixture will look like it's breaking, but continue to whip on medium speed until it comes together and turns glossy and fluffy, about 10 minutes longer. (Buttercream can be stored for up to two weeks in the refrigerator, or six months in the freezer. Allow it to come to room temperature and rewhisk until light and fluffy before using it.)

6 Transfer the buttercream to a pastry bag fitted with a $\frac{1}{2}$-inch plain tip (or a zipper-lock bag with the corner cut off) and pipe about 2 teaspoons of buttercream onto the bottoms of half of the cookies. Top with the remaining cookies and press gently to spread the buttercream to the edges of the cookie. Serve immediately.

FOR THE BUTTERCREAM

$\frac{1}{2}$ cup granulated sugar (3$\frac{1}{4}$ ounces)

2 large eggs

2 teaspoons vanilla extract

$\frac{3}{4}$ cup (1$\frac{1}{2}$ sticks) unsalted butter, cut into $\frac{1}{2}$-inch cubes, room temperature

home-grown & house-made

there's never been **A BETTER TIME TO GROW OR MAKE FOOD in america.**

I THINK IT'S SAFE TO SAY THAT MY MOM, WHO DIED IN 1967, DIDN'T SPEND MUCH TIME GOING TO FARMERS' MARKETS, MUCH LESS FARMS.

She didn't know a vine-ripened tomato from a greenhouse-grown one. Back then farmers were neither seen nor heard—though, ironically, there were many more of them. Now farmers are roaring hot, and not just from the sun beating down on them all day. They are lionized by chefs in every city in the country, interviewed by Martha Stewart on television and the radio, and yes, written about and photographed extensively on Serious Eats. What's more, bread-bakers, sausage-makers, cheese-makers, and butchers get the same treatment all over the food media.

If I had told my mom I was going to go to college and study agriculture so that I could become a farmer, she would have started to cry—and I don't mean tears of joy. Back then, being a farmer was not sexy; it wasn't something a middle-class person would aspire to, not when he could become a doctor or a lawyer or a "professional," as my grandmother would have called it. Farming wasn't considered respectable, in my mother's world. Now, many of the best farmers I know go to fine academic institutions and get graduate degrees to learn how to grow the most complex sweet-tart peaches, the ripest tomatoes, and the sweetest strawberries.

I think it's also safe to say that my mother never bought a fresh-baked hand-formed baguette from an artisan baker (though she certainly knew her way around a corn rye bread). In truth, every aspect of food production in this country has seen some sort of revival. There are farmers who grow tomatoes so good you feel like you're tasting a tomato for the very first time when you bite into one. Likewise, there are bread-bakers in this country who have taken us far, far past Wonder Bread and Levy's Jewish Rye (though those foodstuffs have their place in the world as well).

At Serious Eats, we live to make these discoveries, so in the final chapter of our book we will tell you about some of the people who grow or make terrific food. We know there are others out there, and we look forward to finding them. But these are the stories we know of some of the people who are redefining what and how we eat in America. These folks are the true missionaries of the delicious, and just as important, they are careful stewards of the land they till and the animals they raise and the food they serve to serious eaters everywhere.

Here, you'll meet farmer Rick Bishop and learn why his strawberries are so special, and where you

UNION SQUARE GREENMARKET, NEW YORK, NY

can find them. You're going to meet our favorite peach-grower, Ron Mansfield, who tills his land like the mad agronomist he is, armed with a graduate degree from the University of California. The fact that Ron's Goldbud peaches are so delicious that biting into one is a religious experience is not the result of dumb luck—it's rigorous attention to detail. You'll meet our sculptor-turned-favorite bread-baker Jim Lahey, whose Pizza Bianca (a focaccia-like bread he learned to make at the famous bakery on the Campo De' Fiore in Rome) is the "bread" you are most likely to find if you wander into Serious Eats' World Headquarters on any given day. And prosciutto-maker Herb Eckhouse, who along with his wife took their Harvard educations and fierce intellect and focused on making prosciutto in Iowa the equal of any made in Parma; or Jen Small and Mike Yezzi of Flying Pigs Farm, whose story is just as compelling as their pork, and that's saying something. And yes, you'll meet some of our favorite chefs, because it was chefs who discovered many of these farmers and artisan food-makers well before the rest of us did—and for that we should be eternally grateful.

What's fun about this aspect of the food world is that it's ever-expanding and changing. College students spend summers and postgraduate years in programs like World Wide Opportunities on Organic Farms (WWOOF) that place them on farms all over the world. Young people routinely

apprentice at butchers. And it's not just students. The folks from Flying Pigs Farm host summer weekend camps for urban dwellers to learn how their pork is raised and even slaughtered.

Like any revolution, this one has its messy aspects—and not just standing foot-deep in pig blood and guts. Handmade, carefully grown food can be out of reach, economically, for anyone who doesn't have the wherewithal to make a discretionary spending decision about the food he or she eats. So yes, nutrition advocates say people are going to have to spend more on what they eat—but if you don't happen to have the money to do so, you're still going to send your kids to fast-food joints and to buy produce that has been grown thousands of miles from where it's bought and eaten.

But even this problem is beginning to be addressed. City and state agencies, and even the federal government, have stepped into the breach with subsidized programs that send farmers' markets into depressed neighborhoods. The founder of Growing Power, Will Allen, in Milwaukee, won a MacArthur Fellowship for his work creating urban farms to service undernourished communities. At the Red Hook Community Farm in Brooklyn, disadvantaged kids learn to till the soil and reap the harvest of what they've grown. Farm policies and subsidies are the subject of healthy debate, and Wal-Mart is now selling more organic produce than anywhere else in the country—who'd've thought? This doesn't mean we've created a world in which every citizen has access to honest, healthy food. But we're getting closer, and that gives us hope for the future.

10 CHEFS LEADING THE FARM-TO-TABLE SCENE

1 PALACE KITCHEN, SERIOUS PIE, DAHLIA BAKERY, DAHLIA LOUNGE, LOLA, ETTA'S, SEATOWN SEABAR SEATTLE, WA

TOM DOUGLAS

At all of Douglas's restaurants, chefs try to go as local as it gets, building their menus from whole pigs and lambs raised nearby, locally foraged mushrooms, and Washington wines. This only makes sense—ever since Douglas came to the Pacific Northwest from his native Delaware decades ago, he's been smitten by the region's native bounty. Now he's taken the logical next step by growing wagonloads of vegetables at his own Prosser Farm, a few hours east of Seattle.

For the past three years, Tom's wife and partner, Jackie, along with their family, have coaxed unbelievable produce from the farm: perfect yellow-beet greens, baby rainbow-chard leaves, lush bunches of spicy red and white radishes. Later in the season

BLUE HILL AT STONE BARNS, POCANTICO HILLS, NY

their trucks fill with sweet apricots, ripe tomatoes, and a small mountain of spicy peppers and eggplants, irrigated by the Cascade Mountains' snow melt and ripened in the hot eastern Washington sunshine. From late spring until early fall, these fruits and vegetables appear everywhere on Douglas's menus—from the tomatoes in Lola's Greek salad to the roasted peppers on Serious Pie's pizza. The restaurants have even started canning and preserving to keep the Prosser Farm produce on their winter menus.

2 MAGNOLIA GRILL DURHAM, NC
KAREN AND BEN BARKER

The menu at Magnolia Grill has always been market driven and seasonal—long before those were snappy marketing terms. Husband-and-wife chef team Karen and Ben Barker started out by working with a network of farmers from the markets in Carrboro, North Carolina; and over the years, their businesses have become ever-more closely intertwined. Alex and Betsy Hitt of Peregrine Farm supply their leeks, onions, blueberries (which go into Karen's must-order cobbler), and sometimes as many as 14 to 18 varieties of tomatoes for soups, sauces, and ragouts. The summer deliveries make cooking almost "stupid easy," says Karen, because the flavors are so intense and distinctive. (Maybe "stupid easy" for her, if not for the rest of us.)

In the colder months, they rely on Diane and William Brinkley at Brinkley Farm; William is a North Carolina tobacco grower-turned-greenhouse farmer. He supplies a bounty of greens (turnip, mustard, and collard) as well as newly dug red Pontiac potatoes and Corolla Golds. "The Brinkleys are our link to our Southern agricultural heritage. They're even grinding all the cornmeal and grits," says Karen. And let's not forget the pork. Flo Harley and Portia McKnight operate Chapel Hill Creamery, a pasture-raised sustainable cow's-milk cheese manufacturer, which also raises Berkshire and Tamworth hogs. The oinkers are fed a steady diet of the leftover whey from cheese-making—which may just be why Magnolia Grill's head cheese, ciccoline, porchetta, house-cured hams, and roasted pork butts are so darn succulent.

3 CRAIGIE ON MAIN CAMBRIDGE, MA
TONY MAWS

With such predictably unpredictable weather in the Boston area, Tony Maws never knows exactly what produce will be delivered to his restaurant on a given day. "I have to ask myself, how flexible am I willing to be?" *Very,* tends to be his answer. When you get a first forkful of one of his insanely thought-out dishes, you realize why the intelligent sourcing of ingredients makes such a difference. "It sounds boring, but you bite into carrots from Bay End Farm and you just stop—and you're like, whoa."

Maws and farmer Kofi Ingersoll have become especially close over the years; Tony even got married on the Ingersolls' farm. Supplying produce ranging from the Japanese cabbage-like senposai greens (with a sweet apple taste) to Ingersoll's 30-odd varieties of tomatoes, Bay End Farm is a huge part of Craigie on Main. "I try to be as sustainable as possible," Maws says, "but that means something different in February than it does in July." And the constant flux of the growing process is part of what gets Maws so giddy. He loves that peas have such a short season—you eat them silly while they're around, then are forced to wait the rest of the year.

4 PALEY'S PLACE PORTLAND, OR
VITALY PALEY

Much of the raw, young culinary talent in Portland today—including chefs at Le Pigeon, Beaker and Flask, and Olympic Provisions—started in chef Vitaly Paley's kitchen, absorbing his farm-to-table ethos. For more than 15 years, he's been working with farmers like George Weppler, who grows more than 250 kinds of vegetables on five acres in the Cascade foothills, including 50 types of lettuce and 18 varieties of tomatoes. "He delivers a box of mystery goodies," says Paley of Weppler. "He knows me inside and out: the sizes, the quantities I want. We have this mental connection." What's in those boxes? Maybe green garlic and Walla Walla onions, maybe pinky-size potatoes or two varieties

Meat does magical things in the hands of Tony Maws: a seemingly simple octopus tentacle, say, that's been through a washing machine–like tenderizer, slow-poached for five hours, and aged for two days. But just as important, the chef knows when to get out of the way of good ingredients, as he does with this skirt steak. This preparation, accented with a marinade that includes red chiles, coriander, cumin, and ginger, is really all about the meat.

red chile–marinated **skirt steak**

TONY MAWS, CRAIGIE ON MAIN

SERVES 4

3 dried New Mexican chiles, stems and seeds removed, split in half, and soaked in warm water for 15 minutes

2 garlic cloves

1 teaspoon coriander seeds

1 teaspoon cumin seeds

1 whole clove

3 allspice berries

1 teaspoon ground ginger

1 teaspoon dried thyme

16 black peppercorns

$1/3$ cup canola oil

3 tablespoons soy sauce

2 teaspoons kosher salt

4 skirt or hanger steaks, 6 to 8 ounces each, trimmed of excess fat and silverskin

NOTE With relatively low-fat cuts like hanger or skirt steak, grass-fed beef provides better flavor. Look for grass-fed beef, if available.

1 Remove chiles from the soaking liquid. Add them and the garlic, coriander, cumin, clove, allspice, ginger, thyme, peppercorns, oil, soy sauce, and salt to a blender. Blend until smooth. Add the steaks to a 1-gallon zipper-lock bag. Add the marinade and coat evenly. Squeeze the air out of the bag, seal, and refrigerate overnight, at least 8 hours and up to 24, turning and massaging once or twice to redistribute the marinade.

2 Remove the steaks from the bag and wipe off the excess marinade. Light a large chimney starter full with charcoal (about 5 quarts) and wait until fully ignited and the coals are mostly covered in gray ash, about 20 minutes. Arrange the coals under half of the grill grate and place the grate on top. Cover and preheat for 10 minutes. Remove the cover and brush the grill grates clean with a grill brush.

3 Add the steaks to the hot side of the grill, cover, and grill without moving until the meat is well charred on the first side, about $1^{1}/_{2}$ minutes. Flip the steaks, cover, and grill until the second side is well charred, about $1^{1}/_{2}$ minutes. Transfer to the cool side of the grill, cover, and cook until each center registers 130°F. on an instant-read thermometer for medium rare or 140°F. for medium, about 1 to 4 minutes longer. Transfer to a cutting board, tent with foil, and allow to rest 5 minutes. Slice against the grain and serve.

of kolhrabi. And when Paley doesn't know what to do with any one thing, he just calls up Weppler. In fact, since day one, Vitaly has featured a salad on the menu called George's Gathered Greens: the farmer's beautiful greens get drizzled with a simple lemon juice and olive oil vinaigrette.

Paley's latest obsession is charcuterie-making. The *coppa di testa* sounds daintier than what it really is: a pig's head seasoned and rolled, then sous-vided for 18 hours and sliced like ham. "It's unctuous and tastes like nothing else," Paley promises. And that pig—fed on whey and yogurt at the end of its life—came from Paul Atkinson of Laughing Stock Farm in Eugene, the first guy who sold pigs to famed Berkeley restaurant Chez Panisse. "When he calls up to say, 'I have a pig, do you want it?' I'd be crazy to say no," says Paley.

BLUE HILL AT STONE BARNS, POCANTICO HILLS, NY

5 BLUE HILL AT STONE BARNS
POCANTICO HILLS, NY
DAN BARBER

Talk to Dan Barber, and you feel like you're talking to a food savant. He might be the most thoughtful, articulate chef in America right now. Not only does he work closely with farmers, but he has also started a farm of his own at his restaurant, Blue Hill at Stone Barns, in Westchester County, sourcing right from its own backyard. How seriously does Barber take this farm-to-table movement? You hear chickens clucking and sheep bleating when pulling up to Stone Barns. The high-tech greenhouse he's built on the property with pioneering year-round farmer Eliot Coleman allows Barber to serve at least some locally grown produce at every time of the year.

In addition to the farming operation on the property, Barber works with many breeders from Cornell University, who are breeding varieties of fruits and vegetables that don't even have names yet. In searching for the most vibrant flavors, they're creating new ones altogether. As for the beef, it's prime grass-fed beef (nearly impossible to find anywhere else) and he'll serve it only in the fall, since "the animals still need to graze in the spring and the summer." He swears up and down that grass-fed beef *always* tastes better than the corn-fed alternative—though many would disagree.

6 FORE STREET RESTAURANT
PORTLAND, ME
SAM HAYWARD

Sam Hayward is the chef who really introduced Maine to its own foodstuffs. Before he arrived on the scene in the early 1970s, the only Maine foods that got any attention were lobsters and fried clams . . . and lobsters and fried clams. And perhaps blueberry pie. But he's taken a more expansive view of the state's native bounty, rallying local farmers and playing an active role in the Maine Organic Farmers and Gardeners Association. Besides highlighting locavorism, Fore Street's cuisine is also all about wood-fired cooking. A menu favorite is the Maine Farm Chicken: the bird is from Warren, Maine, and has a slight char from the open flame; underneath, the crackled skin is wet and glistening. It's served with jumbo oyster mushrooms and apple-bacon sherry vinaigrette. None of the food here is too complicated. "We don't interfere with the quality of the raw materials we're buying," Hayward says.

You really get to taste the range of flavor that comes from quality lamb, which Hayward gets from a tiny island farm in the Muscongus Bay off the coast of Maine. Hayward serves three cuts of it on one plate: grilled chop, smoked shoulder, and the turn-spit-roasted leg, alongside fregola sarda, capers, lemon, olives, and aleppo. Hayward's another one of those chefs that will tell you he just gets out of the way of the ingredients he works with—but don't believe they're doing all the heavy lifting. The man can flat-out cook.

7 MICHAEL'S GENUINE FOOD & DRINK MIAMI, FL
MICHAEL SCHWARTZ

In 2007, chef Michael Schwartz was brainstorming names for his new restaurant. He wanted a word that captured his intentions, and it just came to him: *genuine*. "That word has become a measuring stick for every decision we make at the restaurant." For Schwartz, that means rigorous standards for any animals served. He sources local fish you won't see on other Miami menus, like pumpkin swordfish and cero mackerel. The chicken is Poulet Rouge, a French heirloom breed that's now being raised in North Carolina and Georgia. The pork, from Fudge Family Farms in Madison, Alabama, is like the prime rib of pork: rich, sweet, and densely flavored. (He serves the chop and cures bacon, and makes sausage in-house.)

Most of the produce is from surrounding Florida farms, including Paradise Farms in Homestead, where Schwartz gets his organic oyster mushrooms, greens, squash blossoms, raw honey, and herbs. He even prepares his own pastrami, which makes his transplanted New Yorker customers very happy, indeed. Respect for the ingredients, and a kitchen that cares deeply about everything they turn out—that's what we'd call genuine.

8 OSTERIA & PIZZERIA MOZZA LOS ANGELES, CA
NANCY SILVERTON

Nancy Silverton has the culinary equivalent of perfect pitch. What does that mean? The woman simply knows what *good* is, so that when she sets her mind to making something, it invariably turns out well. Her obsessive perfectionism demands not only a refined culinary technique but also the sort of exemplary ingredients she gets at the Santa Monica organic farmers' market every Wednesday. Silverton has a way of wandering the market stalls, from Polito Family Farm citrus fruits to Honey Crisp nectarines to Harry's incomparable strawberries, knowing just what to pluck off the tables. That means that when we wandered into the original La Brea Bakery thirty years ago we found ourselves in a veritable food wonderland, full of perfectly made and curated foods—breads with intense flavor and perfect hole structure, sandwiches that were a model of taste and textural balance, and baked goods worth weeping over. Now, the same thing happens at Mozza2Go, the take-out shop attached to the insanely popular osteria and pizzeria with the same name. From the chicken, tarragon, bacon, and avocado sandwich to the salt-kissed and insanely creamy butterscotch *budino,* every item simply tastes like it's supposed to.

9 CHEZ PANISSE BERKELEY, CA
ALICE WATERS

You can't really write this chapter without bowing in honor of Alice Waters, the patron saint of locavorism and seasonality. Waters founded her Berkeley restaurant in 1971, a landmark operation that served as the inspirational nucleus for bringing fresh-picked, seasonal meals to the table. She has been criticized as overly idealistic, with an all-or-nothing attitude that demands a total and immediate overhaul of the way we eat. But her influence on the way we all dine is undeniable.

What's more, her food can be downright magnificent. Since the menu at Chez Panisse rotates daily, it's impossible to get married to any one dish. If the season's right, you may be dining on Sunny Slope Farms figs with black pepper, crème fraîche, and mint; another day it's the buttermilk-fried quail from Wolfe Ranch, with pancetta, corn bread, greens, and giblet gravy. Whatever the season, it's celebrated at Chez Panisse more fully than anywhere else.

PIZZERIA BIANCO, PHOENIX, AZ

10 PIZZERIA BIANCO PHOENIX, AZ
CHRIS BIANCO

When Chris Bianco moved to Phoenix in 1988, there was no basil farmer in sight. He had trouble finding the most basic ingredients—it was slim pickins at the farmers' markets. But since then he's established relationships with a host of local farmers, including Bob McClendon, who delivers his arugula, favas, the juiciest citrus, and beautiful squash blossoms to Bianco's restaurant. These go into the Market Salad, which rotates with the vegetable supply, just about every week. "Believe it or not," says our favorite *pizzaiolo* in America, "I enjoy making salads more than pizza. It's more of an art than a craft."

Whether he's using escarole hearts with red onion and Point Reyes blue cheese or goat cheese from Black Ranch in Snowflake, Arizona, Bianco always achieves that magical harmony of bitter and sweet, salty and crunchy. "I don't need to make everything," Bianco concedes. He doesn't make his own proscuitto, for instance, but confidently sources it from La Quercia (page 318). Big, long slices of it wrap around ice-cube-size chunks of locally grown watermelons. Chris lets the ingredients sing—and the connection he feels to his ingredients only strengthens the downright mystical connection Chris forges with his customers, through every plate of food he serves.

> ### fruit dessert at chez panisse
>
> The Café at Chez Panisse, which opened in 1980, is where I first confronted the seemingly silly idea of just having a piece of fruit for dessert at a restaurant. Frog Hollow pluots, unadorned, on the dessert menu? When in Berkeley, eat like the Berkeley-ans do. Two pieces of fruit and a serrated knife arrived at the table, and I put the first slices of the juiciest, most perfectly balanced, sweet and tart fruit in my mouth—that's when I finally understood what Alice Waters was talking about. Now the rest of the country does, too.

How often do you go back to a restaurant for their *carrots*? We find ourselves returning to ABC Kitchen, a New York restaurant of Jean-Georges Vongerichten, for the carrot salad. Right around the corner from the Union Square Greenmarket (page 333), ABC Kitchen, under executive chef Dan Kluger, is all about using the best ingredients possible. While there's plenty we loved on the menu, it was this roast carrot and avocado salad we kept talking about for weeks: the roasted carrots are sweet, nutty, and cumin-laced, both soft and spicy, and more exciting than any carrots have a right to be.

carrot salad
with avocado
ABC KITCHEN, NEW YORK, NY

SERVES 4

2 pounds small carrots (3 to 4 inches, ½ inch thick), or large carrots quartered and cut into 3-inch segments, peeled (about 4 cups)

Kosher salt

1 orange

1 lemon

1 teaspoon cumin seeds

2 medium garlic cloves

1 tablespoon fresh thyme leaves

½ cup extra-virgin olive oil

1 teaspoon red wine vinegar

1 teaspoon red pepper flakes

Freshly ground black pepper

1 tablespoon sugar

1 avocado, cut into 12 wedges

2 cups mixed baby sprouts, herbs, and microgreens

4 tablespoons crème fraîche

2 tablespoons toasted sunflower seeds

2 teaspoons toasted sesame seeds

1 Adjust an oven rack to the center position and preheat the oven to 450°F. Place the carrots in a saucepan and cover them with cold water. Season with salt, set over high heat, and bring to a simmer. Reduce the heat to medium and simmer until the carrots are tender, about 10 minutes. Drain the carrots and transfer them to a medium bowl.

2 Cut the orange and lemon in half and juice half of each one, reserving the juice and the unjuiced halves, and discarding the juiced halves. Combine the cumin, garlic, thyme, 2 tablespoons of olive oil, the red wine vinegar, red pepper, 1 teaspoon of the orange juice, and 1 teaspoon of the lemon juice in a blender and blend until smooth. Season the marinade to taste with salt and pepper. Add the marinade and the unjuiced citrus halves to the carrots and toss to combine. Spread the carrots and citrus halves on a rimmed baking sheet and bake until the carrots are slightly shriveled with a few brown spots, about 20 minutes. Allow the carrots to cool to room temperature.

3 Meanwhile, squeeze the juice from the roasted citrus halves into a small bowl. Add the remaining fresh orange juice, lemon juice, remaining 6 tablespoons olive oil, and the sugar. Season the dressing to taste with salt and pepper, and whisk to combine.

4 Divide the carrots and avocado slices onto four plates. Divide the greens among the plates on top of the carrots and avocado. Add a tablespoon of crème fraîche to each salad. Sprinkle sunflower seeds and sesame seeds over each plate.

5 Drizzle several tablespoons of dressing over and around each salad (reserve any remaining dressing for another use), and serve immediately.

FARMERS AND PURVEYORS WE LOVE

Whether they're pig farmers or fig pickers, cheese mongers or peach growers, every farmer and purveyor out there has a story to tell.

TIM STARK
ECKERTON HILL FARM, LENHARTSVILLE, PA: TOMATOES

In New York City, Union Square Greenmarket regulars know to get there early, especially during tomato season—Eckerton Hill Farm runs out of the good ones by noon. Farmer, Princeton graduate, and former shirt-and-tie management consultant Tim Stark, the man behind those tomatoes, can often be found weaving between the tables, dispensing produce wisdom to New Yorkers and chefs. When he's not rhapsodizing about his 100 tomato varieties (pronouncing their names lovingly, like his children: the Brandywines, the Green Zebras, the Cherokee Purples), he's on his farm in Lenhartsville, Pennsylvania, tending to them or the only slightly less famous chiles—of which he sells 40 to 60 varieties, including poblano, habanero, and ají limón.

FLEISHER'S GRASS-FED AND ORGANIC MEATS AT THE NEW AMSTERDAM MARKET, NEW YORK, NY

FLEISHER'S, KINGSTON, NY

RICK BISHOP
MOUNTAIN SWEET BERRY FARM, ROSCOE, NY: STRAWBERRIES

Sweet really isn't a strong enough word for these strawberries, particularly the Tri-star variety. Despite their blackberry size, they're bursting with syrupy nectar juices. It's easy to just keep popping them in your mouth like popcorn—they're one of the more addictive substances Mother Nature has ever created. Rick Bishop, who studied agriculture at Cornell, says his strawberries grow particularly well during the cool nights on his 25-acre farm. You might see him climbing on his parked truck at New York's Union Square Greenmarket, loading those berries eight cases at a time. And once you get a basket, you'll find yourself eating the stem and any dirt crumbs. "It's actually not dirt, it's soil," Bishop corrected us. "And it's a living, breathing thing."

RON MANSFIELD
GOLDBUD FARMS, PLACERVILLE, CA: PEACHES

We are on an eternal search for the perfect peach—one that's so juicy you end up wearing it, one that has a perfect balance between sweetness and acidity. The best peaches we know come from Goldbud Farms in Placerville, in the middle of California gold-rush country. Goldbud's Ron Mansfield employs sophisticated growing and irrigation methods to raise truly remarkable peaches—the kind that, when you bite in, will make you think you're tasting one for the first time.

JOSH AND JESSICA APPLESTONE
FLEISHER'S GRASS-FED AND ORGANIC MEATS, KINGSTON, NY: MEAT

After being a vegan for 17 years, Josh Applestone decided to be a butcher. He and his wife, Jessica, opened their old-fashioned-looking butcher shop in 2004. We can't say with *total* certainty that they sell the best-tasting meat in the country, but it's indisputably delicious. All of their animals come from within 20 miles of their shop, and don't need much embellishment in the kitchen. Fleisher's supplies whole animals to chefs like Dan Barber (page 311); they have a cookbook, have been featured in countless books and magazines, and now run a full-on meat academy for butchers-in-training. Our own writer Chichi Wang went through the program and learned how to butcher a pig after less than a week—and she's no more than 100 pounds, mind you. "You just can't be afraid to dig your fingernails into inches of pristine fatback, and hear the sound of cracking bones and cartilage," she warns. Hands-on: the only way to truly know your meat.

MIKE YEZZI AND JEN SMALL
FLYING PIGS FARM, SHUSHAN, NY: PORK

"We never imagined that we would be farmers," says Mike Yezzi, but when he and his wife, Jen Small, were in graduate school, an old farmstead near them was up for sale and sold to a developer. "We couldn't stand to see that happen." So they bought it in 2000—even though they both had full-time jobs at nearby Williams College. They started with three pigs and now they have closer to 600, along with 3,000 meat chickens and 1,500 laying hens. They strive to preserve rare breeds like Gloucestershire Old Spots and Tamworths to save them from extinction. The moistness and flavor of the resulting meat is superior. You don't need to do much to their meat: the boneless butt is fabulous after a braise; cook it until the meat starts falling off the bone. Flying Pigs Farm pork is not cheap, but we believe it's worth every bit of extra expense.

BOB AND MARY POLITO
POLITO FAMILY FARMS, VALLEY CENTER, CA: CITRUS

Polito Family Farms is a very small operation—"No Harry and David's here, just Bob and Mary running the show," the couple says. Located in the rolling hills northeast of San Diego, Polito's 70 acres of lush groves live through warm days and cool nights—ideal conditions for citrus to grow both sweet and tart. The Valencia and Satsuma oranges are so juicy you might need a bib; the ruby star grapefruits have such sweet red flesh they're easy to peel and eat straight-up like oranges. If you're lucky enough to happen upon the Polito stand at one of the farmers' markets in the LA basin, do not pass up the opportunity to buy some of their grapefruit juice—which is sweeter than most other folks' orange juice.

HERB AND KATHY ECKHOUSE
LA QUERCIA, NORWALK, IA: PROSCIUTTO

Harvard-educated Herb and Berkeley-educated Kathy, the co-founders of La Quercia, are the Iowans who introduced world-class prosciutto-making to this country. If you've never tasted any of La Quercia's truly amazing, antibiotic-free pork products, we hereby declare you pork deprived. The Eckhouses' transcendent prosciutto may actually be better than the highest quality prosciutto di Parma—and that's a high bar to clear. It's beautiful ham: as dark as a burnished mahogany, infused with pink, whose taste builds and lingers, with a complexity far more nuanced than the simple marriage of pork and salt would have you expect. There's a clean sweetness and slightly salty air, with a dark nuttiness and earth at the core—you can almost taste the land the pigs grazed on.

JOHN PRISKE
FOUNTAIN PRAIRIE FARM, FALL RIVER, WI: BEEF

When you spend as much time walking around farmers' markets as we do, it's really frustrating to come upon a fantastic meat purveyor on the road. Why? Because you can't do anything with the meat—it's not as if hotel rooms come equipped with a kitchen. But after meeting Fountain Prairie Farms' John Priske at the Dane County Farmers' Market (page 333) and trying their stellar ground beef in a fantastic burger at Madison's Graze (page 78), we knew we had to sample their other meat. Priske shipped us a dry-aged bone-in ribeye that was delicious, indeed. The pasture-dwelling Highland cattle are raised without growth hormones or antibiotics, and they eat from feed with

JUICES FROM RED JACKET ORCHARDS, NEW YORK, NY

products we get from farmers," Kahan told us. "The arugula, the Italian greens, the Tuscan kale, the milk, the eggs we get from Kinnikinnick Farms—it goes to the very heart of what we do as chefs. It's where every dish in every one of our restaurants starts from."

GREG BATCH
BATCH FAMILY ORCHARDS, LAKE CHELAN VALLEY, WA: CHERRIES

There's more than one state that will assert its cherry-growing superiority, and we're not going to pick sides. But Washington grows more than anywhere else in the nation. The best cherries here are huge and juicy, but not as though they're on steroids—just perfect parcels of cherry juice. Greg Batch and family, on a farm that's grown the fruit since 1936, sell only these sweet, plump tree-ripened cherries, including Bings, Sweethearts, and Lapins.

NICHOLSON FAMILY
RED JACKET ORCHARDS, GENEVA, NY: JUICES

We don't usually get giddy about juices, but these just hit all the right spots: they're tart with just the right sweet backdrop, and each sip is like biting into a different part of the fruit. The pressed-apple ciders are the most popular, but for a few weeks in the spring, Red Jacket makes rhubarb-apple—it has a lemonade's tartness but goes down super-smooth. The Nicholson family has more than 600 acres of orchards in the Finger Lakes Region of New York, where they have formed a tight relationship developing fruit breeds with the local Cornell agrarian studies team. They are also fiddling with all sorts of plum varieties, which also get smashed up and jammified.

ALEX AND BETSY HITT
PEREGRINE FARM, GRAHAM, NC: PEPPERS

Alex Hitt owns the 26-acre Peregrine Farm with his wife, Betsy. He's the only farmer we've ever met

grain thrown into the mix for more marbling; finally, the beef is dry-aged for at least 21 days for maximum flavor.

DAVID AND SUSAN CLEVERDON
KINNIKINNICK FARMS, CALEDONIA, IL: GREENS AND MORE

On their plot of land near the Wisconsin border, about 80 miles northwest of Chicago, David and Susan Cleverdon grow all sorts of certified-organic greens and vegetables. ("We are particularly fond of Italian varieties," they say. "Many of our seeds come from small seed companies in Italy.") They sell at the Green City Market (page 333) and the Evanston Farmers' Market, and some of their best customers are acclaimed chefs like Chicago's Paul Kahan. "First and foremost my food is all about the

who roasts freshly picked peppers on the spot—taking whatever mix of peppers you buy (there are many, including poblanos, shishitos, and padrones, when in season) and roasts them in his hand-cranked propane-fired barrel roaster from Arizona. Adding sea salt, extra-virgin olive oil, and heat does beautiful things; the intoxicating smell of those charred peppers will find you, whatever stall you're at. Allow yourself to eat a couple right then and there—you won't be disappointed.

DAVID AND EVERETT DAVALL
DATES BY DAVALL, INDIO, CA: DATES

The only thing that says dedication more than getting up at 3:00 AM to drive to the market? Getting up at 3:00 AM to drive to the market with a few kids in tow. That's what the DaVall family does every week, and yet they still manage to be relentlessly cheerful. Maybe it's the dates that keep them so happy. Their fresh dates are fascinating, both texturally—they're not dry in the slightest—and in just how different they are. (The DaValls will tell you everything that sets a Medjool apart from a Honey or an Empress—and they know those differences well, as the family's been growing dates since 1912.) You think you know what a date is supposed to taste like, but after a few minutes at DaVall, you realize you didn't know a thing.

MARK TOIGO
TOIGO ORCHARDS, SHIPPENSBURG, PA: PEACHES

You could buy a peach in the supermarket, but it would never taste like those from Toigo Orchards. They actually grow 22 varieties on the 450-acre farm, which has been in continuous operation since the 1700s. About 380 acres are used to grow fruit, and of those, 60 are dedicated just to peaches. Mark Toigo sets up at many of the D.C.-area FRESHFARM markets, selling his prized fruits to local chefs such as Carole Greenwood. At her restaurant Buck's Fishing & Camping, she uses Toigo peaches to make peach ice cream, peach cake, and a much-requested customer favorite—a salad of roasted white peaches, fresh mozzarella, white balsamic vinegar, olive oil, and basil.

ALLAN BENTON
BENTON'S SMOKY MOUNTAIN COUNTRY HAMS, MADISONVILLE, TN: HAM

A first bite of Allan Benton's country ham, prosciutto, or bacon immediately engulfs your senses with the magical elixir of pig, smoke, and salt—the holy trinity of delicious pork. And we're not the only ones who think so. You'll find Benton's products on menus all over the country, from the City Grocery in Oxford, Mississippi, to the Momofuku restaurants in New York City. When you take a

> "Ever since I tried to grow my first garden and discovered I was really lousy at it, I've gone in search of the men and women who grow the food I'd like to be eating. Farmers rock hard!" —organicgal

whiff of this porcine aroma, you not only smell the sweet ham but can also sense Benton's spirit. He has dedicated his life to the craft of traditional salt-curing, smoking, and aging.

HENRY BROCKMAN
HENRY'S FARM, CONGERVILLE, IL: VEGETABLES AND MORE

"Biodiversity Rules!" says Henry Brockman's website—and he practices what he preaches, with more than 600 varieties of 100 vegetables on his multigenerational family farm. Brockman's parents both came from farming families and raised their children on an Illinois farm; while Henry lived all over the world, he ultimately returned to his childhood home to run the farm now respected by eaters and chefs all over the state. "Some of his vegetables look kind of crazy," says chef Paul Kahan, "but they taste great." Brockman is another one of those farmers who's intensely thoughtful about his craft. "He's crazy smart," Kahan says, "a philosopher, a writer—and a farmer."

MARK AND JILL BAKER
BAKER'S GREEN ACRES, MARION, MI: POULTRY, LAMB, AND PORK

In the northern part of Lower Michigan, the Baker family raises animals on the pasture of their highly regarded farm. "Mark Baker and his wife run a real-life American family farm," says chef, teacher, and food writer Brian Polcyn. I've been to a lot of farms, and when you drive up to Mark's place you know in five minutes that he knows what he's doing. He certainly doesn't lead a life of luxury, but even though he raises Mangalitsa pigs, chickens, and lambs, it smells so clean that I just love breathing the air at Mark's farm. How many livestock farms can you say that about?"

MIKE AND TINA WERP
WERP FARMS, BUCKLEY, MI: MICROGREENS

Once a commodity corn and soybean farmer, Mike Werp turned his attention to organic microgreens and baby vegetables. "Mike is amazing," Brian Polcyn told us. "He's so devoted to his crops, his land, and his family. They haven't put in those fancy irrigated greenhouses, but they jury-rigged a small plot of land with six greenhouses that have lots of plastic bags as walls, and wood-burning stoves, so he can grow some stuff for chefs year-round." They drive the 300 miles to Chicago to make deliveries, as well as selling within Michigan. "Without farmers like Mike and Tina we would be lost as chefs," Polcyn said. "I wouldn't even want to think about cooking without their products."

MICHAEL JOHNS AND TERRY COHN
SOW LITTLE FARM, MADISON, WI: RASPBERRIES

You may be familiar with large-scale agri-business farming on hundreds of thousands of acres and small-scale family farming on dozens or hundreds of acres. But then there's what we call micro urban farming—tiny plots on less than five acres. These baby farms are cropping up in cities large and small all over the country, whether on rooftops in Brooklyn or, in Wisconsin, on the outskirts of Madison at Sow Little Farm. Terry Cohn and Michael Johns grow the juiciest, sweetest raspberries imaginable in hoop houses, essentially primitive greenhouses with no heat that allow Johns to extend the growing season (no easy trick in frigid Madison). Varieties, including the yellow 'Anne' and red 'Polana', are plump and delicate and just acidic enough. The entire farm consists of those five acres and two plots of just a few dozen square feet in their backyard. Terry and Michael grow many other things, including explosively sweet 'Black Cherry' and 'Peach' tomatoes, which we watched Michael lovingly harvest with a tiny pair of scissors. According to Terry, "We sell from our front porch pre-ordered via email, and we also sell tomatoes and berries to chefs like Tory Miller at L'Etoile and Graze in Madison."

9 FINE BREAD BAKERS

Bread is a good thing. Very good bread is just about the greatest thing we know. You know what we mean—the kind that doesn't need butter or jam or sandwich fillings; the kind of bread where you tear off one piece to eat, and end up polishing off the loaf in one sitting. It's one of the most basic foods out there, but one of the hardest to perfect. Bread baking has undergone a renaissance in this country, and the following nine bakeries will show you just how far we've come.

1 ACME BREAD
SAN FRANCISCO, CA

Even those who appreciate fine baking may not know that Acme Bread's Steve Sullivan is, in many respects, the father of the artisanal bread movement in this country. Sullivan first became interested in bread-baking during the late 1970s, when he was bussing tables at Chez Panisse restaurant in Berkeley while going to college around the corner; in 1983, Acme Bread was born. After opening four bakeries—our favorite may be the one at San Francisco's Ferry Building, where you can watch loaves plumping up in the hearth oven all day—his goal is still the same: to bake outstanding bread. At their commercial facility in Berkeley, Acme's bakers use modern German-made deck ovens as well as a 1930s Spanish brick oven in three production shifts, churning out their hand-formed loaves and pastries throughout the day and night. He uses only organic flour and works closely with farmers to select grain varieties for each flour he relies on. Acme has managed to do what often seems impossible—expand widely without compromising one crumb in quality.

2 SULLIVAN STREET BAKERY
NEW YORK, NY

When Jim Lahey first opened Sullivan Street Bakery in 1994, he was making three breads with little more than flour, water, and the wild yeast he cultivated by hand in Italy. These breads are now his trademarks: a well-baked dark bread with a crunchy crust and tender innards; his room-temperature pizzas; and the revelatory Pizza

SULLIVAN STREET BAKERY, NEW YORK, NY

BATCH BAKEHOUSE, MADISON, WI

Bianca, soft and pliant and oozing with olive oil. But in recent years, Lahey and his band of bakers have greatly expanded beyond his initial trio into sandwiches and other foods. Lahey has a profound understanding of the inherent appeal of deftly combined flour, water, sugar, salt, and fat—and a deep appreciation of the sanctity of high-quality ingredients and how to use them to maximum delicious effect. And his no-knead method, a beautifully simple baking process he preaches far and wide, has helped make us all realize that we can be bread-bakers, too.

3 CLEAR FLOUR BREAD
BROOKLINE, MA

Walk by this tiny Brookline bakery and the oven fumes will hypnotize you. Inside, there's nowhere to sit, and hardly any standing room—every square foot is devoted to ovens, kneading counters, and

bread displays. Clear Flour's French, Italian, and German loaves turn up in top Boston restaurants, as well as local Whole Foods stores, and their classic pastries are pretty unbeatable, too. If you're there early enough to snag a morning bun, do so. And eat it on the spot. You'll thank us later.

4 STANDARD BAKING CO.
PORTLAND, ME

When you sit down to a meal at Fore Street (page 311), this is the first thing (in a basket) put in front of you—and it instantly raises your expectations of things to come. All these beautiful breads are baked downstairs daily at the commercial bakery, but luckily, even nondiners can grab a loaf from that downstairs operation, Standard Baking Co. The country boule has a sturdy crust and a deep yeasty flavor; the semolina fougasse is simply too easy to keep eating.

5 BATCH BAKEHOUSE
MADISON, WI

If the breads at this tiny corner bakery look something like those at Standard Baking Co. (above), it's no coincidence; head baker Ian Garthwait honed his craft at Standard for two years before opening his Madison bakery. Just as at Standard, the fougasses are worth an order—but so are some less traditional goodies, like a ham, cheese, and sauerkraut-stuffed roll, its innards still warm and oozy from the oven, and Mexican wedding cookies better than any others we've had.

How can we properly state our love for Jim Lahey's Pizza Bianca? It's easily one of our top five foodstuffs in all New York City. It's popped up enough times on Serious Eats to make all the other loaves jealous. And if we were marooned on a desert island, a six-foot-long Pizza Bianca—that's how long the loaves are at Sullivan Street—might just be what we'd want to have with us. More like a focaccia than a pizza in the common sense, it's a simple marriage of flour, salt, rosemary, and olive oil—and that's just about it. It's crisp on the exterior and tender within; there's enough olive oil in it to keep it fresh for at least a day. And it's dangerously easy to re-create at home. Frankly, the world needs more Pizza Bianca. Starting with your home oven. Here is Lahey's recipe (many thanks, Jim).

sullivan street bakery's
pizza bianca

SERVES 6 TO 8

3 cups (15 ounces) all-purpose flour

1 teaspoon salt

¾ teaspoon sugar

1 teaspoon instant dry yeast

3 tablespoons extra-virgin olive oil

1 sprig fresh rosemary

1 Combine the flour, ½ teaspoon salt, the sugar, and yeast in the bowl of an electric mixer. Slowly add 1 cup of cold water.

2 With the dough hook attachment of the machine, mix on low speed until the ingredients begin to combine, about 1 minute. Increase the speed to medium high, and continue to mix for about 10 minutes, until the dough is smooth, elastic, and cleanly pulls away from the sides of the mixing bowl.

3 Oil a medium bowl using some of the extra-virgin olive oil. Place the bread dough in the bowl, and allow it to rest for 2 to 4 hours, until it has doubled in size.

4 Once the dough has doubled, split the dough into halves, and form each into a log. Place each log onto a generously floured surface, and allow it to rest until the dough doubles in size again, at least 1 hour.

5 Place a baking stone in the oven and set the oven to broil, about 520°F.

6 Put the dough on a lightly floured baker's peel. Dimple the dough, creating indents every inch, by pressing it down with your fingertips. Gently pull the dough outward toward the edges of the peel until the dough reaches a thickness of approximately ¼ inch. Drizzle with the remaining olive oil, top with rosemary, and sprinkle with the remaining ½ teaspoon salt.

7 Slide the dough onto the preheated baking stone with the baker's peel. Bake until the bubbles range from golden to deep brown in color, 10 to 12 minutes.

6 KEN'S ARTISAN BAKERY
PORTLAND, OR

Ken Forkish went from being a Silicon Valley engineer to a James Beard Award pastry chef semi-finalist. His Oregon Croissants (filled with sugar sprinkles and Oregon blackberries), pizzas (page 113), and baguettes are all favorites across Portland, and rightfully so. And though you may not think of bypassing any of those for a multigrain roll, it's just as good as all the others: hearty, crusty, chewy, and filling.

MACRINA BAKERY, SEATTLE, WA

7 MACRINA BAKERY
SEATTLE, WA

As we ate our way through many of Seattle's best sandwiches—from the prosciutto at Salumi (page 329) to the roast pork at Paseo Caribbean Restaurant (page 139)—we realized that most of them had one thing in common: they were made on Macrina bread. Leslie Mackie, after a stint as head baker at Seattle's Grand Central Bakery, opened Macrina in 1993 and has steadily earned a reputa-

tion as one of Seattle's premiere bakers, with several James Beard nominations to her name. Today, you'll find her loaves all over the Seattle area, as well as at her several Macrina storefronts, where the doughy fumes will prompt you to buy more bread than you know what to do with. If you're there in the morning, you can't go wrong with a crumbly scone or an airy, sticky-bottomed morning bun.

SALTY TART, MINNEAPOLIS, MN

9 SALTY TART
MINNEAPOLIS, MN

You wouldn't necessarily expect Michelle Gayer, an alum of the West Coast's beloved La Brea Bakery and one of the country's best pastry chefs, to run a tiny Midwestern bakery in a food court—but she does. And her breads, pastries, and savories are worth a trip from anywhere. Puff pastry is a remarkable strength of hers, as it appears in a earthy, herb-scented mushroom galette or a caramelized onion and goat cheese tart; but a tender, yeasty cream-filled brioche, the filling silky and judiciously sweet, or a cinnamon-pluot coffee cake may have you passing up the flaky stuff.

8 ZINGERMAN'S BAKEHOUSE
ANN ARBOR, MI

Ari Weinzweig and Paul Saginaw opened the now-legendary Zingerman's Deli (page 152) in 1982, but soon realized that they couldn't find bread good enough to serve their sandwiches on. So they turned their formidable energies to a bakery, opened with partner Frank Carollo in 1993. It's gone way beyond sandwich scaffolding: their focaccia is cloud-light and oil-laced and easy to scarf down a loaf at a time; their chocolate cherry bread is the stuff of dreams. The sandwich breads have a tender, moist crumb and just enough outside chew. But no matter how phenomenally successful the Zingerman's universe has become, their shops still have a personal touch. The breads look and taste like human beings had a hand in making them.

SALTY TART, MINNEAPOLIS, MN

5 MEAT MAVENS

What's the recipe for the best coppa, chorizo, or salami? Great meats—and meat-curers who know what to do with them. While of course we love Parma for its prosciutto and Salamanca for its *jamón Iberico*, certain American meat mavens create sausages and salumi every bit as good as their European counterparts. Butchers, charcutiers—we salute you.

1 SALUMERIA BIELLESE
NEW YORK, NY

At first glance, the nondescript storefront looks like hundreds of others in the city, but inside, down in the basement, some of the greatest salumi and fresh sausage-makers in the country have been doing their thing since 1925. And Marc Buzzio and his business partner, Paul Valetutti, are still at it. Their meat-making skills are easily appreciated in any sandwich made with coppa, capicola, Genoa salami, sweet soppresata, mortadella, or the house-made mozzarella. All of the above (yes, except the mozzarella) are made with phenomenal Berkshire pork that Buzzio and Valetutti buy from a farmers' cooperative in Iowa. In their hands this meat is transformed into wonderful pork deliciousness in many forms with the aid of salt, pepper, fennel, garlic, and air. And if you stop by their storefront on a Thursday, order a roast pork sandwich with house-made mozzarella and plenty of gravy.

2 OLYMPIC PROVISIONS
PORTLAND, OR

The door separating the Olympic Provisions restaurant-deli from the chamber in the back says it all: MEAT DEPT. Their meat-curing facility is Oregon's first USDA-approved salumeria: while small-batch curers don't need that high-level certification, anyone attempting a wholesale business requires official oversight. That means salumist Elias Cairo makes charcuterie with a USDA inspector watching over him, 40 hours each week. Elias and his charcuterie-making crew, many of whom come from favorite Portland eateries, are not only serving the chorizo, soppressata, and 10 other dry-aged meats at the restaurant, but they are working on a wholesale business, too. Of all the meats, Elias is most proud of the lukanika. "It's my Greek father's recipe," he said of the orange-zesty dry salami.

SALUMERIA BIELLESE, NEW YORK, NY

OLYMPIC PROVISIONS, PORTLAND, OR

Cochon, its big-sister restaurant. Louisiana chef-restaurateur Donald Link makes thick andouille, peppery boudin, house-cured duck pastrami, and one of the finest—really, *the* finest—muffuletta you'll find in the Crescent City. (No offense meant to muffuletta birthplace Central Grocery.) Link grew up in the Bayou, so pork is his first language.

5 BOCCALONE
SAN FRANCISCO, CA

This salumeria from offal-worshiping chef Chris Cosentino is located in San Francisco's Ferry Building (page 335). They sell over 20 cured meats, all handcrafted in small batches across the bay in Oakland, using only sustainably raised, Heritage-breed pork and the best spices and salts. But what we really need to tell you about is the Meat Cone. That's a paper cone filled with slices of meat—your choice of ciccioli, coppa di testa, mortadella, capocollo, lonza—lovingly layered to eat one by one.

3 SALUMI ARTISAN CURED MEATS
SEATTLE, WA

Armandino Batali (you may be familiar with his son Mario?) opened this temple of charcuterie after retiring from an engineering career at Boeing. His Pioneer Square restaurant-cum-butcher-shop, now largely run by daughter Gina Batali and her husband, Brian D'Amato, is cramped and cozy enough to have you envisioning a little hillside shop in Emilia-Romagna. The Batalis honor old-school Italian meat-curing practices. You'll find specimens that just don't show up much elsewhere in America, like the beautifully tender culatello, the prime part of a prosciutto; you'll also find creations all their own, like the ancho-cinnamon-chocolate mole salami.

4 COCHON BUTCHER
NEW ORLEANS, LA

When someone asks where to eat in New Orleans, we invariably point them to Cochon Butcher or

SALUMI ARTISAN CURED MEATS, SEATTLE, WA

5 PICKLERS

Sure, there's an entire supermarket wall dedicated to jarred dills and spears and sweet quarter-size bread-and-butters. But why shouldn't the pickle be a little more interesting? All over America, you'll now find home enthusiasts and small producers alike pickling anything they can get their hands on: collard greens, carrots, okra, watermelon rinds, and so much more.

1 RICK'S PICKS
BROOKLYN, NY

Rick Field of Rick's Picks started pickling for fun in the Prospect Heights neighborhood of Brooklyn in 1997, and now has a whimsical line of jarred veggies, including Phat Beets (beets in a rosemary brine) and Mean Beans (spicy green bean pickles). You'll find them at farmers' markets across the city, always with toothpicked bites for the sampling.

SMOKRA FROM RICK'S PICKS, BROOKLYN, NY

2 HAPPY GIRL KITCHEN
SAN FRANCISCO, CA

Husband-and-wife picklers Todd and Jordan Champagne lived in Norway before they moved to the Bay Area, where you can now find them at many farmers' markets, including Ferry Plaza (page 335). Rows of big glass jars are filled with pickled beets, spicy carrots, bread-and-butter summer squash, cumin-spiced green beans, and all sorts of other inventive takes on standard pickles. And starting with fresh California produce gives any pickler a leg up.

3 PICKLOPIS
PORTLAND, OR

Doesn't Picklopis just make you envision a glorious kingdom of briny things? That's what this Portland-based picklery was going for. Their garlic-dill pickles and thick-cut bread-and-butter pickles are on the sandwiches we love at Bunk Sandwiches (page 135) and other dishes at food carts and eateries around the city. We also love their pickled watermelon rinds and orange-fennel beets.

4 ANGELA'S PEPPER-PICKLED FOODS
WILMINGTON, NC

North Carolina's okra is too beautiful for Angela Cannon *not* to pickle it. She sets up at farmers' markets in the Wilmington area, or you can find her hand-packed, small-batch briny goodness at select markets, too. While her okra is the biggest hit, she also jars Carolina collards, squash, peppers, and the classic cukes.

5 McCLURE'S PICKLES
DETROIT, MI, AND BROOKLYN, NY

Bob McClure lives (and pickles) in Brooklyn while his brother and co-pickle entrepreneur Joe represents the brand in their hometown of Detroit. Their cucumber spears swim in brine with fat garlic cloves and aggressive red chiles—be warned, they don't hold back on the heat. Save their brine for Bloody Marys or to season a stew.

While we love all of Rick Field's pickles, we've found ourselves eating his Smokra by the jar. The okra keeps a fresh crunch and picks up the sweet tang of cider vinegar, but it's the sultry smoked paprika that makes it so memorable.

smokra
RICK'S PICKS

MAKES 1 QUART

¼ pound (about 3 cups) okra, stems trimmed

2 garlic cloves, peeled

1 teaspoon cayenne pepper

1 teaspoon smoked Spanish paprika

1 teaspoon curry powder

½ teaspoon mustard seeds

1 teaspoon red pepper flakes

1½ cups cider vinegar

1 tablespoon kosher salt

1 Add the okra, garlic, cayenne, paprika, curry, mustard seeds, and red pepper flakes to a 1-quart sterilized glass jar with a lid. Pack down until the okra fits.

2 Combine the cider vinegar, 1 cup water, and the kosher salt in a medium saucepan. Bring to a boil, then allow to cool for 2 minutes. Pour the hot brine over the okra until the jar is filled to the brim. Immediately screw the lid onto the glass jar. Allow to sit at room temperature for at least two weeks and up to one year before opening. Refrigerate after opening.

10 FAVORITE FARMERS' MARKETS

PORTLAND STATE UNIVERSITY FARMERS' MARKET, PORTLAND, OR

Picking the best farmers' market is like trying to pick the best heirloom tomato. We love them whatever the form or flavor they take. But here are ten of our favorites, places where you're sure to find a mind-boggling spread of fruits and veggies, meats and cheeses, carefully crafted foodstuffs of all stripes—and, most important, the people who grow, pick, and make them.

1 PORTLAND STATE UNIVERSITY FARMERS' MARKET
PORTLAND, OR

There are six farmers' markets in Portland's urban vicinity, but the grandest of all is the main Saturday market at the Portland State University campus. And it's not just a produce-shopping center; it's a great place to grab a meal. Sure, you should pick up some Rainer cherries and plums from Baird Family Orchards, but for immediate

UNION SQUARE GREENMARKET, NEW YORK, NY

gratification, get a cup of locally roasted Stumptown coffee from the Cafe Velo stand, a baked-right-there biscuit sandwich smothered in gravy with fried chicken from Pine State Biscuits, and a slice of wood-fire baked pizza from the mobile Tastebud oven.

2 UNION SQUARE GREENMARKET
NEW YORK, NY

Equal parts tourist destination, locals' shopping spot, and serious chefs' early morning stop, the greenmarket has evolved into an official urban happening. Vendors at the year-round market spread out on roughly two acres of the city square. And it's far more than just produce you'll find: after getting your strawberries from Rick Bishop's Mountain Sweet Berry Farm, or your apples and pears from 400-year-old Locust Grove Farm, grab pork and leaf lard from Flying Pigs Farm and milk and yogurt from Ronnybrook Farm Dairy.

3 DANE COUNTY FARMERS' MARKET
MADISON, WI

Every Saturday morning from mid-April until the first week of November (moving indoors during the winter to prevent frostbitten shoppers), Wisconsin farmers gather around the Capitol building in Madison for the largest producer-only farmers' market in the United States. (It's so successful there's a four-year wait list for farmers.) It's a study in fascinating diversity—gooey, spicy, scarfable cheese bread from Stella's Bakery, a cheap and indulgent food of the people, next to the sour, crusty loaves of Cress Spring Bakery, whose Jeff Ford is an intensely serious baker who goes so far as to source and grind his own grains. Since the only sellers are the people who make or grow the goods, you'll always have someone to chat with about every delicious bite that ends up in your mouth.

4 GREEN CITY MARKET IN LINCOLN PARK
CHICAGO, IL

Plan to arrive when the market opens for the best pickins, and you'll likely run into acclaimed chef and regular marketgoer Rick Bayless—or any one of the many other Chicago chefs who craft their menus from the Green City goods. We like the purple asparagus and shelled peas from Mick Klug Farms and the French breakfast radishes from Kinnikinnick Farm. And if you're hungry for something a little more substantial, have one of the made-to-order individual pizzas fired in a mobile wood-burning oven.

5 CARRBORO FARMERS' MARKET
CARRBORO, NC

Among the can't-miss vendors at the Carrboro Farmers' Market are Peregrine Farm, who will happily roast the gorgeous-hued peppers you buy from them right on the spot (page 319), and Chapel Hill Creamery, run by Flo Hawley and Portia

McKnight, who make extraordinary farmstead cheeses out of cow's milk, including Thunder Mountain Swiss and the aged raw-milk (unpasteurized) Hickory Grove. It's the market where Karen and Ben Barker (of Durham's Magnolia Grill, page 309) find their raw materials and their inspiration. All these folks together make up the backbone of a truly thriving food culture.

6 SANTA MONICA WEDNESDAY FARMERS' MARKET
SANTA MONICA, CA

The Wednesday, Saturday, and Sunday markets are each a little different, but the Wednesday organic market is a particular treasure. The Wednesday market is a favorite of several LA chefs, including Nancy Silverton. Many of her favorite farmers who frequent the Wednesday market have become ours: we love the incomparable citrus fruit from Polito Family Farms; peaches, plums, nectarines, and pluots from Honey Crisp Farm; gavila strawberries from Harry's Berries. If you do make it on Wednesday, be sure to grab tomatoes from Windrose Farm, whether the heirlooms or the smoked, oven-dried tomatoes. And Sunday, get there early for the breakfast stalls that sell stacks of size-of-your-head pancakes, crepes, and customizable omelets.

7 DUPONT CIRCLE FARMERS' MARKET
WASHINGTON, DC

It's not a huge market, but it makes for a lovely stroll on a Sunday morning through Dupont Circle. Look for the Black and Blue cheese from Firefly Farms—it's oozy, buttery, and has lots of ribbons of blue deliciousness. Chris "the crab cake man" will be there flipping his crustacean fritters (his one-bite sample will have you hooked). For produce, including bourbon peaches and strawberries during the summer, hit up Toigo Orchards.

8 CRESCENT CITY FARMERS' MARKET
NEW ORLEANS, LA

What started in 1995 in a parking lot in the Uptown neighborhood on Tuesdays has grown to include markets three days a week in three different locations. It's the kind of place where you buy a few pies and then scarf them down before you have time to drive them home. You can pick up Creole cream cheese and slather it on a decent baguette, some wonderfully tangy cheesecake made with the same cream cheese from Mauthe's Dairy, and amazing strawberries from Ponchatoula. Food

> " I'm happy to go there and maybe pay a little extra for stuff that is super fresh and very local. . . . The chicken and egg guy has different breeds of hen, so you never know what color the eggs will be. Last time, I had blue and green shells. Yay! "
> —duncan1205

DANE COUNTY FARMERS' MARKET, MADISON, WI

writer John T. Edge recommends B&B Farms' Ben Burkett's sweet potatoes, and he insists that any visitor stop by Lionel Key, the "file powder man" (the powder is a key gumbo ingredient). Chef Donald Link takes his children to the Saturday market for everything from tamales to cantaloupe to frozen fruit pops (called paletas). And Link's forager Ashley Locklear is partial to vegetables and quail eggs she buys from Grow Farm's Nick Ussner and greens from Monica's Okra World.

9 FERRY PLAZA FARMERS MARKET
SAN FRANCISCO, CA

On Saturday mornings, over 100 vendors cover the perimeter of the city's waterfront Ferry Building. Grab the juiciest peaches and nectarines from Frog Hollow Farm or Hamada Farms, California avocados from Will's Avocados, and one of the best coffees you'll ever sip from any of the Blue Bottle Coffee stands. Inside the building itself, splurge on any of the pastries at Boulettes Larder (page 20), cured meats from Boccalone (page 320), sweet and savory yogurt dishes (or cheeses) from Cowgirl Creamery, a warm Acme baguette (page 322), a sandwich from Il Cane Rosso . . . you could eat here for months and never repeat a meal.

10 RANCHO SANTA FE FARMERS' MARKET
SANTA FE, NM

You'll find all the typical fare at the Santa Fe Market, but it's the local produce that makes this market so unique. Green chiles abound—shishito, padron, and the preferred Hatch green chile of New Mexico, used in stews, burritos, and more. Try the local yak meat for sale from Taos Mountain Yak, or pick up some cota (the uncommonly complex tea of the Pueblo Indian), which is grown in nearby San Juan Pueblo.

an opinionated guide to eating at ferry plaza

Yes, the Ferry Plaza Farmers Market arrays a staggeringly impressive spread of California farmers, but regulars also know there is much gratification to be had both within the shops inside the Ferry Building and, on Saturdays, in the stalls outside.

HAYES STREET GRILL Patty Unterman's booth creates a perfect breakfast sandwich: locally made, sweet and smoky Hobbs bacon, softly scrambled eggs, and tomatoes and lettuce from one of their neighbors at the market, on an Acme baguette.

HOG ISLAND OYSTER COMPANY They have a fancy restaurant inside the Ferry Plaza Building, but slurp aficionados know they can also get their grilled oyster fix outside—for the butter-and-garlic fan, a Hog Island char-grilled oyster is one of life's great eating pleasures.

4505 MEATS Cook-turned-butcher Ryan Farr gives the Hayes Street Grill folks a run for their money when it comes to breakfast sandwiches: house-smoked maple pork sausage and cheese do beautiful things together (page 42). He also sells his fine beef and pork hot dog studded with bacon, a crispy, juicy fried chicken sandwich, and some of the best chicharrones we've ever had (page 245).

ROLIROTI Vendor-rotisseur Thomas Odermatt started grilling meats in his family's butcher shop in the Swiss Alps as a child. He launched the rotisserie-on-wheels business in the Bay Area in 2002, and now parks at 27 farmers' markets in northern California; on Saturday mornings, it's the Ferry Plaza market. Rows of glistening birds rotate on the rotisserie, giving the chickens moist white meat enrobed in crispy, herby skin. We're not quite as fond of the porchetta, but the super-juicy chicken and dripping-soaked potatoes are worth every minute of the wait.

CAP'N MIKE'S SMOKED FISH While lox on a cream-cheese–smeared bagel may be the standard smoked fish breakfast, Cap'n Mike's smoked fish on the fantastic crusty sourdough from Acme Bread might be even better. Try the cold-smoked sturgeon served with thin Meyer Lemon slices, capers, and pickled onions, or the fattier San Francisco–style red lox—either way, you can't go wrong.

more serious eats

WE SPENT MONTH UPON MONTH
EATING OUR WAY
ACROSS THE NATION IN SEARCH OF
THE BEST SANDWICHES
& breakfasts & burgers—
but not every remarkable place we visited
fit neatly into such categories. So in these pages,
YOU'LL FIND OUR OUTTAKES:
even more delicious eats,
THE SERIOUS EATS EDITORS' FOOD GUIDES
TO THEIR HOMETOWNS (& ADOPTED HOMETOWNS),
SOME OF OUR OUT-OF-CONTROL
EATING ITINERARIES
& a few places we couldn't keep out of these pages.

day trip to new orleans

While nearly all of the authors of this book had been to New Orleans before—some even for extended book-related eating—we felt that po' boy research deserved its own trip back. The solution? A day trip to New Orleans from our headquarters in New York: flight in, a madcap eating tour, flight out. We don't know if any-one's ever put back as many po' boys in a day.

4:45	LONG ISLAND RAILROAD TO JFK
5:30	ARRIVE AT AIRPORT
6:45	FLIGHT TO NEW ORLEANS
8:45	LAND IN NEW ORLEANS
9:45	MORNING CALL COFFEE STAND BEIGNETS
10:30	ZIMMER'S SEAFOOD
11:15	DOOKY CHASE'S
12:00	McCLANCY'S FRIED CHICKEN
12:30	WILLA MAE'S SCOTCH HOUSE
1:15	MAHONY'S PO-BOY SHOP
1:45	TRACEY'S BAR (RELOCATION OF PARASOL'S KITCHEN)
2:15	DOMILISE'S
2:30	HANSEN'S SNO-BLIZ
3:00	PLUM STREET SNOBALL
3:30	R&O'S PO'BOYS AND PIZZA
4:30	NEW ORLEANS ORIGINAL DAIQUIRIS
4:45	NEW ORLEANS AIRPORT
5:30	FLIGHT TO NYC
9:30	LAND IN NYC

ED LEVINE ON NEW YORK

When visitors ask where to eat in New York, I tend to give them enough suggestions for a week or more. But that's okay—New York is the city that never sleeps, so more than three meals a day is a fine way to go. Here are my can't-misses across the boroughs.

Let's start with breakfast. At **RUSS & DAUGHTERS** on Manhattan's Lower East Side, you get two things you can't find anywhere else in the world: the warm welcome and feeling of camaraderie when you take a number and wait in line making new friends, as smoked fish lovers have done for a hundred years; and the finest "Jewish appetizing food" (smoked salmon, whitefish salad, sable, babka, rugelach) in the city. There may be no tables and chairs, but there is a bench right outside where you can eat your perfect bagel sandwich, washed down with a glass of fresh orange juice.

Frank Falcinelli and Frank Castronovo, better known as "The Frankies," are famous for their Italian-American lunch and dinner fare, but they've perfected breakfast at **PRIME MEATS** in the Brooklyn neighborhood of Carroll Gardens. The hash browns, the egg sandwich, the steak and eggs (it becomes a steak-oriented restaurant at dinner)—it's all great. And once you are in Carroll Gardens, hit up the old-school Italian shops: buy some baseball-sized arancini and sweet soppressata at **ESPOSITO AND SONS**, a slab of Sicilian cheesecake at **F. MONTELEONE BAKERY**, and some mozzarella at **CAPUTO'S**.

If you'd prefer a sit-down breakfast in Manhattan, there's the remarkable truffled egg toast at Italian wine and sandwich bar **'INO**, or, at the cozy **JOSEPH LEONARD**, also in the West Village, the hash browns of my dreams and a fresh take on an egg sandwich made with Brussels sprouts.

Bleecker Street between 6th and 7th Avenues in Greenwich Village is simply one of the greatest eating blocks in Manhattan and in all of New York. (We dubbed it "Sandwich Alley" for the remarkable clustering of notable sandwich shops.) My must-stops: a warm cheese biscuit for breakfast at **AMY'S BREAD**; a grilled cheese sandwich made with fine artisanal cheeses at **MURRAY'S CHEESE SHOP**; a roast pork and smoked mozzarella hero at **FAICCO'S PORK STORE**, an old-fashioned pork store that you don't find many of in Manhattan; and a fine Neapolitan pizza at **KESTÉ** made by legendary picman Roberto Caporuscio. If you'd like a classic New York slice instead, you have two choices: **BLEECKER STREET PIZZA** and **JOE'S**. Just a few paces off Bleecker on Cornelia Street, there's a gooey, just mayonnaisey enough lobster roll at Rebecca Charles's **PEARL OYSTER BAR**, accompanied by her incomparable bacon and scallop chowder. For a lighter lunch, walk a few blocks to Bedford Street and have an open-faced sandwich and a chocolate chip cookie at **BLUE RIBBON BAKERY MARKET**; if you need something sweet, there are three fine gelaterias right on that Bleecker Street block (**CONES**, **GROM**, and **L'ARTE DEL GELATO**)—or head back to Amy's for a slice of carrot cake (our favorite in NYC) or coconut cake.

If you'd prefer an outer-borough food stroll, head to Rego Park in Queens, where you'll find a superb pastrami sandwich (ask to have it hand-cut) accompanied by thick Lincoln Log–like French fries at **BEN'S BEST** (not to be confused with the deli mini-chain Ben's). Then start to walk off that lunch with a stroll down Queens Boulevard to **ANDRE'S HUNGARIAN BAKE SHOP**, where they make New York's best strudel, rugelach, and kugelhopf.

While this book talks about great burgers to no end, I feel compelled to include the restaurants that serve some of my favorite chef burgers in New York that didn't get mentioned: **KEENS STEAKHOUSE**, **THE LITTLE OWL**, **BLUE RIBBON BAKERY**, **TELEPAN**, **DINER**, **UNION SQUARE CAFE**, **PRIME MEATS**, and Michael White's "White Label" burger at **AI FIORI**. All use really good, sometimes dry-aged beef and come with first-rate fries. Less dressed up but still very fine burgers can be found at **FOODPARC**, the **FAIRWAY CAFÉ**, and, at **WHITMAN'S**, the stuffed "Juicy Lucy."

In addition to the New York sandwiches we've already discussed, it's important to mention **DEFONTE'S** roast beef, mozzarella, and fried eggplant sandwich, as well as **SALUMERIA BIELLESE'S** roast pork sandwich (served only on Thursdays) and roast beef sandwich (Mondays). Go early on these days or risk being shut out; and make sure you ask for fresh house-made mozzarella and lots of extra gravy on your sandwich.

Though there are many contenders for the best ramen throne, I still can't resist a bowl at the constantly crowded East Village ramen joint **IPPUDO**. The luxuriant, porky broth, the tender noodles, and the pork belly are all so good on their own, but taking a little bit of each in a single bite will transport you to ramen heaven.

What about Chinese food? The city has multiple Chinatowns (including the neighborhoods by that name in downtown Manhattan; Flushing, Queens; and Sunset Park and Avenue U in Brooklyn), but specialties from that country are spread over the boroughs. In Manhattan, outside of Chinatown, I love the Sichuan food at **SICHUAN GOURMET** and the many branches of the **GRAND SICHUAN INTERNATIONAL** chain. For wonton soup I love **NEW CHAO CHOW** and **GREATER NEW YORK NOODLETOWN**, where many of the noodle dishes and the Chinese barbecue also stand out; for small, succulent spare ribs guaranteed to run up your dry-cleaning bill, head to **BIG WONG**. For cheap dumplings we're partial to the pan-fried *guo tie* at **TASTY DUMPLING** (just a quarter each). In Flushing, at the **PEKING DUCK** kiosk in Chinatown, you can get a carved-to-order Peking duck bun for $1, the greatest food bargain in all of NYC. You'll also find incredible lamb skewers sold just next door, the "Lamb Face Salad" and "Cold Skin Noodles" at **XI'AN FAMOUS FOODS**, and dumplings at **WHITE BEAR**.

If you're looking to partake of New York's finest restaurants without taking out a second mortgage, here's a tip: go for lunch. At **JEAN GEORGES**, Jean-Georges Vongerichten's flagship restaurant, you can eat a two-course lunch for $32 with amuses-bouche and petits fours thrown in as part of the deal. (So it's really like getting four courses.) **DEL POSTO'S** Mark Ladner goes one step further: a $29 three-course lunch with the world's best bread basket thrown in for good measure. And after the lunch hour? Consider **GRAMERCY TAVERN**—the informal front of the restaurant is my favorite no-reservations spot in all of the city for sheer food satisfaction (kielbasa, the $14 lunch special, the pastrami appetizer, and Nancy Olsen's homey yet extraordinarily well-crafted desserts). Finally, for a steal of a $50 prix fixe: **TORRISI ITALIAN SPECIALTIES** (page 134), where by day it's a phenomenal Italian deli, but at night it magically transforms into a gutsy, thrill-seeking, ambitious but insanely focused twenty-seat restaurant where two of America's best young chefs, Rich Torrisi and Mario Carbone, ply their craft.

What about steak? You can't go wrong with **PETER LUGER'S** for insanely dry-aged porterhouse for two. Or you can skip the good-natured abuse and the difficulty in securing a reservation and eat just as well at **PRIME MEATS**; at **PORTER HOUSE NEW YORK**, where Michael Lomonaco serves beautiful steaks with a grand view of Central Park; at **MINETTA TAVERN** for the cote de boeuf and the must-have Black Label Burger (page 81); and finally, at a steakhouse that has not been given its due, **PRIME HOUSE NEW YORK**, where the 56-day dry-aged steak is an edible work of carnivorous art.

Though we've written a fair amount about hot dogs in the book, I would be remiss in not pointing out the foot-long hot dog served at the **BROOKLYN DINER** that is as seriously delicious as it is big, the recession special at **GRAY'S PAPAYA** (two hot dogs and a medium papaya drink), and the slaw dog at **PAPAYA KING**, a Southern tradition done right at a classic New York hot dog emporium. If you've eaten your way through your New York food budget three times over, Papaya King will still do you right for less than $5.

seattle, day 2

When Carey Jones and Robyn Lee hit Seattle for a two-day food blitz, they knew they had their work cut out for them. Their list of places to try was in the high two figures before they started paring it down. Then, to complete the insanity, they loved Paseo Caribbean so much they doubled back and even brought a Paseo sandwich to Serious Eats Headquarters in New York.

8:00	DAHLIA BAKERY
8:45	CRUMPET SHOP
9:15	DAILY DOZEN DOUGHNUT COMPANY
9:30	SEATOWN SEABAR
9:50	MACRINA BAKERY
10:45	CAFE BESALU
10:55	TALL GRASS BAKERY
11:30	PASEO CARIBBEAN
12:00	SKILLET STREET FOOD
12:45	MARINATION MOBILE
1:30	PASEO CARIBBEAN (AGAIN!)
2:15	RED MILL BURGERS
3:00	TOP POT DOUGHNUTS
4:00	OLD-SCHOOL FROZEN CUSTARD
4:45	MOLLY MOON'S HOMEMADE ICE CREAM SHOP
5:30	ARCHIE McPHEE'S
6:00	DICK'S
8:00	SEATOWN SEABAR (DINNER)

CAREY JONES ON THE BAY AREA

There were certain things I took for granted about food until I moved away from the Bay Area at the age of 18: Citrus grew in backyards. Farmers' markets were year-round events. Sandwiches came on sourdough or Dutch Crunch bread. It turns out these assumptions don't always hold in the rest of the country, and it wasn't until I left the friendly verdant shores of Northern California that I learned just how well we eat out there.

FERRY PLAZA FARMERS' MARKET (SEE PAGES 335–336)

Yes, there are other farmers' markets in the Bay Area. Yes, some have greater variety, or have more farmers in attendance, or are less tourist-trafficked. But I go weak in the knees for Saturday mornings at Ferry Plaza—not just the **4505 MEATS** breakfast sandwich and **DOWNTOWN BAKERY** muffins and samples of quark from the **SPRING HILL JERSEY CHEESE CO.**; not just buying a warm baguette from **ACME BREAD** or a log of 'nduja at **BOCCALONE**; not just the bounty of Northern California fruits and veggies from the dozens upon dozens of farmers' stands; but taking your morning's haul and sitting on a bench and munching contentedly while looking out over the Bay. (Or, as is often the case, looking out into the mist over the Bay.) Maybe it's just the three **BLUE BOTTLE** macchiatos I inevitably down, but Saturdays at Ferry Plaza put me in a state of euphoria I just don't feel anywhere else.

TAQUERIA LA BAMBA

There's no consensus that **LA BAMBA**, in Mountain View, serves the best burrito in Silicon Valley, or that they serve the best burrito on the *corner* (rival **LA COSTEÑA** is right next door). But the great thing about California is that there are plenty of contenders for the title. It's how commonplace joints like La Bamba are that should really make West Coasters grateful. Place your order, and a burrito-slinger will stretch out a foot-wide flour tortilla and—*whack, whack, whack*—fling rice and beans and guac and meat (I love the crisp-edged *carnitas*) with devastating aim into the tortilla's bull's-eye, rolling everything up and wrapping it in foil before you've even put your change away. A $7-ish burrito is a good day's worth of food. Thanks to the Salvadorean owner, La Bamba serves delicious pupusas (essentially thick, stuffed corncakes), too.

ARCANGELI GROCERY CO.

Whenever family or friends drove to Pescadero, a small Pacific-side town over the mountains from the Bay Area, they'd come back with a loaf of **ARCANGELI GROCERY CO.**'s artichoke-garlic-herb bread. You can smell it as soon as you wander into the old-time corner store: yeasty and olive-oily and garlicky, studded with tender chunks of artichokes, the crusty squat loaves so big you cradle them in two arms. It's the sort of bread that you buy with the best intentions to bring home . . . and then devour it one torn-off chunk at a time before you're anywhere near your destination. If you've made it out to Pescadero, get a slice of olallieberry pie (page 297) at **DUARTE'S TAVERN**, just a few steps down.

HUMPHRY SLOCOMBE (PAGE 285) AND BI-RITE CREAMERY (PAGE 274)

So deep is my respect for the intensely full-flavored, creamy scoops at BI-RITE CREAMERY that I didn't believe newer establishment HUMPHRY SLOCOMBE could come anywhere close. But when I tasted them back-to-back on one very enjoyable summer afternoon, I realized that even Humphry Slocombe's wackier flavors—bourbon-cornflake, salt-and-pepper—were as well-made as they were ambitious, and every bit as scarf-downable as Bi-Rite's. I can't point you to a favorite, so I'll just recommend you repeat the experiment yourself.

DYNAMO DONUTS

The only way to experience DYNAMO's full range is to go early and often; flavors change all the time and often run out. The chase is frustrating but only ups the appeal. While I've loved blueberry cornmeal and lemon pistachio doughnuts, I've still never gotten a ham-and-Gruyère Monte Cristo, or a sweet-and-salty Caramel de Sel, or the Lemon Sichuan. The more times I visit, the more I have to go back.

ZUNI CAFÉ

You likely don't need to read this book to learn about ZUNI; for decades now, the Market Street restaurant has ranked up there with CHEZ PANISSE as a standard-bearer of California cuisine, and for good reason. It's still an excellent restaurant. I prefer it at lunch, when sunlight streams in through the picture windows and the dressed-up-café feel makes it seem the most civilized place in the world. At any meal, order the roast chicken with bread salad for two. It's about as famous as a chicken dish can be, but it is really that good.

FLOUR + WATER

It's worth putting up with the lines to score a table at FLOUR + WATER—not just for the handmade pasta and vaguely Neapolitan-style pizza, but for the bizarre and wonderful things that end up on top of them: bone marrow pizza; caramelized sunchoke tortellini; rough-cut pasta with pork belly, beans,

and chili oil. This is my favorite kind of dining experience: decidedly informal, wildly creative, and really, *really* good.

TARTINE (PAGE 272)

I have exceedingly high (some might say obnoxiously high) standards for croissants and other baked goods, but TARTINE blew me away. The first time I visited, on a six-stop eating tour, I not only polished off two enormous pastries but stashed leftovers in the car for an unnecessary afternoon snack. The next morning, the enormous pain au chocolat was still better than most other places' oven-fresh versions.

THE SENTINEL (PAGE 139)

Too many cheffy sandwiches are overthought and overcomplicated, but everything I've tried at THE SENTINEL in San Francisco has been a work of sandwich mastery, from the pairings of bread and fillings to the can't-stop-eating them extra gobs of house-made mayo. It's one of those menus that guarantees indecision.

PENINSULA CREAMERY

I won't send you to this 1950s-style diner in Palo Alto for a burger, though I remember them fondly; or for a milkshake, though they're thick and delicious; or for a cup of turkey chili, though it's excellent. I will send you there for the indecently buttery, golden-browned, embarrassingly good tuna melt on sourdough—it's less about the tuna than the cheese, mayo, butter, and bread.

And I'd recommend a cheap burger joint or two, but IN-N-OUT BURGER (page 82) is better and cheaper than all of them.

ERIN ZIMMER ON SOUTHERN CALIFORNIA

I was born and raised in Southern California, smack-dab between San Diego and Los Angeles. I went to a high school that had a surf and longboard team. Translation: we ate a lot of breakfast burritos, fish tacos, and avocado-topped things.

ROSA MARIA'S

My family always stops here for burritos en route to our cabin in Lake Arrowhead. At **ROSE MARIA'S**, house-made, still-steamy flour tortillas are filled with slow-simmered pork, pinto beans, Mexican rice, melted cheddar and fresh, and bright red hot sauce—and they're as heavy as bricks. You'll need a nap after you eat one of these. There are now four locations in the area, but we like the outdoor benches at the original drive-in in San Bernadino.

HUCKLEBERRY (PAGE 27)

I trust whatever pastry-chef-cum-owner Zoe Nathan decides to put behind the glass counter at this Santa Monica bakery and café. Especially the maple bacon biscuit. The layered, flaky, buttery biscuit has a slightly sweet, sugar crystal-sprinkled crust, and just the right amount of salt. The bacon is from Niman Ranch and chopped up into smithereens, so every nibble gets some.

LANGER'S (PAGE 152)

Does Los Angeles have a superior deli culture to NYC? After eating **LANGER'S** pastrami sandwich, you might start to think so. The juicy pastrami has peppery, slightly spicy edges; you wouldn't expect much from the bread but the double-baked loaf is just as much of a reason to eat this.

RUBY'S SHAKE SHACK

Driving up and down the Pacific Coast Highway, my mom used to let us stop at this French's mustard–yellow shack, then called "Crystal Cove Shake Shack." In 2006 it was bought by the retro burger chain Ruby's, but thankfully it's still a flimsy shack with a blender inside churning out date shakes. The sweet, sticky fruits are pureed with vanilla ice cream, and even better when you throw a banana into the mix.

BUTTERMILK TRUCK (PAGE 210)

Of all the new-school trucks popping up in Los Angeles, this is one that's worth following on Twitter. **BUTTERMILK TRUCK** does breakfast and late-night service and, though I'm not usually a sweet breakfast eater, the red velvet pancakes topped with fluffy cream cheese butter (more frosting than actual butter) are the best excuse I can think of to eat cake for breakfast. Not that you need one.

PIE 'N BURGER (PAGE 344)

Los Angeles prides itself on being a burger town, and though they may not use the finest, fussiest ingredients, **PIE 'N BURGER** is still my favorite stop. The decades-old diner with Formica countertops and fading plaid wallpaper serves a quarter-pounder of griddled beef on a toasted squishy bun with American cheese, lettuce, onion, and snappy pickles. Oh, and save room for pie.

PHO THANG LONG

For an enormous bowl of pho, this is my go-to. Unlike what you find at many other pho joints in Westminster (aka "Little Saigon"), here you get good-quality filet mignon.

LOS GOLONDRINAS (MULTIPLE LOCATIONS)

This is what my high school years tasted like. Whether after tennis practice, during a lunch break, or just a sunny day when I could sneak off campus, I'd order two of the carne asada tacos on warm corn tortillas (extra guacamole!) or a machaca breakfast burrito, if I was really hungry.

SCOOPS

Growing up with an Irish mother (her maiden name was McCarthy), I was fed brown bread. If only it were brown bread ice cream from **SCOOPS**! The creamy caramel base is swirled with crunchy beads of Grape Nuts. Owner Tai Kim rotates flavors daily (avocado with banana; raisin and gorgonzola) but the brown bread ice cream is deservedly the most popular.

COLLEGE-TOWN EATS

Maybe it's the number of people coming and going; maybe it's the one-two punch of cash-strapped students seeking cheap eats and professors and guests demanding fine dining. Either way, we've long found that college towns are disproportionately good food towns.

ANN ARBOR, MI

KRAZY JIM'S BLIMPY BURGER (PAGE 78)

It's easy to get excited as you wait in line, watching each patty smashed onto the griddle to absolutely maximize surface area browning, giving you far more crispy bits per bite than your average burger.

ZINGERMAN'S (PAGE 152)

The deli was started by two students at the University of Michigan, Ari Weinsweig and Paul Saginaw; it was followed by **ZINGERMAN'S BAKEHOUSE** (page 327), **ZINGERMAN'S ROADHOUSE, ZINGERMAN'S CREAMERY, ZINGERMAN'S COFFEE COMPANY** . . . and we're probably leaving one out. Each shop is as good as the last, but the Reuben at their delicatessen is one of our favorite bites anywhere.

DURHAM/CHAPEL HILL, NC

MAGNOLIA GRILL (PAGE 309)

Ben and Karen Barker are not only excellent area tour guides (they turned us on to the terrific **NEAL'S DELI**, page 43), they are also the proud owners of one of our favorite restaurants anywhere, the **MAGNOLIA GRILL**. Yes, they use tons of great locally sourced ingredients, but what really makes their food stand out is they know what to do with them—not too much, not too little.

ALLEN & SON (PAGE 202)

You could call Keith Allen one of the last of the barbecue Mohicans—an old-line barbecue purist of the highest order. Beyond the pork, everything else on his barbecue plates is incredibly tasty, too: coleslaw, hush puppies, even French fries and homemade desserts (including ice cream).

LA VAQUITA

The research triangle (Raleigh–Durham–Chapel Hill) is home to many Mexican immigrants, so it's not surprising that excellent taquerias have opened in the area. **LA VAQUITA** makes serious tacos with warm homemade corn tortillas, a little meat, radish slivers, avocado slices, and a lime wedge; we're also fond of their sopes, gorditas, and tortas. We're partial to filling any of these items with carnitas.

PRINCETON, NJ

HOAGIE HAVEN

A no-frills Jersey sandwich shop that's equally good for soaking up beer at 2:00 a.m. or quieting a hangover the next morning. While HOAGIE HAVEN's famous for their knockoffs of the Rutgers GREASE TRUCK sandwiches (page 163), like the "Phat Lady" (a cheesesteak with mozzarella sticks and French fries right in the bun), the standard cheesesteaks and chicken-parm hoagies might be even better.

THE LITTLE CHEF (PAGE 30)

Skip the lines at PJ's Pancake House, and stop in this closet-sized bakery for Edwige Fils-Aimé's perfect croissants and *pain au chocolat* (and a nice Lavazza cappuccino, too). It's hard to imagine there are hidden gems in a town as small as Princeton, but this is the one you should know.

THE BENT SPOON (PAGE 285)

The intensely flavorful ice creams and sorbets here are all New Jersey–centric—whether Jersey corn ice cream, stout ice cream (made with beer from local TRIUMPH BREWERY), or sorbet using nearby TERHUNE ORCHARD's apple cider. And if it's too cold for ice cream, their cupcakes, cookies, and hot chocolate are just as memorable.

MADISON, WI

BATCH (PAGE 323)

Stop by for croissant-dough spiral vanilla swirls, uncommonly delicious blueberry muffins, and crusty, hot stuffed rolls. It's the kind of bakery where you go in for one pastry and walk out with six; they just smell that good.

GRAZE (PAGE 78)

Tory Miller, who bought the restaurant L'ETOILE from pioneering chef Odessa Piper, opened the more casual GRAZE next door in 2010; their $10 pub burger is one of the best (and least expensive) chef burgers we've ever had.

DANE COUNTY FARMERS' MARKET (PAGE 333)

While you should, of course, browse the incredible range of fruits, veggies, meats, and grains at this producers'-only farmers' market, there are plenty of amazing things to grab and eat while you're walking around: squeaky cheese curds by the bag, kettle corn from enormous cauldrons, and a hot and spicy cheese bread from STELLA'S BAKERY that, while it may just look like a grease-laden novelty food, is improbably and irresistibly delicious.

WASHINGTON, DC

SWEETGREEN AND SWEETFLOW

Salads and frozen yogurt may seem a radical departure from the rest of this book, but this small DC chain (started by three Georgetown grads) sets itself apart with top-notch, locally sourced veggies and a frozen yogurt truck, SWEETFLOW, that roams around town. (Breakfast people: Sweetflow serves brûléed oatmeal during the morning hours.)

DOLCEZZA (PAGE 288)

Robb Duncan and his wife/co-owner Violeta Edelman use unusual spice, chocolate, citrus, and nut blends for their Argentine-style gelato (which makes use of more cream than Italian gelato does, and no eggs). The pistachio is earthy and nutty, and the dulce de leche is as good as any in Argentina.

2 AMYS

2 AMYS has the VPN seal of approval, meaning its pizza is certified as "Neapolitan" and must be made according to the ins-and-outs of the Vera Pizza Napoletana association. Official seals aside, this is a great pie. The char, the leopard-spotting, the puffy cornicione (page 112)—it's one of those beautiful pies you stop and admire for a few seconds before chomping into it. It has the soupy, wet center that true Naples pies have, with great balance of cheese and sauce. Be warned: most nights there's at least an hour wait for a table.

AUSTIN, TX

IZZOZ TACOS (PAGE 229)

Steakhouse owner-turned-taco-man John Galindo slow-cooks carne guisada, stewed meat, machaca, and more in his taco trailer. More unusual creations, like the tempura-battered avocado taco, are just as good—and the breakfast tacos are some of the best in the city.

FRANKLIN BARBECUE (PAGE 197)

There was a time when, for the finest brisket, you'd have to drive outside Austin; no longer, with FRANKLIN BARBECUE. Get there early and be prepared to wait: there are often fifty-person lines before the shop even opens, and once they're sold out (which can happen in mere hours), you're out of luck. But it's worth the wait for his insanely tender brisket, achieved with classic low and slow heat.

BANANARCHY

Anyone who's seen *Arrested Development* knows the frozen banana stand, inspired by real ones on Balboa Island in Newport Beach. Co-owners Anna Notario and Laura Anderson decided to start their own in Austin. "We wanted people to treat bananas as if they were a valid dessert, just like cookies or ice cream," said Notario. Try the Afternoon Delight: dipped in chocolate, white chocolate, and peanut butter, it gets coated in graham cracker crumbs and peanut choppings.

BERKELEY, CA

CAFÉ AT CHEZ PANISSE

Though the more formal CHEZ PANISSE is where Alice Waters made her bones in the Bay Area food scene, her café one flight up is where we gravitate to whenever we're in Berkeley. The cooking there is simpler and less elaborate, but the food is just as carefully prepared and delicious—amazing salads, truly tasty fresh vegetables, and extraordinary desserts. The pizzas, if inconsistent, are never less than satisfying.

EMILIA'S PIZZERIA (PAGE 110)

The delicious, straightforward pizza here speaks for itself; bucking all the Neapolitan, artisanal trends, Keith Freilich just makes damn good pies. It's a dead ringer for any of New York's legendary coal-oven pizzerias—a rare thing in the Bay Area—with fresh mozzarella and an open, rustic crumb.

ICI ICE CREAM

The Bay Area is home to much great ice cream, so it's not surprising that Berkeley has an excellent ice cream shop to call its own. ICI owner Mary Canales is a CHEZ PANISSE alum—their pastry chef for nine years—so she is dedicated to both careful process and using great ingredients in her ice cream.

BOULDER, CO

PIZZERIA BASTA (PAGE 112)

Located in a condominium complex near downtown Boulder, PIZZERIA BASTA has fantastic Neapolitan-style pies; toppings are smartly chosen, not strictly orthodox (there's an excellent sausage, rapini, fennel pollen, and chili pizza), and the puffy edges have everything we look for in a pizza crust.

BOULDER COUNTY FARMERS' MARKET

This Colorado non-profit market, organized and run by local agricultural producers, is nestled between the Boulder Creek and the stunning rose gardens at the neighboring DUSHANBE TEAHOUSE. Shoppers can use "market bucks" (a pre-paid market debit card) to purchase goat cheese from HAYSTACK MOUNTAIN GOAT DAIRY, beans from GINGER CAT FARMS, and bison cuts from HIGH WIRE RANCH.

THE KITCHEN

It's hard not to drool over a menu featuring LA QUERCIA prosciutto (page 318) and buratta (a soft, mozzarella-like cheese) on the same sandwich. Sophisticated but laid-back, destination-worthy wine and beer lists—many of the Boulder dining scene's best characteristics show up in this restaurant.

chicago, day 2

Our trip to Chicago was particularly crazy because there were just so many delicious stops we had to make—and because two of our Chicago contributors wanted to show us so much in the city. Note the stop at Old Fashioned Donuts, where the big-as-your-head apple fritters served as an amuse for the next stop at Top Notch Beef Burgers.

10:00	ANN SATHER RESTAURANT
10:15	M. HENRY
11:00	TRE KRONOR
11:45	SUSIE'S DRIVE-THRU
12:30	HONEY 1 BBQ
1:40	OLD FASHIONED DONUTS
2:00	TOP NOTCH BEEF BURGERS
2:45	HAROLD'S FRIED CHICKEN
3:15	CALUMET FISHERIES
3:55	LEM'S BAR-B-Q
4:10	BROWN SUGAR CAFE
4:30	IZOLA'S
5:15	UNCLE JOHN'S BARBECUE
6:00	MK BURGER BAR

FOR YOUR CONSIDERATION

Over the year we spent eating across America, we came across dozens of admirable eating establishments that, due to quirks of chapter topics or geographical distribution, didn't quite make it into the main pages of our book. Here are a few places we couldn't pass up the chance to tell you about.

CITY BAKERY
NEW YORK, NY

Everyone has his or her own reason to love the bakery/lunch spot/takeout destination **CITY BAKERY**, but it's the pretzel croissants that really keep us coming back. Yep, you read that right. A happy oven-fresh love child of Paris and New York, it's just what it sounds like—croissant dough in pretzel form. Now, if you made a pretzel-to-croissant spectrum, this guy would fall about two-thirds of the way toward the latter end; its pretzel tendencies are mainly superficial. The crust is crisp and very salty, studded with sesame seeds and baked long enough to give each little pastry arm a satisfying crunch. The interior, however, is tender and flaky—a pastry dough with nothing pretzel-like about it.

MARCO'S COAL-FIRED PIZZA
DENVER, CO

MARCO'S COAL-FIRED PIZZA serves some of the best wood-fired pizza we've had in the state. Confused? We were, too. But this VPN-certified (see page 114) Denver joint turns out pies that are classically Neapolitan, but not textbook-dull like some orthodox pizzerias can be. The elastic, chewy crust has a great char and hole structure, and the 4-cheese Abruzzo—with the Southern Italian cheese caciocavallo and a whole lot of basil and olive oil—is far more interesting than most white cheese pies we've had.

BIG STAR
CHICAGO, IL

Usually, when chefs do tacos, you'll find them three to a $20 dish, fanned out with sauces artfully streaked across the plate. Not so at **BIG STAR**, a taco and whiskey shack from acclaimed Chicago restaurateurs Paul Kahan and Donnie Madia—where tacos cost $2 or $3. They're tossed on your table in plastic baskets so casually you can't quite believe how *good* they are—the soft corn tortillas filled with gutsy chorizo or pork belly or carnitas. Don't miss the surprisingly affordable cocktails, either; designed by mixologist Toby Maloney of the **VIOLET HOUR**, they're as complex and interesting as that bar's drinks across the street.

MILLER'S TWIST
PHILADELPHIA, PA

All over Philly and New York City, you'll find generic soft pretzels—good if they're fresh and hot, but unremarkable otherwise. Then there are the buttery, crispy on the outside, tender on the inside pretzels that you can get at **MILLER'S TWIST** in the **READING TERMINAL MARKET**. Do your own taste test. Buy a pretzel on the street in Philly and then get one from Miller's Twist. You'll never eat another generic pretzel again.

DICK'S
SEATTLE, WA

Here's the thing about **DICK'S**, a local chain of '50s-style drive-up burger joints in and around Seattle. They may not make the best burgers you've ever had, but they almost certainly make one of the best burgers you've ever had for $1.20. In the style of McDonald's burgers, but an *awful* lot better, they're what we wish all fast food tasted like. "As a meat, cheese, and salt-delivery device," our contributor Adam Lindsley once wrote, "it succeeds marvelously."

BEST PIZZA
BROOKLYN, NY

When you're ballsy enough to call your pizzeria **BEST PIZZA**, you really have to walk the walk. Fortunately for this wood-oven pizzeria in Williamsburg, Brooklyn, there's truth in the advertising. Best Pizza's putting out some great, no-nonsense wood-fired pies (in slice form, no less) that defy easy categorization, with a style of pizza that gives nods to old-school New York–slice joints and coal-oven Neapolitan-American places like **TOTONNO'S** or **PATSY'S EAST HARLEM**. And their meatball sub may now be our favorite in New York.

TONALLI'S DONUTS & CREAM
PORTLAND, OR

Doughnuts and ice cream under one roof: every eight-year-old's dream. The family-owned shop devotes one side to doughnuts, the other to ice cream. It's a corner doughnut shop with super homey old-fashioneds, cruellers, apple fritters, and buttermilk doughnuts, all made fresh daily. The ice creams aren't artisanal, but they're fun. "Hugs & Smooches" swirls in chocolate-covered cherries, and one flavor even has Pop Rocks.

ARNOLD'S COUNTRY KITCHEN
NASHVILLE, TN

From the outside, the squat red corner of a strip mall that houses **ARNOLD'S COUNTRY KITCHEN** doesn't look like much. Don't be fooled. Founder Jack Arnold is an obsessive country cook with impossibly high standards; those standards are carried by his wife Rose and son Kahlil, who now run the show. There are almost no throwaways on this menu: Rare roast beef, squash casserole, fried green tomatoes, two kinds of cornbread (grilled and baked), green beans, and peach cream pie made with fresh local peaches in season—it's all seriously delicious and carefully cooked. It's meat-and-three done right. The line is frequently out the door, but don't fret. It moves fast.

MAGGIE HOFFMAN ON PORTLAND, OR

Portland is one of my favorite food towns, and not just because I grew up there. It's full of young, creative chefs, craft brewers, passionate coffee roasters, and people who care about what they eat. Local farms provide incredibly flavorful produce, and you can drive just over the mountains to catch your own Dungeness crabs. Here are a few of my favorite Puddletown spots:

TASTY N SONS (PAGE 20)

The folks behind the always-packed tapas restaurant **TORO BRAVO** serve an incredible brunch menu all week at **TASTY N SONS**. Be sure to order the Shakshuka (a spicy tomato-egg stew) with merguez sausage. Frittata fillings vary by season, but every one I've tried has been delicious.

LAURELHURST MARKET

You may have to wait across the street at **MUSIC MILLENNIUM**, but the steak at **LAURELHURST** is worth it. Go with the daily steak frites special, and hope its bavette, an underrated, super flavorful cut that is always seared perfectly.

MEAT CHEESE BREAD

Portland's gone so sandwich-crazy that it's hard to pick a favorite, but this little shop on Stark really knows how to fill two slices of bread. Barbecue and bacon waft through the air, so it makes sense to go with pulled pork or the BLB (bacon, lettuce, and beets), though the sweet-savory maple bread pudding sandwich isn't something you'll want to miss.

APIZZA SCHOLLS (PAGE 104)

Portland has become an impressive town for pizza, and this spot is worth lining up for. (Get there ten minutes before it opens.) Though pieman Brian Spangler uses an electric oven, his crusts are bubbled, chewy, and perfectly charred. The Apizza Amore with spicy capicollo is incredible, and the house-made sausage is awesome.

TÁBOR (PAGE 210)

Even when it's been months since I had a Schnitzelwich, I can't get it out of my mind. Juicy pork schnitzel with a miraculously crisp exterior, smeared in ajvar and creamy horseradish sauce and piled in a fresh ciabatta bun with lettuce and caramelized onions: it's a mouthful. Vegetarians aren't an afterthought here: the eggplant sandwich is excellent as well.

GRÜNER

There are a number of ridiculously juicy burgers in Portland (see **LE PIGEON**, page 80) but **GRÜNER**'s may be the most ridiculous of them all. It's beefy, fatty, freshly ground, and bursting with juicy flavor. Fried smashed potatoes on the side don't hurt.

GARDEN STATE

Portland is an excellent place to eat meat, but it's also an excellent place *not* to eat meat. Case in point: this cart in the **MISSISSIPPI MARKETPLACE** pod serves a solid meatball sub, but I actually like the vegetarian option better: it's a chickpea fritter sandwich on Fleur de Lis bread, topped with zucchini, carrots, and aioli.

PARK KITCHEN

It's a special-occasion favorite, especially if you like to experiment with unusual flavor combinations. The excellent flank steak salad with blue cheese and sherried onions is always on the menu, but most other things change seasonally, and the chefs have always fried up something unusual (like a julep cup full of string beans and bacon). **PARK KITCHEN**'s happy hour is a remarkable value, with some of the city's best cocktails marked down to $5. If you like your drinks tart and spicy, order a St. Elizabeth Sour.

CASCADE BREWING BARREL HOUSE

This spot is a treasure; Portland's **CASCADE BREWING** makes fascinating, delicious beers, many of which are tart (thanks to lactic fermentation) and fruity (thanks to local cherries, apricots, and other fruit). Much of what's served in the barrel house is never bottled or served anywhere else.

J. KENJI LOPEZ-ALT ON BOSTON

I was born in Boston but raised in New York, so I've always been torn between the two. But having spent ten years as a student and cook in Cambridge, I've got to say that when it comes to food, I'm a true New Englander. New York may have its pizza and its haute cuisine temples (and the attitude that comes with them), but nobody does seafood like Boston. It's simultaneously a small town and a big city, with all the best parts of both. Here are my favorite spots to eat and drink around town (and please, don't call it Bean Town).

ROSTICERIA CANCUN

The very definition of a hole-in-the-wall, this tiny (read: six chairs and a counter) taqueria serves up the juiciest tacos de lengua around in a fresh double-stack of corn tortillas for under $2. Tongue this good needs only the bare minimum of toppings: a spoonful of chopped onions and cilantro, and a spicy-tart tomatillo salsa.

CRAIGIE ON MAIN (PAGES 80 AND 309)

Chef Tony Maws's mostly locavore, always seasonal Cambridge restaurant is about as gracious, comfortable, and delicious as fine dining can get. I'm also a little biased, because it's where I proposed to my wife. The ring was delivered around the rib of a wild boar chop—who says wild animals can't be romantic?

NEPTUNE OYSTER BAR (PAGE 145)

There are just so many things right about the hot buttered lobster roll at **NEPTUNE OYSTER BAR** that it's now supplanted the traditional New England cold mayonnaise-based version in my mind as the new classic.

TORO

This South End tapas bar was the third restaurant of Chef Ken Oringer's mini Boston empire; it's my favorite of the bunch. Its casual menu mixes traditional tapas (like *patatas bravas* or *gambas al ajillo*) with more uniquely Oringer dishes such as a miniature sea urchin sandwich with miso butter or pork belly with snails and smoked maple. And their insanely creamy, cheesy version of Mexican street corn is required eating on any Boston visit.

FULOON

Fiery bowls of tender steamed beef bubble menacingly under a pool of red hot chili oil. A mouth-numbing salad of crunchy sliced beef tendon and cilantro is dotted with Sichuan peppercorns. Whole crabs are tossed with a mountain of fried garlic and chile peppers. For all you Sichuan chili-heads out there, **FULOON** is the real deal.

S&I TO GO

You'd never expect it from a take-out restaurant serving mostly crab Rangoon and Pad Thai to nearby Boston University students, but this ten-seat hole-in-the-wall has the best Thai food I've had outside of Thailand. Familiar menu items like Gai Pad Gra Pow or fiery Som Tum shine, but the real stunners are the more obscure picks. Try chunks of Thai eggplant and catfish tossed with whole garlands of pickled green peppercorns or crisp and fatty fried pork belly smothered in a sweet and spicy chili sauce.

EASTERN STANDARD KITCHEN AND DRINKS

No one in Boston does hospitality like restaurateur Garrett Harker, and **EASTERN STANDARD** continues to set the bar for classy but inclusive neighborhood dining. They have a solid menu of American classics and a stellar drinks program, but the real draw is the convivial atmosphere. I've spent countless nights closing the bar with a few friends, a couple gin flips, and a plate or two of charcuterie.

DRINK

When it comes to cocktails, John Gertsen, formerly of Barbara Lynch's **NO. 9 PARK**, is both a historian and a genius, and **DRINK** is his baby. There are no menus or visible bottles here, just a team of the most highly trained professional bartenders in the business who know exactly what you want, often even before you do, whether it's a perfectly crafted classic or a brand-new improv piece.

FLAT PATTIES

The smashed griddled patties may look thin, but deep brown crisp edges and plenty of juicy fat deliver huge beef flavor. It's a near perfect California-style burger experience, with plenty of fresh vegetables and a big smear of tangy Thousand Island dressing. In-N-Out ain't got nothing on this one.

BONDIR

"Local, seasonal" cuisine is by now a de rigeur menu description. The difference here is that chef Jason Bond, another alumnus of the Barbara Lynch school of cooking, really means it. The man kills his own chickens, for heaven's sake! I don't know any other chef in the world who can transform a plateful of root-cellar staples—carrots, turnips, parsnips—into a downright inspiring dish. Like the food, the quiet, romantic space is thoughtful and homey.

ADAM KUBAN ON MILWAUKEE

I couldn't have picked a better place to be born than Milwaukee. This is a city that takes its food and drink seriously. Cheese, beer, frozen custard, Friday-night fish-fries—all the comforting stuff that can help you put on an extra layer against the cold winters. And even though my parents moved away (taking me with them, sadly), I still visit regularly. These are just a few of the places to which I make my aunts and cousins chauffeur me when I come to town.

LEON'S FROZEN CUSTARD (PAGE 290)

"Open all year" is what the '50s-era sign proclaims outside **LEON'S** (which was supposedly the inspiration for Arnold's in *Happy Days*). Who would eat frozen custard in the dead of winter? Milwaukeeans. And they think nothing of hopping out of their cars, shivering their way to the walk-up window, and ordering a cone stuffed full of one of the standard flavors or, better yet, one of the rotating flavors of the day. Yes, it is that good.

DIAMOND JIM'S STONERIDGE INN

If you're booking a trip to Milwaukee, make sure a Friday-night fish fry is in your itinerary. It's one of the city's most charming and longstanding traditions, and **DIAMOND JIM'S**, a supper club straight out of 1978, puts on one of the best in the area. The three large pieces of perfectly fried cod have a light, crisp, nicely seasoned batter yielding to moist, flaky flesh. Potato pancakes are the traditional accompaniment; be sure to get them here.

C. ADAM'S BAKERY IN THE MILWAUKEE PUBLIC MARKET

You can't really do full-throttle grocery shopping at the **PUBLIC MARKET**, but if an amazing baked good is on your dance card, you can't do better than one of **C. ADAM'S** cheese danishes. Flaky layers of buttery pastry dough dusted with confectioners' sugar envelop a rich dollop and a half of cream cheese filling. It alone is worth a visit.

ALTERRA COFFEE

If you're looking for a great, well-balanced cuppa joe or a specialty coffee drink, drop into one of the many locations of this local coffee-roasting chain. Many are large, sprawling shops that manage to feel warm, cozy, and neighborhood-y. The non-kiosk locations feature a good food menu, too, with inventive sandwiches and breakfast items served all day long.

MARIA'S PIZZA (PAGE 125)

The trend in pizza is toward wood-fired "artisanal" offerings, but I'd much rather have a **MARIA'S** "Special" pie (plenty of cheese, sausage, mushrooms, and onions) served by the quirky Traxel family, while sitting among paint-by-numbers portraits of religious figures and under swaths of year-round holiday lights. Thin- and flaky-crusted, these pizzas are loaded with toppings until they can take no more and then served on trays far too small for their cheesy, delicious bounty.

KOPP'S FROZEN CUSTARD (PAGE 290)

In Milwaukee, there are burgers with buttered buns and then there are *butter burgers*. **KOPP'S** serves one of my favorite serious butter burgers. There's enough of the dairy product slathered onto the bun of this already juicy burger that it earns its

name—but not such an obscene amount that you contemplate skipping the custard for dessert.

ROOTS RESTAURANT & CELLAR

Milwaukee excels in preserving kitschy, old-school, frozen-in-time type places, but when I want to eat a more contemporary meal, I go to **ROOTS,** where chef-owner John Raymond does the whole farm-to-table thing, with inventive menus (seafood-sausage corn dog, Yucatán smoked chicken, honey-glazed parsnip "ribs") that also take vegans and the gluten-free into account.

KEWPEE LUNCH

If you happen to be driving to Milwaukee from points south, a stop at **KEWPEE LUNCH** in Racine is worth a quick detour. Made from beef ground daily, the small burgers are a throwback to the lunch-counter era. Loosely packed, the patties have a nice sear on them and are just juicy and salty enough. They're not sliders, but they are small. I'd suggest going with a double. And a malt.

NATIONAL BAKERY

Another Milwaukee thing? Hot ham and rolls on Sunday. Bakeries in the area typically offer a half-dozen "hard rolls" with the purchase of a pound of deli ham. Customers take the ham and rolls home and assemble the sandwiches themselves, typically slathering on a generous amount of butter (this is Wisconsin, after all). The rolls are shatteringly crisp on the outside with a tight, dry crumb that holds the butter exceptionally well.

FRANKS DINER

FRANKS in Kenosha is known for its garbage plates, big ol' hashes of potatoes, eggs, green peppers, onions, jalapeños, and your choice of meat(s). It's good, if a bit gut-busting, but perhaps even better is their French toast, made with thick slices of diner-baked bread. The atmosphere at Franks matches the quality of the food, too. It's that friendly brand of sassiness—tough love dished out when it's needed by the cook-owners. Patrons seem to abide by it and take it in stride.

ACKNOWLEDGMENTS

There would be no *Serious Eats* book without the devoted, passionate, and lively Serious Eats community that has grown together over the last four years. Our community of contributors, commentators, and food enthusiasts inspires us every day to do the work that we do. Without Ed's brother, Mike, and his wife, Carol, there would be no Serious Eats in any form. Our agent, Vicky Bijur, believed in this book and the site from its first day. Our editor, Emily Takoudes, and her trusty assistant, Peggy Paul, kept their sense of humor and kept us on track throughout. Many thanks to Lauren Shakely, publisher of Clarkson Potter, whom we met at a party and who was immediately taken by the spirit of the Serious Eats crew. Thanks to Harriet Bell, who helped turn our torrent of ideas into a coherent proposal.

While part of the Serious Eats team worked tirelessly on the book, the rest of the crew at World HQ made sure everything kept humming along: Erin Adamo, Christine Tsai, Leandra Palermo, and Donna Brucale.

Maggie Hoffman, SE's Slice and Drinks Editor, contributed lots of Portland food intel and the guide to Portland in the back of the book. Midtown Lunch visionary Zach Brooks shares our love of street food and sandwiches and chauffeured us around Los Angeles. Holly and Terry Cohn showed us where to eat in Madison, Wisconsin; Pableaux Johnson was the greatest New Orleans tour guide serious eaters could ask for, and on twenty-four hours' notice, no less. Thanks also to the rest of our NOLA crew: Brett Anderson, Lolis Eric Elie, and Will Benjamin. We couldn't have written this book without Robb Walsh, our go-to man for everything edible in Texas; John T. Edge, our mouth in the south; Kathleen Purvis, friend and Charlotte source; or chef Bryan Polcyn, our Detroit taste buds and long-distance pizza courier. Hamburger America auteur George Motz supplied crucial burger context; Paul Kahan shared his love for Chicago-area farmers and their crops; Karen and Ben Barker, first couple of the current Raleigh-Durham food scene, ate with us and introduced us to the treasures of the Carrboro farmer's market; and Michael Schwartz of Michael's Genuine Food and Drink, along with Jackie Sayet, showed us around Miami with the help of Miami food blogger Sef Gonzales and Miami über-chef Michelle Bernstein and her husband and partner, David Martinez.

Our eating tours through Chicago were made possible by Serious Eats writers, drivers, and local experts Nick Kindelsberger and Daniel Zemans, who gave up half a week of their lives to stuff themselves silly with us; we were also helped along by former SE man in Chicago Michael Nagrant. Nick Solares, Serious Eats hamburger authority, chimed in with burger knowledge concerning a number of cities and also contributed photos. Kathy YL Chan told us what's what in her native Hawaii.

David Lewis, Danica Kombol, and John Kessler contributed Atlanta inside knowledge. Samantha Blatteis showed us around Portland, Maine. Chichi Wang taught us all about New Mexico, with additional research from John Edwards, who was always a willing driver. Former Serious Eats intern Alison Herzog and her husband, Chris, hosted us in Salt Lake City (and braved twenty-two restaurants in one day); Ron and Fay Stanford drove us around Philly; Roger Marmet chauffeured us around D.C. in record time. We can't forget Tyler Williams, our doughnut connection in Lexington, Kentucky.

We're always indebted to our interns, our partners in researching, writing, and editing (not just eating). Leah Douglas and Faye Leong contributed directly to the text, and Rachel Heise Bolten was a truly fine fact-checker.

The good folks at Kimpton Hotels, including Vanessa Bordman, Sara Nielsen, and Jamie Law, found us wonderful hotel rooms at their lovely hotels around the country. Jason Stone, GM of Kimpton's Harbor Court Hotel in San Francisco, not only scored us some serious ramen, but also had it perfectly hot when we finally arrived.

We slept soundly across the country thanks to the hospitality of James and Melinda Edwards, Claudia Christman-Skieller, Jennifer Cheng, Rebecca Kim, Julie Ann Elefante, and Rosamund Lannin.

Serious Eats wouldn't exist without our supportive investors, including Mike and Carol Levine, Marc and Cathy Lasry, Steve Trost and Beryl Snyder, Henry and Vanessa Cornell, Bob Rosen and Marcia Golub, Chandler and Alanna Bocklage, and Sol and Elizabeth Kumin. They are last, but certainly not least; to them we owe a debt of gratitude that cannot be quantified, no matter how many spreadsheets we produce.

DIRECTORY

ALABAMA

Big Bob Gibson Bar-B-Q
1715 6th Avenue Southeast
Decatur
(and other locations)
www.bigbobgibson.com

ARIZONA

Aqui Con El Nene
1500 West Wetmore Road
Tucson

The Fry Bread House
4140 North 7th Avenue
Phoenix

Matt's Big Breakfast
801 North 1st Street
Phoenix
www.mattsbigbreakfast.com

Pane Bianco
4404 North Central Avenue
Phoenix
pizzeriabianco.com/pane

Pizzeria Bianco
623 East Adams Street
Phoenix
www.pizzeriabianco.com

Sweet Republic
9160 East Shea Boulevard
Scottsdale
www.sweetrepublic.com

Truckin' Good Food
Phoenix
www.truckingoodfood.com

CALIFORNIA

A's Burgers
34344 Pacific Coast Highway
Dana Point
(and other locations)

Acme Bread
1 Ferry Building Marketplace
15
San Francisco
www.ferrybuildingmarket-
place.com/acme_bread_com-
pany.php

Apple Pan
10801 West Pico Boulevard
Los Angeles

Bakesale Betty
5098 Telegraph Avenue
Oakland
(and other locations)
www.bakesalebetty.com

Bi-Rite Creamery
3692 18th Street
San Francisco
www.biritecreamery.com

Boccalone
1 Ferry Building Marketplace
21
San Francisco
www.ferrybuildingmarket-
place.com/boccalone_shop_
page.php

Bouchon Bakery
6528 Washington Street
Yountville
www.bouchonbakery.com

Boulettes Larder
1 Ferry Building Marketplace
48
San Francisco
www.bouletteslarder.com

Buttermilk Truck
Los Angeles
www.buttermilktruck.com

Chez Panisse
1517 Shattuck Avenue
Berkeley
www.chezpanisse.com

Comme Ça
8479 Melrose Avenue
West Hollywood
(and other locations)
commecarestaurant.com

Crème Brûlée Cart
San Francisco
thecremebruleecart.com

Culture Organic Frozen Yogurt
340 South California Avenue
Palo Alto
culturefrozenyogurt.com

Dottie's True Blue Café
522 Jones Street
San Francisco

Duarte's Tavern
202 Stage Road
Pescadero
www.duartestavern.com

Emilia's Pizzeria
2995 Shattuck Avenue
Berkeley
emiliaspizzeria.com

Ferry Plaza Farmers' Market
1 Ferry Building Marketplace
San Francisco
www.ferrybuildingmarket-
place.com

4505 Meats
1 Ferry Building Marketplace
San Francisco
(and other locations)
www.4505meats.com

Hapa Ramen
San Francisco
haparamensf.com

Happy Girl Kitchen
173 Central Avenue
Pacific Grove
(and other locations)
www.happygirlkitchen.com

Huckleberry Bakery & Cafe
1014 Wilshire Boulevard
Santa Monica
www.huckleberrycafe.com

Humphry Slocombe
2790 Harrison Street
San Francisco
www.humphryslocombe.com

It's-It
San Francisco
www.itsiticecream.com

Joe's Cable Car Restaurant
4320 Mission Street
San Francisco
joescablecarrestaurant.com

La Farine
6323 College Avenue
Oakland
(and other locations)
www.lafarine.com

Langer's
704 South Alvarado Street
Los Angeles
www.langersdeli.com

Let's Be Frank Dogs
3318 Steiner Street
San Francisco
(and other locations)
www.letsbefrankdogs.com

Little Lucca
724 El Camino Real
South San Francisco
(and other locations)
www.littlelucca.com

Ludotruck
Los Angeles
www.ludolefebvre.com/
ludotruck

Marisco's German Taco Truck
3504 University Avenue
San Diego
(and other locations)

Mozza2Go
6610 Melrose Avenue
Los Angeles
www.mozza2go.com

Nina's Food
240 North Breed Street
Los Angeles

Oki Dog
860 North Fairfax Avenue
Los Angeles
(and other locations)

Osteria
6602 Melrose Avenue
Los Angeles
(and other locations)
www.osteriamozza.com

Philippe's
1001 North Alameda Street
Los Angeles
www.philippes.com

Pie 'n Burger
913 East California
Boulevard
Pasadena
www.pienburger.com

Pink's
709 North LaBrea Avenue
Los Angeles
www.pinkshollywood.com

Pizzaiolo and Boot & Shoe Service
5008 Telegraph Avenue
Oakland
(and other locations)
www.pizzaiolooakland.com

Pizzeria Mozza
641 North Highland Avenue
Los Angeles
(and other locations)
www.pizzeriamozza.com

Pizzeria Picco
316 Magnolia Avenue
Larkspur
www.pizzeriapicco.com

Poco Dolce
2419 3rd Street
San Francisco
(and other locations)

Recchiuti Confections
1 Ferry Building Marketplace
30
San Francisco
(and other locations)
www.recchiuti.com

**Santa Monica Wednesday
Farmers' Market**
2nd Street & Arizona Avenue
Santa Monica
www.smgov.net/farmers_
market/wednesday.htm

The Sentinel
35 New Montgomery Street
San Francisco
www.thesentinelsf.com

Serpentine
2495 3rd Street
San Francisco
www.serpentinesf.com

Sweet Rose Creamery
225 26th Avenue, Suite 51
Brentwood
sweetrosecreamery.com

Tartine
600 Guerrero Street
San Francisco
www.tartinebakery.com

Tcho Chocolate
Pier 17, The Embarcadero
and Green Street
San Francisco
(and other locations)
www.tcho.com

Top Dog
2534 Durant Avenue
Berkeley
(and other locations)
www.topdoghotdogs.com

Umami Burger
850 South La Brea Avenue
Los Angeles
(and other locations)
www.umamiburger.com

Una Pizza Napoletana
210 11th Street
San Francisco
www.unapizza.com

COLORADO
Biker Jim's Gourmet Dogs
2148 Larimer Street
Denver
(and other locations)
www.bikerjimsdogs.com

Bud's Bar
5453 Manhart Street
Sedalia

Pizzeria Basta
3601 Arapahoe Avenue
Boulder
pizzeriabasta.com

CONNECTICUT
Colony Grill
172 Myrtle Avenue
Stamford
(and other locations)
www.colonygrill.com

**Flanders Fish Market &
Restaurant**
22 Chesterfield Road
East Lyme
www.flandersfish.com

Sally's Apizza
237 Wooster Street
New Haven
www.sallysapizza.com

Zuppardi's Apizza
179 Union Avenue
West Haven
www.zuppardisapizza.com

DISTRICT OF COLUMBIA
Ben's Chili Bowl
1213 U Street NW
www.benschilibowl.com

Dolcezza
1560 Wisconsin Avenue NW
(and other locations)
www.dolcezzagelato.com

**Dupont Circle Farmers'
Market**
1560 20th Street NE
www.freshfarmmarket.org/
markets/dupont_circle

Market Lunch
225 7th Street SE # 11

Red Hook Lobster Pound
www.redhooklobsterdc.com

Teaism
800 Connecticut Avenue NW
(and other locations)
www.teaism.com

FLORIDA
El Mago De Las Fritas
5828 Southwest 8th Street
West Miami
www.elmagodelasfritas.com

El Palacio de Los Jugos
5721 West Flagler Street
Miami
(and other locations)

**La Camaronera Seafood
Joint & Fish Market**
1952 West Flagler Street
Miami
www.lacamaronera.com

**Michael's Genuine
Food & Drink**
130 Northeast 40th Street
Miami
(and other locations)
www.michaelsgenuine.com

GEORGIA
The Colonnade
1879 Cheshire Bridge Road
Atlanta
www.colonnadeatl.com

**Holeman & Finch
Public House**
2277 Peachtree Road, Suite B
Atlanta
www.holeman-finch.com

Moto Bene
2744 Peachtree Road NW
Atlanta
www.motobenepizza.com

The Silver Skillet
200 14th Street
Atlanta
www.thesilverskillet.com

Varasano's
2171 Peachtree Road NE
Atlanta
www.varasanos.com

HAWAII
Shave Ice
2135 Waiola Street
Honolulu
(and other locations)

Ted's Bakery
59-024 Kamehameha Hwy.
Sunset Beach
www.tedsbakery.com

IDAHO
Hudson's Hamburgers
207 East Sherman Avenue
Coeur d'Alene

ILLINOIS
Burt's Place
8541 North Ferris Avenue
Morton Grove

Calumet Fisheries
3259 East 95th Street
Chicago
www.calumetfisheries.com

David Burke's Primehouse
616 North Rush Street
Chicago
davidburkesprimehouse.com

Gene and Jude's
2720 River Road
River Grove

Great Lake
1477 West Balmoral Avenue
Chicago

**Green City Market in
Lincoln Park**
1750 North Clark Street
Chicago
www.greencitymarket.org

Honey 1 BBQ
2241 North Western Avenue
Chicago
www.honey1bbq.com

Hoosier Mama
1618 1/2 Chicago Avenue
Chicago
www.hoosiermamapie.com

Hot Chocolate
1747 N Damen Avenue
Chicago
hotchocolatechicago.com

Hot Doug's
3324 North California Ave.
Chicago
www.hotdougs.com

Ina's
1235 West Randolph Street
Chicago
www.breakfastqueen.com

Izola's
522 East 79th Street
Chicago

Lem's Bar-B-Q
311 East 75th Street
Chicago

M. Henry
5707 North Clark Street
Chicago
www.mhenry.net

Old Fashioned Donuts
11248 S. Michigan Avenue
Chicago

Scooter's Frozen Custard
1658 West Belmont Avenue
Chicago
scootersfrozencustard.com

17th Street Bar & Grill
214 North 17th Street
Murphysboro
17thstreetbarbecue.com

Superdawg
6363 N. Milwaukee Avenue
Chicago
(and other locations)
www.superdawg.com

Top Notch Beef Burgers
2116 West 95th Street
Chicago

Uncle John's Barbecue
337 East 69th Street
Chicago

Wiener and Still Champion
802 Dempster Street
Evanston
wienerandstillchampion.com

Xoco
449 North Clark Street
Chicago
www.rickbayless.com/restaurants/xoco.html

INDIANA
Stop 50
500 South El Portal Drive
Michiana Shores
stop50woodfiredpizzeria.com

Workingman's Friend Tavern
234 North Belmont Avenue
Indianapolis
www.workingmansfriend.us

IOWA
Coffee Cup Cafe
616 4th Street
Sully
www.coffeecupcafe.com

KANSAS
Bobo's Drive-In
2300 Southwest 10th Avenue
Topeka

Cozy Inn
108 North 7th Street
Salina
www.cozyburger.com

KENTUCKY
Homemade Ice Cream & Pie Kitchen
2525 Bardstown Road
Louisville
(and other locations)
www.piekitchen.com

Spalding's Bakery
760 Winchester Road
Lexington
www.spaldingsbakery.com

LOUISIANA
Angelo Brocato
214 North Carrollton Avenue
New Orleans
www.angelobrocatoicecream.com

Casamento's
4330 Magazine Street
New Orleans
casamentosrestaurant.com

Central Grocery
923 Decatur Street
New Orleans

Cochon Butcher
930 Tchoupitoulas Street
New Orleans
www.cochonbutcher.com

Crescent City Farmers' Market
200 Broadway Street
New Orleans
(and other locations)
www.crescentcityfarmersmarket.org

Domilise's
5240 Annunciation Street
New Orleans

Mahony's
3454 Magazine Street
New Orleans
www.mahonyspoboys.com

McHardy's Chicken & Fixin'
1458 North Broad Street
New Orleans

Morning Call Coffee Stand
3325 Severn Avenue
Metairie

Stanley
547 Saint Ann Street
New Orleans
www.stanleyrestaurant.com

Willie Mae's Scotch House
2401 Saint Ann Street
New Orleans

Zimmer's Seafood
4915 St. Anthony Street
New Orleans
zimmersseafood.webs.com

MAINE
Duckfat
43 Middle Street
Portland
www.duckfat.com

Fore Street Restaurant
288 Fore Street
Portland
www.forestreet.biz

Micucci's Italian Groceries
961 Riverside Street
Portland
www.micucci.com

Hot Suppa
703 Congress Street
Portland
www.hotsuppa.com

Standard Baking Co.
75 Commercial Street
Portland

MARYLAND
Mia's Pizzas
4926 Cordell Avenue
Bethesda
miaspizzasbethesda.com

Pitango Gelato
802 South Broadway
Baltimore
(and other locations)
www.pitangogelato.com

MASSACHUSETTS
Clear Flour Bread
178 Thorndike Street
Brookline
www.clearflourbread.com

Cutty's
284 Washington Street
Brookline
www.cuttyfoods.com

Craigie on Main
853 Main Street
Cambridge
www.craigieonmain.com

Flour Bakery
12 Farnsworth Street
Boston
(and other locations)
www.flourbakery.com

Galleria Umberto
289 Hanover Street
Boston

L.A. Burdick
52 Brattle Street
Cambridge
(and other locations)
www.burdickchocolate.com

Mike & Patty's
12 Church Street
Boston
www.mikeandpattys.com

Modern Pastry
257 Hanover Street
Boston
www.modernpastry.com

Mrs. Blake's Pies
515 State Road
Vineyard Haven

Picco Restaurant
513 Tremont Street
Boston
www.piccorestaurant.com

Sofra
1 Belmont Street
Cambridge
www.sofrabakery.com

State Road Restaurant
688 State Road
West Tisbury
stateroadrestaurant.com

Straight Wharf Fish Store
6 Harbor Square
Nantucket
straightwharfrestaurant.com

Toro
1704 Washington Street
Boston
www.toro-restaurant.com

Toscanini's
899 Main Street
Cambridge
www.tosci.com

MICHIGAN

Grand Traverse Pie Company
525 West Front Street
Traverse City
(and other locations)
www.gtpie.com

Krazy Jim's Blimpy Burger
551 South Division Street
Ann Arbor
www.blimpyburger.com

Motz's Burgers
7216 West Fort Street
Detroit

McClure's Pickles
Detroit
(and other locations)
www.mcclurespickles.com

Tomatoes Apizza
24369 Halsted Road
Farmington Hills
(and other locations)
www.tomatoesapizza.com

Zingerman's Bakehouse
422 Detroit Street
Ann Arbor
www.zingermansdeli.com

MINNESOTA

Al's Breakfast
413 14th Avenue Southeast
Minneapolis

Salty Tart
920 East Lake Street
Minneapolis
www.saltytart.com

MISSISSIPPI

Big Bad Breakfast
719 North Lamar Boulevard
Oxford
www.bigbadbreakfast.com

Taylor Grocery
4 County Road 338 # A
Oxford
www.taylorgrocery.com

MISSOURI

Askinosie Chocolates
514 East Commercial Street
Springfield
www.askinosie.com

Big T's BBQ
5912 Blue Parkway
Kansas City
(and other locations)
Bluestem

900 Westport Road
Kansas City
www.bluestemkc.com

Carl's Drive-In
9033 Manchester Road
Brentwood

L.C.'s Bar-B-Q
5800 Blue Parkway
Kansas City

Oklahoma Joe's
3002 West 47th Avenue
Kansas City
(and other locations)
www.oklahomajoesbbq.com

Stroud's
5410 Northeast Oak Ridge Drive
Kansas City
(and other locations)
www.stroudsrestaurant.com

Ted Drewes
6726 Chippewa Street
St. Louis
(and other locations)
www.teddrewes.com

Town Topic
2121 Broadway Street
Kansas City

NEVADA

Bouchon Bakery
3355 Las Vegas Blvd. S.
Las Vegas
www.bouchonbakery.com

NEW HAMPSHIRE

The Friendly Toast
113 Congress Street
Portsmouth
(and other locations)
www.thefriendlytoast.net

Polly's Pancake Parlour
672 Route 117
Sugar Hill
pollyspancakeparlor.com

NEW JERSEY

The Bent Spoon
35 Palmer Square West
Princeton
www.thebentspoon.net

Grease Trucks
58 College Avenue
New Brunswick

Jimmy Buff's Italian Hot Dogs
354 River Road
East Hanover
(and other locations)
www.jimmybuff.com

The Little Chef
8 South Tulane Street
Princeton
www.littlechefpastries.com

Santillo's Brick Oven Pizza
639 South Broad Street
Elizabeth

White Manna
358 River Street
Hackensack

White Rose System
1301 East Elizabeth Avenue
Linden

NEW MEXICO

Bobcat Bite
418 Old Las Vegas Highway
Santa Fe
www.bobcatbite.com

Ranco de Chimayo
300 County Road 98
Chimayo
www.ranchodechimayo.com

Rancho Santa Fe Farmers' Market
16079 San Dieguito Road
Santa Fe
www.ranchosantafefarmers-market.com

Tecolote Café
1203 Cerrillos Road
Santa Fe
www.tecolotecafe.com

NEW YORK

Barney Greengrass
541 Amsterdam Avenue
New York
www.barneygreengrass.com

Big Gay Ice Cream Truck
New York
biggayicecreamtruck.com

Biryani Cart
West 46th Street & 6th Avenue
New York
www.biryanicart.com

Blue Hill at Stone Barns
630 Bedford Road
Pocantico Hills
www.bluehillfarm.com/food/blue-hill-stone-barns

Bouchon Bakery
10 Columbus Circle
New York
www.bouchonbakery.com

Charles' Country Pan Fried Chicken
2839-2841 Frederick Douglass Boulevard
New York

Charlie the Butcher
1065 Wehrle Drive
Williamsville
(and other locations)
www.charliethebutcher.com

Country Boys
176 Lafayette Avenue
Brooklyn
(and other locations)

Dessert Truck
6 Clinton Street
New York
(and other locations)
www.dt-works.net

Di Fara
1424 Avenue J
Brooklyn
www.difara.com

Doughnut Plant
379 Grand Street
New York
(and other locations)
www.doughnutplant.com

Duff's
3651 Sheridan Drive
Amherst
(and other locations)
www.duffsfamouswings.ca

Egg
135 North 5th Street
Brooklyn
www.pigandegg.com

Freddy, the King of Falafel
30th Street & Broadway
Astoria
www.thekingfalafel.com

Grom
2165 Broadway
New York
(and other locations)
www.grom.it

Hallo Berlin
626 10th Avenue
New York
halloberlinrestaurant.com

Hot Truck
660 Stewart Avenue
Ithaca

Katz's
205 East Houston Street
New York
katzsdelicatessen.com

Locanda Verde
377 Greenwich Street
New York
www.locandaverdenyc.com

Maialino
2 Lexington Avenue
New York
www.maialinonyc.com

Minetta Tavern
113 MacDougal Street
New York
www.minettatavernny.com

Motorino
349 East 12th Street
New York
(and other locations)
www.motorinopizza.com

Papaya King
179 East 86th Street
New York
(and other locations)
www.papayaking.com

Paulie Gee's
60 Greenpoint Avenue
Brooklyn
www.pauliegee.com

Peking Duck Stand
40-28 Main Street
Flushing

Pizza Moto
176 Lafayette Avenue
Brooklyn
(and other locations)
www.pizzamoto.com

Rick's Picks
176 Lafayette Avenue
Brooklyn
(and other locations)
www.rickspicksnyc.com

Roni-Sue's Chocolates
120 Essex Street
New York
www.roni-sue.com

Sal, Kris, and Charlie's Deli
33-12 23rd Avenue
Astoria

Salumeria Biellese
376-378 8th Avenue
New York
www.salumeriabiellese.com

Shake Shack
Madison Square Park
New York
(and other locations)
www.shakeshack.com

Shopsins
120 Essex Street
New York
www.shopsins.com

Steve's Authentic Key Lime Pies
204 Van Dyke Street
Brooklyn
www.stevesauthentic.com

Sullivan Street Bakery
533 West 47th Street
New York
sullivanstreetbakery.com

Taïm
222 Waverly Place
New York
www.taimnyc.com

Torrisi Italian Specialties
250 Mulberry Street
New York
www.piginahat.com

Totonno's
1524 Neptune Avenue
Brooklyn
(and other locations)

Two Little Red Hens
1652 Second Avenue
New York
www.twolittleredhens.com

Union Square Greenmarket
East 17th Street & Broadway
New York
www.grownyc.org/
unionsquaregreenmarket

Walter's Hot Dogs Stand
937 Palmer Avenue
Mamaroneck
www.waltershotdogs.com

Yura on Madison
1292 Madison Avenue
New York
www.yuraonmadison.com

NORTH CAROLINA
Allen & Son
6203 Millhouse Road
Chapel Hill

Angela's Pepper-Pickled Foods
2105 California Beach Road
Wilmington
(and other locations)
www.angelasppf.com

Bella Mia Coal-Fired Pizza
2025 Renaissance Park Place
Cary
www.bellamiacoalfire.com

Lexington Barbecue
10 US Highway 29-70 South
Lexington

Louise's Old Fashioned Baked Goods
Carrboro Farmers' Market
301 West Main Street
Carrboro
carrborofarmersmarket.com

Magnolia Grill
1002 9th Street
Durham
www.magnoliagrill.net

Neal's Deli
100 East Main Street
Carrboro, NC
www.nealsdeli.com

The Pig
630 Weaver Dairy Road
Chapel Hill
www.thepigrestaurant.com

Price's Chicken Coop
1614 Camden Road
Charlotte
www.priceschickencoop.com

Scratch Bakery
111 Orange Street
Durham
www.piefantasy.com

Sunrise Biscuit Kitchen
1305 East Franklin Street
Chapel Hill

Skylight Inn
1502 South Lee Street
Ayden

Wilber's Barbecue
4172 Highway 70 East
Goldsboro
www.wilbersbarbecue.com

OHIO
Jeni's Splendid Ice Cream
900 Mohawk Street
Columbus
www.jenisicecreams.com
(and other locations)

Johnnie's Tavern
3503 Trabue Road
Columbus

OREGON
Apizza Scholls
4741 SE Hawthorne Blvd.
Portland
www.apizzascholls.com

The Big Egg
4233 N. Mississippi Avenue
Portland
www.thebigeggfoodcart.
blogspot.com

Bunk Sandwiches
621 SE Morrison Street
Portland
www.bunksandwiches.com

Garden State
4237 N. Mississippi Avenue
Portland
gardenstatecart.com

Kenny and Zuke's
1038 SW Stark Street
Portland
www.kennyandzukes.com

Ken's Artisan Bakery & Pizza
304 SE 28th Avenue
Portland
www.kensartisan.com

Le Pigeon
738 East Burnside Street
Portland
www.lepigeon.com

Nong's Khao Man Gai
1003 SW Alder Street
Portland
www.khaomangai.com

Olympic Provisions
107 SE Washington Street
Portland
www.olympicprovisions.com

Paley's Place
1204 NW 21st Avenue
Portland
www.paleysplace.net

**Picklopis
(at Three Square Grill)**
6320 SW Capitol Highway
Portland
www.picklopis.com

Pok Pok
3226 SE Division Street
Portland
www.pokpokpdx.com

Portland State University Farmers' Market
SW Park Avenue and
SW Montgomery Street
Portland
portlandfarmersmarket.org

Sahagun Chocolates
Portland
sahagunchocolates.com

Tabor
433 SW Stark Street
Portland
www.schnitzelwich.com

Tasty n Sons
3808 N. Williams Avenue
Portland
www.tastynsons.com

Wy'east
3131 SE 50th Avenue
Portland
www.wyeastpizza.com

PENNSYLVANIA

Café Estelle
444 North 4th Street
Philadelphia
www.cafeestelle.com

Capogiro Gelato Artisans
3925 Walnut Street
Philadelphia
(and other locations)
www.capogirogelato.com

Il Pizzaiolo
703 Washington Road
Mt. Lebanon

Pamela's Diner
60 21st Street
Pittsburgh
(and other locations)
www.pamelasdiner.com

Pizzeria Stella
420 South 2nd Street
Philadelphia
www.pizzeriastella.net

Primanti Bros.
46 18th Street
Pittsburgh
(and other locations)
www.primantibros.com

Robert Wholey & Co.
1711 Penn Avenue
Pittsburgh
www.wholey.com

Tessaro's
4601 Liberty Avenue
Pittsburgh

RHODE ISLAND

Garrison Confections
72 Ledge Street
Central Falls
garrisonconfections.com

Gray's Ice Cream
16 East Road
Tiverton
(and other locations)
www.graysicecream.com

Hewtin's Dogs Mobile
Providence
www.chez-pascal.com/
HewtinsDogsMobile.htm

SOUTH CAROLINA

Scott's Bar-B-Que
2734 Hemingway Highway
Hemingway
www.thescottsbbq.com

The Hominy Grill
207 Rutledge Avenue
Charleston
www.hominygrill.com

Sweatman's BBQ
1427 Eutaw Road
Holly Hill

TENNESSEE

B.E. Scott's Barbecue
10880 Highway 412 West
Lexington

Bailey and Cato
1307 McGavock Pike
Nashville

Cozy Corner BBQ
745 North Parkway
Memphis
www.cozycornerbbq.com

Gus's World Famous Fried Chicken
310 South Front Street
Memphis
(and other locations)

Martin's Bar-B-Que Joint
7238 Nolensville Road
Nolensville
www.martinsbbqjoint.com

The Sands Soul Food Diner
937 Locklayer Street
Nashville

TEXAS

Amy's Ice Creams
1012 West 6th Street
Austin
(and other locations)
www.amysicecreams.com

Babe's Chicken Dinner House
104 North Oak Street
Roanoke
(and other locations)
www.babeschicken.com

Barbecue Inn
116 West Crosstimbers Road
Houston

The Breakfast Klub
3711 Travis Street
Houston
www.thebreakfastklub.com

City Market
633 East Davis Street
Luling
(and other locations)
www.lulingcitymarket.com

Dough Pizzeria Napoletana
6989 Blanco Road
San Antonio
www.doughpizzeria.com

East Side King
1618 East 6th Street
Austin
(and other locations)
eastsidekingaustin.com

Franklin Barbecue
900 East 11th Street
Austin
www.franklinbarbecue.com

Frenchy's Chicken
757 West Little York Road
Houston
(and other locations)
www.frenchyschicken.com

Gourdough's
1219 South Lamar Boulevard
Austin
www.gourdoughs.com

Izzoz Tacos
1503 South 1st Street
Austin
www.izzoztacos.com

Juan in a Million
2300 East Ceser Chavez St.
Austin
www.juaninamillion.com

Kreuz Market
619 North Colorado Street
Lockhart
www.kreuzmarket.com

La Cocina De Consuelo
4516 Burnet Road
Austin
www.consueloskitchen.com

Los Barrios
4423 Blanco Road
San Antonio
www.lhdlb.com

Louie Mueller Barbecue
206 West 2nd Street
Taylor
louiemuellerbarbecue.com

Magnolia Cafe
2304 Lake Austin Boulevard
Austin
(and other locations)
www.themagnoliacafe.com

Mi Madre's
2201 Manor Road
Austin
mimadresrestaurant.com

Odd Duck Farm to Trailer
1219 South Lamar Boulevard
Austin
oddduckfarmtotrailer.com

Pierson & Company Bar-B-Que
5110 West T C Jester Blvd
Houston

Shipley Do-Nuts
3410 Ella Boulevard
Houston
(and other locations)
www.shipleydonuts.ws

Smitty's Market
208 South Commerce Street
Lockhart
www.smittysmarket.com

Snow's
516 Main Street
Lexington
www.snowsbbq.com

Southside Market
1212 Highway 290 East
Elgin
www.southsidemarket.com

Tacodeli
1500 Spyglass Drive
Austin
(and other locations)
www.tacodeli.com

Thelma's
3755 Southmore Boulevard
Houston

UTAH
Banbury Cross
705 South 700 East
Salt Lake City

Bruges
336 West Broadway
(300 South)
Salt Lake City
www.brugeswaffles.com

Chow Truck
Salt Lake City
www.chowtruck.com

The Copper Onion
111 East Broadway, Suite 170
Salt Lake City
www.thecopperonion.com

Les Madeleines
216 East 500 South
Salt Lake City
www.les-madeleines.com

VERMONT
Penny Cluse Café
169 Cherry Street
Burlington
www.pennycluse.com

VIRGINIA
24 Crows
650 Zachary Taylor Highway
Flint Hill

Ray's Hell-Burger
1713 Wilson Boulevard
Arlington

Rebel Heroes
Arlington
www.rebelheroes.com

WASHINGTON
Cafe Besalu
5909 24th Avenue Northwest
Seattle
www.cafebesalu.com

Crumpet Shop
1503 1st Avenue
Seattle

Cupcake Royale
4556 California Avenue
Southwest
Seattle
(and other locations)
www.cupcakeroyale.com

Dahlia Bakery
2030 5th Avenue
Seattle
www.tomdouglas.com

Dahlia Lounge
2001 4th Avenue
Seattle
www.tomdouglas.com

**Daily Dozen Doughnut
Company**
93 Pike Street
Seattle

Delancey
1415 Northwest 70th Street
Seattle
www.delanceyseattle.com

Etta's
2020 Western Avenue
Seattle
www.tomdouglas.com

Fran's Chocolates
1325 1st Avenue
Seattle
(and other locations)
www.franschocolates.com

Lola
2000 4th Avenue
Seattle
www.tomdouglas.com

Macrina Bakery
2408 1st Avenue
Seattle
www.macrinabakery.com

Mallard Ice Cream
1323 Railroad Avenue
Bellingham
www.mallardicecream.com

Marination Mobile
1412 Harvard Avenue
Seattle
(and other locations)
www.marinationmobile.com

**Molly Moon's Handmade
Ice Cream Shop**
917 East Pine Street
Seattle
(and other locations)
mollymoonicecream.com

Monster Dogs
2302 1st Avenue
Belltown
(and other locations)
seattlemonsterdogs.com

**Old-School Frozen
Custard**
1316 East Pike Street
Seattle
(and other locations)
www.oldschoolfrozen
custard.com

Palace Kitchen
2030 5th Avenue
Seattle
www.tomdouglas.com

Paseo Caribbean
6226 Seaview Avenue NW
Seattle
(and other locations)
www.paseoseattle.com

**Salumi Artisan
Cured Meats**
309 3rd Avenue South
Seattle
www.salumicuredmeats.com

Seatown Seabar
2010 Western Avenue
Seattle

Serious Pie
316 Virginia Street
Seattle
http://tomdouglas.com/
index.php?page=serious-pie

Skillet Street Food
Seattle
www.skilletstreetfood.com

Veraci
500 Northwest Market Street
Ballard
(and other locations)
www.veracipizza.com

WISCONSIN
Batch Bakehouse
1511 Williamson Street
Madison
www.batchbakehouse.com

**Dane County Farmers'
Market**
330 West Mifflin Street
Madison
(and other locations)
www.dcfm.org

Graze
1 South Pinckney Street
Madison
www.grazemadison.com

Jake's
1634 West North Avenue
Milwaukee
www.jakesmilwaukee.com

Kopp's Frozen Custard
5373 N. Port Washington Rd.
Glendale
(and other locations)
www.kopps.com

Leon's Frozen Custard
3131 South 27th Street
Milwaukee
www.leonsfrozencustard.us

Maria's Pizza
5025 West Forest Home Ave.
Milwaukee

Northpoint Custard
2272 North Lincoln
Memorial Drive
Milwaukee
www.northpointcustard.com

Solly's Grille
4629 N. Port Washington Rd.
Glendale

INDEX

A

A16 pizza, 96
Abate, Lou, 122
ABC Kitchen, 314
Acme Bread, 20, 76, 139, 322
Adult Brownies (recipe), 280–281
African-American barbecue ribs, 194–195
African-American soul food traditions, 178
Ai Fiori, 340
Al Forno pizzeria, 100
All American hot dogs, 166
Allen, Keith, 179, 202, 345
Allen, Will, 307
Allen & Son, 157, 202, 345
Almond Joy Pancakes, 24
Al's Breakfast, 36
Alterra Coffee, 354
American Royal Barbecue Competition, 175
Amoroso's Baking Company, 143
Amy's Bread, 339
Amy's Ice Creams, 287
An Xuyen bakery, 135
Anchor Bar, 246
Anderson, Brett, 171
Anderson, Laura, 347
Anderson, Walter, 84
Andre's Hungarian Bake Shop, 339
Angela's Pepper-Pickled Foods, 330
Angelo Brocato, 289
Ann Sather's Restaurant, 348
Anna's Daughters' Rye, 20
Apizza Scholls, 103, 104, 351
Apple Pan, 72
Apple Pie (recipe), 300–301
Appleman, Nate, 134
Applestone, Josh and Jessica, 317
Aqui con el Nene, 168
Arcangeli Grocery Co., 342
Archie McPhee's, 341
Arnold, Jack, 350
Arnold, Kahlil, 350
Arnold, Rose, 350
Arnold's Country Kitchen, 350
Arthur Bryant's, 174
artisanal sandwiches, 142, 145, 146
A's Burgers, 22
Askinosie Chocolates, 277
at-home burgers, 83–89
Atkinson, Paul, 311

B

Babe's Chicken Dinner House, 255
Babiel, Rolf, 235
Bacon and Egg Sandwich (recipe), 44
Bacon Banh Mi (recipe), 150

Bacon Dog Carts, 167
Bailey and Cato, 255
Baird Family Orchards, 332
Baker, Mark and Jill, 321
Baker's Green Acres, 321
Bakers Pride pizza ovens, 93
Bakesale Betty, 139
Ballinger, Melissa, 122
Bananarchy, 347
Banbury Cross, 264
Banh Mi, Bacon (recipe), 150–151
bar pizza, 99, 100, 108
Barakat, Alison, 139
Barbecue Brisket (recipe), 195
barbecue festivals, 174–175
Barbecue Inn, 250
barbecue joints, 134, 188, 194, 197, 200–203,
barbecue meat cuts, 186–187
barbecue rib recipes, 190–193
barbecue sandwiches, 157–161
barbecue sauce traditions, 177, 178, 192–193
barbecue-style guide, 176–181
Barber, Dan, 311
Bardol, Chris, 122
Barker, Karen, 296, 297, 309
Barker, Karen and Ben, 334, 345
Barney Greengrass, 27
Bartolotta, Joe, 244
Basinski, Sean, 212
Bastianich, Joe, 104
Batali, Armandino, 135, 329
Batali, Gina, 135, 329
Batali, Mario, 104, 294
Batch, Greg, 319
Batch Bakehouse, 31, 323, 346
Batch Family Orchards, 319
Bay End Farm, 309
Bayless, Rick, 137, 293, 333
B&B Farms, 335
BBQ Ribs, Kansas City (recipe), 190
BBQ Spareribs with Five Spice Rub and Sticky Ginger Glaze (recipe), 192–193
B.E. Scott's Barbecue, 178, 201
beef cuts (barbecue), 186
Bella Mia Coal-Fired Pizza, 116
Belmont Lunch, 72
Ben's Chili Bowl, 166
Ben's Nest, 339
Bent Spoon, The, 271, 285, 346
Benton, Allan, 320
Bernstein, Michelle, 159
Best Pizza, 350
B&G Oysters, 261
Bianco, Chris, 104, 111, 135, 313
Big Apple Barbecue Block Party, 175, 180
Big Bad Breakfast, 23
Big Bob Gibson's Bar-B-Q, 157, 201
Big Egg, The, 210
Big Gay Ice Cream Truck, 207, 208, 215
Big Happy Farms, 225
Big Nasty Biscuit, 24
Big Star, 349

Big T's BBQ, 178
Big Wong, 340
Big-A** Sandwiches, 216
Bigelow, Fran, 276
Bigelow's, 260
Biker Jim's Gourmet Dogs, 167
Bi-Rite Creamery, 271, 274, 342
Biryani Cart, 209–210
Biscuits and Gravy (recipe), 28
Bishop, Rick, 11, 306, 317, 332
Bissonnette, Jamie, 69
Bite, The, 261
BK Carne Asada, 168
Black Angus beef, 80
Black Label burger, 81
Blackberry Blisscakes, 37
Blackbird Farm brisket hash, 43
Blake, Eileen, 299
Blake's Lotaburger, 83
Bleecker Street Pizza, 339
Bloomfield, April, 161
Bloop oatmeal cart, 211
Blue Bell ice cream, 270
Blue Bottle Coffee, 335
Blue Hill at Stone Barns, 311
Blue Ribbon Bakery Market, 339, 340
Blue Smoke, 174, 180
Bluestem, 79, 138–139
Bob Red Mill, 211
Bobby's Burger Palace, 57
Bobcat Bite, 62, 68
Boho's Drive-In, 72
Bob's Clam Hut, 261
Boccalone, 329, 335
Bon Chan Chicken, 259
Bond, Jason, 353
Bondir, 353
Boo, James, 201
Boot & Shoe Service, 96
Borek, Teena, 32
Bosnian street food, 216
Boston eats, 352
Boswell, Scott, 26
Bouchon Bakery, 148, 273
Boulder County Farmers' Market, 347
Boulettes Larder, 20, 335
Boulud, Daniel, 57
Bowl, Sonny, 211
Bracewell, Bryan, 194
Bracewell, Ernest, Sr., 194
bread bakers, 322–327
breakfast burritos, 22–23
Breakfast Klub, The, 24
breakfast sandwiches, 42–43, 336
breakfast tacos, 50–51, 228, 229
Brinkley, Diane and William, 309
Brinkley Farm, 309
Brisket, Barbecue (recipe), 195
Brockman, Henry, 321
Brooklyn Diner, 340
Brooks, Zach, 208
Brown Sugar Cafe, 348
Browne, Alaina, 9
Brownies (recipe), 280–281
Bruges, 162
Bryant, Arthur, 175, 198

Buchanan, Gail, 210
Bud's Bar, 76
Bunk Sandwiches, 135, 330
Burdick, Larry, 276
Burger Blend (recipe), 86
burger recipes, 65, 74, 86, 88, 89
burgers, 56–57, 59–60, 62–63, 64, 68–79, 80–81
Burkett, Ben, 335
Burmeister, Brett, 216
Burt's Place, 106
Butcher, Jaszt, 69
Buttercream (recipe), 302
Buttermilk Truck, 210, 344
Buzzio, Marc, 328
Byrd, Errin, 237

C

C. Adam's Bakery, 354
Café at Chez Panisse, 347
Cafe Besalu, 30, 341
Cairo, Elias, 328
Calexico, 206
California-style pizza, 101
California-style burgers, 353
Callaghan, Kenny, 180
Calumet Fisheries, 244, 348
Canales, Mary, 347
candy makers, 276–279
Cannon, Angela, 330
Cannondale pizza, 110
Capogiro Gelato Artisans, 288
Cap'n Mike's Smoked Fish, 336
Caporuscio, Roberto, 124
Caputo's, 339
Caramel Sticky Buns (recipe), 34
Carangi Bakery, 142
Carbone, Gabrielle, 285
Carbone, Mario, 340
Carl's Drive-In, 70
Carnitas Tacos (recipe), 230–231
Carollo, Frank, 327
Carrboro Farmers' Market, 333
Carrot Salad with Avocado (recipe), 314
Casamento, Joe, 246
Casamento's Restaurant, 246
Cascade Brewing Barrel House, 351
Cascade Natural Beef, 80
Castronovo, Frank, 339
C.C. Brown's ice cream, 270
Central Grocery, 146
Champagne, Todd and Jordan, 330
Chang, David, 255
Chang, Jerome, 235
Chang, Joanne, 30
Chapel Hill Creamery, 309, 333
Charles' Country Pan Fried Chicken, 251
Charlie the Butcher, 138
Cheeseburger, All-American (recipe), 87

cheffy burgers, 80–81, 340, 346
cheffy fried chicken, 255
cheffy trucks, 234
Chez Panisse, 113, 313
Chicago eats, 348
Chicago pizza, 96, 101
Chicago thin-crust pizza, 99
Chicken and Rice with White Sauce, Halal Cart–Style (recipe), 218–219
Chilaquiles Verdes (recipe), 52–53
Chinese food (New York), 340
Chocolate-Chip Cookies (recipe), 282–283
chocolates, 276, 279
Choi, Roy, 208, 232
chorizo, 53
Chow, SuAn, 225
Chow Truck, 225
Chubby Melt, 64
Ciminieri, Cookie, 116
City Bakery, 349
City Market, 194
Clam Box, 261
Clark, Kat, 211
Cleverdon, David and Susan, 319
Cochon Butcher, 146, 329
Coffee Cup Cafe, 38, 299
Cohn, Terry, 321
Cole, Kent, 36
Coleman, Eliot, 311
Colicchio, Tom, 57
college-town eats, 345–347
Colonnade, The, 255
Colony Grill, 108
Comme Ça, 81
Cones, 339
Connecticut-style lobster, 220
Consiglio, Salvatore "Sally," 95, 122
cookie recipes, 282–283, 302–303
cookies, chocolate-chip, 271, 282–283
Copper Onion, The, 77
Corned Beef Brisket (recipe), 156
Corned Beef Hash (recipe), 47
Cosentino, Chris, 329
Country Boys, 229
Cowgirl Creamery, 335
Cozy Corner BBQ, 201
Cozy Inn, 72, 85
Crabby Jack's, 140
Craigie on Main, 80–81, 309, 310, 352
Creekstone Farms, 81
Crème Brûlée Cart, 225
Creole gumbo, 170
Crescent City Farmers' Market, 334
Cress Spring Bakery, 333
Creuzot, Percy "Frenchy" Jr., 251
Crown Burger, 63
Crow's Dairy, 225
Crumpet Man, 23
Crumpet Shop, 23, 341
Cuban sandwiches, 159, 161, 220

Cubano Mixto Sandwich (recipe), 160–161
Cunetto, Frank, 70
Cupcake Royale, 273
Currence, John, 23
Cutty's, 137

D

Dahlia Bakery, 42, 295–296, 341
Dahlia Lounge, 308
Daily Breads, 299
Daily Dozen Doughnut Company, 263, 341
Daisy Mae's BBQ USA, 174, 180
D'Amato, Brian, 135, 329
Dane County Farmers' Market, 333, 346
Dates by Davall, 320
Davall, David and Everett, 320
David Burke's Primehouse, 80
DB Burger, 57
De Julio's Sausage Co., 108
Deen, Paula, 61
DeFabritus, Rich, 101
Defonte's, 340
Del Pesto, 340
Delancy, 110
delicatessens, 152
DeMarco, Dom, 104
DeMasco, Karen, 279
Dessert Truck, 235
Detroit-style pizza, 101
Di Fara Pizza, 104
Diamond Jim's Stoneridge Inn, 353–354
Dick's, 341, 350
Dinosaur Bar-B-Que, 180
DIY burgers, 83–89
Dolcezza, 288, 346
Domilise's, 140, 338
Dooky Chase, 140, 171, 338
DOP (Denominazione di Origine Protetta), 115, 128
Dottie's True Blue Cafe, 27
Double-Double burgers, 83
Dough, Pizza (recipes), 120, 127
Dough Pizzeria Napoletana, 106
Doughnut Plant, 262
doughnut street carts, 224
doughnuts 262–265,
Douglas, Jackie, 308
Douglas, Tom, 42, 68, 76, 295, 308
Down East–style barbecue, 177
Downyflake Restaurant, 299
Drink (Boston), 353
Duarte's Tavern, 297
Duckfat, 245
Duff's, 246
Dulce de Loco, 225
Duncan, Robb, 288, 346
Dupont Circle Farmers' Market, 334
Dutch Crunch sandwich, 159, 163
Dutchman Delight, 272
Dynamo Donuts, 343

E

East Side King, 234, 242
Eastern Standard Kitchen and Drinks, 353
Ebert, Roger, 83
Eckerton Hill Farm, 316
Eckhouse, Herb, 307
Eckhouse, Herb and Kathy, 318
Edelman, Violeta, 288, 346
Edge, John T., 23, 63, 158, 201, 251, 335
Edison, Roz, 209
Egg (Brooklyn), 26–27
egg-in-toast variations, 40
Egg Sandwich, Your Favorite (recipe), 44
Eggs Rothko, 26–27
Eggs Stanley, 26
Eggs, Super-Eggy Scrambled (recipe), 41
El Güero Canelo, 168
El Mago de Las Fritas, 79
El Milagro taco factory, 50–51
Elie, Lolis Eric, 176, 198, 201
Emilia's Pizzeria (Berkeley), 110–111, 347
Emilia's Pizzeria (San Francisco), 96
Errico, Matt, 285
Esposito, Raffaele, 95
Esposito and Sons, 339
Essex Seafood Restaurant and Fish Market, 261
Etta's, 308
Exotic Grains of Paradise ice cream, 287
Extra-Virgin Olive Oil Gelato, (recipe), 294
extreme burgers, 61

F

Faicco's Port Store, 339
Fairway Café, 340
Falafel (recipe), 222–223
Falcinelli, Frank, 339
fancy-pants burgers, 60–61
Farm on Adderley, 45
farmers and farmers' markets, 306–307, 316–321, 332–334
farm-to-table scene, 308–313, 354
Farr, Ryan, 245, 336
fast-food–style burgers, 60, 82–83
Fat Darrell sandwiches, 163
Fatty Melt, Hamburger (recipe), 65
Ferry Plaza Farmers' Market, 335, 336, 342, 42
Field, Rick, 330, 331
Fils-Aimé, Edwige, 11, 30, 346
Firefly Farms, 334
Five Guys, 57, 83
5-8 Club, 62
Five-Spot sandwich, 25
Flanders Fish Market & Restaurant, 245
Flat Patties, 353
Flay, Bobby, 57
Fleischman, Adam, 72

Fleisher's Grass-Fed and Organic Meats, 317
Fleur de Lis bakery, 135, 214
Flour + Water, 96, 343
Flour Bakery, 30–31
Flying Pigs Farm, 307, 318, 333
F. Monteleone Bakery, 339
food carts, 206–208, 216
food trucks, 225–226
Foodparc, 340
Fore Street Restaurant, 311, 323
Forkish, Ken, 113, 326
4505 Meats, 42–43, 245, 336
Fountain Prairie Farms, 78, 318
Fox, John, 165
Frank Pepe's, 95, 100, 106
Franklin, Aaron, 197, 347
Franklin Barbecue, 197, 347
Franks Diner, 354
Fran's Chocolates, 276
Freddy, the King of Falafel and Shawarma, 220
Freilich, Keith, 110–111, 347
French Fries (recipe), 248–249
French Laundry, 229
Frenchy's Chicken, 251
fried bites, 242–246
Fried Catfish (recipe), 243
fried chicken, 250–255
Fried Chicken (recipe), 256–257
Fried Oysters with Tartar Sauce (recipe), 247
Friendly Toast, 24
Frita Cubana burger, 79
Frog Hollow Farm, 335
frozen custard, gelato, and ice cream, 286
frozen custard spots, 290–291
Fry Bread House, The, 245
Frying Scotsman, The, 216
Fudge Family Farms, 312
Fuloono, 352
Funky Monkey doughnuts, 224
fusion burgers, 61

G

Gabriel, Charles, 251
Galindo, John, 50, 229, 347
Galleria Umberto, 111, 246
Gapultos, Marvin, 225
Garcia, Nina, 214
Garden State, 214, 351
Garrison Confections, 276
Garthwait, Ian, 323
Gastelum, Salvador, 168
Gayer, Michelle, 327
Gelato, Extra-Virgin Olive Oil (recipe), 294
gelato, ice cream, and frozen custard, 286
gelato spots, 288–289
Gendusa Bakery, 170
Gene and Jude's, 166
George's Gathered Greens, 311
Gerdes, C.J. and Linda, 246
Germon, George, 100, 117

Gertsen, John, 353
Gialina, 96
Giannone, Paul, 121–122
Gilmore, Bryce, 221
Ginger Cat Farms, 347
Godby, Jake, 285
Goldbud Farms, 307, 317
gooberburgers, 63
Gordon, Ken, 152
Gorham, John, 20
Gourdough's, 224
Gramercy Tavern, 340
Grand Sichuan International, 340
Grand Traverse Pie Company, 298
grandma-style pizza, 99
Granola with Pepitas and Cranberries (recipe), 46
Gray's Ice Cream, 287
Gray's Papaya, 340
Graze, 78, 346
"Grease Trucks," 163
Greater New York Noodle-town, 340
Greek-style pizza, 99
Green, Ike, 203
Green City Market in Lincoln Park, 333
Green Eggs and Ham, 24, 27
Greengrass, Gary, 27
Greenpointer pizza, 122
grilled cheese sandwiches, 64–65
Grilled Cheese, The Best (recipe), 149
Grilled Pizza Dough (recipe), 120
Grilled Pizza Margherita (recipe), 118–119
Grom, 289, 339
Grow Farms, 335
Growing Power, 307
Grüner, 351
Guerra, John, 116
Gus's World Famous Fried Chicken, 251
Gutman, Liz, 278

H

Habetz, Tommy, 135
Hallo Berlin, 235
Hallowell, Charlie, 113
Hamada Farms, 335
hamburger buns, 59, 66, 67
Hamburger Express, 56
Hamburger Fatty Melt (recipe), 64–65
hamburgers. See burgers
Haney, Paula, 296
Hansen's Sno-Bliz, 338
Hanson, Lee, 81
Hapa Ramen, 217
Happy Girl Kitchen, 330
Hardaway, J.C., 175, 198
Harker, Garrett, 353
Harley, Flo, 309
Harold's Fried Chicken, 348
Harry's Berries, 334
Hash, Corned Beef (recipe), 47
Hash Browns, Super-Crispy (recipe), 48

Hawaiian-Asian-Mexican fusion fare, 209
Hawley, Flo, 333–334
Hayes Street Grill, 336
Haystack Mountain Goat Dairy, 347
Hayward, Sam, 311
Heavenly Hots, 22
Henry's Farm, 321
Herrell, Steve, 271
Hewtin's Dogs Mobile, 43
High Wire Ranch, 347
high-end burgers, 80–81
Hill, Bruce, 110
Hill Country, 180
Hitt, Alex and Bitsy, 309, 319
Hoagie Haven (Princeton), 346
Hoffman, Maggie, 350–351
Hoffy Hollywood's Original Natural Casing Beef Frankfurters, 164, 166
Hog Island Oyster Company, 336
hole structure (pizza dough), 104, 122
Holeman & Finch Public House (Atlanta), 79, 255
Homemade Ice Cream & Pie Kitchen, 298
Hominy Grill, The, 23–24, 255
Honest Tom's Tacos and Coffee, 228
Honey 1 BBQ, 178, 197, 348
Honey Blue Cheese ice cream, 287
Honey Crisp Farm, 334
Hoosier Mama, 295
Horn, Doug, 106
Horn, Terri, 273
Horseshoe sandwich, 158
Hot Brown sandwich, 158
Hot Chocolate (Chicago), 274
hot dogs, 165–168, 336
Hot Doug's, 165
Hot Suppa, 26
Hot Truck, 163
Howell, James Henry, 198, 202
Huckleberry Bakery and Café, 27, 344
Hudson's Hamburgers, 76
Huevos Yucatecos, 24
Humphry Slocombe, 271, 285, 342

I

ice cream, gelato, and frozen custard, 270–271, 286
ice cream spots, 285–287
Ici Ice Cream, 347
Iggy's bakery, 137
Il Pizzaiolo, 112
Illinois-style barbecue, 178
Ina's, 22
Indian burritos, 210
Ingersoll, Kofi, 309
In-N-Out Burger, 56–57, 82–83, 343
'Ino, 339
Insta-Burger King, 56
Ippudo, 340
Iris Café, 45
Isreal, Mark, 262

Italian Tipo "00" flour, 118–119, 127
Ithaca Bakery, 163
It's-It, 272
Izola's, 253, 348
Izzoz Tacos, 50, 229, 347

J

Jahn's ice creams, 270
Jake's, 152
Jar, 255
Jasper, Melissa and Robert, 24
Jean Georges, 340
Jeni's Splendid Ice Cream, 285, 271
Jerry's Nut Company, 267
Jersey hot dogs, 166
Jesus Juice ice cream, 285
Jett, Marshall, 237
Jewish appetizing food, 339
Jewish English muffins, 27
Jibarito sandwich, 159
Jimmy Buff's Italian Hot Dogs, 165
Jobe's Drive-In, 63
Joe's (Manhattan), 339
Joe's Cable Car Restaurant, 72
Joe's Tomato Pies, 94
Johnnie's Tavern, 68
Johns, Michael, 321
John's Pizzeria, 95
John's Roast Pork, 142
Johnson, Pableaux, 169
Johnston Family Farm, 237
JoJo potatoes, 248
Jones, Bruce, 202
Jones, Carey, 9, 169, 296, 342–343
Jones, Pete, 202
Jonnie's Grill, 63
Joseph Leonard, 339
J.T. Farnaham's, 261
Juan in a Million, 50
juice bars, 275
Juicy Lucy burger, 62–63

K

Kahan, Paul, 321, 349
KA-POW! chocolate bar, 276–277
Kassler ham, 42
Katsanevas pastrami burgers, 63
Katz, Burt, 106
Katz's (New York), 152
Kaul, Deepak, 76
Kave, Rhonda, 279
Keens Steakhouse, 340
Keller, Thomas, 57, 148, 273
Kelsey, Charles, 137
Kenny and Zuke's, 152
Ken's Artisan Bakery, 326
Ken's Artisan Pizza, 113
Kentucky-style barbecue, 178
Kesté, 339
Kewpee Lunch, 354
kewpie mayo, 234, 242
Key, Lionel, 335
Killeen, Johanne, 117
Kilpatrick, Maura, 26
Kim, Tai, 345

Kimball, Curtis, 225
Kimchi Quesadillas (recipe), 233
Kindelsperger, Nick, 165
King, Jen, 278
Kinnikinnick Farms, 319, 333
Kitchen, The (Boulder), 347
Kluger, Dan, 314
Knaus Berry Farm, 32
Kobe beef burgers, 79
Kobe/Wagyu burgers, 60
Kogi BBQ, 206, 232
Kopp's Frozen Custard, 290, 354
Korean Fried Chicken (recipe), 258, 259
Kouing Aman, 30
Kraus, Jeff, 224, 236
Krazy Jim's Blimpy Burger, 78, 345
Kreuz Market, 178, 194
Kroc, Ray, 56
Kuban, Adam, 9, 353–354
Kurtzman, Meredith, 294
Kwik Meal, 208

L

L.A. Burdick, 276
La Camaronera Seafood Joint & Fish Market, 138
La Cocina de Consuelo, 51
La Farine, 31
La Frieda, Pat, 81
La Quercia, 27, 313, 318, 347
La Vaquita, 345
Ladner, Mark, 340
LaDou, Ed, 101
Lafayette Coney Island hot dogs, 166
Lahey, Jim, 307, 322, 324
LaMar's Doughnuts, 174
Lang, Adam Perry, 180
Langer, Norm, 152
Langer's, 152, 344
Laredo Taqueria, 51
L'Arte del Gelato, 339
Lasater, Gary, 23
Latham, Dan, 237
Laughing Stock Farm, 311
Laurelhurst Market, 351
Lawless, Phoebe, 297
Lawry's Seasoned Salt, 138
L.C.'s Bar-B-Q, 178, 188
Le Pigeon, 80
Leary, Dennis, 139
lechoneria (pig emporium), 274, 275
Lee, Robyn, 9, 296, 302
Lefebvre, Ludo, 234
Leidenheimer Baking Company, 140
Lemon Ricotta Pancakes (recipe), 39
Lem's Bar-B-Q, 178, 200, 348
Leon's Frozen Custard, 290, 353
Les Madeleines, 30
Leslie, Austin, 251
Lessins, Nick, 111
L'Etoile, 78, 321
Let's Be Frank Dogs, 167
Lewis, Edna, 255

Lexington Barbecue No. 1, 202–203
Lexington-style barbecue, 177
Lilly, Chris, 181, 201
Link, Donald, 146, 329, 335
Little Burger, 83
Little Chef, The, 30, 346
Little Lucca, 163
Little Owl, The, 340
lobster food carts, 220
Lobster Rolls, Hot Buttered (recipe), 144–145
Locanda Verde, 32,
Lochmead Dairy, 287
Locklear, Ashley, 335
Locust Grove Farm, 333
Loeb, Josh, 287
Lola, 308
Lomanoco, Michael, 340
Lombardi, Gennaro, 94
Lombardi's pizzeria, 94
Long Island pizza, 99
Lopez-Alt, J. Kenji, 9, 12, 352
Los Barrios, 245
Los Golondrinas, 345
Louie Mueller Barbecue, 188
Louise's Old Fashioned Baked Goods, 273
Lowder, Ryan, 77
Lucky Dogs hot dogs, 166
Ludotruck, 234
Lupo's pizza, 95
Luther Burger, 61

M

M. Henry, 37, 348
Macarons (recipe), 302–303
Machacado tacos, 50
Mackie, Leslie, 326
Macrina Bakery, 135, 139, 326, 341
Madagascar chocolate, 279
Madia, Donnie, 349
Magician (El Mago), The, 79
Magnolia Cafe, 36
Magnolia Grill, 309, 334, 345
Mahony's Po' Boys, 338
Maialino, 37–38
mail-order biscuits, 29
Maine Farm Chicken, 311
Maine Organic Farmers and Gardeners Association, 311
Maine-style lobster, 220
Mallard Ice Cream, 287
Maloney, Toby, 349
Mancini's Bakery, 163
Mangieri, Anthony, 108, 111, 124
Manila Machine, 225
Mansfield, Ron, 307, 317
Marco's Coal-Fired Pizza, 349
Margherita di Savoia, 95
Margherita pizza, 98, 113, 122
Margherita, Grilled Pizza (recipe), 118–119
Margherita, Neapolitan Pizza (recipe), 128–129
Margie's Candies ice cream, 270
Maria's Pizza, 125, 354
Marin pizza, 110

Marinated Skirt Steak (recipe), 310
Marination Mobile, 209, 341
Marisco's German Taco Truck, 229
Market Lunch, 38
Maron, Joe, 203
Maron, Margaret, 203
Martin, Patrick, 200
Martinez, Fernando, 229
Martinez, Yolanda, 229
Martin's Bar-B-Que, 200
Mary's Family Pie Shop, 197
Mary's Fish Camp, 261
Matt's Bar, 62
Matt's Big Breakfast, 24–25
Matt's Place Drive-In, 63
Mattus, Herman, 271
Mauthe's Dairy, 334
Maws, Tony, 80, 309, 310, 352
McClancy's Fried Chicken, 338
McClendon, Bob, 313
McClure, Bob, 330
McClure, Joe, 330
McClure's Pickles, 330
McCusker, Tom, 228
McFaul, Nancy, 23
McHardy's Chicken & Fixin', 253
McKnight, Portia, 309, 333–334
McNally, Keith, 81
Mean Beans, 330
Meat Cheese Bread, 351
Meat Cone, 329
meat mavens, 328–329
meat-to-fat ratio in burgers, 68, 69, 77
Medianoche sandwich, 159
Medjool Date ice cream, 287
megaburgers, 61
Memphis Minnie's, 174
"messy" burgers, 69
Meyer, Danny, 37, 57, 73, 180, 291
Meza, Juan, 50
Mi Madre's, 50
Mia's Pizzas, 122
Michael's Genuine Food & Drink, 312
Mick Klug Farms, 333
micro urban farming, 321
Micucci's Italian Groceries, 125
Midwest-style pizza, 99
Migas tacos, 50
Mike & Patty's, 19
Mike's Pastry, 272
Miller, Amy, 287
Miller, Cecilia, 245
Miller, Jamie and Kaire, 30
Miller, Tory, 78, 321, 346
Miller's Twist, 349
Mills, Mike, 175, 176, 178, 181, 201
Milwaukee eats, 353–354
Milwaukee Public Market, 354
Minetta Tavern, 81, 340
mini hamburgers, 60
Missouri-style barbecue, 178
Mister Softee ice cream trucks, 207

Mitchell, Ed, 175, 181
Mitraillette sandwich, 162
MK Burger Bar, 348
Modern Apizza, 100, 106
Modern Pastry, 272
Molinare, Ron, 112
Molly Moon's Handmade Ice Cream Shop, 293, 341
Momofuku Noodle Bar, 255
Monica's Okra World, 335
Monk, Wayne, 202
Monster Dogs, 167
Montes, Elizabeth, 276–277
Moonlight Bakery, 221
Moore, Sue, 167
Morehea, Elizabeth, 210
Morf, Heidi, 287
Morgan Valley Lamb, 162
Morning Call Coffee Stand, 264
Mossy Creek Cafe, 64
Moto Bene, 237
Motorino, 108, 129
Motz, George, 57
Motz's Burgers, 73, 85
Mount Vesuvius, 94
Mountain Country Hams, 320
Mountain Sweet Berry Farm, 317, 333
Mozza2go, 274, 312
Mrs. Blake's Pies, 299
Mrs. Fields cookies, 271
Mueller, Louie, 188
Muffuletta (recipe), 147
muffulettas, 146, 329
Mulligan's Pub, 61
Murray's Cheese Shop, 339

N

Nagrant, Michael, 197, 296
Nakano, Richie, 217
Nana's House Special, 113
Nantucket Bake Shop, 299
Narvaez, Dahlia, 274
Nasr, Riad, 81
Nathan, Zoe, 27, 287, 344
National Bakery, 354
Naughty & Nice doughnuts, 224
Neal, Bill, 43
Neal, Matt and Sheila, 43
Neal's Deli, 43
Neapolitan Pizza Dough (recipe), 127
Neapolitan Pizza Margherita (recipe), 128–129
Neapolitan-style pizza, 96, 98, 108, 114, 122, 129, 237
Neapolitan-American–style pizza, 98–99, 104
Neptune Oyster, 145, 261, 352
Nevin, Ira, 93
New Chao Chow, 340
New Haven–style pizza, 99, 122
New Orleans Original Daiquiris, 338
New Orleans po' boys, 169–171, 338
New York–style barbecue, 180
New York–style pizza, 99, 237

New York–Neapolitan–style pizza, 98, 116
Nguyen, Tan, 220
Nicholson family, 319
Niman Ranch bacon, 344
1955 and 1964 pizzas, 125
Nina's Food, 214
Nong's Khao Man Gai, 209, 216
nonna pizza, 99
Normas, 45
North Carolina barbecue traditions, 177
Northpoint Custard, 244
Notario, Anna, 347
Nutella, 224, 277–278
Nu-Way weiners, 166

O

Obama, Barak, 70
Obegi, Joe, 72
Odd Duck Farm to Trailer, 221
Odermatt, Thomas, 336
Oki Dog, 168
Oklahoma Joe's, 178, 188
Old Fashioned Donuts, 265, 348
Old Forge–style pizza, 101
Old-School Frozen Custard, 291, 341
Oleana, 26
Olive Oil, Extra-Virgin, Gelato (recipe), 294
Olsen, Nancy, 340
Olympic Provisions, 328
onion burgers, 63, 69, 77, 84
Orange-Scented Yeast Waffles (recipe), 33
Oregon Croissants, 326
Original Tommy's, 62–63
Oringer, Ken, 352
Osteria & Pizzeria Mozza, 312
Otto tacos, 51

P

Padrón pizza, 110
Paesano's, 142
Palace Burger Royale, 68
Palace Kitchen, 68–69, 308
El Palacio de Los Jugos, 274, 275
Paley, Vitaly, 309
Paley's Place, 309
Palombino, Mathieu, 108
Pamela's Diner, 37
Pancakes, Lemon Ricotta (recipe), 39
Pane Bianco, 135–137
Papaya King, 164, 165, 340
Paradise Farms, 312
Parasol's, 140
Park Kitchen, 351
Parker, Ricky, 201
Parmigiano-Reggiano pizza, 106
Parrish, Louise, 273
Pascual, Gigi, 210
Paseo Caribbean Restaurant, 139, 341
Patty Melt (recipe), 74–75
patty melts, 72, 76

Paulie Gee's, 121–122
Peacock, Scott, 255
Pearl Oyster Bar, 339
Peking Duck Stand, 217
Peninsula Creamery, 343
Penny Cluse Cafe, 18
Pepe, Frank, 95, 100, 122
Peregrine Farm, 309, 319, 333
Pero, Anthony "Totonno," 94
Peruvian chocolate, 279
Peter Luger's, 340
Pete's Famous hot dogs, 166
Petroff, Bryan, 208
Pettinger, Jim, 167
Pettit, Brandon, 110
Phat Beets, 330
Philippe's, 135
Philly cheesesteak, 143
Pho Thang Long, 344
Picco Restaurant, 121
picklers, 330
Picklopis, 330
Pie Crust (recipe), 300–301
Pie 'n Burger (Los Angeles), 344
Pie 'n Burger (Pasadena), 69
Pierson & Company Bar-B-Que, 194
pies, 295–299
Pig, The, 134·135
Pike Place Market, 42
Pine State Biscuits, 332
Pinkney, Ina, 22
Pink's, 166
Piper, Odessa, 78
Pitango Gelato, 289
pitmasters, 198
pizza, 92–95, 98–101
Pizza Bianca, 307, 322–323
Pizza Bianca (recipe), 324
pizza cognition theory, 123
pizza dough (recipes), 120, 127
Pizza Margherita, Grilled (recipe), 110–119
Pizza Margherita, Neapolitan (recipe), 128–129
Pizza Moto, 237
pizza ovens, 93, 102–104, 114, 126
Pizza Paradiso, 122
pizza renaissance, 96–97
Pizzaiolo, 96
Pizzaiolo and Boot & Shoe Service, 113
pizza-making at home, 126–129
Pizzeria Basta, 112, 347
Pizzeria Bianco, 104, 111, 313
Pizzeria Delfina, 96
Pizzeria Mozza, 104, 111
Pizzeria Picco, 110
Pizzeria Picco, 96
Pizzeria Stella, 111–112
Pizzeria Uno, 95
pizzerias, 104, 108–116, 121–122, 124, 125
Plain White Squishy buns, 66, 76
plain-Jane burgers, 76
Plum Street SnoBall, 338
po'boy sandwiches, 140, 170–171
Poco Dolce, 278
Pok Pok, 235

Polcyn, Brian, 321
Polito, Bob and Mary, 318
Polito Family Farms, 312, 318, 334
Polly's Pancake Parlor, 36
Pompeii, 94
Pool, Erenia and Matt, 24–25
pork cuts (barbecue), 187
Pork Love pizza, 106
Pork, Pulled, Sandwiches with Coleslaw (recipe), 182–183
Pork, Pulled, Tinga, Mexican-Style (recipe), 184–185
Porter House New York, 340
Portland eats (Oregon), 350–351
Portland State University Farmers' Market, 332
Portland street food (Oregon), 216
Postmodern Pancakes, 20
Poulet Rouge, 312
Povich, Susan, 220
Prather Ranch, 76
Prechter, Diana, 36
Price's Chicken Coop, 252
Primanti Bros., 162
Prime House New York, 340
Prime Meats, 339, 340
Prime Steak Burger, 81
Priske, John, 318
Prosser Farm, 308
Pruett, Elisabeth, 272
pub burgers, 60
Pulled Pork Sandwiches with Coleslaw (recipe), 182–183
Pulled Pork Tinga, Mexican-Style (recipe), 184–185
purveyors, 317–321
Purvis, Kathleen, 252

Q

Queen City Cayenne ice cream, 285
Quesadillas, Kimchi (recipe), 233
Qui, Paul, 234
Quickel, Dan, 236
Quint, Doug, 207–208, 215, 236

R

Rack and Soul, 251
Rahman, Mohammed, 208
ramen joints, 340
ramen noodles food cart, 217
R&O, 140, 171
Rancatore, Gus, 285
Ranch de Chimayo, 242
Rancho Santa Fe Farmers' Market, 335
Rasmussen, Romina, 30
Rawley's hot dogs, 166
Ray, Rachael, 57
Raymond, John, 354
Ray's Hell-Burger, 70
Rebel Heroes, 220
Recchiuti, Michael, 276
Recchiuti Confections, 276

Red Chile-Marinated Skirt Steak (recipe), 310
Red Hook Community Farm, 307
Red Hook Lobster Pound, 220
Red Jacket Orchards, 319
Red Mill Burgers, 341
Red, White, and Blues, 174
Red's Eats, 145, 166
Reitano, Stephanie and John, 288
Reservoir Tavern, 95
Reuben (recipe), 154
Ribs, BBQ, Kansas City (recipe), 190
Richardson's Grape Nut ice cream, 266
Ricker's Andy, 235
Rick's Picks, 330, 331
Robert Wholey & Co., 163
Roberts, Adam, 25
Robert's Grill, 63
Robinson, Ray, 175, 201
Robson, Doug, 136
Rocca, Emmanuelle, 95
Rodbones, 174
Rodgers, Judy, 57
Roesch, Charles, 138
Roliroti, 336
Roman-style pizza, 99
Roni-Sue's Chocolates, 279
Ronnybrook Farm Dairy, 333
Roots Restaurant & Cellar, 354
R&O's Po-Boys and Pizza, 338
Rosa Maria's, 344
Rosa pizza, 106
Roseland Apizza, 100
Rosticeria Cancun, 352
rotisserie-on-wheels, 336
Ruby's Shake Shack, 344
Rucker, Gabriel, 80
Ruiz, Rosanne, 225
Russ, Joel, 206
Russ & Daughters, 329
Russian Dressing (recipe), 155

S

Sabrett All Beef Natural Casing Frankfurters, 164, 207
Sadowski, Walter, 139
Saginaw, Paul, 152, 327, 345
Sahagun Chocolates, 276
Sal, Kris, and Charlie's Deli, 163
Sally's Apizza, 95, 100, 106–107
Salsiccia pizza, 122
Salty Tart, 327
Salumeria Biellese, 328, 340
Salumi Artisan Cured Meats, 135, 329
Samdri, Kevin, 214
San Antonio pizza renaissance, 96
San Marzano plum tomatoes, 128
Sands Soul Food Diner, The, 20

sandwiches, 42–43, 44, 134–139, 142, 145, 146, 158–159, 162–163
Sandy's Fish and Chips, 261
Santa Monica Wednesday Farmers' Market, 334
Santarpio's pizza, 95
Santillo, Al, 125
Santillo's Brick Oven Pizza, 125
Sarja, Rose, 299
Sasso, John, 95
Saxton, Kamala, 209
Schmidt, Edgar "Smitty," 194
Schmidt, Fred, 158
Schnitzelwich, 210
Schrafft's ice cream, 270
Schwartz, Michael, 32, 312
Schwertner, Amaryll, 20
Sciortino's pizza, 95
Sclarow, Dave, 237
Scoops, 345
Scooter's Frozen Custard, 291
Scott, Rodney, 179, 201
Scottish street food, 216
Scott's Bar-B-Que, 201
Scrambled Eggs, Super-Eggy (recipe), 41
Scratch Bakery, 297
Sea Swirl, 260
Seaton, Kerry, 251
Seaton, Willie Mae, 251
Seatown Seabar, 42, 308, 341
Seattle food blitz, 341
Secret Breakfast ice cream, 285
Segal, Mindy, 274
Sentinel, The, 139, 343
Serious Pie, 107, 308
Serpentine, 76–77
17th Street Bar & Grill, 201
Sevier, Mack, 197
Sewell, Ike, 95
Shake Shack, 57, 73, 291
Shave Ice, 293
Shere, Lindsey, 271
Shiner Bock ice cream, 287
Shipley's Do-Nuts, 263
Shirley, Wilber, 203
Shopsin, Kenny, 20, 21
Shopsins, 20, 85
S&I Thai to Go, 352
Sichuan Gourmet, 340
Sicilian street-cart food, 214
Sicilian-style pizza, 99, 111, 125
Sid's Diner, 63
Sifton, Sam, 123
Sikder, Meru, 209
Silver Skillet, The, 25
Silverton, Nancy, 104, 111, 271, 274, 312, 334
Singleton's barbecue, 174
Skillet Street Food, 214, 341
Skirt Steak (recipe), 310
Skylight Inn, 202
Sliders, The Ultimate (recipe), 84–85
Slutty Cakes, 20
Small, Jen, 307, 318
smashed burgers, 62, 78, 79, 88
Smitty's Market, 157, 178, 194
Smokra (recipe), 331
Snow's, 194

Snowville Creamery, 285
Sofra, 26
Sohn, Doug, 165
Solly's Grille, 76
Something Natural, 299
Sonoran hot dogs, 168
Sorton, Ana, 26
Soul Burger Number One, 70
soul-food barbecue traditions, 178
South Beach Wine & Food Festival, 57
South Carolina barbecue traditions, 177
Southeast Asian street food, 235
Southern California eats, 344–345
Southern Foodways Alliance, 251
Southern Fried Chicken (recipe), 256–257
Southside Market, 157, 194
Sow Little Farm, 321
Spacca Napoli Pizzeria, 96
Spalding's Bakery, 263
Spangler, Brian, 103, 104, 351
Spareribs, BBQ, with Five Spice Rub and Sticky Ginger Glaze (recipe), 192–193
Spiedies sandwich, 158
Spot, The, 106
Spotted Pig, 161
Spread (San Diego), 45
Spucky sandwich, 158
Squish and Red, 237
St. Louis–style pizza, 101
St. Louis–cut ribs, 178, 187
Standard Baking Co., 323
Stanley, 26
Stark, Jim, 316
Starr, Stephen, 111–112
state fair foods, 267
State Road Bakery, 24
Steak 'n Shake, 83
Steamed sandwich, 158
Stehling, Robert, 23–24, 255
Stella's Bakery, 333, 346
Stern, Jane, 153
Stern, Michael, 153
Steve's Authentic Key Lime Pies, 296–297
Sticky Buns, Caramel (recipe), 34
Stone, Jason, 220
Stop 50, 122
Straight Wharf Fish Store, 139
Strauss Family Creamery, 292
street carts, transience of, 211
street carts turned restaurants, 235
street food, 206–208, 209–210, 214–217, 220–225
Street Vendor Project, 212
Stroud's, 254
Stumptown coffee, 332
"stweet" vendors, 236
Suchoff, Sam, 134
Sueyoshi, Sakai "Jimmy," 168
Sullivan, Steve, 322
Sullivan Street Bakery, 322, 324

Sunrise Biscuit Kitchen, 43
Super Johnnie Burger, 68
Superdawg, 165–166
Super-Duper Weenies, 166
Superstition Farms, 225
Susie's Drive-Thru, 348
Swamp Shack, The, 216
Swanky Franks, 166
Sweatman's BBQ, 200
sweet bites, 272–274
Sweetflow, 346
Sweetgreen, 346
Sweet Republic, 287
Sweet Rose Creamery, 287
Swingle pie, 296

T
Tabor, 210, 351
taco trucks, 228–229
Tacodeli, 50–51
Tacos, Carnitas, with Salsa Verda (recipe), 230–231
Tacos Garcia, 229
Taïm, 242
Tall Grass Bakery, 341
Taos Mountain Yak, 335
tapas bars, 69, 352
Taqueria La Bamba, 342
Tartar Sauce (recipe), 247
Tartine Bakery, 25, 272, 343
Tasty n Sons, 20, 351
Tasty Dumpling, 340
Taylor Grocery, 244
Tcho Chocolate, 279
Teaism, 273
Tecolote Café, 24
Ted Drewes, 57, 272
Ted's Bakery, 299
Ted's Resetaurant, 62
Teena's Pride Farm, 32
Telepan Diner, 340
Tennessee-style barbecue, 178
Tessaro's, 68
Texas-style barbecue, 178
Thai Coconut Milk gelato, 288
Thai food, 352
Thai street food, 209, 216, 235
Thelma's, 196
Three Little Pigs, 42
Thunder Mountain Swiss cheese, 334
Tillamook cheese, 80
Timrek, Ek, 234
Tinga, Mexican-Style Pulled Pork (recipe), 184–185
Tips, 39, 47, 89
Toigo, Mark, 320
Toigo Orchards, 320
tomato pies, Trenton, 101
Tomatoes Apizza, 122
Tommaso's pizza, 96
Tonalli's Donuts & Cream, 350
Tony's Pizza Napoletana, 96
Toomey, Rachel, 137
Top Dog, 167
Top Notch Beefburgers, 77–78, 348
Top Pot Doughnuts, 341
Toro, 69, 352
Toro Bravo, 350
Torrisi, Rich, 340
Torrisi Italian Specialties, 134, 340

Toscanini's, 285
Totonno's, 116
Totonno's pizzeria, 94
Town Topic, 79
Tracey's Bar, 140, 338
Tracht, Suzanne, 255
Traxel, Bonnie, 11, 125
Tre Kronor, 348
Trenton tomato pies, 101
Tres Leches doughnut, 262
Trillin, Calvin, 174
Triple Chocolate Adult Brownies (recipe), 280–281
Truckin' Good Food, 224
24 Crows, 287
2 Amy's, 346
Two Little Red Hens, 273

U
Umami Burger, 72–73
Umberto I, 95
Una Pizza Napoletana, 96, 108, 111
Uncle John's Barbecue, 178, 197, 348
Union Square Cafe, 340
Union Square Greenmarket, 333
Unterman, Patty, 336
urban barbecue, 174, 178
urban farms, 307, 321
Usinger's Natural Casing Pork and Beef Frankfurters, 164
Ussner, Nick, 335
Utsonomaya, Moto, 234

V
Vandamme, Pierre, 162
Vanilla Bean doughnut, 262
Vanilla Macarons (recipe), 302–303
Vanilla Swirls, 31
Varasano, Jeff, 113, 126
Varasano's, 113
Varsity hot dogs, 166
Vendy Awards, 208, 212–213, 214
Veraci, 237
Vietnamese food carts, 220
Vinyard, Mary Beth, 255
Virgil's barbecue, 174, 180
Vitek, Karel, 214
Vitek, Monika, 214
Vongerichten, Jean-Georges, 314, 340
VPN (Associazione Verace Pizza Napoletana) accreditation, 106, 112, 114–115, 346, 349

W
Waffles, Orange-Scented Yeast (recipe), 33
Waiola, 293
Walsh, Robb, 51, 196, 252, 347
Walter's Hot Dog Stand, 165
Wang, Chichi, 318
Waters, Alice, 97, 113, 313, 347

Weinstein, Mike, 122
Weinzweig, Ari, 152, 327, 345
Weld, George, 26
Weppler, George, 309
Werp, Mike and Tina, 321
Werp Farms (Buckley, MI), 321
Wheel In Drive-In, 63
Whitaker, Kelly, 112
White, Michael, 340
White Bear, 340
White Castle, 69, 73, 83, 84
White Mana (Jersey City), 70
White Manna (Hackensack), 70, 85
White Rose System, 69
White Sauce, 219
Whitman's, 340
Wholey's whaler sandwich, 163
Wichayanuparp, Jan, 287
Wicks, Benjamin, 11, 170–171
Wiener and Still Champion, 246
Wilber's Barbecue, 203
Wildrose Farm, 334
Wiley, Kathy, 278
Willie Mae's Scotch House, 251, 338
Will's Avocados, 335
Wilson, Ruby, 201
Wiseguy pizza, 106
Wizenberg, Molly, 110
Wood, Nick, 135
Wood Stone Corporation, 103
Workingman's Friend Tavern, 72
World Champion Barbecue Cooking Contest, 175
World Wide Opportunities on Organic Farms (WWOOF), 307
Wy'east Pizza, 237

X
Xi'an Famous Foods, 340
Xoco, 137, 293

Y
Yezzi, Mike, 307, 318
Yoshikawa, Shiho, 287
Yung, Helen, 287
Yura on Madison, 298

Z
Zambazo sandwich, 214
Zeidaies, Freddy, 220
Zephyr Farm Sunnyside Egg sandwich, 43
Zero Zero, 96
Ziba's Pitas, 216
Zimmer, Erin, 9, 344–345
Zimmer's Seafood, 338
Zingerman's Bakehouse, 152, 327, 345
Zukin, Nick, 152
Zuni Café, 57, 343
Zuppardi's Apizza, 100, 107